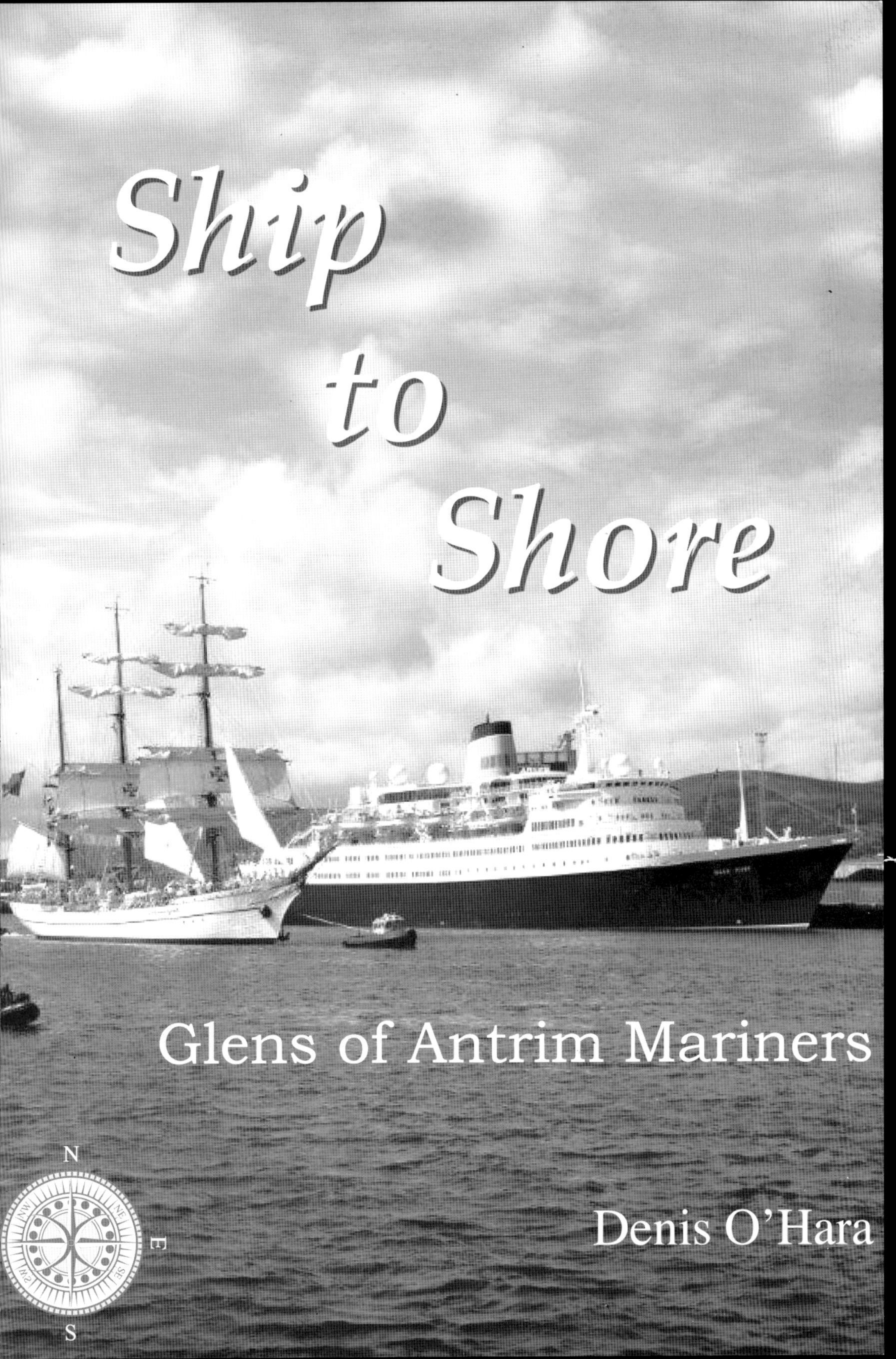

Ship to Shore

Glens of Antrim Mariners

Denis O'Hara

ISBN. 978 - 1 - 906689 - 52 - 0

Front Cover: Old and New - a 'Tall' ship berths beside a passenger boat in Belfast Harbour (courtesy Northern Ireland Tourist Board).

Back Cover: Famine ship replica, *DUNBRODY* (courtesy Dunbrody Centre, New Ross), with inserts of Captain Mick McCormick and the *S.S. BALLYDOUGAN.*

Printed by Impact Printing, Ballycastle and Coleraine, in association with Glendun Publishing, Cushendun (denisjohn@utvinternet.com)

Book cover design by Impact Printing, Ballycastle, County Antrim

ACKNOWLEDGEMENTS

Editor: Colin McAlpin

Sub-Editors: Daniel V O'Hara, Orla Wilkinson, Eamonn O'Hara, Elizabeth Stewart.

Commercial Consultant: Catherine O'Hara

Image Scanning: Glendun Publishing. .

GRATEFUL thanks for the research use of the Web site facilities of *Google.com and Wikipedia*, Newspapers - *Irish News, Belfast Telegraph, Larne Times, Northern Whig*, and *News Letter.* Magazines - *Glensman,* and *The Glynns.*

Appreciation of help received from the Newspaper Library staff at Central Library, Belfast.

Thanks to the patient staff at Impact Printers, Ballycastle, County Antrim - especially Tommy McDonald.

This book would also not be possible but for the generous co-operation of all interviewees - Chris Barrett, Don Black, Margaret Black, Patsy Black, Brian Blaney, Dr Sean Blaney, Gerry Blaney Snr, Gerry Blaney Jnr, Margaret Blaney (nee Black), Margaret Blaney (nee McKeegan), John Blaney, Willie Blaney, Ian Bradley (Camlin Books), Murray Brogan, Leo Burns, Paddy Burns, John Carson, Pat Close, George Darragh, Lawrence Darragh, Malachy Darragh, James Docherty, Rita Eley, John and Ann Gore, Monica Graffin, Michael Graham, Arthur Harvey, John and Josephine Healy, Danny Healy, John Higgins, Tony Hoey, Sheila Magee, Brendan Mitchell, Joe Mitchell Snr, Joe Mitchell Jnr, John Mitchell, Louis Monaghan, Roy and Sean Mort, Marie Mort, Ian Mort, Danny Murphy, Joe Murphy, Alex Murray, Norris and Margaret Murray, Joe McAfee, Andrew McAlister, Greta and Mary McAlister, Eileen McAllister, Charlie McAuley, Barry McCartin, Margaret McCausland, Sean McClements, Hugh McCormick, Eric and Eileen McCullough, David McCurdy, Randal McDonnell (Cushendun), Randal McDonnell (Laney), Ian McElheron, Anna McEvoy, Francis McGinty, Eugene, Paul and Kevin McHugh, Hugh McIlwaine, Alex McKay, Alistair and Jim McKay, Denis McKay, Harriet McKay, Nellie McKay, Kathleen McKay, Kate McKay, Rosemary McKay, Dan McKillop, Denis McKillop, Neil, Alex and John McKillop, Michael McKillop, Patrick McKeegan, Sarah and Sean McKeegan, Barbara McLaughlin, Jim and Debbie McLaughlin, Eugene and Canon Alex McMullan, Oliver McMullan, Archie McNaughton, Fergus McNaughton, Kevin McNaughton, Margaret McNaughton, Kieran McNeill, Sean, Seamus, and Paddy McNeill, Seamus (J.J.) McNeill, Danny and Pearl McQuillan, Angela McWilliams, Paul Newe, Johnnie O'Boyle, Daniel V. O'Hara, Johnny and Jim O'Hara, Vincent O'Hara, Paddy O'Neill, Donnell O'Loan, Hugh O'Mullan, Dan O'Neill, John O'Neill, Mickey Quinn, John Robbin, Anona Robertson, Alistair Rowan, Tommy and Margaret Rowan, Ita Small, Philip and Rose Sharpe, Anne Sharpe. Alex and Colm Thompson.

Photographs courtesy of Margaret Black, Dr Sean Blaney, Gerry Blaney Snr, Gerry Blaney Jnr, Margaret Blaney (nee McKeegan), Margaret Blaney (nee Black), Willie Blaney, Ian Bradley (Camlin Books), Leo Burns, Paddy Burns, Lawrence Darragh, Malachy Darragh, Carmel Delaney (Adm; Dunbrody Famine Ship, New Ross), John Gore, Monica Graffin, Michael Graham, John and Danny Healy, John Higgins, Joe Mitchell Jnr, John Mitchell, Ian Mort, Roy, Sean and Marie Mort, Norris and Margaret Murray, Eileen (Patterson) McAllister, Greta and Mary McAlister, Charlie McAuley, Gerry and Catriona McCartin, Margaret McCausland, Hugh McCormick, Patrick McCormick, Charlie McDonnell, Ian McElheron, Anna McEvoy, Paul McHugh, Hugh McIlwaine, Alastair and Jim McKay, Denis McKay, 'Wee' John McKay, Kathleen McKay, Patrick McKeegan, Sarah McKeegan, Denis McKillop, Neil and Alex McKillop, Jim McLaughlin, Eugene McMullan, Fergus McNaughton, Kevin McNaughton, Paddy McNeill, Danny and Pearl McQuillan, Angela McWilliams, N. I.Tourist Board (Lynette Conlon), Kate Oliver, Johnnie O'Boyle, Daniel V. O'Hara, D. J. O'Hara, Johnnie O'Hara, Vincent O'Hara, Kate Oliver, Donnell O'Loan, John O'Neill, Tommy and Margaret Rowan, Ita Small, Anne Sharpe.

Sponsored By:
Blaney Agri Services. 36a Warden Street, Ballymena.

CONTENTS

1 - MASTERLY MARINER 1
2 - LETTER BOOST 5
3 - TROOP SHIP TRAUMA 11
4 - PAY MASTER 17
5 - SLOOP SHOCKER 20
6 - ROYAL COMMAND 24
7 - SHORE STREET SKIPPER 29
8 - CAPE FEARS 32
9 - PRISONER of WAR 36
10 - NIGHT of HORROR 40
11 - DOCKSIDE SAGAS 47
12 - SPIRITS of the GLENS 51
13 - LIMESTONE CARRIERS 58
14 - SHOOTING STAR 64
15 - CONVOY CAPERS 67
16 - A BRIDGE TOO FAR 70
17 - PAIN BLAME 77
18 - CAPTAIN CHARLIE 81
19 - TORPEDO TERROR 85
20 - BAY of PLENTY 88
21 - BURMA RUN 100
22 - FRIENDLY FOLK 102
23 - GRAHAM GRIEF 106
24 - BITTEN by the BUG 110
25 - INSPIRED DECISION 123
26 - MERCY MISSION 127
27 - FAMILY AFFAIR 133

28 - PERILS of PENZANCE 139
29 - TERRIBLE WASTE 147
30 - CLOSE CALLS 152
31 - OIL SLICKS 163
32 - CATTLE CROSSING 170
33 - AMERICAN DREAMS 172
34 - TAX RELIEF 177
35 - NUCLEAR NERVES 183
36 - LUXURY LINE-UPS 191
37 - CURRY FAVOURED 197
38 - ISLE of CALM 209
39 - LEAP of FAITH 214
40 - RABBIT RUN 218
41 - GOOD SAMARITAN 223
42 - HAPPY WANDERER 225
43 - SMALL WONDERS 230
44 - VILLAGE PEOPLE 232
45 - CULTURE CLASH 239
46 - BLACK MARKERS 245
47 - DOUBLE DESPAIR 248
48 - WALL of WATER 251
49 - PLAIN SAILING 254
50 - CHARLIE'S CHOICE 263
51 - FERRY TALES 268
52 - HARBOUR LIGHTS 271
53 - DIVING DILEMMA 275
54 - CABLE GUY 278
55 - CREWS CONTROL 284

INTRODUCTION

THIS book is dedicated to past and present mariners from the Glens of Antrim, who have not, I feel, been adequately recognised for decades of instinctive valour when battling the elements on the high seas.

A nostalgic journey down a misty memory lane may go some small way to paying tribute to the life, times, and often spectacular exploits of those sturdy sailors. My humble chronicle, with no claim to being the definitive article, attempts to place a reasonable record of the days of the billowing sails on those majestic cutters of the 19th century to the 21st century's sophisticated seamen, who have sailing demands down to a fine art, through the assistance of computerised equipment.

Throughout lengthy research, and wonderfully generous help from so many loquacious friends along the Antrim Coast, from Glenarm to Torr Head, I knew there would be numerous stories of heroic and tragic incidents in equal measure. It is difficult enough to try and work with the waves, and the inherent dangers, during normal circumstances, but to negotiate mine-strewn and U-boat infested waters during the war-torn years of 1914-1918 and 1939-1945 must have been frightening experiences.

Danger lurked everywhere for those trying to make a living for their families back home. Most of the sailors from small holdings, where many farmers had to double up as mariners during winter months, and face the hazards of the sea. Lives of many seamen were lost throughout these isles, and families from the Glens were not without heartbreak.

Worldly adventurers were drowned in severe storms, during shipwrecks, and also there were fatalities from accidents on board sailing, steam, and oil-driven ships. There are also many jaunty tales of ocean travel. This hardy breed made full use of opportunities to better themselves.

Seafaring was an obvious escape route from the poverty trap, a stairway to success as many became Masters of the oceans. What is fascinating is the fact this proud insular race of sea-faring folk contributed so greatly to the world of industry and commerce. I took so much for granted, without ever looking behind the reasons why a voyage was necessary.

It may have been an urgently required shipment of coal or oil to an area fast running out of fuel. It may have been a container cargo of fruit from Tasmania or the West Indies, with the products soon to reach shops in the Glens.

The world of high finance floated to the surface when cargoes to and from countries were revealed, where oil and gas deposits are being discovered below the sea bed, where underwater telephone lines are laid or repaired for global requirements.

Ever since boats took to the water I found Glensmen not far away from a ship's poop-deck, some heartily involved in the daring escapades of smugglers trying to avoid the Custom and Excise cutters when making clandestine trips across the testing neck of water from that once hotbed of whisky distilling, the Mull of Kintyre, and passage to the Antrim coast.

Before the completion of the Antrim Coast Road, the Glens of Antrim was an area generally inaccessible from inland. Most of the trade and trafficking involved Campbeltown, Southend, and Dunaverty on the Mull of Kintyre, and the little ports at Cushendun and Waterfoot.

However, the building of the Coast Road, lasting from 1832 to 1842, soon put an end to the old traditional ways of bartering and smuggling. Sir Charles Lanyon, born at Eastbourne, and later to become Mayor of Belfast, was the architect responsible, and the Chief Engineer was William Bald. The Coast Road project included the serenely imposing Glendun Viaduct, which was completed in 1839.

Nautical necessity took on greater impetus after the Great Famine, when farming on the confined holdings in the Glens and the nearby hinterland could not support family survival. Young men emigrated to the Americas, to the Antipodes, and others went to work on the waters of the world.

The old-time weather-beaten ocean adventurer donned homemade, hand-knitted, ganseys to stand on an open bridge and brave the often howling gales on cruel seas. What was also spellbinding during my most satisfying research was the memory retention of many old salts, who loved their lives at sea, and looked back with a warm glow of satisfaction. It takes a special kind of person to face the perils of passage on the oceans.

The mariners I had the privilege of meeting in the course of trying to put the yarns together were more than willing to chat over old times. I suspect they believed themselves to be a forgotten race. Everyone, including family members who preserved memorabilia, had a tale to tell. Most of the sailors could recall the name of every ship they worked on, the tonnage of those vessels, and what cargo hauls were taken from where to what port in some exotic location.

To start the journey I felt it fitting to add to the numerous raging endorsements of the staggering world achievements by a Glensman who carved out a special place in sea-faring folklore Captain Charles McDonnell of Glenariffe became a . . . 'lord of the seven seas'.

My research ranges from the high-masted sailing ships, the wind-jammers of McDonnell's 19th century record-making runs to the changing face of seamanship so highlighted by the mammoth high-tech tankers and liners of the late 20th century, and through to the early 21st century. This compilation is awash with mini-style biographies that include long, short, and tall tales.

The circumstances and yarns of ocean travel deserve a special place in the history of the coastal area that produced a multitude of exceptional mariners. I found this bow-to-stern examination, of stoic seamen in their often life-threatening journeys, an absorbing exercise. Using part of a biblical line - 'Write down all that you see' - I decided to search out as much as possible on the past and the more recent history of our coastline mariners, and their bravery on the briny.

I include an excerpt from a poem by John Masefield, the Poet Laureate of the United Kingdom from 1930 until his death in May 1967. I feel the inclusion of a part of Masefield's 'Sea Fever' is appropriate in many respects, not least the fact he had a close connection with Cushendun, and lived at Rockport for a time.

Born in June 1878, in Herefordshire, he first joined the Royal Navy, and in 1894 moved to the Merchant Navy. He went on a windjammer to New York, jumped ship, and worked as a barman and also in a carpet factory before returning to England in 1897 to settle to writing poems and books.

He was 23 when he married Cushendun-connected Constance Crommelin, who was a 35-year-old mathematics teacher. Her wealthy family created Newtowncrommelin, and owned the Cave House and Sleans properties in Cushendun. Her sister was married to ex-Royal Navy officer Oscar Wayne Walker. The Walkers once lived at Linton Lodge, Cushendun.

This tome takes on a broad canvas. It indulges in some light-hearted anecdotes. It attempts to give an insight into the rigorous duties and pressures of being a sea captain, a first mate, an engineer, to the dedicated deck hand.

At the risk of inadvertently overlooking anyone, or any Glens family with links to seamanship, I hope the assembled tales of the trials, trauma, tribulations, tensions, and triumphs in the face of harsh adversity during global adventures will be accepted as a comprehensive and compelling collection.

'I must go down to the seas again,

To the lonely sea and the sky

And all I ask is a tall ship

And a star to steer her by.'

(Extract from John Masefield's 'Sea Fever')

Masterly Mariner

EXCEPTIONAL seafarer Charles McDonnell of Kilmore, Glenariffe, ruled the waves like no other Glensman. He established a spectacularly special brand of ocean travel in the 19th century. During his short and dramatic life he became a legend in seamanship.

One of the finest, and certainly one of the most famous of seamen from these isles, Captain McDonnell was a visionary in understanding the whims of wind, time, and tide. Tragically, he died from a sudden illness, aged 31, in his mother's home at Glenariffe on the 26th of January 1859. Like so many intrepid adventurers and explorers of an almost forgotten time, he was born to conquer the seas.

McDonnell is best remembered for speed of sail travel. He was the first mariner to make the journey 'Down Under' in 63 days, from Liverpool to Melbourne. Indeed, his vessel, the majestic sailing ship *JAMES BAINES*, is also warmly recalled for some record-breaking feats, passages under sail and masterminded by the shrewd McDonnell. He should also be revered for his sea-distance discovery of a quick way to conquer horizons, and is regarded as the man to prove what is known at sea as the 'Great Trade Circle Sailing'.

He attended Talmaght School up Glenariffe Glen, where he was taught by a wise sage with seafaring navigation knowledge, his schoolteacher George Doran. From regular discussion with Master Doran, head of Glenariffe National School from April 11, 1842, it was figured the fastest way to travel on a sea voyage was by using lines of the earth's circumference . . . to follow the curvature of the earth, and not plot a voyage by a straight line on a map. He was first to test the theory of wind pressures, instigated by Dutch meteorologist, Buys-Ballot.

I doubt if there is any moving object so elegant as a sailing ship in full flight. Captain McDonnell belonged to that colourful age of chartering unknown territory, and achieving fresh feats of seamanship. Ever since the mists of time, transport by sea proved to be such an ingenious method of covering vast treks of ocean. The thrill of sailing as a way of travel has endured. Sixth century Saint Brendan the Navigator was one of the early pioneer explorers of the seas.

High-mast sailing ships brought this method of making the world smaller to a higher level. Long before the discovery of radar, telephones, Morse code, and other electronic devices to make sea travel a precise science, the cry of 'three bells and all is well' - and measuring the depth of an inlet's water level by lowering over the side a stone on a strong cord, was part of this fascinating old-time adventure.

Overcoming the forces of nature, when negotiating the oceans, helped to map out the islands and land masses of the globe. The safest and fastest routes became the original handbook, thanks to the enterprising and fearless masters of sailing ships. Captain McDonnell was such a man, achieving so much in such a short time.

Mercurial McDonnell, brother of Alexander, went to sea at 18 years of age. He quickly made an impact, almost from the moment he started serving his time. Local historian and retired college lecturer Donnell O'Loan, married to a relation of the Captain, nurse Elizabeth McDonnell, explained: "He served his time with the Belfast shipping company of David Grainger and Sons. This firm had five full-rigged clipper ships, and some smaller ships.

"The vessels were mostly built in Quebec, and registered in Liverpool. When they built the 665 tons *RIVERDALE* in 1847 Charles McDonnell was placed in command. So, he became a ship's master at 20 years of age. The Grainger ships traded mostly to New Orleans and Australia. After completing a number of voyages on the *RIVERDALE* he decided to move, and joined the Black Ball Line.

"The *MARCO POLO* was built for that company in 1851. He worked on her as First Mate, and under a notorious Captain named 'Bully' Forbes, when it notched a world record for a round trip to Australia in 1852. McDonnell later became Master of the *MARCO POLO,* and established the sailing ship record run that has never been equalled, covering 428 nautical miles in 24 hours."

The indomitable McDonnell masterminded what were described as 'unparalleled passages' to Australia. He was aboard two of the world's fastest sailing ships of the 19th century - the *MARCO POLO* and the *JAMES BAINES.* The first major success was with the *MARCO POLO*, and the owners were so thrilled by his achievement they presented him with an inscribed gold watch.

The legend states: "Presented to Mr Charles McDonnell by the owners of the *MARCO POLO* as their testimony of their high opinion of his service as Chief Officer, when she made her phenominal passage of 68 days to Melbourne, and 78 days home, the voyage, including detention, being completed in 5 months and 21 days.' He became that ship's captain at the age of 25.

Also preserved from that heady time is a photograph of the Captain, taken by the 'American Photographic Gallery, 162, Capel Street, Dublin. P. O'Reilly, Proprietor'. Charlie McDonnell, a descendent of the sea specialist, kindly gave me use of the sepia image. He said: "It was first discovered by my cousin, Dr Alasdair McDonnell. He gave me the photograph. My family link with Captain Charlie is through my father, Alex, and his father Randal."

In 1854, after nine years at sea, the now 27-year-old McDonnell's next challenge was to skipper the three-skymasted *JAMES BAINES*, and achieve forever fame. The ship, painted black outside and white inside, had sister ships, the *LIGHTENING*, the *DONALD McKAY*, and the *CHAMPION of the SEAS.* The 2,275-tons *JAMES BAINES*, featuring 13,000 square feet of sail, was built for the Black Ball Line by a Donald McKay in Boston, USA, for James Baines and Company of Liverpool, and was launched on June 25, 1854, from east Boston.

The record run across the Atlantic, timed from Boston docks to Mersey Lighthouse, started on September 12. During a period of tall-masted wooden vessels, when sailors were generally dubbed as 'Jack Tars', the ship shattered the world record for a crossing of the Atlantic. She clocked 12 days and six hours, and during parts of the voyage reached 20 knots an hour. This remarkable time still stands for a sailing ship effort from Boston to Liverpool.

After that, Captain McDonnell made the clipper ship trip from Liverpool to Melbourne, setting out on December 9, 1854, this time in 63 days 18 hours. The now packet ship's return sailing began with departure from Melbourne on March 12, 1855, with a cargo of 40,000 ounces of gold and 360 passengers. It took 69.5 days. The Saloon passengers were so delighted they presented McDonnell with a silver tea service, in May 1855.

The return passage from a second trip, leaving Melbourne on August 8, 1856, was not so noteworthy from a time factor, as it took 105 days. However, the precious cargo included 174,000 ounces of gold. His crew featured two other Glensmen, George McKillop of Glenballyeamon, and a Mr McGalliard of Carnlough.

The Indian Mutiny began in 1857, and the *JAMES BAINES* became a troop ship, departing Portsmouth with a regiment of British soldiers on board for Calcutta. The story goes Queen Victoria, now aware of McDonnell's superior skills as a navigator, went to Portsmouth. Many Mercantile Marine vessels were used to transport the troops, and the Queen greatly admired the *JAMES BAINES*. Rumour has it she offered McDonnell £100 for every day he could slice off his contract sailing time to India.

Research reveals he took 103 days to get there, but the return was to prove the beginning of the end for both the sleek ship and the masterful mariner. On New Year's Day, 1858, the *JAMES BAINES* left Calcutta, bound for Liverpool with a cargo of 2,200 bales of jute, 6,213 bags of linseed, 6,583 bags of rice, and 40 bales of cow hides. She docked 101 days later. Unfortunately, on April 22, 1858, the ship's cargo went on fire while being unloaded, and the boat, a charred hulk, was a total loss. This proved a shattering setback for the first and last master of the *JAMES BAINES*.

Donnell O'Loan remarked: "According to family beliefs, the loss of the *JAMES BAINES,* through fire damage, led him to a state of depression. To see this great vessel consumed by fire broke his heart. He was an excellent mariner. The facts speak for themselves regarding Captain McDonnell's relatively short sea career."

Shortly after this numbing disaster, and serving 13 years at sea with such distinction, the celebrated voyager retired from service, and returned to Glenariffe, to live with his widowed mother. McDonnell sadly died of suspected pneumonia at his home. He went out into Red Bay to help in a near-drowning incident involving a barc. He took ill afterwards. A few month's later, on January 26, 1859, the Captain died at 31 years of age, and is buried in the Bay Cemetery, Glenariffe.

A devotee of McDonnell is Captain Hugh McIlwaine, whose bungalow in Waterfoot is named 'James Baines', and a hallway wall is adorned by a painting of the fabled yet ill-fated vessel. "He is a legend in seamanship. Captain Charles McDonnell was one of the finest mariners ever to come out of the Glens, and certainly the most famous seaman from these isles," insisted McIlwaine.

"An exceptional man, he did not enjoy a long life. In her maiden voyage the *JAMES BAINES* shattered the world record for a crossing of the Atlantic. Charles McDonnell cleverly figured the fastest way to travel on a sea voyage was by using lines of the earth's circumference, and not by a straight line."

2

LETTER BOOST

CAPTAIN Patrick McDonnell was the perfect example of how family connections are paramount in the Antrim glens. Immense pride in such a closely-knit community helped to create a special bond, and in a variety of ways, McDonnell was no exception. Mariners made their own crucially important impact in a bygone era, when work at sea helped to finance family survival during extremely difficult times.

Captain McDonnell's willingness to assist fellow Glenaan men was fulsome, and is preserved in a letter written in 1937. He vouched for John McKillop, who wanted to return to work at sea. The Captain penned the recommendation on October 2, 1937, when he was skipper of a Dorey boat, the *SARNIA.*

The letter reads . . . 'This is to certify that the bearer, John McKillop, sailed with me as sailor and bo'sun from 1924 to 1930 at different times on the *ARRAN ISLAND* and the *TYNAN of BELFAST.* Yours faithfully, P McDonnell, Master.' The *SARNIA,* built at South Shields for the Dorey Shipping business in 1923, was sold to Hargreaves Coal and Shipping Company of London in June 1957. She was renamed *HARDALE,* and 16 months later broken up in Rotterdam.

Incidentally, McKillop sailed on the Dorey's coaster *TORFEY.* The ship was renamed *YORK RIVER* in 1929, and six years later sold to an

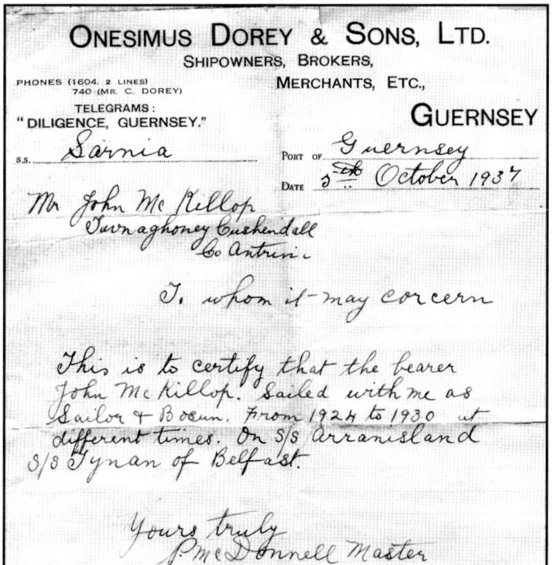

ONESIMUS DOREY & SONS, LTD.
SHIPOWNERS, BROKERS,
MERCHANTS, ETC.,
PHONES (1604. 2 LINES) 740 (MR. C. DOREY)
TELEGRAMS: "DILIGENCE, GUERNSEY."
GUERNSEY

S.S. Sarnia PORT OF Guernsey
DATE 2nd October 1937

Mr John Mc Killop
Turnaghoney Cushendall
Co Antrim

To whom it may concern

This is to certify that the bearer
John Mc Killop. Sailed with me as
Sailor & Bosun. From 1924 to 1930 at
different times. On S/S Arranisland
S/S Tynan of Belfast.

Yours truly
P McDonnell Master

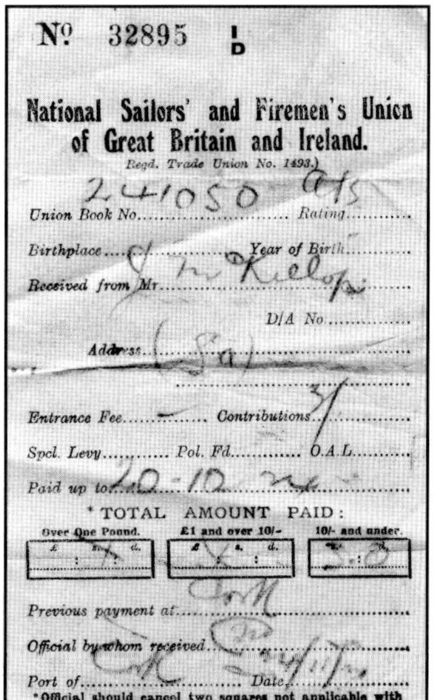

Nº 32895

National Sailors' and Firemen's Union of Great Britain and Ireland.
Regd. Trade Union No. 1493.

Union Book No. 241050 ... Rating ...
Birthplace ... Year of Birth ...
Received from Mr J McKillop
D/A No. ...
Address ...
Entrance Fee ... Contributions 3/
Spcl. Levy ... Pol. Fd. ... O.A.L. ...
Paid up to 10 - 10 ...
* TOTAL AMOUNT PAID:
Over One Pound. | £1 and over 10/- | 10/- and under.
Previous payment at ...
Official by whom received ...
Port of ... Date ...
* Official should cancel two squares not applicable with pencil and Branch Stamp.

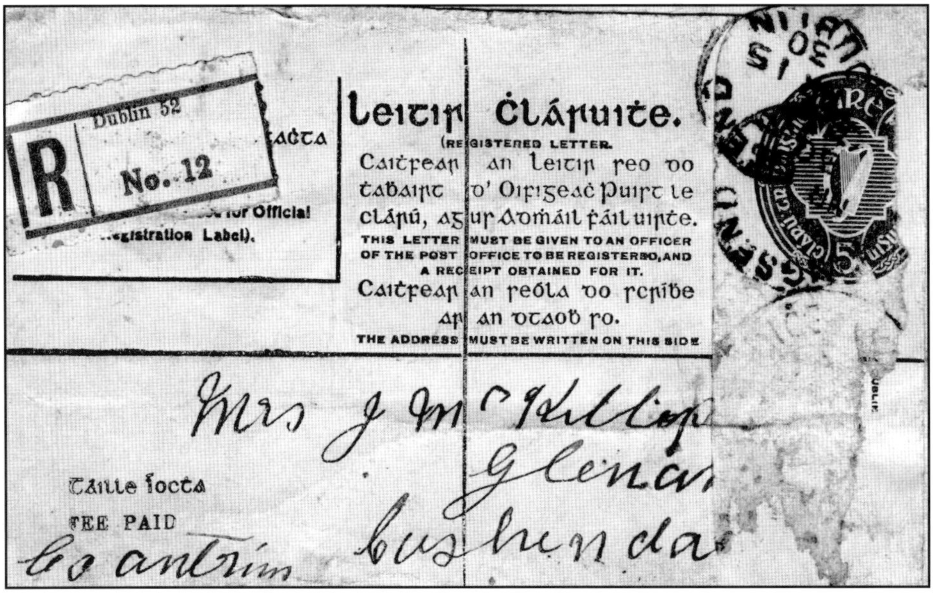

Italian ship-breaking firm. Born in 1872, and a brother-in-law of 'Captain Paddy', he (McKillop) was a grandfather of Denis McKillop, who was of great help in providing some information for this chronicle. Denis said: "My grandfather (John McKillop) sailed a lot to and from the 'Free State'. He posted his wages home to this wife. He was an AB, and a bo'sun. He first enrolled in Cork, then again, on October 11, 1912, in Plymouth. He was back and forth to work at sea."

Captain McDonnell was part of a seafaring family. He was a nephew of Captain James McKeegan of the ill-fated *GEM*. Paddy's four brothers, Hugh, John, Archie, and James also went to sea. Originally from the townland of Echery, at the head of Glenaan, the McDonnell's moved to live at Middle Road, close to Cushendall.

Denis McKillop added: "A great, great nephew of Captain Paddy is Captain Danny McNaughton. All of the 'Horley' nickname breed. Danny is also a nephew of James Hugh McNaughton, and his father was Charlie McNaughton, and mother Mary McDonnell."

Mrs Rose Sharpe (nee McDonnell), recalled sea tragedy in the family: "Hugh McDonnell, my uncle, was drowned at sea, when 21 years of age. I heard it was during a blackout in the Second World War. He was crossing from dockside onto his ship when he fell into the harbour. He is buried in France. My aunt Nellie, the youngest, died in 2009. She recalled those happenings. Her brother Pat went to sea, while my grandfather Paddy McDonnell was a sea captain.

"The Captain's sons were Johnny, Pat, Hugh, Jamie, and Neil. Pat and Hugh went to sea. After the death of Hugh, I'm led to believe Pat came home, gave up the sea, and took up farming. Johnny, Neil, and Jamie did not go to sea. My mother was a sister. Her name was Mary McDonnell, and she married a McDonnell, connected to Randal McDonnell of Munaroe, Laney. My daddy and Randal's daddy were brothers. Sarah McKeegan is my cousin. Pat McDonnell was her father."

Randal McDonnell's father Randal had another Randal McDonnell, a cousin and seaman, as his best man when he married. "It seems a bit confusing, so many Randal McDonnell's. I am a distant relative of captain Paddy McDonnell," said Randal of Munaroe, Glencorp, "My granny, Mary McDonnell was a sister of the Captain. Once I saw the sea book of Randal McDonnell, who was best man at my father's wedding. The book was kept between two rafters in the old house.

"P. K. McKillop, Denis McKillop's uncle, went to sea for a short time. He told me so, and I also recall him telling me about old Johnny McDonnell, of Eshery, who felt the boat he was on was about to sink. He was sailing with his brother, Captain Paddy, through a bad storm. Johnny went into the room on the boat where the skipper was eating at a table that had edges to prevent plates from sliding off. He told his brother he felt the ship was about to go down.

"The Captain was unmoved, continued to eat meat from a plate that kept slipping one way and then another, with the violent swaying of the boat. Captain Paddy told Johnny to calm down, and that he would survive worse storms than the one they were in. He did. Johnny didn't stay long at sea. It was very sad that Captain Paddy's son Hugh was drowned at sea."

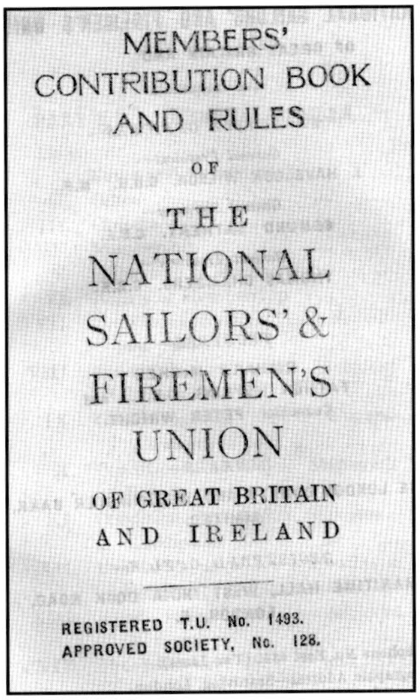

MEMBERS'
CONTRIBUTION BOOK
AND RULES
OF
THE
NATIONAL
SAILORS' &
FIREMEN'S
UNION
OF GREAT BRITAIN
AND IRELAND

REGISTERED T.U. No. 1493.
APPROVED SOCIETY, No. 128.

The McDonnell-McKeegan-McNaughton family ties had to endure the ravages of war from the sinking of the *GEM*. It was one of the many harrowing events of the 1914-1918 conflict. The War, both on land and on sea, impacted with excruciating anguish throughout the world, including the small parochial pockets of the Glens. The generally peaceful Glenaan area had to suffer particularly despairing heartbreak, when an innocent hard-working set of seamen were sent to watery graves.

The sickening saga of the despicable sinking of the *GEM*, by German mines on Christmas Day 1914, and the multiple loss of the lives of merchant seamen, brought enduring sorrow to many families. It is a tragedy that remains palpable a century later. The veteran skipper of the *GEM* since 1895 was Captain James McKeegan, a man who provided endless openings for strapping young men of his own area to make a living at sea.

The steamer of the Robertson Company, known as 'The Training Ship of the Glens', sank off Scarborough on December 25, 1914. Captain James, 65, was a son of Hugh and Mary McKeegan of Falmacrilly, Glenaan. Hugh died on November 24, 1891 aged 76, and Mary died on May 17, 1914, aged 90. A brother of the Captain, Hugh died, aged 15, on February 4, 1869.

The *GEM*, the last ship to escape from a port in Belgium before German forces confiscated all 'foreign' boats after World War One began on August

4, 1914, was on passage from Mostyn to Tyne with a cargo of 460 tons of salt cake when it struck a mine at 6.15pm. The ship broke in two, following a massive explosion. Ten lives were lost, including some from Glenaan, Carnlough, and Glenarm. The First Mate and one Ordinary Seaman were saved.

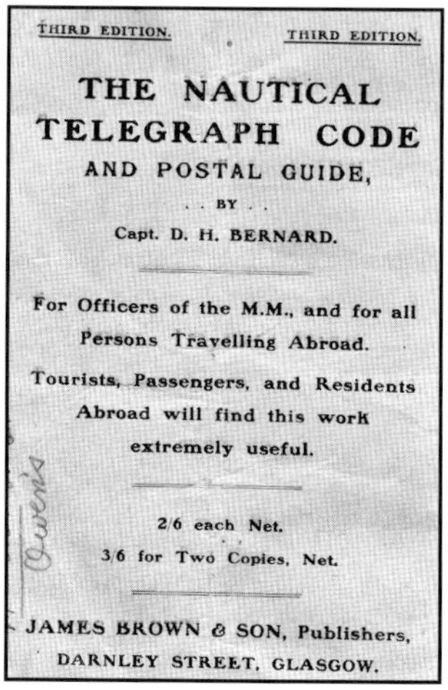

THIRD EDITION. THIRD EDITION.

THE NAUTICAL TELEGRAPH CODE AND POSTAL GUIDE,

BY

Capt. D. H. BERNARD.

For Officers of the M.M., and for all Persons Travelling Abroad.

Tourists, Passengers, and Residents Abroad will find this work extremely useful.

2/6 each Net.

3/6 for Two Copies, Net.

JAMES BROWN & SON, Publishers,
DARNLEY STREET, GLASGOW.

Along with Captain McKeegan, other Glensmen to perish were Hugh McKeegan, a 27-year-old steward and a son of Hugh and Margaret McKeegan, Glenaan - and a nephew of Captain James - and also the skipper's grandnephew, James Hugh McNaughton, a 22-year-old Able Seaman of Lubitavish, Glenaan. McNaughton was the son of Alex and Mary McNaughton. Another Antrim coast man to drown was Willie Graham, a fireman from Spring Hill, Glenarm.

It appears Captain James and James Hugh McNaughton went below to help shipmates, when the stern broke away. The two men, along with five colleagues, drowned at that point. The remaining members of the crew were now trying to survive in the ice-cold sea, including James McCambridge, of Glenballyeamon, and Hugh McKeegan, a 27-year-old ship's cook from Falmacrilly.

James McCambridge was one of two survivors, and later revealed that Hugh McKeegan, regarded as a strong swimmer, decided to swim in the direction of lights, some two miles away. The gallant idea was to try and raise an alarm. Hugh was never seen again. James McCambridge, reputed to have sailed with Captain Alexander McKillop of Clough on the *EGLANTINE* towards the close of the 19th century, also stated that one by one the men in the water succumbed to the freezing cold water.

The other crew men to die were - Duncan McInnes (Chief Engineer), Hugh O'Dornan (Fireman), Thomas Simpson (Second Engineer), James Humphrey (AB), Ted Williams (AB), and John Witherspoon (Second Mate). Loss of lives and ships during this wartime incident was colossal. Historians reveal that along with the *GEM,* a minesweeper, *NIGHT HAWK*, and another cargo steamer, *ELI,* were also lost on the same day, after running into mines.

What happened on the water followed the German's shelling of the Yorkshire seaside town of Scarborough. There was a heavy loss of life in December 1914, when 19 people were killed and 80 injured. Records show the shelling of Scarborough, by German battle-cruisers *VON der TANN* and *DERFELINGER,* was all part of a ruse to lay deadly five-horn mines, each packed with 350lbs of explosives, in the bay area, by the German light-cruiser *KOLBERG.* It was believed the Germans felt this densest minefield ever known in the history of naval warfare would lure the British Grand Fleet into an ambush.

Denis McKillop provided interesting memorabilia of that and many other Glenaan-related sea stories. Of the *GEM* disaster he stated:

"Captain James was a brother of old Mrs Arthur's (McAlister) mother. 'Wee' Archie McKeegan's mother Mary and Sarah were sisters of the Captain, and lived at Lubane. One was married to a McSparran. Mrs Arthur was Mary McSparran, and a brother of Hugh McSparran. From that family line to go to sea was James McKeegan, a nephew of Captain James, and a brother of 'wee' Archie. James was a deep-sea sailor."

Captain McKeegan had another brother, Patrick, also a sea captain, who emigrated with his family to America in 1912. Sean McKeegan and his wife Sarah (McDonnell) disclosed Patrick was shipwrecked a couple of times, and survived. "He ran aground in the Goodwin Sands, a 10-mile sandbank in the English channel, six miles east of Deal, Kent. He was on the *AXIMITE* - and later at the Bishop Rock, at the Scilly Isles off Cornwall, where he went down again, this time on the *EMERALD.* Again all hands were saved."

Glens captain's eventful career

A wide circle of friends in Ireland, Britain and America will learn with regret of the death of Captain Patrick McKeegan of Glenaan, Cushendall, at the age of 76 years.

The late Captain McKeegan began his sea-faring career on the old sailing ships and later was master of several of Messrs William Robertson's (Glasgow) ships.

While in charge of the 'Aximite', she was run down off the Goodwin Sands, all hands escaped after a thrilling experience.

He went back to the 'Emerald' and had again the experience of being run down, this time off the Bishops. Again all hands were saved.

Captain McKeegan emigrated to the United States 26 years ago and his family of four sons and one daughter reside there.

A brother, Captain James McKeegan, was master of the SS Gem when she was sunk by a mine off Scarborough on Christmas Eve 19014 during the Great War.

All hands with the exception of Mr James McCambridge, a Cushendall man, and a young lad from Dundalk, were lost.

Captain McKeegan was an enthusiastic supporter of Gaelic games, horse-racing and dog racing.

He is survived by his children, his wife and by his sisters, Mrs Hugh McKeegan, Mrs James McKeegan and Mrs S McSparran, all of Glenaan.

The funeral to the family burying-ground in St Patrick and St Brigid's cemetery, Glenariff was eloquent of the esteem in which he was held.

The Belfast morning daily *Irish News* edition of Saturday June 7, 2007, related the June 9, 1935, passing of Captain Patrick McKeegan, with the story headlined . . . 'Glens Captain's eventful career'. "A wide circle of friends in Ireland, Britain, and America will learn with regret of the death of Captain Patrick McKeegan of Glenaan, Cushendall, at the age of 76 years. The late Captain McKeegan began his seafaring career on the old sailing ships, and later was master of several of Messrs William Robertson's (Glasgow) ships.

"While in charge of the *AXIMITE*, she was run down off the Goodwin Sands, all hands escaped after a thrilling experience. He went back to the *EMERALD*, and had again the experience of being run down, this time off the Bishops. Again all hands were saved.

"Captain McKeegan emigrated to the United States 26 years ago, and his family of four sons and one daughter reside there. A brother, Captain James McKeegan, was master of the *GEM,* when she was sunk by a mine off Scarborough on Christmas Eve, 1914, during the Great War.

"All hands, with the exception of Mr James McCambridge, a Cushendall man, and a young lad from Dundalk, were lost. Captain Patrick McKeegan was an enthusiastic supporter of Gaelic Games, horse racing, and dog racing. He is survived by his children, his wife, and by his sisters, Mrs Hugh McKeegan, Mrs James McKeegan, and Mrs S McSparran, all of Glenaan. The funeral to the family burying-ground in St Patrick and St Brigid's cemetery, Glenariffe, was eloquent of the esteem in which he was held."

Sean McKeegan added: "The McKeegan clan originally came from the Scottish western isle of Uisk in the 16th century, as galloglass, fighting men for the McDonnell's. They returned to Scotland, and some of them later came back to Glenaan, to work as road builders and weavers. Six brothers came over from Uisk to build roads at the top end of Glenaan. They stayed here."

From seafaring records, other McKeegan names to emerge include a J McKeegan. He is listed a Mercantile Mariner from the Cushendall area, who was lost at sea, on June 10, 1917. He was a steward on board the 572-ton *KEEPER*, an Irish steamer out of Limerick. The *KEEPER* was on voyage from Belfast to Limerick with a cargo of grain, when it was sunk by a German submarine. All 12 lives were lost.

3 TROOP SHIP TRAUMA

GERRY BLANEY Snr, a celebrated skipper from the prominent Cushendall seafaring family, and like all men from the Glens who braved the erratic elements of the oceans, had many tales to tell. Always a genial and affable big man, he proudly recalled an extremely important troopship-saving episode near New Zealand. This was one of the drama highlights of Blaney's long and rewarding career at sea.

Born on June 23, 1925, Captain Gerry described how the incident developed during the Korean War. "In the 1950's, when the Korean War conflict was happening, we picked up New Zealand soldiers after their transport ship ran aground on a barrier reef. I was with the Standard Vacuum Oil tanker, *STANVAC KARACHI*, when we were first at New Zealand's north island and then shifted to the south island to complete our load.

"This was before the sea rescue. I remember a strange thing happening in Wellington Harbour. Our ship was the biggest ever to go into that harbour at that time. The pilot took us in, but only when the tide was right. I was the chief officer, and said to the skipper - what is that other ship doing, going round and round in the harbour?

"I was told it was a ship about to set off to Korea, and on board were 575 New Zealand troop replacements for the conflict up there, and their skipper was adjusting his compass. The ship, named the *WAHINE,* and filled with the New Zealand soldiers, left a week ahead of us.

"However, we had a faster ship, and overtook it. There was an S.O.S from it, and we responded. Other ships in the area picked up the request for help. We said we'd go, as we knew the ship from the harbour incident. We were 60 miles from the troubled vessel when we received the call, and then found it aground on a reef with the stern dipping into the water - a ship of over 4,000 tons almost ready to go down."

Records reveal that on August 15, 1951, the 38-year-old 4,436 tons New Zealand troopship *WAHINE* ran aground on the Masela Island Reef, off Cape Palsu (Indonesia) in the Arafura Sea. All aboard were rescued by the Standard Vacuum Oil's *STANVAC KARACHI* - and taken to Darwin. Salvage attempts were unsuccessful, and the vessel was abandoned as a total loss. The troopship was carrying a number of 25-pounder artillery guns for the 16th Forward Regiment. Steps were taken by the army to remove the breech blocks from the guns on board.

During an absorbing interview with Captain Blaney at his Cushendall bungalow in December 2012, he added: "They had bigger lifeboats than ours. We had steel lifeboats, with diesel engines - four all told. The mate and me were the first to go out to the sinking ship, and start taking off the first batch of the soldiers. We got down there, and then back for another load. We were working from 11 o'clock in the morning and the whole operation ended around midnight.

"We used their motorised steel lifeboats, because they were longer and speedier than ours. After the rescue we were again back in Wellington, and coming out of the harbour was another ship loaded with soldiers for the war in Korea. The pilot taking us into harbour knew of our rescue of the New Zealand troops. He congratulated us, and kept saying we would be thanked and recognised in the highest possible manner by his country's officials.

"He'd say: 'You'll get something special. You will surely be awarded recognition for what you did. You'll probably get gold watches'. Once we anchored there, sure enough we were invited ashore to meet the Prime Minister and all his fellow government officials. We were thanked, given cups of tea and sandwiches - and that was it. No gold watches, nothing to remember. After that, we used to kid each other on the ship - saying - What time is it with your gold watch?"

It was reported, at the time, the *WAHINE*, which left Darwin, was 23 miles off the usual channel route, grounded on a reef 320 air miles north-north-west of Darwin. The *WAHINE* had a crew of 80, and left Wellington for Japan on August 2. The *STANVAC KARACHI*, built in the USA in February, 1950, had a gross tonnage of 10,612, and was renamed *COMET DEFENDER* in 1965. One year later, it was altered to become a bulk carrier, and renamed *UNION DEFENDER*.

"I spent most of my working life in that area of the Far East - New Zealand, and Australia - and based out of Singapore. After being home on leave, I'd have to take flights to Singapore, to start work again. I was on several of the Stanvac ships. Stanvac was one of the best shipping companies in the world to work for.

"On one of my trips down to New Zealand's south Island I met a member of the Blaney clan - Ma Blaney. She owned 'Ma Blaney's Hotel'. I was in it. All the seafarers went there when they stopped off, anchored in the south island.

"I first met Ma Blaney when I was a Chief Mate. Our ship docked in Dunedin on a Sunday morning. The harbour was deserted. We managed to get alongside the dock. I had my own men get the hoses off. I went to the old man, Captain Campbell, and told him we were ready to unload. When we were getting things sorted out with the local harbour agent, Captain Campbell told him my name was Blaney. This man said his wife was a Blaney.

"We shook hands. Later he came down to Captain Campbell to say - 'Ma Blaney wants to see the Blaney man from Ireland.' My captain said 'You got to go and see her, so go with her husband, the agent. Captain Campbell suggested to me I should put on my uniform, so as to make a good impression. At the time I was the only one of the officers who was out of uniform, and wearing khaki trousers. I went up to the hotel, where I was dropped off at the steps leading to the front of the hotel. There was this elderly lady coming down. She was in her 80's, I guess.

"Ma Blaney had a gleam on her face. She hugged me, would hardly let me go, held onto me, and cried and cried. She was from Ireland. The agent came back with me to my ship on the Sunday night, and asked me if I knew of a place in Ireland named Cushendun. Ma Blaney was from Cushendun. I told him I lived next door, in Cushendall - and also that my Blaney family had a strong connection with Cushendun."

Gerard Patrick Blaney, who passed all 'ticket' examinations in Belfast, followed a family trait by taking to the waves at 16 years of age. The Blaney household history of seafarers starts deep into the 19th century. It is mingled with triumphs and tragedies.

He said: "My grandfather, John Henry Blaney, went to work on the sailing ship *LOCH TORRIDON*. He was the skipper during the 19th century. He died in 1910, aged 85. The ship, a clipper, traded mainly between New Zealand and Australia. He often made passage from Glasgow, and went round either Cape Horn or the Cape of Good Hope. On the way to the Antipodes, the ship would come in from the Clyde to anchor in Cushendun Bay, and change or add crew members."

John Henry Blaney married Mary O'Hara of Knocknacarry and had an only child, who also became a sea captain. "He was also John Henry 'Jack' Blaney, my father, and he married Mary O'Hara of Shore Street, Cushendall," explained Captain Gerry. "Sadly, my father was killed at sea, in the Mediterranean during the Second World War. He was on a ship carrying explosives to Italy. My father was in the Canadian Army during the First World War.

"During the Second World War he brought over a boat from Canada, to help sweep the channels for mines. It was thought at the time the boats used for fishing on the banks in Canada would help. He was on one of those. The boat he was in charge of, when crossing the Atlantic, was attacked by a German plane. The boat sank.

"Fortunately, Jack had a dog on board, and when he landed in the water he held on to the dog. As he was unable to swim, the dog helped to save his life. Jack and the boat's other survivors were picked up by another ship, and landed in County Donegal. He went back to sea after that close shave, yet I feel he should not have. But, that was his way. I was just starting out on my career, when I got word he had been killed."

Maritime records reveal Jack Blaney was on board the *BRINKBURN*, when the steamer was sunk on June 21, 1943. The listed captain was Norman Johnston. His ship was part of a convoy carrying ammunition bound for Italy. The *BRINKBURN* was torpedoed by German submarine U-73, west of Algiers. The Master, 21 crew members, and five gunners were lost. One crew member and five gunners were rescued by landing craft and also a fishing vessel, and taken to Algiers. This dreadful outcome was part of a sickening Second World War double disaster for the Blaney family.

"My brother Harry was also killed at sea at the start of the Second World War. He was with the cargo steamer, the *CHELDALE* when it was involved in a collision in 1940, with the motor vessel *GREYSTOKE CASTLE*," added Captain Gerry.

Tragedy struck another Cushendall family in that horrific incident of February 17, 1940, Brian McKillop of Chapel Road, son of Michael and Anne McKillop, was also killed. Michael McKillop, a nephew living in Canada, explained his family lost not only Brian but also another uncle, Paddy, when they worked at sea.

The disasters were unrelated. "The uncle who perished at sea during the Second World War was Brian, who was lost, along with Harry Blaney. Their ship, the *CHELDALE*, was in collision at night with another ship, the *GREYSTOKE CASTLE*, about 24 miles off Durban, South Africa. Apparently, there had been a warning of a German U-boat in the area, and ships were ordered to sail without lights - in retrospect, not the best advice. Anyway, I think that 16 men on the *CHELDALE* were lost that night when she sank."

Paddy McKillop became a sea captain, but before then ran on convoys with Kelly coasters during the opening years of the Second World War. After the fall of France, in 1940, convoys loading at ports in the South of England for dangerous midnight trips across the Channel included Kelly boats. Paddy McKillop is recorded as First Mate under skipper Andy Barron, when the they sailed out of Shoreham and Dover on the *SAINTFIELD*, a boat built for the Kelly company in 1937, and renamed *BALLYKELLY* (1) in 1952.

Barron's crew also included Chief Engineer John Golding of Newry and Second Engineer James Balmer of Glenarm. McKillop survived the conflict, yet suffered a heart-wrenching demise during his maiden voyage as a ship's master. Michael McKillop said: "It became a double family tragedy at sea. Uncle Paddy, as captain of his own vessel for a first time, suffered a burst appendix. This led to peritonitis, and the ship sailed under full steam for Liverpool, which apparently was the closest port.

"Though he lived long enough to land in Liverpool, he died in hospital, on May 21, 1945. There was additional sadness to his death as he planned to be married on his return to Cushendall immediately after this voyage. My father, Michael, went over to Liverpool to claim his body, and Paddy is buried in the family grave at the Bay, Glenariffe. On the family headstone Brian McKillop is listed simply as - 'Lost at Sea'."

A nephew of the same name (Paddy McKillop) also lives in Canada, a brother of Michael, and also of St Malachy's College, Belfast, teacher, Paddy - whose athletic son Michael became world famous when winning two track gold medals in the 2012 Paralympic Games.

Despite the numbing setbacks the Blaney family had to endure, Gerry was not put off from making a career on the waves. He said: "Harry was one of four brothers. He was the first of us to start at sea, then Jim, me, Paddy and Mick. My brother Jim and I were at sea then. Younger brother, Captain Paddy went to sea when the Second World War was just over. I started my career at Liverpool, and shortly afterwards news came through of my father's death.

"I studied all the while I was at sea, and eventually gained my captain's ticket. I sat all my examinations in Belfast, where we had a very good teacher. My brothers went there also, to sit their tickets. Jim was the first to become a Captain. He was a skipper on coasters. I was next, becoming a deep-sea captain, as was my brother Paddy. Mick was chief officer when he passed his Master's Ticket just before he was killed at sea.

"Something happened to the cargo on the ship as it was going up the English channel. He went down the hold to investigate, fell, and was killed. Mick was the third member of the family to be killed at sea, and was buried in Belfast. Jim was a skipper with the Stevenson Clark company from Newcastle-Upon-Tyne. He married Mary McNaughton, and they once owned a pub in Harryville, Ballymena. They lived in Leighinmohr Avenue, Ballymena, and Jim was buried in Crebilly Cemetery."

Gerry Blaney held a great admiration of fellow Glensmen who went to sea. "The Antrim Glens area once supplied more seamen than any other coastal part of Ireland, or the British Isles - and we never got much thanks for it. Quite a few of the seamen from the Glens went and did their tickets to become Masters. I think of great sailors such as Con Connolly, who was a student at St Malachy's College, Belfast, and Glenariffe's Mick McCormick. A brilliant home coast captain was Tommy Scollay. He was a great sailor.

"Tommy was with me when we were on one of Ireland's two tankers. Often I had to go to see Tommy, who was older than me, and ask his advice. I remember on one voyage to France we went to Mass, and then dinner in Bordeaux. In the early days I thought Tommy, who was the same age as our Harry, had a Foreign Masters' ticket. I found out he didn't. He had the coastal one.

"So, I persuaded him to study from my old books, and sit the examination for the Foreign Masters' ticket. He did, and took it. In my young days, in Cushendall, I remember having great chats with old-time sailors such as Tommy Rennicks. He used to cut the hedges around the barracks. Tommy was a very decent man."

Blaney's beginnings on the oceans began close to home: "I started out at sea on the coast, and then moved to deep-sea in 1943. My first job at deep-sea was on a Canadian company-owned ship, the *MOWATA PARK*. I joined her in Bangor Bay, in April 1943. It was part of a convoy of ships there. This was towards the latter stages of the Second World War. They were short of men. The Pool sent for me, and enquired would I go. I said, 'fair enough'.

"I was an AB then. The Second Mate was on watch on the *MOWATA PARK* when the boat anchored up and was ready to go. He asked me to steer the ship out of Bangor Bay, so I took the wheel. The captain was also on the bridge, and on the way up the North Channel and along the Antrim Coast I pointed out Cushendall, and said - 'That's where I live'.

"Our cargo back from Canada was plane parts, all boxed up, and then assembled in Britain into fighter aeroplanes to take on the Germans. The last cargo we took back from Canada was a bit scary. We had 4,000 tons of bombs in the number three and number four holds. It was a dangerous business.

"The amazing part of that convoy journey happened after we steered up the English Channel, and the pilot took over to guide us up the River

Thames to our berth. On the way over from Canada our ship's carpenter told us he picked up news on a radio network that the Germans had a new invention, a pilotless aeroplane that was bombing targets in England.

"It was called the Doodlebug, a small plane with bombs, but with no pilot, and mostly aimed at London. At first we didn't believe him, that this could be possible. Anyhow, on the way up the Thames the pilot confirmed Germany's use of the Doodlebug, and pointed out places right and left on the river bank that had been bombed.

"When we berthed we heard this strange noise. On our ship we had two large poles at the front and two more at the back - to hold up a wire net. It was meant to try and catch torpedoes. The net needed to be lowered and quickly, once we heard the Doodlebug was coming in our direction. The wire net was down the whole length of the ship. This other man from the crew went south on the ship, and I went north, and we furiously worked at the mechanism to get the net lowered, and just got it down in time.

"The pilotless plane buzzed narrowly over our ship, and exploded on the other side of the harbour. Imagine what would have happened had the Doodlebug caught our net and crashed into our ship, loaded with all those bombs. I seemed to be lucky all the time during my career at sea. I was once on convoy duty during the Second World War to Russia, sailing in around Finland to ports in northern Russia. I believe every convoy that went this dangerous route there was the risk of losing three ships, through German torpedoes. Many lives were lost.

"I was fortunate to be on ships that managed to safely get there and back. One of my great memories of those trips was the way we were greeted by the Russians. They were very generous to us, very polite, very grateful. They erected big headstones in their village ports, as a mark of respect - to recognise all the ships that didn't make it.

"Immediately after the War, and before going to the Far East, I continued to work deep-sea from Canada. I recall a cargo of trains we once brought back to England. The Germans bombed most of the railway trains off the tracks during the War. The engines were built in Canada. We didn't bring over railway carriages."

PAY MASTER

MONEY MATTERS required stringent supervision by a ship's Captain during the 19th century, and one very meticulous master was Alexander McKillop of Cloughs, Cushendall. His grandson, Neil McKillop retained a diary belonging to the old skipper, detailed notes that included wages paid to his crew members following coastal trading aboard the *EGLANTINE.*

The Captain's log reveals exactly how much, and down to the last old-time penny, his sailors, mostly from the Glens, took home. Neil, a retired accountant who lives near the family homestead at Glenburn, Cushendall, said: "Even from the time he left the sea, to farm, he lists the cows calving, the prices made for stock sold, and the wage of £5 for six months paid to Dick Mullan, also of Cloughs, for working on the farm. The sea wages list suggests most members of the crew came from the Glens.

"Before that, Captain Alexander was on three-masted clipper ships involved in the tea trade, sailing tea cargo from Ceylon to London. It is believed he was skipper of the first commercial ship to go through the Suez Canal, when the seaway was opened."

The Suez Canal, Egypt's artificial sea-level waterway that connects the Mediterranean Sea and the Red Sea opened to shipping on November 17, 1869. It took ten years to construct. The north-end terminus is Port Said, and the southern end has Port Tawfiq. The first vessel through was the Imperial yacht *L'AIGLE*, belonging to the French empress Eugenie.

The first ship to follow was the P&O sail and steam passenger/cargo liner *DELTA*. This ocean liner, one of the earliest vessels to be sail and steam propelled, also made voyages across the Atlantic with passengers for Ontario, Canada. The *DELTA* was built at Sunderland in 1862, and in November 1891 was seriously holed from a collision with an old sunken wreck off the coast of what is now Vietnam. The vessel became flooded, and was then beached.

Captain McKillop, it seems, guided the next ship after the *DELTA* through the Suez, and in later years became master of the *EGLANTINE.* His recorded pay sheet for the crew of that ship, from September 17, 1880, until April 15, 1881, is an illuminating read, and is as follows.

W.H. McDonnell - 6 months and 29 days at £5.10 shillings per month = £24.7 shillings 8 pence.

Neal Darragh - 3 months and 2 days, and another 26 days at £2.17.6 per month = £10.19.0. A further payment to Neal Darragh for 2 months and 25 days at £2.17.6 per month = £8.2.11.

Michael Kelly (Mate) - 2 months and 24 days at £5 per month = £14.

A McQuillan - 2 months and 23 days at £2.17.6 per month = £7.19.1.
Lawrence Johnston - 2 months and 5 days at £2.17.6 per month = £6.4.7.
John McAuley (2nd Mate) - 3 months and 5 days at £4 per month = £12.8.0.
Arthur Tegart - 2 months and 5 days at £2 per month = £4.4.0.
Thomas Sergue (cook) - 6 months and 1 days at £3 per month = £18.2.0.
Henry McAuley - 3 months and 4 days at £2.17.6 per month = £9.19.4.
James McAuley - 5 months and 25 days at £2.17.6 per month = £16.15.5.
James McCambridge - 5 months and 25 days at £2.17.6 per month = £16.15.5 Total wages = £149.17.5.

When Captain McKillop retired, he was presented with a painting of the *EGLANTINE*, an ivory cane with a gold top, and a ship's chronometer - a specialist timekeeper used for marine navigation. Born in 1839, he died on the 24th of March, 1919. His sons were John and Danny. "The Captain's father was also Alexander McKillop, and the mother was Mary McCloey from Sloan, Cloughs," added Neil. "She was a member of the Church of Ireland congregation. Her sister, Margaret became Mrs Whiteford, grandmother of Bobby Whiteford. My father, Daniel was born on January 19, 1886, and his brother Michael John was born on the 28th of January 1888."

The Captain's father's brother was Daniel McKillop. He was Commanding Officer of the Coastguard Station at Arthurstown, County Wexford. Two of his sons went to sea, Michael and Alexander. The latter was drowned off the west coast of Africa, while Michael, the eldest, was a deck hand on the Graves-owned 'famine ship', the *DUNBRODY*.

Distant relative, Neil McKillop retains a copy of Michael's Certificate of Discharge, dated the 15th of July, 1856. The Able Seaman returned from a trip delivering emigrants to Quebec. The date of departure from Wexford, for this voyage, was the 14th of April, 1856. The vessel's registered tonnage was 458. The master of the ship was Captain W. Williams, who signed the now faded discharge document for Michael McKillop, whose place of birth is listed as Wexford.

The original *DUNBRODY* was built in Quebec, in 1845. The first master was Captain John Baldwin. It was initially used as a cargo ship, taking timber out of Canada. In 1845, the first year the potato crop failed in Ireland, the ship was converted, with cabins fitted, and used to transport famine survivors to North America. This was to facilitate the mass exodus of people, and when not enough conventional passenger ships were available.

From 1845 to 1881, the *DUNBRODY* transported Irish emigrants, mostly to Canada, and the port quarantine landing was Grosse Ile, Quebec. In 1847, she took 313 passengers, cabin and steerage, to Quebec. The Captain was John W. Williams. In 1869 the ship was sold, and in 1875 shipwrecked with a cargo of timber at Labrador.

A magnificent replica of the *DUNBRODY* lies at anchor in New Ross Harbour, County Wexford, and is a massive tourist attraction. History and nostalgia are sure to create big business. This project offers a trip back in time to a part of Irish history that can never be airbrushed. The reproduction of this emigrant vessel proves authentic interpretation of the ghastly famine experience. The *DUNBRODY* provides a unique insight into the tenacious bravery and hardships of the Irish emigrant.

Michael McKillop's brother Alexander was tragically drowned off the west coast of Africa on the night of the 6th of March, 1865. Ncil (McKillop) added: "The teenager's father received two letters from the young man's shipmate, Patrick Doran of Tramore, to describe what happened." Alexander started his sea career as a cabin boy on the Royal Navy's HMS *ESPOIR*. The name of the ship is French for 'hope' - and was launched on January 6, 1860. In 1869, she was converted to work as a dredger.

In a letter, dated May 13, 1865, Patrick Doran explains, in detail, how two gigs left the ship around 6.30pm, with a crew of four sailors and one officer, and with rations for two days. 'At 11.30 on the same night, when the boat was 30 miles from the ship, a sea struck her on the starboard beam, and she capsized. Two of the men were asleep, and were never seen again.

'The coxswain of the boat and another man held onto her until half-a-mile off the shore, and one of them could not hold any longer and was drowned. The one man who would be saved, yet couldn't swim, reported young Alex, decided to swim for the shore, but was never seen again.' It was believed he may have died from a shark attack.

Doran sent another excellently crafted letter to the Arthurstown McKillop family, dated July 10, 1865. He confirmed crew members went ashore, and combed the shoreline for a number of days, but did not find any bodies.

Other sea tales of the McKillop family include a second cousin of Captain Alexander, also named Alexander McKillop, who was captured in Hamburg Harbour on the boat he was a crew member - on the day the First World War started. He was taken off the boat, and held in a German prisoner-of-war camp for four years, until the conflict ended.

Neil McKillop said: "He was captured on the 14th of August 1914. Old Captain Jim Mitchell, also captured, was married to his sister. She was Mitchell's second wife. Alexander was a skeleton when he came home from Germany. Still, he went back to work at sea, and was involved in an accident on the boat, and lost a leg. My granny was Lizzie McAllister, married to the Captain. One of their two sons, Danny, was my father. He was named after my grandfather's brother Danny, who went to Arthurstown, Wexford."

John McKillop, a nephew of Neil, said: "Captain Alexander was born on the night of the 'Big Wind' of January 6, 1839. The wind was so strong it blew the roof off the family home at the 'Lowtown', in the townland of Cloughs. Captain Alexander was at sea for over 40 years. To mark his retirement he was presented with a painting of his ship, the *EGLANTINE*."

The painting inscription reads '*EGLANTINE*, Liverpool. A McKillop, Commander' John's brother Alex, whose wife Margaret runs the 'Village' B&B in Cushendall, is guardian of the prized mementoes. Their father was also named Alex, married to nurse Annie Smith, whose grandmother was a McDonnell, and her great uncle was Captain James McKeegan of the GEM.

5

SLOOP SHOCKER

THE MURRAY family of Waterfoot has a long and proud tradition in assorted seafaring issues ever since the middle of the 19th century. Affectionately known locally as 'The Divers', to distinguish the mariners from other Murray families in Glenariffe, and also to highlight how the men folk diversified into a lucrative ship salvage business.

The versatile Murray seamen, once also prominent on the north Antrim coastline as major salmon fishermen, were progressive owners of sailing ships, mainly of the sloop variety and trading across the Sea of Moyle.

However, one enterprise turned to disaster when their boat, the *THOMAS & MARY*, went to the bottom of the sea off Garron Point, County Antrim. Norris Murray, the youngest of the 20th Century generation of salmon fishermen and seamen from Waterfoot, kindly supplied me with confirmed details of the incident and subsequent inquest

The report of the sinking of the 60-tons *THOMAS & MARY* sloop, owned by John and Paddy Murray of Red Bay, and with direct connections to the brothers John, Alex, Archie and Norris Murray, reveals the tragic happening of December 19, 1852, with the loss of one life. It is an engrossing episode. A wooden vessel, with rigging style listed as 'sloop', it was a sail coaster built in Belfast, and first registered in 1841, by a T McIlwaine of Islandmagee.

The Murrays purchased the boat in 1847, and it was used for transporting cargo to and from the Antrim Coast and Belfast to the Scottish western isles. The official summary on the demise of the boat begins: 'On Saturday morning, the 18th inst (1852) the vessel sailed from Lamlash, in the island of Arran, in Scotland, bound for Belfast, having a crew of three hands and a general cargo on board.

'The wind was fair, and everything went well, till after passing the Castle Light, when she sprung a leak, which, notwithstanding the utmost exertions of the crew at the pump increased upon them. They hoisted all sail, and ran before the wind, hoping to get into some port on the Irish Coast, and when off the Point of Garron, about half past three o'clock that afternoon, she went right down.

'Fortunately, as she was sinking, the boat which was on deck floated, and the three men sprang into her having but one oar which they immediately lost, and were driven by the wind and tide past Tournamona Point.

'In this fearful extremity they tore up one of the seats of the boat, which they endeavoured to guide her with. They were, at length, between six and seven o'clock, driven into a little creek called Port Scally, when,

Name	Thomas & Mary
Location	Garron Point, Co.Antrim
Nationality	Irish
Date Lost	1852
Port	Belfast
Material	Wooden
Weight Tons	60
Ship Type	Sail Vessel
Ship Role	Coaster
Rigging Style	Sloop

Owner and Registration History	Owner in 1841	T.McIlwaine
	Owner in 1847	J. and P.Murray, Red Bay

Location	Garron Point, Co.Antrim
Date Lost	19 – 12 – 1852
Cause	Sank
Captain	P.Murray
Crew Lost	1
Passenger Lost	0.

On Saturday morning the 18th.inst. the above vessel sailed from Lamlash, in the island of Arran, in Scotland, bound for Belfast having a crew of three hands and a general cargo on board.
The wind was fair and everything went on well till after passing the Castle Light when she sprang a leak, which not withstanding the utmost exertions of the crew at the pump increased upon them. They hoisted all sail and ran before the wind hoping to get into some port on the Irish Coast; and when off the Point of Garron, about half past three o'clock that afternoon, she went right down. Fortunately as she was sinking the boat which was on deck floated and the three men sprang into her having but one oar which they immediately lost and were driven by the wind and tide past Turnamona Point.

In this fearful extremity they tore up one of the seats of the boat which they endeavoured to guide her with. They were at length between six and seven o'clock p.m. driven into a little creek called Port Seally when unfortunately the boat swamped and they were all washed out. The night was dark and the surge raged about them depriving them of every ray of hope.

Providentially, however the Master and one of the hands were driven on shore in an exhausted state, but one melancholy to relate the other poor fellow, Denis McLaughlin, of The Waterfoot, Red Bay, was lost. His body was washed ashore the next day, greatly bruised and disfigured by dashing against the rocks. An inquest was held on the body on Tuesday by Alexander Markham, Esq. Coroner and a respectable jury when the verdict of 'Found Drowned' was recorded. – Belfast Whig.

The Standard, London, Saturday 25th December 1852

The Belfast Shipping Register Lists a vessel from 1844 to 1856 Thomas & Mary 25 T Coaster owned by J.& P. Murray, Red Bay?. A note in 1856 says she was lost in 1855.

unfortunately, the boat swamped, and they were all washed out. The night was dark, and the surge raged about them, depriving them of every ray of hope.

'Providentially, however, the Master and one of the hands were driven on shore in an exhausted state, but one melancholy to relate, the other fellow, Denis McLaughlin of the Waterfoot, Red Bay, was lost. His body was washed ashore the next day, greatly bruised and disfigured by dashing against the rocks. An inquest (reported by the *Northern Whig* of Belfast) was held on the body on Tuesday by Alexander Markham, Esq; Coroner, and a respectable jury, when the verdict of 'Found Drowned' was recorded.'

Norris Murray indicated his industrious ancestors of the late 19th and early 20th century switched from owning and sailing such vessels to sea salvage work and salmon fishing. The last major diving job undertaken was when repairing a lock gate in Newry Canal during the 1950's.

Norris related the work was given to his family by the main contractor, McLaughlin and Harvey, following an IRA bomb that twisted the gate in one of the locks, and the gate fell into the canal water. It also appears the final diving job was to repair a small coaster in Carnlough Harbour.

Back in the distant past, Murray brothers did all sea salvage work in the area, and when possible hauled the salvage into the shallow harbour mouth of the River Dun, at Cushendun. The shipwrecked *CLEMENTINA* was a good example, with salvage taken ashore beside the old Ropeworks that became the Cushendun Hotel, and what is now known as 'The Blue Room'. The main drive shaft of this vessel was sold, and transported up the coast to be used by the Glenarm Limeworks.

The ship's mahogany staircase and landing, and also a carved cabin door, were purchased by Alex O'Hara, a Parkmore and Retreat Stations goods and passenger haulier, and used in the second-floor development of his house at nearby Knocknacarry. The *CLEMENTINA* went down on February 16, 1916.

The *CLEMENTINA* was once a Belgium Royal Yacht that was converted for warship use by the Royal Navy during the First World War. It ran aground, and the wreckage eventually salvaged by the Murray brothers. It was claimed by Cushendun folk the ship went down off Layd Point, near the south side of Cushendun Bay, and did not founder in Red Bay as logged in written memoirs.

Also salvaged by Murrays was the 216 tons *IRISHMAN* , a steam coaster than ran onto the rocks at Torr Head in January 1925. **Some material gratefully gathered from the excellently detailed hardback issue of *'Shipwrecks of the Ulster Coast'* by Ian Wilson, and first published by Impact Printing of Coleraine in 1979.

The first of the next generation of Murrays to go back to the sea was John. Born on January 30, 1924, he was an AB on coasters, and when home also involved himself in the diving business. He was followed to the sea by his brothers, Archie and Alex. Norris, who did not go to sea, explained the normal procedure was for his brothers to return from ocean travel to work the extensive family salmon fishing, and then take off again. That was the way it was in those days, with other local seamen arriving in to help save the summer crops.

Alex Murray said: "I worked deep-sea, and mostly heading up the St Lawrence River, I was with a Scottish company for a time, sailing to Quebec and Dalhousie. That is a part of the world you have to be out of by the end of September, or you will be trapped because of the winter ice coming in. I was also on one of the Head Line trips to Canada, when we took a cargo of 40 head of quality milk Friesian cows, and lots of crates of Scotch whisky. On the way back to England, we had a cargo of giant paper rolls. I think we had five tons of those rolls. We also took back timber.

"Early in the 1950's, shipping companies were looking for men, and I signed on out of Belfast. You were given your card, and all the necessary work papers, before you went abroad. Many men from the Glens worked on their farms during the summer, and went to sea during the winter months. It was a way of life then.

"I was back and forth at sea work for almost three years, and made the trip to Canada three times. I was also in other jobs, and did some fishing near home, and up the Causeway Coast. My brother Archie went to work at sea before me. He was mostly coasting with the Dorey company. Like myself, he worked back and forth at the seafaring.

"I also worked for a while on Dorey boats. Guernsey is a lovely place, indeed anywhere on the Channel Islands. In those days it took three to four days to unload a cargo of coal. We had to take the coal off in tubs. It was a slow process - just as that used to discharge coal at Red Bay pier.

"Of the old Murray family, the generation before me, I had three grand uncles - John, Archie and Alex. They never married. They had a sister who went to America, and lived at Cleveland, Ohio. They had sailing ships. Then my uncles became involved in the sea salvage business. They did quite a lot of diving, after shipwrecks happened around Rathlin Island, and from there right up the coast."

Born in 1935, he added: "I did very little diving. My brother John dived a lot. Archie did a bit of diving too. That business was on the way out in the 1950's. I remember we were working on a job in Carnlough Harbour. I was probably manning the air pump. Also there with us was Jack Mitchell. The diver's gear then included a telephone system inside the big heavy brass helmet.

"That gave the diver contact via a telephone line up to the people on the boat or the pier. In olden times the only system of communication between the diver and the workers on the air pump, and so forth, was by tugging a rope."

Norris Murray had further sea association through his wife Margaret (nee McKay). Her brother Jim from Layd, who lived at Cairns, Cushendall, spent time coasting, and then moved to deep-sea. He was known as 'Red' Jim. "My brother Jim, who had sandy hair, started off coasting with Captain Jim McGonnell on the *BALLYGILBERT*," said Margaret.

"He moved to join Captain John Mort on the *PASS of GLENOGLE.* He also worked alongside Danny O'Loan, Snr, who lived down Dalriada, Cushendall, before moving to deep-sea sailing when he joined Esso tankers, including the *ESSO YORKSHIRE* out of London. He travelled all over the world."

6

ROYAL COMMAND

ALEXANDER Smith McDonald rose from a humble background in Cushendun village to the pinnacle of success in the Royal Navy. He achieved the high rank of Lieutenant Commander. His protracted service, during the Second World War, the Korean War, and the Suez Crisis, earned him the O.B.E in 1967

Born on December 9, 1922, he devoted 47 years to the Royal Navy, serving with distinction mainly under the waves as Commander of submarines. McDonald enjoyed a meteoric rise from schoolboy days at Knocknacarry Primary to the podium of power in the Royal Navy. He died, aged 84, in Birmingham, on March 19, 2007, after a lengthy battle against cancer.

The third of six children in the family of Edinburgh-born Smith McDonald and his Cushendun-born wife Anne Veronica (nee McNeill), he left home in May 1938 to join the Royal Navy. In a personal summary of his career, Alex once revealed he joined the Royal Navy at the age of 15, direct from school. He advanced his education and promotion prospects through extensive studies, including Public Speaking, Instructional Techniques, and the Senior Officers' Business Appreciation Course, and Management Decision Making Course at Bristol University in 1971.

The sedulous sailor stated his specialisation as submarines. On May 3, 1939, he joined the RN Boys' Training ship, HMS *CALEDONIA*, at Rosyth, Scotland, and completed the initial training course in September 1939, the month the Second World War broke out. He was three months short of his 17th birthday.

In December 1939, his first posting was on the light cruiser HMS *CERES*, for service in the North Atlantic, Mediterranean, East Indies, and Indian Ocean, and he remained for two and a half years on this tour of duty, before returning to England in July 1942.

His next ship was the HMS *DRAKE,* from September to December 1942, when taking in an Educational Course prior to the Upper Yardman's Course, and spending the opening eight months of 1943 on the MS *COLLINGWOOD*, for the Upper Yardman's Course. He was commissioned in August 1943.

Four months were spent on a Sub-Lieutenant's Course at various RN schools, and from January 1944 until June 1951 he covered submarine service in the North Sea, the Mediterranean, and Far East. He was below the waves in vessels such as the *UNA, THRASHER, SATYR, TAKLENT, SIDON, AUROCHS THULE, ALARIC,* and *SANGUINE.*

From August to December 1951, he switched to serve on the

destroyer, HMS *CHAPLET,* and from January 1952 to July 1953, he was Staff Officer (Administration) to S.O.R.F. Portsmouth. He then concentrated on a six-month course at RN Tactical School, Woolwich. It was back to sea in February 1954, until December of that year, on the frigate HMS *CARDIGAN BAY,* for duty in the Far East

Following a January 1955 Instructional Technique Course at RNB Portsmouth, he was appointed Course Officer on the HMS *ROYAL ARTHUR* at the RN Leadership School, and from August to December 1955 was on the destroyer HMS *ST KITTS,* for stints in the Mediterranean and Home Stations.

Duty continued with one year, from February 1957, on the fast minelayer HMS *MANXMAN* in the Mediterranean, followed by the Executive Officer's job on reserve ships in Malta and Commanding Officer of the HMS *LOFOTEN.* From January 1960 to May 1962 he was the Commanding Officer of reserve ship sub-division at Hartlepool. From August 1962 through 1973 Alex was the Regional Careers' Staff Officer at West Midlands.

A synopsis of his hugely successful career, by his eldest son John, included: 'On completion of his training, the Second World War had begun, and he was sent into active service in the North Atlantic, and on Russian convoy escort duty. During the War, he trained as an officer, and on completion of that training he joined the submarine

in
Loving Memory
of
Patrick (Pat)
Joseph MacDonald

Pat was born Saturday, August 3, 1918 at Cushendun, County Antrim, Northern Ireland. He received his education at the Christian Brother's School, Belfast, Northern Ireland and at Heriot Watt College in Edinburgh, Scotland.

Pat immigrated to Canada in the 1950s. He resided in Ontario and was employed with Ontario Hydro, then in Quebec City and was employed with Davie Shipbuilding and Anglo Pulp and Paper and at The Pas in 1971 being employed with Manitoba Forestry Resources until his retirement in 1983 from his position as Manager of Maintenance and Engineering.

It was during his employment with Davie Shipbuilding that he was involved with the construction of the Hundah Hydroelectric project in the South Western Region of India. So, he was quite surprised years later to find that Father Marshall Joseph, when in The Pas, came from the same region.

Pat was united in marriage to Helen Logue, August 16, 1942 at Loanhead, Midlothian, Scotland.

In 1939 Pat enlisted with the Royal Navy-Fleet Air Arm serving his country with this division until the end of World War II and then worked with the Royal Canadian Navy Reserve for some years later.

Pat was very generous with his time to his church community. He was a faithful parishioner of Our Lady of The Sacred Heart Cathedral Parish.

He was involved in various ministries including Reading, Altar Serving, and as a Eucharistic Minister, many times going to people's homes when they were unable to attend services at the church. He helped Father Gerard Nogue monthly with the Services at St. Anthony's Hospital.

Pat reached further with his gifts being a Lay Presider at liturgies, both at the Cathedral and at Cranberry Portage, when a priest was unavailable. Many times, as well, Pat presided at Christian Wake Services at the Church and at the Funeral Home and also gave the Hemauer's and their replacement, Norm Harris, a helping hand with funerals when they were on holidays.

He was Past President of Parish Council of Our Lady of the Sacred Heart Cathedral, and was a former member of The Pas Health Complex Board of Directors.

After a lengthy battle with cancer, Pat passed away Saturday, August 6, 1994 at St. Anthony's General Hospital, The Pas, at the age of 76 years.

He is survived by his loving wife, Helen; sons and daughters, Patrick Smith (Lynn) of Ear Falls, Ontario, Joanna (Germain) Levesque of St. Redempteur-De-Levis, Quebec, Daniel Joseph (Micheline) of Neufchatel, Quebec, Ferne (Doug) Kinley of Rockyford, Alberta, and Alexander Francis (Sandra) of The Pas; 14 grandchildren; 4 great grandchildren; sisters, Anne (Jack) Murphy of Brighton, England, Kathleen (Johnnie) Bernier of Beaumont, Quebec; brother, Alex S. (Betty) of Birmingham, England, and Reverend Brother Angelo C.P. of Northern Ireland.

Pat was predeceased by his parents, Smith and Annie Veronica (McNeill) of Northern Ireland; granddaugther, Mary, beloved daughter of Patrick and Lynn, and sister, Mary Margaret McCauley.

service, seeing action in both the Mediterranean and Far East. After the end of the War, Alex continued to serve at sea, including both the Korean and Suez conflicts.

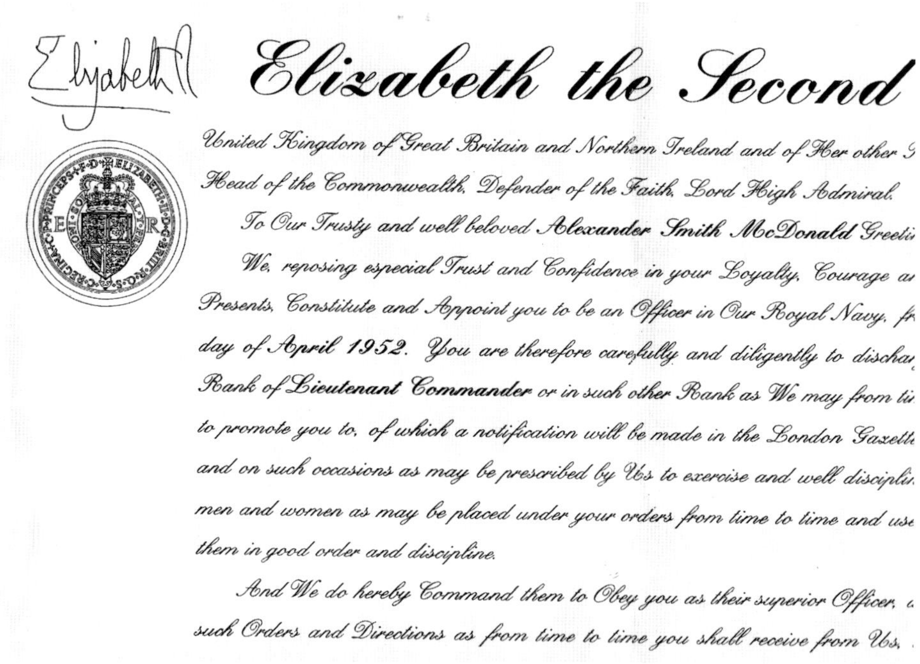
Elizabeth R

Elizabeth the Second

United Kingdom of Great Britain and Northern Ireland and of Her other

Head of the Commonwealth, Defender of the Faith, Lord High Admiral.

To Our Trusty and well beloved Alexander Smith McDonald Greeti

We, reposing especial Trust and Confidence in your Loyalty, Courage a

Presents, Constitute and Appoint you to be an Officer in Our Royal Navy, fr

day of April 1952. You are therefore carefully and diligently to discha

Rank of Lieutenant Commander or in such other Rank as We may from ti

to promote you to, of which a notification will be made in the London Gazett

and on such occasions as may be prescribed by Us to exercise and well discipli

men and women as may be placed under your orders from time to time and use

them in good order and discipline.

And We do hereby Command them to Obey you as their superior Officer,

such Orders and Directions as from time to time you shall receive from Us,

'In 1944, he met and married Elizabeth (Betty), who was, at the time, a serving WREN. In 1958, Alex was posted to Malta, where for the first time the family (by now five children) lived permanently together. Betty remembers their time in Malta as one of the happiest periods of their lives. A fifth, and last, child was born in Malta.

'On their return from Malta, Alex was posted to West Hartlepool. In 1962. he was given his last posting as a Royal Naval Officer (and promotion to Commander) to Birmingham as Regional Staff Officer for the West Midlands and Wales.

'In 1967, he was invested with the O.B.E. by Her Majesty The Queen, in recognition of his military service. Upon retirement from the Royal Navy, in June 1973, Alex joined the *Birmigham Post* and *Mail* as Competitions' Manager. He also became an active member in his parish of Adcocks Green, Birmingham, where he served as School Governor. His pastimes included swimming, and also golf at Olton Golf Club. He took an interest in boxing, and was Vice-President of the Gynodd Sporting Club.'

The O.B.E parchment is signed top left corner - Elizabeth R - and states: 'ELIZABETH the SECOND, by the Grace of God of Great Britain and Northern Ireland and of Her other Realms and Territories Queen Head of the Commonwealth, Defender of the Faith Lord High Admiral.

'To Our Trusty and well beloved Alexander Smith McDonald Greeting! We, reposing especial Trust and confidence in your Loyalty, Courage and good conduct do by these Presents Constitute and Appoint you to be an Officer in our Royal Navy from the first day of April 1952.

'You are therefore carefully and diligently to discharge your Duty as such in the Rank of Lieutenant Commander or in such other Rank as We may from time to time hereafter be pleased to promote you to, of which a notification will be made in the *London Gazette,* and you are in such manner and on such occasions as may be prescribed by Us to exercise and well discipline in their duties such officers, men and women as may be placed under your orders from time to time and use your best endeavours to keep them in good order and discipline.

'And We do hereby Command them to O.B.E. you as their superior Officer, and you to observe and follow such Orders and Directions as from time to time you shall receive from Us, or any your superior Officer, according to the Rules and Discipline of War in pursuance of the Trust hereby reposed on you.

'Given at Our Court at Saint James's, the fifteenth day of December 1964 in the Thirteenth Year of Our Reign. By Her Majesty's Command.'

The Commander's niece, Mrs Angela McWilliams, who lives with husband Bernie in Knocknacarry, keeps close contact with her cross-channel cousins. Her mother, Mary Margaret McDonald, who married Charlie McAuley of Glenaan, was one of three girls in the McDonald family that also produced another top echelon seafarer, the Commander's older brother Patrick Joseph.

Nurse McWilliams said: "All members of the McDonald family went to the old Knocknacarry Primary School. The three boys were - uncle Donnie (Brother Angelo CP Ardoyne), who died aged 72 in 2010, served in Ardoyne Monastery, P J, who died in Canada, and Alex.

"It is quite remarkable that uncle Alex, after leaving Knocknacarry School went from there to the Sea Training School and as a young teenager straight into the Second World War. My aunts are Anne and Kathleen - the youngest of the family. She went to Canada, where she married a French-Canadian."

The sea career of Pat McDonald was also colourful. Born on Saturday August 3, 1918, his formative education switched from Knocknacarry to a Secondary education at the Christian Brothers' School, Belfast, and on to Heriot Watt College, Edinburgh. In 1939, he enlisted in the Royal Navy - Fleet Air Arm, serving with this division until the end of the Second World War. He married Helen Logue at Loanhead, Midlothian, Scotland, on August 16, 1942.

Pat emigrated to Canada in the early 1950's, and joined the Royal Canadian Navy Reserve for a number of years. He resided in Ontario. where he was employed by the Ontario Hydro. Then it was into Quebec City, where he worked for Davie Shipbuilding, when the firm built the Hundah Hydroelectric project in the south-west region of India.

Later, he was with Anglo Pulp and Paper, and at The Pas, Manitoba, and in 1971 Pat was employed as Manager of Maintenance and Engineering by Manitoba Forestry Resources until his retirement in 1983. After a lengthy battle with cancer he passed away, aged 76, on Saturday August 6, 1994, at The Pas, once the home of Native American tribe, the Cree Indians. The Pas lies 630 kilometres north west of the provincial capital, Winnipeg.

At that time, his sister Anne was married to Jack Murphy, living in Brighton, and Kathleen was married to Johnnie Bernier in Beaumont, near the St Lawrence River at Quebec. Pat was preceded then by his parents, and by his sister Mary Margaret McAuley.

Anne 'Nan' McDonald was first married to a Jack Walsh, and lived for a time at Riverside Crescent, Cushendun. They later separated. They had two sons, John and Tom.

Angela McWilliams surmised her grandfather probably met Ann Veronica McNeill in Edinburgh, and came with her to live in Cushendun. She said: "My grandfather, I believe, had been at sea, and came from Edinburgh. We are connected to McNeill's of The Rocks, and this is probably a reason they came to live in Cushendun. Aunt Nan and Jack Walsh had two sons. John Jnr was born and reared in Cushendun.

"He joined the Royal Marines in 1962, aged 17. He served in Aden, the Middle East, Borneo, Singapore, Malaya, Norway, and France. His brother Tommy joined the Royal Navy in 1974. He served on the HMS *EAGLE* - then the largest warship in the Navy."

Sean 'The Rock' McNeill said: "Mrs McDonald was probably a second cousin of my father. I remember Smith McDonald and his wife working and living at Miss Ada McNeill's house, Cushendun, before moving into the house behind McBride's pub in Cushendun Village. I recall a young Alex McDonald coming to chat with my father when we lived at Rockport. He seemed a very modest man, the submariner."

7 SHORE STREET SKIPPER

CAPTAIN JIM McGONNELL of Cushendall went to sea at 16 years of age, at the start of the Second World War. He began in late 1939 with the Kelly Company, working on coasting coal boats. He was also involved in convoys during the War.

In December 2012, during a chat with Mrs Eileen McAllister, better known as Eileen Patterson, of Shore Street, Cushendall, I was fortunate to glean background information on Jim McConnell. A niece of the dapper skipper, she sadly died aged 77 on February 1, 2013.

Her detailed recall included: "Uncle Jim survived working at sea during the Second World War, and then went to join the Dorey Shipping Company in Guernsey, where he became their Head skipper. He also sat a Ship Pilot's ticket, and worked at that until he retired. Jim settled in Guernsey, where he lived out his years there. He met his wife in Guernsey, a girl of French extraction, Kathleen LeLacher, and they raised six of a family.

"Captain Jim, who was from Tully, Cushendall, took a lot of local men to sea, including Captain Danny McNaughton. Jim usually called into the McNaughton house for a yarn when he was home on a break from sea, and often a young Danny would ask him: 'When are you taking me to sea?'

"Uncle Jim eventually agreed, but on condition Danny would not remain on the low rung of the work ladder . . . not just stay an ordinary seaman, but study for the Tickets. Uncle Jim wanted him to work his way to the top, and Danny did just that. Danny worked his way through all the Ticket examinations, and became a captain. Jim, who was a very modest man, had Jim McElroy of Dalriada with him on the boats, as cook. The First Mate for many, many years was Paddy Mooney, a brother of Alex Mooney and Mrs Thompson."

From Cairns, Paddy Mooney lived for a time in Guernsey. His road to the sea apparently started on a surreptitious 7.30am bus trip out of Cushendall. A nephew, Alex Thompson said: "I was told Paddy's older brother Alex intended to go to sea. Paddy went instead, taking off with Pat McNaughton, Kevin's (Mogey) father. I believe they were very young, just left school. I think they went to Larne on the bus."

Mooney worked on Dorey coasters, often on the McGonnell-skippered boat. He moved to Weymouth in the south of England, eventually married, and settled to live there the rest of his days, rearing two of a family. For a time he was a vesper in the local church. He suffered cancer in one lung. However, successful surgery helped him to live a further 25 years after the removal of the lung.

Mrs McAllister added: "Over the years many other local men who went to sea with Captain Jim McGonnell included James and Robert Emerson, sons of Tommy Emerson. From Waterfoot, he had Patsy McAllister and his brother Mickey with him."

Incidentally, the golden age of assured employment with the Dorey company fizzled after the Fastnet Race of 1979, when many lives were lost during storms off the south coast of Ireland. Peter Dorey, boss of the famous Guernsey coaster shipping firm that was launched in 1887 by his grandfather, Onesimus Dorey, was an avid and competitive yachtsman. Tragically, the head of the company since 1963, drowned while participating in the 1979 Fastsnet Race. His wife carried on the business until 1983. The Dorey company, facing liquidation, was sold to James Fisher and Sons, Limited, of Barrow-in-Furness.

Eileen McAllister remarked on a time when Captain Jim was very pally with the Blaney brothers, Jim and Captain Gerry: "They were great friends, and when they were home on leave were always chatting about life at sea. I think they sat most of their different Ticket examinations together. Jim McGonnell lived with my mother, Lily McGonnell, better known as Lily Patterson. He was her half brother.

"My mother's mother died of what was called 'Galloping Consumption', when my mother was four years of age. That was my grandfather's wife, and two other sisters of my mother also died of the same illness. They lived at Carnlough at that time, and had a butcher's shop there. After my grandfather's wife died, he came back home to Cushendall, and took my mother with him. Two maiden aunts reared her, along with another aunt - Margaret McGonnell - who was a schoolteacher at Ballyeamon Primary. They were aunts of Captain Jim.

"Maggie McGonnell also taught music, and to people such as Dr O'Kane and Fr Black. At one time, she assembled a small orchestra in Cushendall, to take part in concerts as a way of raising money for the restoration of the churches that had been burned - at The Bay and Cushendall. Money was badly needed to pay for the rebuilding. Maggie taught the piano and the violin.

"The orchestra had people like Dan O'Loan and Joe Doyle on the fiddle. Somebody else played the cello, and so forth. Maggie was a teacher first at the Bay, and then moved to take up a post at Ballyeamon School. For years, she walked every day up and back to Cushendall, to teach in the school. She was once engaged to be married to a man named McGaughey, but he was lost at sea. She never married, and died in 1935.

"My great, great grandfather was Dan McGonnell. Two of his brothers went to sea during the 19th century, on sailing ships. They were Patrick and Alex McGonnell. My great, great grandfather came down into Cushendall from the side of Lurig Mountain, and opened the wee shop in Shore Street in the 1840's.

"He used to travel to the Mull of Kintyre to bring back beef, and sometimes it was a case of vice versa. It was during one of those sailings he met Betty McAlonan of Campbeltown, and eventually married her. They had a family of eight children, including the poet, Dan, who was to become a butcher in the house on Shore Street.

“Dan and my grandfather, Alex McGonnell, served their time to become qualified butchers in the Brogan butcher shops in Glasgow. John Brogan was friendly with old McGonnell, and he took Dan and my grandfather to their business in Scotland to learn the trade.

“Apparently old Brogan used to say to Dan: ‘You know Dan, if you were half wise you’d own Cushendall’. My uncle Dan, of course, liked a good time. He was some character, a bit wild at times - when he’d go on the rip. Dan had three sisters. Lizzie was the housekeeper. Kathleen was a schoolteacher, and Ellen was a dressmaker.

“I recall a story of how mischievous Dan could be. Once there was a man up High Street, old Ketty Nicholl, who had a beautiful rose garden - and grew gooseberry bushes. He used to sell a pennyworth of gooseberries. He also had a notion of my aunt Lizzie. He was always looking into the house on Shore Street, when Lizzie would be cooking on an open fire.

“Because he was a small man he would climb up the iron bars outside the shop to take a closer look through the window at Lizzie. Then uncle Dan McGonnell decided to do something when coming back from the slaughterhouse. He was about to hang the carcases on the bars when he saw Nicholl.

“So, he took a bucket of blood, crept up to the iron bars, and poured the contents all over the unsuspecting Nicholl. Some folk on the street thought the poor man had his throat cut, because there was so much blood on him, and blood running onto the pavement.

“The District Nurse was sent for by a passerby, but the nurse was soon satisfied there was no damage done, no sign of a wound on Nicholl, just a prank. Dan McGonnell was a rogue. He killed sheep and goats in the slaughterhouse down the back lane, and for people such as the O’Hara’s in Knocknacarry.”

8 CAPE FEARS

HAZARDOUS passage around Cape Horn was often an inevitable consequence for old-time mariners. Perhaps there is nowhere in the world's sea lanes more treacherous to navigate than this South American stretch of gigantic waves and wicked winds.

Before the opening of the Panama Canal, many Glens of Antrim seafarers braved and survived the high-rigged sailing ship voyage past the Horn, on the way from Europe to North America's west coast ports. One man from Lower Cloughs, Cushendall, made many of these ever-testing trips. He was Captain Patrick McAuley.

A grandson, Paddy Burns, related: "Both my grandfather, Patrick McAuley and his son James were deep-sea mariners. Captain Patrick spent his working life on the oceans, and was a skipper of deep-sea sailing ships that often made the very tough passage around Cape Horn.

"I never knew my grandfather. He died in 1936, a year before I was born. Mary, his widow, often told how her husband used to describe the trips he made around the Horn. At times it was a pretty horrendous experience, but they never thought much about it in those days. My grandfather went to sea in the 19th century, working on riggers. His wife ran the farm at home. They reared a family of one son and three daughters.

"He worked a very long time on the seas, until he was 70 years of age, and ironically died shortly after he retired. After travelling to all parts of the globe, surviving many rough voyages, he collapsed and died while taking home a load of turf from the mountain, at Tievebulliagh. On the way back with the horse and cart, he got down to open a gate and slumped on the spot.

"His son, James also became a sea captain, and worked deep-sea. Tragically, as a young man he died on board his ship when it was coming up the Clyde to berth in Glasgow. He suffered an appendicitis problem. The appendix burst, and he died there of peritonitis. The medical people could not save him. I never knew James. He married Charlotte McCollam from Rathmullan, County Donegal. They had a family of three girls, who retained the house at Rathmullan."

The Burns family had another direct link with seafaring, through Paddy's older brother Frank, who was at sea for around ten years. He was a stoker on Kelly boats. Captain 'Count' Johnny McCormick of Waterfoot took Frank to sea. The 'Count' was a relation of ours, as his wife was a full cousin of my mother. She was Anne McAuley. Her father was George McAuley, a brother of my grandfather, Captain Paddy.

"Frank left the sea to work in England, and did contracts for British Telecom in laying cables. He often brought men from here over to work for him in England. I was 76 in April, 2013. Frank, who is dead, was five years older than me. The eldest member of our family is Mary, who is 83. I was 15 when Captain Paddy's wife died, 61 years ago, in 1952."

Burns added: "My father was James Burns. Frank and me were grandsons of Captain James. So Frank continued on the family tradition of going to work at sea, making it three successive generations. James McAuley, who died in a Glasgow hospital, was a brother of my mother, Rosetta McAuley. While I am still on the sea theme, I remember a great kindness shown by the late Pat Connolly. When he was at sea he once brought me a nice coffee table as a present, following his journey to and from Buenos Aires."

Captain Hugh O'Mullan of Waterfoot, added: "I knew Frank Burns very well. He was at sea some time before me. I sailed with him on Kelly boats. He was at sea a long time before he gave it up, and went to work on land, in construction in England."

One of the saddest stories of a seaman from the Glens is that of John Darragh. Born up Glenballyeamon, in the shadow of Tievebulliagh - once a factory to make weapons of war during the Stone Age - he collapsed at his new Cushendall village home, and died of a massive heart attack. Surviving the hardships of Merchant Marine work for over 30 years was quite an accomplishment, yet his life came to a crushingly cruel end.

In the most unpredictable fashion, he suffered a tragic demise on Monday, Septembcr 3, 1962. Born on the 12th of July 1911, and a seaman since he left primary school, John Darragh, from Murroo, Cloughs, on Gault's Road, he died aged 51. The passing of such a young and seemingly powerful man in his prime remains one of the tragic tales of the Glens.

The irony of his shocking death in his new home on Chapel Road, was that he'd just returned from Dublin, after witnessing the All-Ireland hurling championship final of Sunday September 2. He was an avid follower of the sport, and secured time off from sea duties to make the trip to Croke Park, where he was one of a 75,039 gate.

On that afternoon, the final featured a Jimmy Doyle-skippered Tipperary defeating Wexford, led by Billy Rackard. The outcome was 3-10 to 2-11. Referee was John Dowling (Offaly), and the glamour game heralded the first live screening of the final by Teilifis Eireann.

His son Malachy said: "He died on a Monday, after arriving back from Croke Park around two o'clock in the afternoon. He felt unwell, said he would lie down for a while, and after a cup of tea went to bed. Shortly afterwards, my mother Ann - who was O'Neill from Glenarm - heard him falling out of the bed because of the intense pain he suddenly suffered from a massive heart attack.

"Walking along the road outside was nurse Annie T (Smyth) McKillop, who came in, saw what was happening - and sent for the local doctor. A locum arrived, driven in a car by a young Alastair McSparran, not then fully qualified. The locum went upstairs, gave my father an injection, but it didn't save his life.

"A week earlier, he took me on the crossbar of his bicycle down from Murroo Bridge to start my job as an apprentice motor mechanic in Frankie McCormick's garage in Cushendall. Paul McKeegan was also starting work there. At that period, we were moving down from Murroo to the house on Chapel Road, and completed the move on the Sunday of the hurling final."

John Darragh, whose brother Neil emigrated to New York in the 1920's and played in the successful 'Antrim' hurling team there, also did a bit of farming. Malachy added: "When he took time away from the sea, he used to dig out lint dubs with John McCurry. They went around the country digging dubs for farmers. He also had his own lint dub. It is still there at the front of my house.

"My mother did the farming after they were married. He was at sea long before that. I think sea work was his only job, apart from a bit of farming. He worked mostly on Kelly coasters, although namesake George Darragh of Carnlough, suggested my father once worked on the *ULSTER PIONEER*. There was a period when my father worked a lot in and out of Liverpool and Heysham."

The *ULSTER PIONEER*, a cross-channel passenger service, was first owned by Coast Lines, until 1958, when purchased by William Sloan of Glasgow. In 1963, she was bought by the Belfast Steamship Company, and renamed *TALISKER*. She was sold on in 1965 to Burns and Laird; then to an Israeli company in 1970, and renamed *SNAPIR*. In 1973, she became the *WOODBINE*, then the *HONG SHEN* in 1975, and after being sold on to a Malaysian firm in 1978 sunk ten years later.

Malachy Darragh continued: "I believe my father sailed at one time with a young John Graham of Cushendun. John, who later became a Captain, used to call at our house." The Darragh family included the eldest son Eamonn, then the twins Neal and Malachy, and the youngest - Martin.

Malachy's wife Kathleen, a retired schoolteacher, revealed: "Martin worked at sea for three years. He was a butcher on cruise ships. He made trips on passenger liners to Australia, once meeting a cousin down there. I remember Martin telling us how discipline was so strict on those ships."

Also to take to the mix of temporary sea work and farming from the Murroo area was Mick Quinn. His son of the same name, local TV engineer, said: "My father worked on Kelly coasters before he was married. He lived at Clougheen, Clough Road, Ballyeamon, and went to sea when a young man. He came from a farming background, and started at sea before he was married. He sent money home to help with the running of the farm."

Casting the net around the Cloughs - Glenaan vicinity, other men to test the waters included the Gore brothers - Pat, Archie, and John. A nephew, John Gore, a retired schoolteacher, said: "Of the men in the family, my father, Jim, was the eldest. He was born in 1907. John was next, then Archie, Patrick, and Denis. Pat, Archie, and John worked at sea.

"Sadly, uncle John was killed at sea, on the River Clyde. He was docked in Glasgow. The accident happened on December 8, 1939, at the start of the Second World War, when there was a blackout in place. On the way back to his ship he lost his footing, slipped between his boat and the dock wall, and was drowned. The body wasn't recovered until five days later."

Born at Mill Hollow, at the bottom end of Gault's Road, on August 12, 1909, John, who was a vital member of the Cushendun Emmets' hurling side that won the 1931 Antrim Championship, started at sea when he signed on as a fireman at Dublin on February 16, 1937. Archie, born on January 5, 1911, first registered as a fireman on January 31, 1946.

Archie's career opened on board the Kelly coaster *COLERAINE*. He later worked on boats such as the *MELISSA, CREWHILL, BALLYBRYAN*, and in 1952 the *BALLYGALLY*, when he was promoted to Second Engineer. Nephew John added: "Uncle Pat was on coasters, and I met him once at his boat, the *PALM*, when it was berthed in Belfast. I was up there working at the time. Pat was a ship's cook, and spent his days on Kelly boats.

"I have other sea connections. My mother Cassie's brother was John McQuaige from Cushendun, who was a seaman for a long time. My wife Ann's sister, Sheila is married to Captain Hugh O'Mullan of Waterfoot. I'm also a cousin of John Mitchell of Glenariffe. His mother, who married Jack Mitchell, was a McLernon - my grandfather's sister."

Other seamen from the Glenaan-Ballyeamon area included Charlie 'Pat' McKeegan of Tavanaghan. He spent a short spell at sea during his teenage days, working on coasters, before deciding to return to dry land and become as a lorry driver for Graham's road repair firm of Glenariffe. Others from that area included Sam Moore of Cloughs, and Alex Quinn of Tavanaghan, who worked on coasters alongside Hugh Healy.

9 PRISONERS of WAR

CAPTAIN James Mitchell found himself in the wrong place at the wrong time, when he berthed his ship in Hamburg, just as the dreadful First World War erupted. The German forces impounded his vessel, and placed the Glenariffe man, his wife Rose, and members of his crew in the slammer. They were frog-marched off to prisoner-of-war facilities, a desolate area a few miles outside the city limits.

As master of the *INDIANOLA*, Captain Mitchell was able to bring his wife on trips with him, but this journey turned into a horror story. She was Rose Henry, and also from Foriff, Glenariffe. Her father was a sea captain, James Henry. Captain Mitchell and his wife were taken to the Ruhleben camp, a compound set up by the Germans for civilian prisoners such as merchant seamen.

Grandson Joe Mitchell of Waterfoot said: "Both were placed in prisoner-of-war camps. After six months or so his wife became very ill. She was released, and allowed to come back home, but never recovered from that horrific experience in Germany. She had to go to hospital, and later died there. Captain Jim was detained in his prison camp for the duration of the war."

On Tuesday, August 4, 1914, Britain entered war with Germany, after the German invasion of Luxemburg, and the following violation of Belgian territory. The *INDIANOLA*, registered in 1912, was owned by Leyland Shipping of Liverpool. The ship was detained on the River Elbe, north Germany, at Hamburg.

Ruhleben internment camp, once a racecourse, lay six miles west of Berlin, and held up to 5,500 prisoners. It was a civilian detention centre, and it housed citizens of the Allied Powers - including merchant seamen, fishermen, students, holidaymakers, or workers stranded there when the War erupted in 1914. Crew members of ships stranded in German ports, and those captured at sea when rescued from boats sunk by U-Boats were taken to the camp.

James P. Mitchell, whose father Alexander was the captain of a tugboat working out of Belfast, is listed in the POW groupings of merchant seamen held in Ruhleben. He is registered as Chief Officer of the *INDIANOLA*, and it also states the year he was born, 1874. Along with Captain Mitchell, the names are listed of the other members of the crew who were captured on the ship. The crew members detained were seaman mostly from England.

His great, great grandson, Joe Mitchell, son of Joe Jnr, states the captain's wife Rose took ill in the camp, was repatriated - released to return to the Glens - but died a year later, in 1915, in an Antrim hospital.

Joe Mitchell III said: “While he was interned, Captain Jim Mitchell carved out a model of a German Taube reconnaissance aeroplane, made out of a bullet and a bullet casing, with soldered wings and undercarriage. This remains a proud possession in the Mitchell family.

“He was detained for the length of the First World War. His ship was impounded, and then used by the Germans. Ironically, it was torpedoed by the British in the Baltic. It didn’t sink. It was salvaged, and refurbished to be given back to the original company at the end of the War. My great, great grandfather was back in the seafaring business in 1919, and on board his old ship. However, this time he worked as First Mate. The ship’s first passage after the war was to New York.

“Captain James married again, to Rose McKillop of Cushendall. She became a surrogate mother for my grandfather Joe, and his brothers Jack and Jim. The old Captain died in the mid-1930’s, and is buried in Glenariffe Cemetery. My other grandfather, my mother Deirdre’s father, Hugh O’Brien from Belfast was also a seaman. He died aged 79 on November 24, 1985, and is buried with wife Eithne in the Bay Cemetery.

“He was a ship’s cook for most of his life. Before he went to sea he fought in the Irish Civil War. On one of his sea trips, to New Orleans, his ship was berthed at Baton Rouge, the Louisiana State capital, and was in the city with his crew colleagues when former State Governor Huey Long was assassinated.” Long, a Democrat, was a US Senator when he was gunned down in Baton Rouge on September 10, 1935. He was 42.

During the Second World War, Hugh O’Brien was torpedoed on convoy duty, and survived. He did the Momansk and Halifax runs. Hugh’s grandfather was Captain Tom O’Brien of the sailing ship *WALTER J CUMMINS*. In 1892, he died on his ship when it was moored at Tarbert, County Kerry. The O’Brien’s originally came from Ardglass. County Down.

The Mitchell family maintained a sterling association with sea work. Captain Joe Mitchell, born and reared on a small farm near the top end of Glenariffe glen, once held the hugely important post of Commander of the Mosquito Fleet. The romantic-sounding name of the small Esso-owned tankers in the Caribbean Sea matched the exotic surroundings at the island of Aruba

His son Joe revealed: “My father spent a long time working out of Aruba, on oil tankers belonging to the Esso Company. At one time, Aruba, an island 20 miles long in the southern Caribbean and 17 miles north of the coast of Venezuela, was the biggest oil refinery in the world. The crude oil was shipped out of nearby Venezuela to the refinery. Because it was a shallow bay off Venezuela only boats of shallow draft could be used to transport the oil. I believe a ship of 5,000 tons was all that could be used, and the Esso boats became known as the Mosquito Fleet.”

Aruba, equidistant from the Colombian shoreline town of Maicao, on the La Guajira Peninsula, was once a smuggler’s home during the olden times of pirate plunder, and the need for privacy in the Caribbean. For a lengthy period of the 20th century, the paradise island was known as the distribution centre for the American giant cigarette company, Philip Morris. The company’s Marlboro brand filtered throughout the Caribbean and South America from Aruba.

Joe Mitchell Jnr added: "My father was in Aruba during the Second World War, when it was shelled by German U-Boats. The Germans tried to prevent fuel leaving there, to help in the war effort of America and England. I recall my dad telling about a German blockade, and a bombardment that resulted in some oil-tank farms in Aruba going up in flames, after being hit by shells. He was near the scene, but not hurt."

Joe Jnr's son, Joseph supplied more detail on the adventures of the Mitchell family in the Caribbean: "During periods of the Second World War my grandfather was involved it taking cargo of oil, petroleum, from Venezuela to Texas. The tanker convoy run was perilous, and regarded the 'Happy Time' by German U-boat captains."

Joe Jnr added: "His employer was the Lago Oil and Transport Company, owned by Esso. He became Commander Captain of the Mosquito Fleet, when the viability of oil shipped from Aruba became less and less - because of oil now gushing out of the Middle East, from Abadan. Ceru Colorado was the name of the fashionable area in Aruba. At that time, this select part of the island was full of rich Americans, who built big houses there.

"With the changing circumstances regarding the oil business the American influence diminished, and the wealthy Yanks gradually left the island. This resulted in his American employer altering his work. He changed to be Training Officer for the indigenous sailors, and his job was to help them improve their seamanship, and get their Tickets to be tugboat officers."

Brendan Mitchell, a retired schoolteacher and the youngest of Captain Joe's three boys, remembers with warm affection a special time in the posh part of Aruba. "When we were very young, we used to go out there every second summer. I also lived with my father and mother for 18 months, and attended primary school. I would have been six years of age.

"At one period or another we all went to school in Aruba. My brother Joe was out there for a long period, and went to High School for one year, before coming back here to attend St MacNissi's College. Jim, the eldest, who became a veterinarian, was ahead of us at Garron Tower. He was born in March 1940, and would come out to join us in Aruba during the summer time."

After living in Aruba for almost two years, the boys were sent back home, just before the 11-plus examination. They split up to stay with their uncle Dan McKillop at Foriffe, or with their aunt Betty O'Rawe at Tully, Cushendall. "My father was with Shell UK for a while, working back and forth from Britain to America," added Brendan, "He fell in with somebody in America, who told him the Esso oil company was looking for sea captains for their fleet. Esso USA was taking oil from Maracaibo Bay to Aruba.

"It eventually came to the stage when the natives, who were well educated, decided they wanted to do the work, take over the jobs done only by whites - Americans mainly, with some Irish and English included. The Lago colony, where we lived, was only for white residents. That is the way it was then. It was a fantastic place. It had self-contained units, and had absolutely everything. There were several beaches, a golf course, a bowling alley, a number of restaurants. It was like a top-class holiday resort at that time, with one thousand homes.

"The people who lived in the bungalows were all employees of Esso USA. When the change happened, and as people left to return to their native countries - most of them going to the USA - their houses were knocked down. The Americans made sure their houses could not be used by anyone else. They all knew they were being phased out.

"After my father left being a tanker captain, he became a tug master in Ceru Colorado Harbour - taking tankers through the reefs into the harbour. The natives started to be trained to do the jobs. My father was the only one left behind by Esso USA, to train the locals.

"He stayed there up to 1964. By that stage, I was boarding in Garron Tower. So was brother Joe. Jim travelled there at the start, and then boarded when he was sitting his finals. I remember Jim being my dormitory monitor at the Tower."

The Mitchell boys were left with glowing memories of an idyllic time of sun, azure seas, and loafing on soft sand in Aruba, but it was not all plain sailing for their father. Indeed, Captain Joe Mitchell's career at sea stalled, and almost ended when he sustained a serious back injury. He was confined to a hospital bed in Ballymena for close on 18 months, and during this period he studied the ways of the waves.

Joe Jnr added: "He also became an excellent chess player during the time he was recuperating. He spent 18 months lying on a board in a hospital. He studied a bit, obviously had a lot of time on his hands. When he came out of hospital he had to wear a brace around his back. He was advised it might be unwise to go to sea again. The chance to join Lenehans came about, so he threw away the brace, and went back to sea.

"My father got his Master's Ticket when 26 years of age. On one occasion he was stranded in South America, when working for the Irish Bay Line. This firm was owned by Lenehans, who were former farmland owners of an area in County Down, now occupied by the Ulster Folk Museum at Cultra, Craigavad. There was, I believe, a financial problem involving the ship owners, so my father was sent down to Buenos Aires as stand-in captain.

"It may have been, I believe, to Bahia Blanco. He was put in charge, and had to stay there with the crew. Lloyds of London would not allow the ship to move. I remember him telling me he was put up in a very grand hotel until the matter involving the ship's owners and the authorities there was resolved. He also said members of the crew soon began to get fidgety - some became very annoyed, because they had not been paid.

"The three sons of my grandfather Captain Jim Mitchell all went to work at sea . . . my father Joe, and my uncles, Jack, and Jim, who was a boilermaker and spent a short while as a seaman. I believe my uncle Jack came home after spending many years at sea, and joined the Murray family in the diving business. My father came home from Aruba, and bought the house 'Tieve Tara' at the top of Barrack Brae, Cushendall. Sadly, he suffered a heart attack, and died aged 67, in 1987."

10 NIGHT of HORROR

CELEBRATED Carnlough-based skipper James Kelly was awarded the O.B.E. in 1953, honoured for his heroic part in helping in the rescue of some survivors during the heartbreaking *PRINCESS VICTORIA* disaster.

He was one of four skippers of small merchant vessels that joined in the rescue operation off the County Down coast near Donaghadee. James Kelly poured oil on the water, to try and calm the waves so that survivors could be picked up out of the viciously stormy sea.

On January 31, 1953, one of the most sickening sea disasters in these isles happened when the *PRINCESS VICTORIA*, a ferry vessel sailing from Stranraer to Larne, sank in the North Channel during a severe storm. At that time, it was the biggest maritime disaster since the Second World War.

Built in 1947, at Dumbarton, Scotland, the *PRINCESS VICTORIA* was the first purpose-built ferry for these island coastal routes. Brought into service in 1947, with a gross tonnage of 2,694, and one of the earliest roll-on/roll-off ferries, she was owned by the British Transport Commission, and operated out of Stranraer by British Railways.

The boat could facilitate 1,500 passengers, plus 70 tons of cargo and 40 cars, and had sleeping quarters to accommodate 54 passengers. For a journey that normally lasted two and a half hours, the *PRINCESS VICTORIA* managed to stay afloat in near hurricane conditions for seven hours, before sinking. During one of the most dreadful spells of weather to afflict Europe, floods also swept the UK to claim 307 lives. In Holland, it was reported 1,300 people died during tidal flooding.

The skipper of the *PRINCESS VICTORIA* was 55-year-old James Millar Ferguson of Stranraer when the vessel left the Scottish port's railway loading pier at 7.45am on that fateful Saturday, and sailed out into the open sea from Lough Ryan with 44 tons of cargo, 128 passengers, and 51 crew. The boat foundered off Mew Island, at the Copeland Islands, Donaghadee. There were 133 deaths. Of the 44 survivors not one was a woman or a child, nor a ship's officer. In the noblest of seafaring traditions, Captain Ferguson went down with his ship.

Helping out during the very difficult rescue operation, were four small boats that were sheltering in Belfast Harbour. They answered SOS calls, and went to the scene of the stricken ferryboat. The small ships included the coastal oil tanker, the *PASS of DRUMOCHTER*, whose master was Captain James Kelly

The four captains were honoured with Order of the British Empire medals. The other skippers of the merchant vessels with their brave crewmen were James Alexander Bell of the *LAIRDSMOOR*, Hugh Angus of the *ORCHY*, and David Brewster of the *EASTCOTES*.

The imperturbable Kelly tried to pour oil on the troubled waters, hoping to calm the waves, but the well-meaning ploy didn't really help. Carnlough-born crew member Patsy Black explained: "Oil on the water didn't work, because the fuel we used was heavy black oil. It had to go through a heater, and whenever it hit the water it just went into lumps. A Glenarm seaman, who lives in Larne, was also on the boat that night. Mervyn McKay, an AB, who was doing relief for a few weeks.

"On the night before the *VICTORIA* disaster we were in Belfast Harbour, discharging oil. Discharging our cargo was very slow. The process of pumping oil to the Gasworks, situated at the bottom of the Ormeau Road, in the middle of Belfast, took a long time, as it was a very slow pump. It was too dangerous to rush the pumping, and risk bursting a pipe.

"Along with two other seamen, I worked all night discharging. At nine o'clock in the morning we got the ballast in, when we heard the weather forecast, which was very bad. Captain Kelly decided to go and anchor off Carrickfergus. Having been up working all night I went to bed, but the boat was rolling all over the place. So, I got up out of bed. We were making our way across to Corswell Point.

"We received word when we were half-way across. We heard the ferryboat was in trouble somewhere near the Maidens. We had to turn back, all the boats had to turn back. The trouble with the *PRINCESS VICTORIA* was it couldn't communicate with other boats, as all messages had to go through Portpatrick radio.

"People didn't know for sure where the boat was. Then we got word of the bad news of the *PRINCESS VICTORIA* at the Copelands. We turned back, and that was when we came across one of the lifeboats that had 28 to 30 people in it. We stood by her, and gave the lifeboat protection.

"One of the survivors, a man, tried to get into our boat, but he fell off the rope ladder, and dropped into the sea. He got his arms around the ropes, but our boat raised up, way up higher than the lifeboat, and he couldn't get his feet onto the ladder. He was saved. He was trying to hold by both hands. That man, John McKnight from Larne, attended the 60th anniversary of the tragedy."

Cushendall's Sean Mort sailed with a survivor: "I knew and worked with Jimmy Blair. I was on the *MOYLE,* belonging to the Shamrock Company, Larne, and our chief steward was Jimmy. Paddy 'the Rock' McNeill also sailed with him on the *MOYLE.* Whenever we would be going to Casablanca, for potash cargo for Cork and Dublin, and we'd hit stormy conditions you would find Jimmy Blair walking on the deck in the middle of the night. He couldn't sleep, or sit still, when the weather was really bad. It was the aftermath of his experience on the *PRINCESS`VICTORIA.*"

Three weeks after the 60th anniversary of the disaster, John McKnight, who served with the RAF during the Second World War and was the last survivor of the *VICTORIA* sinking - and was chief cook on the boat - passed away.

Patsy Black, who resides in Cushendall, added: "For the 60th anniversary of the sinking of the ferryboat, a special Sunday service was held. I was in the Larne Lifeboat up to Donaghadee, and there the Donaghadee Lifeboat went out with us. We sat off the Copelands, where we laid wreaths. The shore service at Larne was the following Thursday."

The poignant anniversary brought back that bleak night, when the coasters provided shelter from the worst of the seas until the Donaghadee lifeboat, the *SIR SAMUEL KELLY*, arrived, and was able to bring survivors on board. Lieutenant Commander Stanley Lawrence McArdle and Chief Petty Officer Wilfred Warren of HMS *CONTEST* were each awarded the George Medal for exceptional bravery. They dived into the water to help survivors.

The wreck site of the *PRINCESS VICTORIA* was not discovered until 1992. A team of Scottish divers found the wreck five miles north/north-east off the Copeland Islands, in 90 metres of water. Following the tragedy, a special service was held at Larne Harbour. As wreaths were tossed on the water, as a mark of respect for the dead, the crowd sang: 'Lord, hear us when we cry to thee. For those in peril on the sea.'

The opening month of 1953 was a depressingly gloomy one in Northern Ireland, as the *PRINCESS VICTORIA* shocker followed the January 5 loss of 27 lives, when a British European Airways Vickers 610 Viking 18 airliner crashed on approach to Belfast Airport, at RAF Nutt's Corner. The domestic flight from RAF Northolt Airport, in west London, carried 31 passengers and four crew members.

Three crew members and 24 passengers perished after the plane apparently lost height when approaching the runway. The plane first crashed into a pole supporting an approach light, then into further light poles, a mobile standard approach van, and finally into a brick building that housed equipment some 200 yards from the runway.

The last impact caused the plane to break up. Ten years later the airfield was shut down, as Belfast Airport moved six miles away to the site at Aldergrove. The casualty list from the Nutt's Corner debacle and from the sinking of the *PRINCESS VICTORIA* made it a very sad time for all the families concerned.

Captain Kelly carved a special place in Irish seafaring history. No doubt, the monumental tragedy that was the *VICTORIA* plunging to the deep, had a lasting memory for him. His sea adventures began in the late 1920's. His grandson, Jonathan Kelly, kept a record of the great man's career. "My grandfather was born in Glasgow, in September 1906. The family moved back to the Dunloy-Rasharkin area, closer to Glenwherry, County Antrim. His parents were from that Dunloy area.

"I remember being taken there by my grandfather, to show me the house where he once lived. The family moved to Carnlough at one point, and as a young man he worked in the lime quarries. His first job as an Ordinary Seaman was on the *BENGORE HEAD*, starting on January 24, 1929. He made five runs to the Baltic on her, and then switched to deep-sea, sailing to locations such as Canada, America, and the Persian Gulf.

"He was on ships such as *WICKLOW HEAD, FANAD HEAD, ROXBY,*

and *BRITISH COLONEL.* After serving an apprenticeship of 'three years before the mast', he progressed to become an Able Seaman. He went back to Glasgow in the 1930's, when he advanced to be a First Mate, but then left the sea for a term, from October 1937.

"He worked on Glasgow Corporation trams as a conductor, probably to help financially as he studied for a Master's ticket. He returned to seafaring on July 13, 1940, as First Mate and sometimes as Second Mate, trading from Greenock to Newhaven, before taking a five-month Admiralty engagement as Mate in the Scapo Flow on August 5, 1940."

It was at the historic Scapa Flow stretch of sheltered water, within the Orkney Islands on Scotland's north-east coast, he obtained a German submarine's brass clock that featured a swastika on the face. Susan McPherson, niece of Captain Kelly, and Jonathan's cousin, said: "My mother's sister Kathy Jamison was married to Captain Kelly. I remember he had a special clock, a trophy taken off a German submarine at Scapa Flow. Captain Kelly was on Merchant Navy convoy duty then.

"The clock was round, the size of a large tea plate and made of brass. When you looked into the face there is a print of a German swastika. I believe some members of a German submarine crew badly wanted tea, and swapped the clock for bags of tea. When I was young I joined my aunt Kate and her daughter Margaret. We took trips on the *PASS of DRUMOCHTER.*"

Jonathan (Kelly), a Belfast-born, Larne-reared TV Programme Editor living in the south of England, continued the good Captain's Log: "He obtained his Certificate of Competency, Master (Home Trade) on the 17th of March, 1938, but it is again as a Mate or sometimes as a Second Mate that he goes back to sea. At this time, he was living in the east end of Glasgow, in Dunchattin Street.

"He is first named a Master on the *ADHERENCE,* on November 4, 1941. He appears to skipper both British and Irish vessels - settling into a pattern of 'Empire Ships' such as *EMPIRE SETTLER* and *EMPIRE LUNDY.* In 1943, he obtained a Certificate of Proficiency, to show he had 'completed the MN A/A Gunnery Course, and is qualified in the firing and cleaning and oiling of ALL A/A WEAPONS and DEVICES FITTED TO D.E.M.S." (D.E.M.S being - Defensively Equipped Merchant Ships).

"I have heard he assisted at the Dunkirk evacuation. The earliest war record I have is dated June 1940. Family members tell me he was there, and he told me this also when I was a child. Of course he was at the D-Day landings on a petrol tanker ('a floating bomb' - he called it). The ship was *EMPIRE SETTLER*, a tanker of 334 GRT, registered at Grangemouth. The entry starts May 18, 1944 in Grangemouth, and ends November 8, 1944 in Southampton."

After the Second World War, Captain Kelly worked for the Bulk Oil Steamship Company, later bought by William Corry and Son. Jonathan Kelly said: "I think his first boat as peace-time skipper was the *PASS of BALLATER,* in the 1940's. He moved to the *PASS of DRUMOCHTER*, and joined her for a first time as skipper at South Shields in April 1952.

"He became a Senior Captain with the company. I believe his last ships were the *PASS of GLENCLUNIE* and *PASS of DALVEEN.* He retired in 1977, and returned to live in Carnlough, where my grandmother, Mrs Kathy Jamison, lived. He remained in Carnlough the rest of his days."

Back to the views of Patsy Black, who met his Cushendall-born wife Ann (McCann) while she worked in the Carnlough Post Office, and who confessed he was a reluctant seaman. "I was 18 when I went to sea. I had no intention of going, because I was quite happy at home in Carnlough, until I just happened to meet Captain Kelly on a street in Carnlough, one Saturday. He said there was a job going on his boat, if I wanted it. I decided to give it a go.

"I left Carrickfergus on the Sunday, and was at sea for the next 14 years. I joined my first boat at Carrickfergus, where she was discharging a cargo of petrol. She was the *PASS of BALLATER.* Always, I worked on 'Pass' boats, and from start to finish I worked in the engine room.

"The *PASS of GLENOGLE* was the one I was on whenever I got married. John Mort was the skipper. Brian, the brother-in-law was with us, and two other Cushendall men - James Mort and Alistair McKay. After I was married, Ann came with me quite often, always cruising. We would be on runs to the Continent. Ann had to take her chance with the weather

"One time, down the Bristol Channel, the weather was so bad we had to anchor off an island. I was in the engine room. Ann was in the cabin, but everything there, bits of furniture, including drawers of desks, were flying all over the place."

Captain Kelly closed out his sea career on the Larne-Stranraer ferries, and Captain Hugh McIlwaine of Waterfoot recalled working for him: "I was with James Kelly on one of the ferry boats out of Larne. He was a Coastal Master. When I first met him he was on a ship named the *DALRIADA*, for Sealink Ferries. It was also during my final years at sea.

"I spent three and a half years working on the Larne-Stranraer run. James Kelly was ashore, mostly, looking after crews, getting seamen to work on the boats. He proudly signed his name James Kelly OBE, and must have been around 70 years of age at that time."

Glenarm seaman Eugene McMullan also praised Captain Kelly: "He influenced me to go back to sea, I knew him well. He did great work on the *PASS of DRUMOCHTER* during the *PRINCESS VICTORIA* disaster. He was a very popular mariner. Captain James was the man who came to me and said I was mad to be working seven days a week on my milk run in Glenarm, when I could be working

Larne Times, Thursday, May 9, 1957. 7

Ellesmere Port salutes brave Carnlough seaman

HE SHOWED HIMSELF as a prize example of his race in giving his own life to save the life of another man." With these words Rev. Father Down, of the Apostleship of the Sea, paid tribute to a Carnlough seafarer who lost his life in a 30-minute drama in the gas-filled compartment of an oil tanker at Stanlow Dock, Ellesmere Port, on New Year's Day.

CEREMONY.

The priest was speaking at a ceremony held in Ellesmere Port's Council Chamber on Wednesday night, when the Mayor of the Borough, Alderman H. G. Black, presented the "Daily Herald" Order of Industrial Heroism, which had been posthumously awarded to Mr. Daniel McNeill, aged 40, whose home was at 49 High Street, Carnlough, Co. Antrim.

better hours and earning good steady money as a seaman on the ferryboats out of Larne Harbour.

"He got me a job on the Sealink Ferries. I became a bo'sun there. Also employed by Sealink then were the Montgomery brothers, Jim and George from Carnlough. At that stage, Captain Kelly was no longer working full-time on the seas. After he quit Kellys, he joined Sealink, when it was owned by British Railways. He looked after the boats. He was Captain-in-Charge of all boats for Sealink, and would take them personally into dry-dock when needed."

One sad note concerns the tragic death of a Captain Kelly crew member, Dan McNeill, an AB from Carnlough, who was killed on the famous coaster while berthed in Elsmere Port. Cushendall's Roy Mort was also a member of the crew when the horrific incident happened. He said: "There was a leak in the pump, and the chief engineer went down to fix it, but was overcome by fumes. Dan McNeill saw this, and went down the ladders to help bring him up. Unfortunately, Dan was overcome by the fumes, and died. The ship was kept in quarantine for a few days. We were not allowed to smoke or put on lights, before the all-clear - that there was no further risk of fumes."

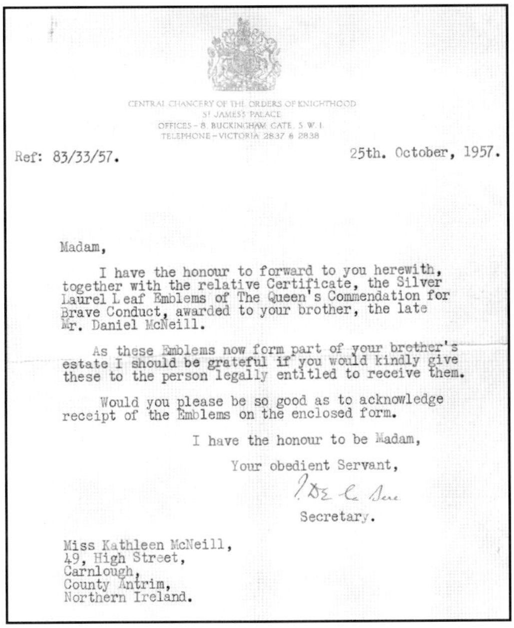

CENTRAL CHANCERY OF THE ORDERS OF KNIGHTHOOD
ST JAMES'S PALACE
OFFICES - 8, BUCKINGHAM GATE, S.W.1.
TELEPHONE - VICTORIA 2837 & 2838

Ref: 83/33/57. 25th. October, 1957.

Madam,

I have the honour to forward to you herewith, together with the relative Certificate, the Silver Laurel Leaf Emblems of The Queen's Commendation for Brave Conduct, awarded to your brother, the late Mr. Daniel McNeill.

As these Emblems now form part of your brother's estate I should be grateful if you would kindly give these to the person legally entitled to receive them.

Would you please be so good as to acknowledge receipt of the Emblems on the enclosed form.

I have the honour to be Madam,

Your obedient Servant,

Secretary.

Miss Kathleen McNeill,
49, High Street,
Carnlough,
County Antrim,
Northern Ireland.

The brave McNeill's niece is Cushendun man Joe Magee's wife Sheila, who said: "Uncle Dan was on leave when the oil tanker helped in the rescue drama during the *PRINCESS VICTORIA* sinking of 1953, but four years later lost his life. Dan was overcome by fumes in the hold of the boat." Sheila, whose maiden name is McKernan, lived with the family near Drumnasole, outside Carnlough, when the *VICTORIA* went down. She was at home listening in on the trawler radio shipping channel news when the disaster unfolded.

She recalled: "We wondered if uncle Dan was on the *DRUMOCHTER*. Next morning, he appeared at our house. He cycled out from Carnlough, to visit, and told us he was on ship's leave. He had the weekend off. Sadly, he died on New Year's Eve, 1957, when he attempted to rescue another member of the *DRUMOCHTER* crew, named Kerr from Carrickfergus.

"The alarm was raised by my uncle Dan, who was on duty that night, when he discovered the man Kerr lying in a collapsed state down in the engine room. Dan went down, and carried the man up the steps, but didn't reach the top rung. Kerr was saved by other seamen, but Dan was gassed, overcome by the fumes, and died. His father was also named Dan McNeill, a Glenarm man and also a sailor man. Granda Dan was a great hurler in his youth, and played for Glenarm in the first Feis na nGleann final against Carey, at Waterfoot in 1904."

Sheila Magee also has family ties to the legendary schoolteacher, George Doran, a specialist in sea work during the 19th century. "He was a grandfather of Charlie McKernan. My father's mother was Maria Doran, before she married," she added. "George Doran spent 16 years in the Glens, finishing up at Drumnasole School, before being appointed, in 1857, to the Belfast Maritime Nautical Model School.

"He was a respected specialist in nautical teaching, and is regarded the influence behind the theory of 'Great Circular Sailing'. He taught a young Charles McDonnell, when he was appointed teacher at Glenariffe National School in April 1842."

Mrs Magee also reeled off the names of many seaman from the Carnlough area: "Eamonn Hyndman, the Montgomery brothers, George and Jim, Eamonn McCart, Johnny McGill, Dan McCart, Freddie Hegarty, Willie Granville, George Darragh Snr, and Glenarm-born Sean O'Neill. Davy Smyth was the Harbour Master at Carnlough for many years."

DOCKSIDE SAGAS

TRIUMPH and tragedy from dockside incidents arrived in equal measure to the Connolly family of Cushendall. Pat Connolly was awarded a special bravery commendation for trying to save the life of fellow sailor, while his older brother Con cruelly died in a drowning accident in the River Foyle.

The sons of Captain Patrick 'Patsy' Connolly followed the family pattern, with Pat Jnr working as an AB for an extensive period. During the early part of his career, he sailed on the Kelly coaster, *CARRADORE.*

Another brother, Frank, a retired schoolteacher, said: "Pat was at sea for well over ten years. I believe he started with Captain Jim McGonnell. Later on, he sailed deep-sea with Blue Star Line, and was with Alistair McKay to America, and down to Australia and New Zealand. I know he made many trips to South America, to places such as Montevideo and Buenos Aires. On one occasion, he rescued a man who fell overboard. Pat received an award."

Pat Connolly's widow Maura, (nee McCambridge, Ballymena), clarified her husband's award. "It was from the Royal Humane Society based at Watergate House, London. The parchment was awarded on the 7th of May, 1963. That was a year after we were married. The rescue incident happened earlier in 1963, in Brazil."

The honour from the Humane Society includes part inscription - 'It was resolved unanimously that the Honorary Testimonial of the Society's inscribed parchment be given to Able Seaman, Patrick Connolly, Merchant Navy.' On the 29th of January, Pat, 'at personal risk', went to the rescue of a man who had unfortunately drowned in Santos Harbour.

Maura added: "Pat told me it was a member of the ship's crew that fell overboard, between the ship and the pier, but also struck his head on the way down into the water. Pat dived into the harbour, helped to bring the man up, but by then the man was dead. The ship he was on then, I believe, was the *BRAZIL STAR.*

"He sailed on that ship a number of times, back and forth to South America, before he quit the sea in 1964. Pat, who was born in 1936, lied about his age to get to sea, claiming he was 16, when he was 15. Overall, he was 13 years at sea, starting on coasters. I recall him saying he called in quite a few times to Newry, with coal cargo, before going deep-sea. He was on the Blue Star Line, and sailed with Alistair McKay.

"Often, Pat chatted about sailing to Australia and New Zealand, and when we had a very young family he talked about emigrating to New Zealand, but I'm a home bird, and wouldn't go. Pat, when he left the sea, went into the pub business, including once in Glenarm, where he had 'The Schooner' pub. I had my own knowledge of the business, as I used to help my uncle Paddy McQuillan and his sister Mary in their McQuillan's Fountainville pub in Ballymena."

The tragic death of Con Connolly remains a strong part of the Antrim Coast's seafaring history. He was 48 years of age, and left behind wife Sheila, and three children - Colette, Pat, and Brigeen. Colette, the eldest who became Mrs O'Hagan, and a Past Lady Captain at Cushendall Golf Club, understandably can never erase those days of darkness, when her father's body was missing for up to six weeks. It is surmised he fell between his boat and the pier at Derry.

She said: "Dad died on December 30, 1970, and his body was found at New Buildings up the River Foyle, on the 6th of February 1971. I was 16 then, and was a student in the St Louis Grammar, Ballymena. My brother Pat was 15, and at St Aloysius School in Cushendall, and my sister Brigeen was 13, and also at St Louis school. It was a terrible time for the family.

"I remember when I answered the ring of the doorbell at home, when a telegram came to state my father was missing. My mother, who was Sheila McLaughlin from County Donegal, turned white. It was nearly six weeks after that before the body of my father was found. It was an awful period for us. Sergeant Joe Campbell was a great comfort to my family. He went up to Derry to help identify the body.

"My mother's sister, Eilish was married to St MacNissi's College, Garron Tower, teacher Pat Clerkin, and it was Pat who came to the St Louis School on the day we were told my father's body was found. He took me and my sister Brigeen home.

"Until then, the waiting was dreadful. We continued to go to school, but you could not concentrate on studies. I knew the news was going to be really bad when the St Louis Vice-Principal, Mr Keenan, a brother of Mrs Helena Crummey, took me out of the Library. It was on a Monday. Brigeen was taken out of her class. That was in the early afternoon. It was the worst possible news.

"I will never forget the day. My father, was buried on Monday the 19th of February, 1971. It was such a massive heart-breaking period for our family. My father sailed deep-sea before his marriage, and for a short time afterwards. He obtained his 'Certificate of Competency as Master of Home Trade - Passenger Ship', on the 2nd of March 1956.

"I believe the boat on which he was sailing at the time of his death was the *TILLERMAN*. Despite the horror of his death, I look back on happier times. I was around eight years of age when he was First Mate on the Shell Mex tanker, the *REFINER*, that called in at Cushendall Bay. The family went out to the ship in one of Dixie McElroy's rowing boats. Mammy and my brother Pat stayed on the boat, and went with my father on up the coast to Derry. Myself and Brigeen were taken home.

"My father's grandfather, also named Con, was a sea captain. I believe he sailed at one time on the *CUSHENDALL*. Patsy Connolly was my grandfather, and his sister was Rosie Emerson."

Frank Connolly continued the family's seagoing history: "Danny, or 'DC', my youngest brother, was not very long at sea, and with coasters. I was a traitor to the family's seafaring cause. Along with Jamie, the cobbler, we were the only male members in three generations of the Connolly clan to stay on dry land."

His father, the aforementioned Patsy Connolly, carved out a solid skipper's career, and at one time had the strangest duty to perform - taking butter from farms at Glendun to the McSparran family shop in Glasgow. The creamery crusader of the early 20th century regularly brought home-churned butter exported from the Antrim Coast. It was a prized commodity in Glasgow.

Frank, a respected historian, said: "One of my father's early tasks was to take butter made in Glendun to Glasgow, to be sold in the McSparran shop. 'Butter from Home' was the sale logo in the shop window. I heard my father saying Mrs McSparran was a very fine woman.

"During his early days, he often stayed at Mrs Ellen Cavanagh's B and B accommodation in Belfast's dockland, near Corporation Street, while waiting to go on a boat. He also mentioned being looked after by the McSparran family in Glasgow. He was a captain of Kelly boats. One boat I recall he was master of was the *CORTEEN*." The *CORTEEN* was built at Glasgow in 1920, re-named by the Kelly Company as *BALLYCLARE* in 1952, and sold in 1959.

Incidentally, Mrs Cavanagh (nee McKillop) and her sister Kate, both born at the 'Big Bridge', Glendun, had an 'eating house' and also kept boarders in their B&B beside the 'Sunflower Bar' on Garmoyle Street. Ellen, who died in 1930, married Carnlough seaman James Cavanagh, while Kate also married a seaman from Carnlough, named Regan.

Frank Connolly added: "My mother, Evelyn Burns, was from County Donegal. She worked in Glasgow for Dan 'Mick' McAuley of Clough, Cushendall, who ran a shop over there. My father met Evelyn in Glasgow. He probably went to sea when he left school, at 14, going deep-sea first. He started as a deck hand, and worked his way up to be a captain. He moved to coasters, and joined Kellys. He died in 1949, just a couple of years after he retired from the sea.

"During both the First and Second World Wars he was at sea. In the First World War he was twice torpedoed by German submarines while in the Dardanelles. From the first torpedo attack he was rescued, and then the boat that picked him up was torpedoed. He was saved again. During the Second World War, while not part of the D-Day landings, he was on the first ship to bring supplies into France."

Patsy Connolly's father Con was also a sea captain with Kellys. "The whole Connolly family went to sea, apart from my uncle James and me. My father's brother Jamie was a cobbler in Cushendall," added Frank. "My uncle Frank - I was named after him - went to sea. He was a Mate on the *CASTLEREAGH*, when he was drowned at sea, on February 23, 1925." The 443 gross tons *CASTLEREAGH*, a Kelly cargo steam coaster en-route from Ayr to Shoreditch, foundered two miles south east of Swanage, Dorset. All ten members of the crew perished.

"My father had another brother, Con Connolly, named after his father," added Frank. "He was with Kellys also, and ended up working for the Limerick Shipping Company. He married a girl from Limerick, and lived down there. During the Second World War, he was on a ship that came under German gunfire, even though the ship flew a big Irish tricolour.

"Incidentally, my grandfather, Captain Con Connolly, before he joined Kellys, started out working deep-sea, and sailed round Cape Horn. At the beginning of his career he was on windjammers, and then finished up on coasters.

"My brother Con, tragically drowned at Derry harbour in 1970, when he slipped on the pier, was then a Mate on Kelly boats. He went to sea when he left school, and first worked overseas, on deep-sea voyages, before changing to coasters.

"James, another brother, became a bo'sun, and for many years was on Head Line boats out of Belfast, sailing to Canada. He worked alongside Charlie McKay of Cushendun for a while. He was also on Manchester Liners sailing to America."

Kevin McKillop of Mill Street, Cushendall, was a close friend of James Connolly. McKillop also worked deep-sea, and mainly for the Manchester Liners, back and forth across the Atlantic. McKillop and Connolly worked together on those liners, and then both settled to live in Manchester.

A significant connection with the Connolly clan, through blood ties and sea links, is the Emerson family, one that also suffered tragedy. Frank Connolly revealed: "My aunt Rosie married Johnny Emerson, whose brother Tommy had two sons who went to sea. Sadly, James Emerson was killed when he fell into the hold of his ship in Spain. Tragically, this type of accident and loss of life happened very often to seamen.

"The other son of Tommy Emerson was Robert, who became a First Mate. His grandfather was also at sea. He was Captain Robert Emerson, who was from Portaferry, County Down, and came to Cushendall where he married a Murray girl, a sister of Ian and Jamie, who was once the greenkeeper at Cushendall Golf Club."

12

SPIRITS of the GLENS

THE ENDURING resiliance of Glens of Antrim seamen has been in evidence for centuries, many carving special places in the exploration of the oceans, involvement in many wars, and always with an inquisitive eye for good trading opportunities.

Most of their adventures were born of necessity, a means to make a living and help ease the hardships of their families back home, who were trying to eek out an existence on small hill farms, others surviving through fishing, and quite a few teenagers nudged into reluctantly offering their services at hiring fairs and very often into the Irish version of slave labour.

Looking out to sea instilled the obvious, an outlet to escape from land drudgery, and the chance of betterment. There was the close proximity of being able to trade with Scotland, mainly to the Mull of Kintyre. A little bit of smuggling on the side never did any harm, unless you were scuttled by the Excise men. A dominant player in that clandestine cottage industry was Cushendun skipper James O'Hara, who ran the gauntlet with mixed success.

He was given the fanciful and colourful nickname of 'The Pirate.' In truth, he was a basic smuggler working his sloop *JAMES* out of Cushendun, and trading to and from the Mull of Kintyre. He regularly took part in cat and mouse games with the Revenue Cutters, often escaped the net with his cargo of contraband - but was also nicked and fined. O'Hara worked a lucrative business with folk at Campbeltown on the Mull.

Another Revenue runner was John McVey, also of Cushendun. A committed smuggler, he skippered his own sloop, the *COVE.* It may seem a romantic period of derring do, secretive midnight sailings across the Irish Sea, and on a grander scale of 'whisky running' to north America, when trying to avoid paying taxes on the goods.

However, here is a reminder of a time when the 'Excise Men' were successful in nabbing smugglers. In September, 1965, the Reverend Webb from Campbeltown arrived in from the Mull of Kintyre, armed with records of Excise captures for his guest lecture to members of the newly-formed Glens of Antrim Historical Society. He highlighted the strong connection of western Scotland with the Antrim coast, a brisk shipping lane.

The sea corridor not only opened a natural route for trade but also raiding warring tribes. Campbeltown was once regarded the 'whisky capital of the world' when the peninsula proudly boasted 34 distilleries that produced barrels galore of a distinctive tasting single malt whisky. Merely three distilleries survived after the financial fall-out in the United States from the 1930's Depression.

The Webb lecture highlighted Customs' records to prove a daily ferry service for goods and passengers existed from 1739, from Cushendun to Dunaverty on the Mull. Revenue hauls included the following: 1756-Smuggled into Cantyre, and seized, were 66 casks of brandy, 42 casks of rum, 24 bottles of white wine, and one boat. 1772-Commissioners in Edinburgh sent to Customs man in Campbeltown 2 muskets, 3 pistols, and a suite of colours. 1773-Seizure of shipment of wool to Ireland.

1780-John Morrison intercepted, on voyage from Cushendun by American privateer from Boston, the *BLACK PRINCESS.* On her were mounted 18 carriage guns. Two Revenue cutters went out to intercept her. Hadn't much chance. Apparently, this schooner, built in 1774, was once used by Benjamin Franklin to capture British ships during the 1776 American War of Independence, and later along with a sister ship, *BLACK PRINCE* became part of the lucrative Atlantic smuggling scene.

1784-Revenue cutters of Campbeltown seized a 24.5 chest of black tea from a long rowing boat in Red Bay, 1785-16 stone of wool seized. Salt smuggled to the fishing industry. Took it in barrels to the boats at the fishing grounds, where fish gutted, and salted on board. Boats also carried one or two coopers. 1786- Sloop *JAMES,* with its master James O'Hara seized off Campbeltown, landing 13 tons of Irish meal. 1787-Seized 6,000 lbs of leaf tobacco from Rathlin. American privateers stored it in Rathlin Island - sugar too. Last ferry boat to Cushendun was in 1843.

Cushendun Bay, during in the 18th and 19th centuries, was a hive of boating action, vessels of all shapes and sizes involved in vibrant trade across the neck of water to the Mull of Kintyre, and big ships calling back in again from Glasgow to pick up crew members for another long haul to Ceylon, to the Americas, or ports in the southern Hemisphere.

There was also a strong bond between western Scotland and the valleys of Glendun, Glenballyeamon and Glenaan, ever since young tradesmen - weavers, joiners, stone masons - poured in from the western isles. Included was the McSparran family of Gigha's first-footing onto the Antrim coast around 1800.

This is a cue to relate a strange but true incident, when a ship from Glasgow anchored in Cushendun Bay. Lowered was a filled coffin into a rowing boat, and the deceased carefully taken to the shoreline. It proved a nostalgic occasion, a final return home for Innispollan (Cushendun)-born Margaret Ann (McCormick) McSparran.

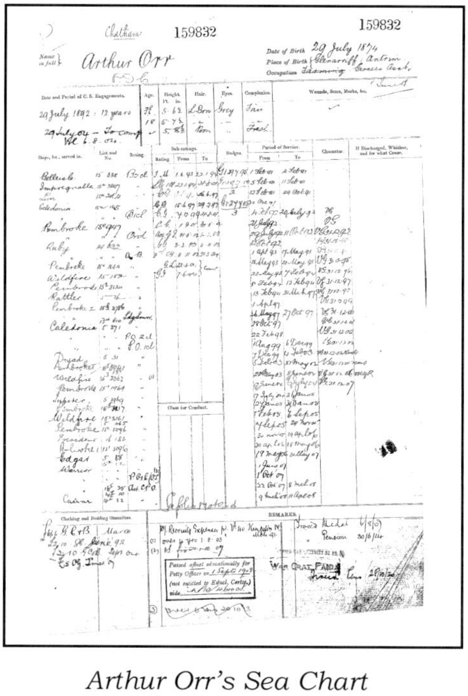
159832
159832
Arthur Orr
Date of Birth 29 July 1874

Arthur Orr's Sea Chart

In March, 1886, Mrs McSparran was transported from Scotland to Cushendun on board a steamer. She was the daughter of Dan and Mary McCormick (nee O'Hara, of Sleans, Cushendun). In 1848, she married James McSparran, a sailor and schooner owner, and died in Glasgow on March 5, 1886. The steamer anchored in Cushendun Bay to enable the body to be brought ashore for burial in the nearby Cregagh Cemetery.

It was a fitting farewell, with the Irish Channel yet again playing a prominent role. James McSparran was one of seven children born to Archy McSparran, who came from Scotland to the Antrim glens around 1800, and married Ann McNeill of Layd, Cushendall.

James, who traded between the Antrim coast and Scotland, later opened a business at Commerce Street, Glasgow, to supply provisions to ships departing the Clyde for foreign parts. In 1848, he married Margaret Ann, and they had eight children. One member of the family, Sarah, married sea captain Arthur Hamilton of Ballindam, Cushendun. Her sister Mary married Captain Hamilton's brother John, who was a lighthouse keeper.

The eldest McSparran child was Archy, and he became a sea captain. He married, for a second time, Sarah Ann McKeegan of Cushendall, who died, aged 83, in 1948. He died, aged 43, in 1894. They had two children - Mary, who married Arthur McAlister of 'Arthur's' at Shore Street, Cushendall, and Hugh, who remained a bachelor, and was a butcher at Mill Street, Cushendall. He died in 1949, aged 56. **Information on the McSparran sea-faring interest gleaned from the family's written history - *'From Gigha to the Glens'* - by Malachy McSparran.

Glensmen looking beyond the home horizon, usually emigrated to foreign parts or took off on proud clipper ships and three-masted schooners that provided elegant passage on the oceans, and also with an added sense of high drama. Many men, working for months 'before the mast', were often dropped off by their clipper ship skipper in Cushendall and Cushendun Bays. It was time out to visit family and friends, and bring home money after lengthy passage.

During the days of the Spanish Main - doubloons, pieces of eight, hidden treasure - through to slave ships, and wool and tea cargo vessels, I suspect Irish mariners were heavily involved. Many of our greatest sailors from the Glens, along with the legendary Captain Charles McDonnell, included another Glenariffe luminary of the seas, Denis Black of Kilmore. He was a contemporary of McDonnell, and worked at the same time on sailing vessels, during the 1850's, for the Black Ball Line.

The shipping company requisitioned four three-masted sailing ships. Along with the *JAMES BAINES*, the sister ships were the *LIGHTENING*, the *DONALD McKAY*, and the *CHAMPION of the SEAS*. Historic research suggests Black as a sailor man of considerable substance. Like Charles McDonnell, he also appears to have been a formidable seafarer, one filled with feverish self-belief.

Black worked on the *LIGHTNING*, and later became chief officer of an American-owned cargo vessel *THE YOUNG MECHANIC*. He made one passage from Hull to Bombay. He left Bombay in January 1858, and in August of that year was appointed chief officer of the 12,000 tons *HOPE*, departing Liverpool for Cork, and on passage with troops to Bombay. In 1862, he was Mate of the *ALIPORE*

From the townland of Foriff, Glenariffe, came the Orr brothers, Arthur and James. The following information on the Orrs was garnered through the invaluable help of historian Iain Bradley of Camlin Books, Glenarm. He revealed the brothers joined the Royal Navy towards the end of the 19th century. Arthur's sea chart lists his birth as July 29, 1874, and his occupation as a grocer's assistant, when he signed on.

It appears James signed on for 12 years on July 29, 1892, his 18th birthday, and re-joined from July 29, 1904, until September 1, 1908. He sailed as Ordinary Seaman on a number of ships, including *IMPREGNABLE, CALEDONIA, PEMBROKE, RUBY, WILDFIRE, RATTLER*, and then as Petty Officer on the *CALEDONIA, DRYAD, PEMBROKE, WILDFIRE, PRESIDENT WARRIOR* and *CARINO.*

Perhaps, the most poignant and historic tale of sea sadness is the one gouged out on the horizontally placed 'Fulldiew' headstone in Craigagh Graveyard, Cushendun. Local old-time sailor Charles McAlister, who once worked before the mast with a young Nelson, before the latter became famous as an Admiral, had the carved sentiments on the slab forever logged in Glens folklore, following the tragic death of his teenage son.

McAlister's family connection with ocean travel ended in a gut-wrenching homecoming incident. His 18-year-old son, John slipped and fell off a sailing ship's rigging, and plunged to his death a short distance from Cushendun Bay. This numbing story behind the death, on the 11th of March, 1803, is hacked out on the headstone in almost indecipherable fashion.

Respected local historians unravelled parts of the traumatic tale. The young man was returning to meet his betrothed, and the schooner he worked on dropped anchor in Cushendun Bay. Shortly before that, when climbing to the Crow's Nest, to take a longing look at his homeland, young McAlister lost his footing, fell from the main mast, and died instantly.

On a chilly March day, locals waited on the beach to watch a lifeboat being lowered, and what appeared to be a canvas covered lifeless body placed in it. Four rowers and a ship's officer brought the boat crunching up the sand. The officer asked if anyone knew of the McAlister family. Charles, by then a privateer and owner of the *RATTLESNAKE* ferryboat that traded from Cushendun to the Mull of Kintyre, arrived to identify the body of his son.

His grief is expressed on the tombstone that he apparently requisitioned. The tragic romantic tale took a further dark turn when the broken-hearted young bride's frozen body was found on the morning after the funeral, lying inert across the grave.

The headstone, with phonetically sounding words on it, (Fulldiew means Full Due) includes crude carvings of a ship and what is perceived to be the outline of a goat, or a stag. The meaning and reason for the latter drawing is unknown. In the spelling of the day, the inscription is laid out as follows:

CHARLES McALASTERS BURR
ING PLACE
HERE LIES THE
BODDY OF JOHN
HIS SON DIED 11
MARCH 1803
AGED 18 YEARS
YOUR SHIP
LOVE IS MOR
ED HEAD AND
STARN FOR A
FULDIEW

Incidentally, Charles McAlister ferryboat enterprise, on his *RATTLESNAKE* vessel, continued across the Sea of Moyle after the death of his son. Following the creation of the Coast Road, including the building of the Glendun Viaduct - and later the narrow gauge railway system from Parkmore inland - passage from Cushenden to Kintyre, through the ferry service to Dunaverty, ceased in 1843. This really ended the once bristling indigenous sea trading in this part of the old Kingdom of Dalriada.

And so came a closing countdown to a way of life that was generally curtailed to friends, relations, and business associates trading back and forth with goods such as whisky, Shetland ponies, Cushendall ponies, cattle, sheep, and not forgetting the annual regattas played out during summertime at Cushendun Bay, Cushendall Bay, Red Bay - between Glens rowers and rope-muscled men from the Mull of Kintyre and the western isles.

On Thursday July 11, 2013 - 210 years after the death of John McAlister - the Cushendun & District Development Association, backed by the Moyle Community Cohesion Project and Peace 111, unveiled the significant tribute to that incident - a wonderfully designed and constructed 'Fulldiew' Seat, located in Riverside Car Park at the mouth of the River Dun.

The occasion, overseen through the eloquent delivery of CDDA Secretary Alistair McIlhatton, and acknowledged by Moyle Council Chairperson Cara McShane, was suitably 'launched' by a special guest, 99-year-old Mary McAuley of Cushendall (nee Glendun-born Mary 'Archie' McNeill). McIlhatton has his own family links to the sea. Carved on a headstone in Cregagh graveyard is the death of his great, great uncle, John McKillop, of Beaghs, Glendun, who drowned at sea on the 4th of December, 1856. McKillop, son of Bernard and Catherine (nee McAllister) McKillop, was 29.

LIST OF SHIPPING
REGISTERED AT THE PORT OF BELFAST, ON THE FIRST OF JANUARY, 1855.

EMPLOYED IN THE FOREIGN TRADE OF THIS PORT.

Vessels.	Tons.	Owners.
America ...	1,683	J and T Sinclair
Dalriada ...	1,507	David Grainger & Son
Ultonia ...	1,474	John Dunn
Asia ...	1,395	David Grainger & Son
a The Crown ...	1,284	Thomas Carey, Carrickfergus
Oliver ...	1,283	Hugh Wardlow
United Kingdom	1,267	Robert Corry
Epaminondas ...	1,105	D Grainger & Son, James Lemon, S M'Causland
James Carson ...	1,164	John Dunn
Childe Harold...	1,124	W C Gregg
Tara ...	1,123	John Harrison & W Lepper
a Danube ...	1,103	David Grainger & Son
Scotland ...	1,079	J and T Sinclair
Hibernia ...	1,065	John Dunn & Capt M'Mahon
York ...	1,015	John Martin & James Ireland
Gulnare ...	1,101	John Dunn
Lincluden Castle	991	John Dunn
Nimroud ...	987	H Wardlow
Beloochee ...	967	J and T Sinclair
Roscoe ...	898	J and T Sinclair
Alarm ...	895	J and T Sinclair
African ...	889	James Cranston Gregg
St. Helena ...	811	R and J P Corry
Free Trader ...	803	J and T Sinclair
Eliza Morison ...	797	David Grainger & Son
Robina ...	791	J & T Sinclair & W Milford
Digby ...	787	D Grainger & Son
Salem ...	786	J Milford and W Sinclair
Sarah ...	729	J Gardiner and J Rounds

Vessels.	Tons.	Owners.
Emily ...	83	Henry Joy
Earl Grey ...	83	John Clarke, Whitehouse
Elgin ...	162	D Mogey, Carrickfergus
Eliz. and Joanna	30	Geo. M'Quaid, Donaghadee
Elizabeth, ...	28	G Laird, Islandmagee
Emma Hamilton,	24	S Thompson & others, I.magee
Elizabeth, ...	[illegible]	E Murray & others, Cush.dall
Elizabeth, ...	20	John Dunn
Ellen, ...	20	Henry Johnston
Eliza, ...	19	E Smith
Favourite, ...	[illegible]	J D and P Delargy
Fairy, ...	101	J Delargy and others
aFanny, ...	125	D Mogey, Carrickfergus
Fanny, ...	91	W Austen and W Coey
Four Brothers,	47	Wm M'Clean
Francis and Isabella	47	John Millar
Frederick ...	42	John Gaussen and Co
Friendship ...	42	David English, Islandmagee
Fame ...	[illegible]	A M'Laughlin, Cushendall
Farmer ...	35	Daniel M'Laughlin
Fawn (yacht), ...	19	Richard Davison
Friends, ...	79	Thos Mark and John M'Minn
Gleaner ...	94	Martin Harper
Gnat, ...	96	P Wright and J Wallace
Grace Darling	67	Hugh Morrison and others, Carrickfergus
Grand Junction,	62	Wm Dargan
Greyhound ...	29	Wm Cousins
Grace Gillespie	34	J Wallace & others, B.water
Grace ...	22	H M'Comb and others
Hero ...	114	James Brown
Hero ...	83	P Wright and J Wallace
Hope ...	67	S M'Kee and others
Halcyon ...	18	P Cuming
Harmony ...	65	J Massey
Harmony ...	61	Isaac Arrott

1855 Ship's Register

Incidentally, there may be a connection between the 'Fulldiew' McAlister family and that of a J McAlister of Cushendun, who is listed in the Port of Belfast bulletin of January 3, 1855, as the registered owner of a boat named *SAILGEM*. In the lengthy list there are Antrim coast owners of various sized vessels such as A McAlister, Cushendall, the registered owner of *ORLANDO*; D McLaughlin, Cushendall, and his *ISABELLA*; William Stewart of Glenarm is the named owner of the *MARY*.

In the list is the *MARGARET*, owned by J McNeill, Carnlough; another *MARGARET*, registered by J McBride and A and J Blaney; *CARES*, owned by Edward O'Neill, Cushendall; *CALEDONIA*, registered to Patrick O'Neill, Red Bay; *EDWARD AZIZ*, owned by Richard Halloran, Glenarm; *RESOLUTION*, registered to James Delargy; *BROTHERS*, owned by Daniel O'Hara; *AGNES*, owned by J McMullan, Glenarm, and *BALLOT*, registered to Bridget, Alex and J Blaney.

Thirteen years earlier, there were many ships officially registered to Glens of Antrim owners including A McMullen (Glenarm), P Delargy of Cushendall, G Halloran and P O' Hara of Glenarm, and other Cushendall/ Red Bay folk such as D McCart, James Coulter, and J Herdman.

Other eminent seamen of the distant past include Captain Arthur Kane of Tampagh, Glenariffe. He died aged 60 on August 27, 1895. Also, as revealed by Canon Alex McMullan of Glenarm, there is the noted Captain Michael Coulter, buried in the Bay Cemetery, Glenariffe. "Captain Coulter, a skipper of schooners, donated a hurling trophy. It was named after him. Teams from along the coast once played for the Captain Coulter Cup. It was first used for team competition, but this faded. In the 1970's, the Glenarm club resurrected the Captain Coulter Cup, and it was awarded for the Long Puck competition at their annual Sports Day."

Captain Coulter of Glenariffe, and later Glenarm, died in the 1930's. In 1907, he presented the Cup. His father was a coastguard, who married in Waterfoot. His brother, William became a distinguished marine painter in San Francisco. William Alexander Coulter, born March 7, 1849, died on March 13, 1936, in his home at Sousalito, beside San Francisco Bay.

He left Glenariffe at 13 years of age, to work on sailing ships for seven years before deciding to stay on dry land in California, and become an artist. In the late 1870's, this man with a special flair went to Europe to make a close study of marine painting. One of his most outstanding productions is his painting of the San Francisco fire of 1906. He died aged 87.

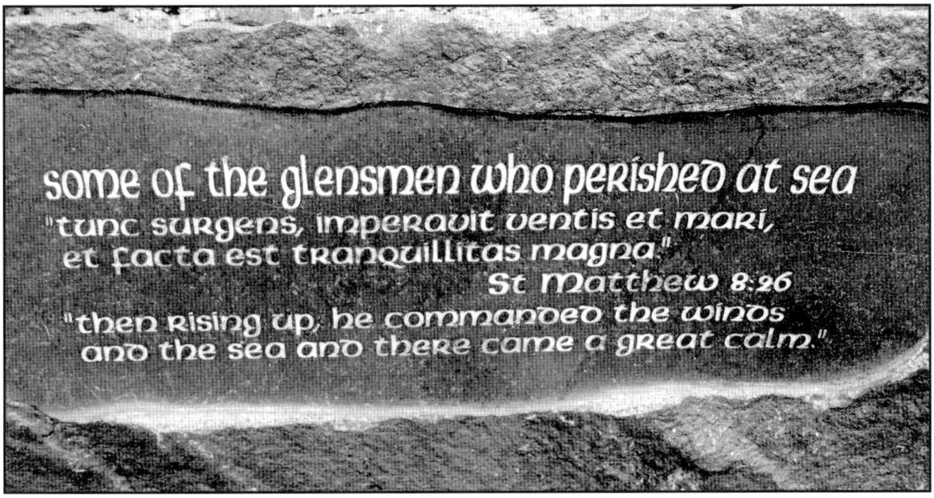

Another noteworthy was a Captain Walsh of Glenariffe, who managed to quickly move his boat, the Dorey's *PORTELET* out of Spain, and just in time, as the Spanish Civil War was getting under way. Of course, headstone hunting also reaped many other names of past Glens seamen such as Captain Patrick Hamilton, who died, aged 56, at Gloucester on July 24, 1854, and Captain Alexander Hamilton, who died at sea on August 14, 1872, aged 24.

There are the two black marble tribute plaques in the Bay Cemetery to - 'Some of the Glensmen who perished at sea.' The lists, also featuring seaman who did not die at sea including Charles McDonnell, heralds the names Bernard McQuillan, John McNaughton (1914), James McAllister (1861), Denis Black, Paddy O'Boyle (1940), James Emerson, Patrick Dunphy (1847), John Harvey (1866), Alex Robbin, James McKeegan, John and Arthur McAllister (1853), Denis (1861) and John McKillop (1863), Hugh Lynn, James McGaughey (1901),

John McMahon (1905), James (1914) and Andrew McGonnell (1895), Frank Connolly (1925), Charles McKeown (1928), John McLernon (1939), Jack and Harry Blaney, Hugh McDonnell (1940), Brian McKillop (1940), Con Connolly, Joseph Burns, James McCormick (1907), John Murray (1918), Seamus McCormick (1951), and James McAllister of Garron Point, who was drowned at sea, aged 31, on the 1st of January 1949.

13

LIMESTONE CARRIERS

THE COMPACT ports of Glenarm and Carnlough once punched well above their respective weights, and it was all down to the export of limestone. Glenarm, one of the oldest towns in Ireland - granted charter by King John (1199-1216) - reared many steadfast seafarers. The lure of the lapping waves seemed a natural outlet from the compact harbour that once housed a battery of small puffers taking limestone out and across the North Channel to Scotland.

Those halcyon days are but a misty-eyed memory. Larne-born Tony Hoey, married into the Hegarty family of Glenarm that held strong sea-going interests, was once close to the closing of the limestone trading. "I worked in the office of the Carnlough Lime Company from 1969 to 1971. Before that, the shipping of lime out of Carnlough Harbour was over, the old railway down to the Harbour long gone," said Hoey,

"However, the lime was still quarried, but then the 'smalls' brought to Glenarm by the lorry load, where it was processed through the hoppers, crushed down, and put into the wee ships at Glenarm Harbour. There was also a time when boats, some with sails - clipper ships, would gather at the mouth of the river to await their turn - while maybe two other boats would be loading lime in the Glenarm Harbour.

"Back in the early part of the 20th century, the port of Carnlough exported peat, or turf, which was grounded up Glencloy, and from the factory there it was then shipped out to Germany. The peat, I believe, was used to make explosives."

The two delightfully claustrophobic villages also, during the past two centuries, spawned a surfeit of top-class seaman. One of the key mariners was a sturdy man from Glenarm. He was Captain James McKendry, skipper on coasters. He was a near neighbour of Eugene McMullan, who said: "James was a big man. I knew him very well. His daughter Sally married Dale Lough of Ballygalley, parents of sprinter Gary Lough. Dale Lough became Captain and President of Cairndhu Golf Club. He (Dale) was also a top official at Houstons of Larne, a subsidiary of the Kelly Company."

Eugene's brother, Fr Alex, who sadly died on April 23, 2014, added: "I believe Captain James, for a time, worked on the East Downshire Company boats. The Downshire boats were coal cargo coasters that traded in and out of ports such as Garston, Derry, Ayr, and Dublin. Captain McKendry lived three doors from us. I knew the family well."

Other neighbours in Mark Street, Glenarm, were Tommy and Hughie Robinson, who was an engineer on coasters. Fr Alex said: "When I was a small boy I ran a week-end errand for the Robinson family, to collect the Sunday newspapers." Iain Bradley of Camlin Books, Glenarm, supplied further information on the sea-going Robinson family. "Johnny Robinson served on the HMS *NITH*, a river-class destroyer. I was told that he drowned at sea. He was the son of Owen Robinson and Mary McGavock of Mark Street, Glenarm, and was born in 1886. I am not aware of when he died. A brother Hugh was also at sea. There was another brother named Joey.

"Hugh Robinson made a habit of sending regular postcard letters home from sea. For example, he leaves Fleetwood on the *BURN NAZE* on February 2, 1907, and notes -' Mother, going to London. Hugh'. He also informs home of a sea tragedy. Writing from the *FLUOR* in Liverpool he states- 'Mother, sorry about John Magill. Loading grain for Cork, Hugh.'

"He worked on numerous vessels, including the *LOCH DOON, EMERALD* and *FELSPAR.* His brother Johnny's postcards begin in September 1906, from Belfast, when leaving on boats such as the *TOPAZ, RUBY, BARSHAW,* and *OBSIDIAN.*"

Eugene McMullen's excellent memory of old Glenarm seamen included Eddie Lavery. "Eddie was an ordinary seaman. There was a very high number of sailors from my area, many working on Robertson boats to such an extent that the Robertson fleet became known as 'The Glenarm Navy'. Mark Street used to be jam-packed with sea-going men. Some of the other Glenarm seafarers included Captain Billy Balmer, who was on coasters, and then worked for Sealink. His brothers, James and Tommy also went to sea. Tommy was an outstanding rower, who competed at regattas.

"Glenarm also had Captain Bill Kerr, and his brother Bertie, who was an AB. There was Captain Bertie Rea, from down Castle Street, who was related to Anna Sullivan - who married Captain Brian McEvoy. Another famous Glenarm sailor, who lived on his own in Castle Street, was nicknamed 'Bottle Bill'. He was Billy McNeill."

Glenarm-born sailors also featured Dan Cassidy, who lived near Drumnagreagh, and chief engineer Sean O'Neill, who moved up the coast to live in Waterfoot, where he married Sarah Ann Black of Glenariffe. Before leaving Glenarm, there is the tragic tale of a member of the McKay boat-owning family.

In 1878, a young skipper, Alexander McKay was drowned when his brigantine, the *PYKE* was crushed and sunk in a collision with the *ADRIATIC* during fog off the County Wexford coast. His uncles, Pat and James McKay worked on coasters. His brother, Daniel McKay was also a seaman. From the early 20th century another Glenarm man, born on July 28, 1899, was Michael Kane, a fireman on coasters, and Frank Bunting, who was a fireman on the *BASUTO*, during the First World War, and died on December 9, 1918..

Moving north from Glenarm village, around the little mud-sliding headland, lies charming Carnlough Bay, and right on the ocean edge of the village rests the picturesque wind-protected harbour. This is a special place, with a history all of its own, through the limeworks, and grooming many seamen.

Included is Captain Francis Black, once First Mate of the *FALLOFIELD*, when Hugh McIlwaine worked with him: "He had been a skipper, but when I sailed with him he worked as Mate on a Savage's boat. I was the Second Mate on the *FALLOWFIELD*. He went to live in Larne, where he died. Captain Black had all the qualifications to get a good job on the Larne ferries."

Eugene McMullan added: "I also sailed with Francis Black on coasters, when he was skipper of the *GIRASOLE*. He had a brother, James, who worked as a fireman with me on a Charlie Brown coal burner out of Larne. I recall delivering coal cargo to Deptford Power Station. Also on board then was Johnny McClure of Glenarm, who was the cook.

"From Carnlough came Captain Willie Granville. He was skipper on Sealink when Bertie Kerr was on watch. One time, I was on the ferryboat when we felt a bump. We saw a hull going below the waves, and we thought we'd rammed and sunk some wee boat out in the middle of the channel, on the way from Larne to Stranraer. What happened was that a submarine decided to surface, right in front of us, took a knock, and quickly dived under. We saw the sub's hull disappear very quickly. There was no harm done, no damage all round."

Captain Granville decided to end the long-haul run of deep-sea voyages, and join the ferry trail with Sealink. A man with Masters' Foreign Ticket, he was with Sealink when Captain Hugh McIlwaine decided to do the same. McIlwaine, who worked under Captain Granville, said: "I believe his parents were from the South of Ireland, and that his father was once the lighthouse keeper on Rathlin Island. He was a Master with Sealink, when I sailed with him out of Larne.

"On one trip from Larne to Stranraer I was in charge of down aft. I told the bo'sun to make sure the stern door was closed, and went up to the bridge to join the skipper. We were out of Larne when an urgent message came in from another ship sailing close by. It warned us: 'Your stern door is still wide open!'

"That was a close call. It was shock news, and the mistake could have proved very dangerous. Willie said: 'My God, Hugh, what have you done.' I explained I did order the bo'sun to shut the door before we set sail. The order was overlooked. It could have been a serious situation had weather conditions been rough. Fortunately, it was flat calm."

Eugene McMullan added: "From Carnlough too were the two Montgomery brothers, Jim and George. I knew George, who ended up working for the P&O Ferries. Also on the Ferries were Eamonn Watterson and Donal McGuckian, who had been a deep-sea man in his younger days. I believe Eamonn Watterson was on the P&O boats for over 35 years."

The area around Glencloy produced many other great seaman, including War hero, Charles Kevin Magill, a Second Engineer from Oscar Cottage, Carnlough, who was awarded the King's M.B.E. (Civil Division). In November 1944, Magill's ship was torpedoed, and was rapidly sinking when he and another officer jumped together into the sea.

Magill was seriously injured when the ship's propeller struck him on a leg. Despite that, he went to the assistance of the other officer, who was in trouble. He helped him onto a raft, and both men were eventually rescued.

Not so fortunate were Able Seaman Pat Black (24), and Captain John O'Gorman (35). Both were killed on November 2, 1917, after the 332 gross ton steam cargo ship *JESSIE*, built in 1901, was attacked by German submarine UB-35 off the east coast of England. The *JESSIE* , with a crew of ten, was en-route from Calais to Middleborough when shelled near Filey.

The boat was beached, a total loss. Captain O'Gorman, along with the chief engineer and two crew members were drowned when their lifeboat capsized.

Also from that part of the Antrim Coast came Captain Joseph McGavock, Captain John Robinson, Captain George McGavock, and the Wilson brothers (both captains) - William and the much decorated Joseph - and their father David Wilson, who was also a skipper.

Other seaman from the district included Captain Alex Hamill, James Kelly (lost at sea on April 13, 1918), Master Mariner Hugh McNeill (died November 3, 1931), John McSparron, Master Mariner John Gribben emigrated to New Zealand (born 1850. Died 1918), his half-brother Philip, also a sailor, died in Auckland, Captain Willie O'Kane, Chief Petty Officer Hugh Duffin - and lost at sea, in October 1940, was James O'Kane.

Captain Sam Pollock, who lives at the south side of the Bay, was an acclaimed lecturer on the ways of seafaring. His wise words were greatly appreciated by such future skippers as Cushendun's Paddy McNeill.

The Burns brothers, John and Paddy, went to sea. Leo stayed on dry land. Related to the seafaring Connolly clan of Cushendall, John Burns was an AB on world travel with his close friend Eugene McMullan. Paddy also worked deep-sea routes, out of Liverpool and London. He was, for a time, with the Bulk Oil Shipping Company. He was also coasting, and, during a short period, served under Captain John Mort on the *PASS of GLENOGLE.*

Many retired seamen, including members of the Burns family, once assembled for a wreath-laying ceremony at Carnlough harbour to mark the *PERIDOT* disaster. The ill-fated coal coaster went down with all hands, a crew of nine, lost at Brown's Bay, Islandmagee, on October 25, 1905. The 200-ton steam driven *PERIDOT*, built in 1890, was part of Robertson's Gem line in Glasgow, and traded across the Irish Sea from Scotland to Carnlough. During ferocious conditions the boat, en-route to Carnlough, made for the shelter of Larne Lough, but floundered. She ran aground, and broke in two, at Skernaghan Point, Brown's Bay. the bell was recovered by divers in 1995.

A plaque in Carnlough recalls this dreadful loss of life - 'Majority of them came from Carnlough'. The names of those who perished included Alexander McNeill, a ship's cook and grandfather of John, Paddy and Leo Burns. McNeill lived for a time at Garron Point. The other crew members were - Hugh O'Kane (Captain), Patrick Black (Mate), John McMahon (Chief Engineer), John Darragh (seaman), James McKinty (fireman), James Stewart (fireman), Alexander Ferguson (Second Engineer), and Robert McKeller (seaman - from Scotland).

Former World Flyweight boxing champion Dave 'Boy' McAuley, born in Larne but with firm family links up the coast in Carnlough, disclosed a sea connection through his grandmother. He said: "She was a McKenty, from Carnlough, and my grandmother's brother John went to sea. I believe he was first a schoolteacher, but then decided on a career at sea. I was also told he was close to sitting his finals for a ship's Masters Ticket when he was lost at sea in September 1908."

Regrettably, I remain on further sea sadness in the Carnlough area - the loss of Tom Marquis off Land's End. The boat sunk, and it was said all crew members were never seen again. On a brighter note, I can recall the town being 'on the bread line' during the 1960's, and solving the sliced pan shortage by going Dutch. During a bread strike in Northern Ireland, enterprising sailors from Holland, coming into Carnlough Harbour to load up with lime cargo, decided to make a few guilders on the side.

Glensman's Brave Action in War

The King has been pleased to approve the following award: MBE (Civil Division) to Charles Kevin Magill, second engineer officer, Oscar Cottage, Carnlough, Co Antrim. Mr Magill's ship was torpedoed and sank rapidly. As she was sinking the second engineer officer and another officer jumped into the sea together. Although Mr Magill was seriously injured when the propeller struck him on the leg, he went to the assistance of the other officer who was in difficulties and helped him onto a raft. They were both rescued eventually.

Sean McClements, one-time bar owner and bookmaker in the village. was right in the middle of an exciting and colourful time. "I remember a Dutch ship, the *HANS*, bringing in bread during a bread strike in the 1960's. It solved the crisis. The *HANS* came to our rescue. When many people in Northern Ireland were doing their level best in trying to obtain bread from the south of Ireland, the folks at Carnlough had their bread delivered dockside from the Continent.

"The crew of the *HANS*, coming in from Amsterdam, saw a great opportunity to make a few bob on the side. They loaded their boat with loaves of bread on the Continent, and sold the bread at Carnlough docks. It proved a nice wee sideline for the sailor men. I remember a queue of local people down at the harbour to buy bread from the boat.

"Also, I remember when a Dutch boat came in you could see the crew placing their very colourfully painted clogs on the side of the boat, so as not to harm the wooden deck when the sailors were about to take shore leave in the village. A member of the crew of the *HANS*, Jan Schmidt, later left the sea and came to live in Carnlough.

"At that time, there was a lot of coming and going at Carnlough Harbour. The place was a bustle of activity. Sadly, those days are long since gone, but no harm in a bit of nostalgia. I recall with great affection that period in the history of Carnlough, when those small ships loaded up with limestone. It was astonishing how the boats could manoeuvre into and out of such a small harbour.

"Seafaring was also a way of life then for many family members in Carnlough. I remember meeting deep-sea sailors when they arrived home on leave, and went to dances in the Carnlough Parochial Hall. Often, I used to listen as they related their adventures in the Waterfall Bar, which was often a haven for seamen coming in to talk over their trips.

"There was always great craic. They used to tease other mariners from Carnlough, those who worked the coasters - calling them 'Lunch Box Seamen'. One deep-sea man I recall was Eamonn 'Frosty' McCart, definitely quite a character. Another who worked as a deep-sea mariner, was Eamonn Hyndman. He was a dead ringer for Cliff Richards. Apparently he left ship in Australia, and remained there.

"Of course, the lively limestone business was a big earner for Carnlough in the old days. My father Pat, originally from Dunloy, did the explosive charges at the Carnlough limestone quarry. Occasionally, repairs would be necessary on some boats in the harbour. I recall watching the Murrays of Waterfoot having to dive to repair a boat in the harbour.

"Once I bought a diver's helmet from a man in Carnlough. The weight of the helmet is incredible. I also bought a ship's bell, from a wreckage. It was very heavy, and lay for years under a table in the corner of the Waterfall Bar."

14 SHOOTING STAR

INSTINCTIVE bravery probably saved the lives of his fellow crew members, yet Cushendall sailor Johnny O'Hara remained modest about a single act of heroism that also probably preserved the lifespan of Kelly coal coaster *PARKNASILLA* during the Second World War.

In April 1942, O'Hara, without any consideration of personal protection, fought off two attacking German aircraft by lying on his back on the ship's deck, and firing 30 rounds from a Lewis gun. It appears some bullets hit one of the fighter planes, and the German airmen decided to scamper. For this act of bravado, O'Hara was awarded the B.E.M (British Empire Medal).

The issue of April 16, 1942, in the Belfast morning newspaper, the *Irish News* published the derring do of courageous O'Hara. 'Glensman's bravery under air attack' - The heroism of a Cushendall seaman has been recognised by the award of the B.E.M (Civil Division). The seaman is John Henry O'Hara, a lamp-trimmer of Shore Road, Cushendall. The story of how he helped to repel an attack by German aircraft on his ship is told in the *London Gazette*.

'The ship was sailing along when she was attacked at night by German aircraft. Two assaults were made by bombs and machine-guns. O'Hara took the Lewis gun, firing it lying on his back without any cover. He shot 30 rounds, most of which hit and drove off the attack.'

During the 1939/1945 conflict, 18 Kelly boats were requisitioned by the British Government for use. There were awards of one M.B.E., eight B.E.M. and one George Medal. Captain William Gibson of O'Hara's vessel, the *PARKNASILLA,* was commended, as was his son, Captain Robert Gibson - master of the *INISHTRAHILL.*

O'Hara's exploits on the *PARKNASILLA* became legendary. The boat was sailing to Belfast with a cargo of coal, and was - 'heavily attacked north of Bishop Rock, at the Isles of

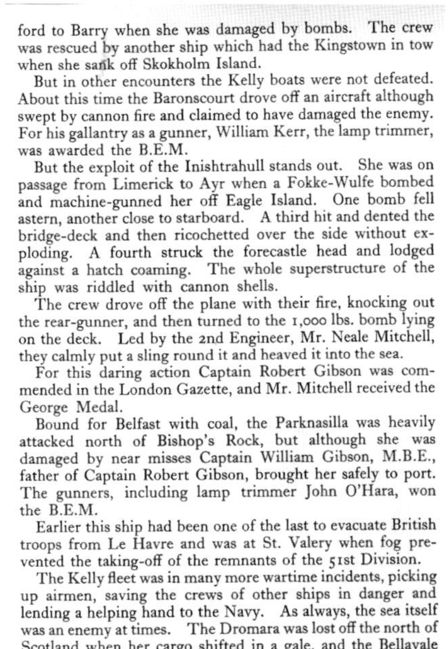
ford to Barry when she was damaged by bombs. The crew was rescued by another ship which had the Kingstown in tow when she sank off Skokholm Island.

But in other encounters the Kelly boats were not defeated. About this time the Baronscourt drove off an aircraft although swept by cannon fire and claimed to have damaged the enemy. For his gallantry as a gunner, William Kerr, the lamp trimmer, was awarded the B.E.M.

But the exploit of the Inishtrahull stands out. She was on passage from Limerick to Ayr when a Fokke-Wulfe bombed and machine-gunned her off Eagle Island. One bomb fell astern, another close to starboard. A third hit and dented the bridge-deck and then ricochetted over the side without exploding. A fourth struck the forecastle head and lodged against a hatch coaming. The whole superstructure of the ship was riddled with cannon shells.

The crew drove off the plane with their fire, knocking out the rear-gunner, and then turned to the 1,000 lbs. bomb lying on the deck. Led by the 2nd Engineer, Mr. Neale Mitchell, they calmly put a sling round it and heaved it into the sea.

For this daring action Captain Robert Gibson was commended in the London Gazette, and Mr. Mitchell received the George Medal.

Bound for Belfast with coal, the Parknasilla was heavily attacked north of Bishop's Rock, but although she was damaged by near misses Captain William Gibson, M.B.E., father of Captain Robert Gibson, brought her safely to port. The gunners, including lamp trimmer John O'Hara, won the B.E.M.

Earlier this ship had been one of the last to evacuate British troops from Le Havre and was at St. Valery when fog prevented the taking-off of the remnants of the 51st Division.

The Kelly fleet was in many more wartime incidents, picking up airmen, saving the crews of other ships in danger and lending a helping hand to the Navy. As always, the sea itself was an enemy at times. The Dromara was lost off the north of Scotland when her cargo shifted in a gale, and the Bellavale was driven ashore at St. John's Point and became a total loss. The Clapham was run down by a naval trawler in fog and sank, her crew being rescued.

HONOURS AND AWARDS

Name.	*Place of Birth*	*Present Address*	*Rank*	*Name of Ship*	*Nature of Honour or Award*
Neale Mitchell ..	Birr, Offaly, Eire	45 Pim's Avenue, Strandtown, Belfast	Second Engineer	Inishtrahull	George Medal
Samuel Montgomery ..	Belfast	Deceased	Second Engineer	Lagan	M.B.E.
Samuel McCluskey ..	Portaferry	Portaferry	Lamp Trimmer	Melissa	B.E.M.
F. Barbour ..	Belfast	70 University Street, Belfast	Cook	Clapham	B.E.M.
Albert Inch ..	Belfast	20 Templemore Avenue, Belfast	Cook	Glenmaroon	B.E.M.
John Coyle, ..	Belturbet, Co. Cavan (of Ulster parents)	Cloughfin, Islandmagee	Cook	Annaghmore	B.E.M.
A. Tout ..	Brixham	—	Fireman	Glengarriff	B.E.M.
Wm. Kerr	Islandmagee	Ferndene, Islandmagee	Lamp Trimmer	Baronscourt	B.E.M.
David Young ..	Portavogie	Deceased	A.B.	Corteen	B.E.M.
John H. O'Hara ..	Cushendall	Shore Street, Cushendall	Lamp Trimmer	Parknasilla	B.E.M.

17

Scilly, Cornwall'. Bishop Rock is listed as the smallest island in the world to have a building on it, which is a lighthouse. The story, related through the Kelly shipping company bulletin, stated: 'Although she was damaged by near misses Captain William Gibson, M.B.E., father of Captain Robert Gibson, brought her safely to port, the gunners, including lamp trimmer John O'Hara, who won the B.E.M.

Glensman's bravery under air attack

THE heroism of a Cushendall seaman has been recognised by the award of the BEM (Civil Division). The seaman is John Henry O'Hara, a lamp-trimmer of Shore Road, Cushendall. The story of how he helped repel an attack by German aircraft on his ship is told in the London Gazette.

"The ship was sailing along when she was attacked at night by German aircraft. Two assaults were made by bombs and machine-guns. O'Hara took the Lewis gun, firing it lying on his back without any cover. He shot 30 rounds, most of which hit and drove off the attack."

'Earlier, this ship had been one of the last to evacuate British troops from Le Havre, and in mid-June 1940 was at the small French port of St Valery-en-Caux, when fog prevented the taking-off of the remnants of the 51st Division.' The 1,180 tons *PARKNASILLA,* built in 1932 at Aberdeen, had a name change to *BALLYKERN* in 1956, and was scrapped in 1963.

O'Hara belonged to an iconic Cushendall seafaring family. His son Vincent proudly recalled the shooting incident. "My father was commended for his action against German aircraft fighters that attacked the ship he was on. He was a young man then. He took hold of the boat's machine gun, lay on his back on the deck and fired upwards and at the German fighters. He wasn't injured.

"He was aged 27 when the shooting incident against the Germans happened. He was awarded the B.E.M, which seemed the customary honour for seamen, and he received the medal from King George. He wasn't married at that time. He married in 1943. My sister Mary is the eldest of the family, born in 1944. After the War, he stayed at sea. He was First Mate a good part of his life with the Kelly boats, and sailed mostly on the *BALLYDUGGAN*. Then he was forced to retire through ill health.

"He went to sea at 14-years-of-age, starting out from Cushendall Beach. A merchant ship anchored in Cushendall Bay, so he went out to it, asked for a job, got it, and off he went. He progressed through examinations, from AB Seaman to First Mate. He never became a captain. My father retired from working at sea at 58-years-of-age, so he spent a total of 44 years as a seaman.

"Generally, he sailed on coasters, but was once deep-sea for a spell during the last war. He was also on convoys of ships bringing coal cargo to northern Russia. His brother Brian went to Dublin, where he was a Ship's Pilot in Dublin Harbour. My father's sister Mary married Gerry Blaney Snr's father - Captain Jack."

Vincent's grandfather, Captain Dan O'Hara was also involved in a wartime incident, one that took place during the First World War. "With him on board the boat was his nephew Eddie. His vessel was one of the first merchant ships to be sunk by a German U-boat. It was his first sighting of a submarine, and for a moment didn't know what it was. This was during the month of March - likely at the beginning of the 1914-1918 War. This was a very bad attack on the boat."

The other members of the O'Hara sea-going fraternity included Captain James Edward O'Hara, Senior Pilot of Dublin Port and Docks. He died at his home in Dublin, one hour before he was due to retire. His obituary read - 'He was a member of a well-known seafaring family from Cushendall, County Antrim.' There was also Captain John O'Hara, who died on January 2, 1950, whose wife Mary (nee McCormick of Glenaan) died on December 11, 1943. Their daughter Mary married Captain John Henry (Jack) Blaney.

CONVOY CAPERS

SECOND WORLD WAR convoys proved a crucial part of survival for everyone associated with the varied forces that combined to overcome Hitler's tyranny. The wee ships played a big part in the overall operations, with many local seamen involved, including Brian McEvoy of Glenarm.

Long before he became a noted captain of Kelly coal coasters, he was an AB on convoy duty through the icy Arctic blasts, sailing on tenterhook passage up to the Soviet ports of Archangel and Murmansk. One of his crew colleagues out of Belfast was the loquacious Gerry Fitt, who retained the distinctive sailor's swagger right through his colourful political career.

Those were uneasy and tense times for men of the sea. The Arctic convoys generally ran twice a month. There were various routes, including the Canadian and USA fleets across the north Atlantic, and out of Iceland. The risky Russian convoy was uncomfortably close to German forces, and obviously around the treacherous enemy-infested waters off the coast of Norway to the two ports. The main UK departure port was Liverpool.

The convoys were escorted on their high-anxiety voyages by ships of the Royal Navy and Royal Canadian Navy. It has been estimated there were around 80 convoys, involving 1,400 mercantile ships, from August 1941 to May 1945. Lost were 85 merchant ships, and 16 of the Royal Navy.

Captain Brian McEvoy's widow, the charming Anna, said: "Brian worked on the convoys right through the Second World War. It was before I met him. I know he sailed up the

SHIPS OWNED BY HOWDENS LTD.
and by their forerunners

This information about Howdens' vessels came to hand after the issue of the previous issue of the magazine. We now print this for the information of anybody interested.

□□□

ss COMET. Gross Tonnage 94. Built in Dumbarton in 1821. Engines of 24 h.p. Converted to Schooner and acquired by John Smiley & Son, Larne and sailed until 1876.

ss BLACK DIAMOND. Gross Tonnage 259. Built in Troon in 1864. A wooden steamer, she was acquired by Howden Brothers in 1888. Ran aground on Gobbins, Islandmagee on 28th May, 1892.

ss FERRIC. Gross Tonnage 335. Built in Belfast in 1883. Acquired by J. S. Howden (Howden Bros. Manager) in 1899. Transferred to W. J. R. Harbinson in 1903. Lost 16th January, 1905, by stranding at Black Arch, 2 miles north of Larne on passage Ayr to Belfast with coal.

ss MONARCH. Gross Tonnage 310. Built in Belfast for Alexander King Ltd. (a Company later acquired by John Kelly Limited) in 1905. Sold in 1917 to Manchester company. Foundered on 12th June, 1919, 10 miles off Ailsa Craig.

ss ROMA. Gross Tonnage 181. Built Larne by Larne Shipbuilding Co. in 1903 for W. J. R. Harbinson and C. L. McKean. Sold in 1917. Scrapped in 1959.

ss KILCOAN. Gross Tonnage 456. Built in Troon for W. J. R. Harbinson and C. L. McKean. Sunk by German submarine on 15th January, 1915 off Liverpool Bar.

ss NELLIE. Gross Tonnage 109. Built in Belfast in 1895. A wooden steamer, she was acquired by Howden Brothers in 1908. Broken up 1919.

ss SKERNAHAN. Gross Tonnage 530. Built in Workington in 1902. Acquired by Howden Brothers in 1915. Originally named the Cape York she was sold in 1915. Lost on 11th August, 1916 in collision.

ss CARNDUFF. Gross Tonnage 257. Built in Belfast in 1910 for Howdens. Scrapped in 1955.

ss COLLIN. Gross Tonnage 287. Built in 1915 for the Company and was sold to Alexander King Ltd. in 1919. Sold in 1949 to a Cardiff shipping company. She was converted to a sand suction dredger, re-named ISABEL. Sold to Tay Sand Co. Ltd, Dundee in 1965.

ss GLENO. Gross Tonnage 187. Built in Larne in 1902, she was acquired by Howdens in 1916. Sold by them in 1917. Foundered in March, 1917 off Godrevy, Cornwall.

ss SALLAGH. Gross Tonnage 325. Built in Alloa in 1916. She was scuttled on 10th February, 1917 after capture by submarine off Bardsey Island.

ss CARGAN. Gross Tonnage 274. Built in Alloa in 1916 for Howdens. Sold in 1921. Scrapped in 1956.

ss STRAIDE. Gross Tonnage 326. Built in Alloa for Howdens in 1917. Sold in 1953 and scrapped in 1954.

ss DROMAINE. Gross Tonnage 234. Built Alloa in 1917 for Howdens. Sold in 1945. Reported broken up in 1952.

ss FALAVEE. Gross Tonnage 338. Built Alloa 1918 for Howdens. Wrecked in Carlingford Lough on 14th January, 1942 on passage Belfast to Newry.

ss GALGORM. Gross Tonnage 453. Built Alloa in 1918 for Howdens. Sold in 1922. Scrapped in the Far East in 1934.

ss GRACEHILL. Gross Tonnage 452. Built in Alloa in 1918 for Howdens. Wrecked on Sanda Island on passage from Londonderry to Ayr on 8th March, 1957.

ss FINVOY. Gross Tonnage 374. Built in Alloa in 1918 for Howdens. Sold in 1957. Scrapped in 1958.

ss NELLIE. Gross Tonnage 235. The second of that name, she was built in Larne for Howdens. Sold in 1923.

Baltic on the Russian run. In those days a member of the crew was Gerry Fitt of Belfast. They became great friends. In later life, Gerry used to call down to visit us, and chat with Brian at our home in Glenarm.

"They loved to yarn about the past. Gerry Fitt once pushed for recognition for all seamen who took part in those dangerous voyages. In recent years medals were presented to seaman who participated in that time of the conflict, yet there has been no award for Brian. Incidentally, during convoy duty the small Kelly boats flew a balloon from the masthead to deter low-flying aircraft."

Brian McEvoy, who died in July 2007 when he was 80, quit sailing at 63 in 1985. He was joined in retirement that year by two other veteran Kelly/Howden's skippers - Bill Bailie and Bob Preston. McEvoy served 46 years at sea - mostly on Kelly boats. A brother, Nicholas, was drowned during a blackout at Oban, Scotland, in 1942.

Mrs McEvoy added: "Before we married, in April 1947, Brian worked on deep-sea ships. He was two years older than me. After he left deep-sea work, he joined Kellys, and was on their coasters the rest of his days at sea. He moved around the Kelly boats, starting as Mate. The vessels included the *BALLYKELLY*, the *BALLYHALFT*, and the *BALLYLORN*."

Twenty four years after working as Mate with captain Bob Gibson on the *BALLYHAFT* at Shoreham-by-Sea, Brian skippered the diesel-powered *BALLYKERN* 11 on October 1981, when loading grain cargo at the same Sussex port. The *BALLYKERN* 11 was launched as *BAXTERGATE* in 1976, and had the name changed four years later. *BALLYKELLY* (2) was built in Copenhagen in 1976, as *LIS DANIELDSEN*, and given the name change in 1979.

By the way, Bob Gibson's father was William Gibson M.B.E. skipper of the *PARKNASILLA* that was involved in sensationally warding off German fighter planes during the Second World War. John O'Hara of Cushendall was the hero of that gunfire exchange. Later, O'Hara and Glenariffe's Neil O'Boyle worked on Kelly boats with Brian McEvoy, whose son Brian emigrated to New Zealand to work on a ferry.

During his retirement, Captain McEvoy enjoyed his favourite pastime, a game of golf. He was a member of the nearby Cairndhu Club. In August 1982, and on his home course, he won the stableford section Kelly Cup in the annual outing of the NI Coal Importers' Association Golf Society.

Anna McEvoy has her own very strong connection with a variety of seafaring folk from Glenarm: "Bertie Rea, a deep-sea captain, who did some coasting later in life, is related to me. His mother and my mother were half sisters. My late father and my brother Bobby Sullivan, who lives in New Zealand, both went to sea. My father, Mickey Sullivan was born in Glenarm, and worked on minesweepers during the Second World War.

"One ship I know he was on was the *SARDONIC*. He forged his age, to join the Royal Navy at 15 years, before the First World War. He survived both Wars, and after that joined the merchant navy to work on the cross-channel ferry from Belfast to Liverpool. He took a bad heart problem, and had to retire to live at home in Glenarm. But he became restless, and decided to go to New Zealand, where my two brothers were living.

"He went to Christchurch, and was tragically killed when crossing a street - hit by a motorcar driven by a drunk driver. His two sons, Mickey Jnr and Bobby, were also at sea. They decided to emigrate to New Zealand. Mickey Jnr died there, from a heart attack. Bobby went to sea out there, but before he emigrated he married Mena Cassidy from Glenarm, and they have five of a family.

"After Bobby went to New Zealand, he was joined out there by Tom McMullan of Glenarm village. Tom's father Jim owned McMullan's Bar in Glenarm. Tom went to sea locally. Our son Brian then left to settle in New Zealand. He is married to Teresa Robinson of Larne. Brian emigrated when he was 21 years of age. He works as bo'sun on the ferry that crosses the Cook Strait, between the north and south islands."

During his sea career, and it seems for a time when working as a deck hand on the *QUEEN MARY* passenger liner, Bobby Sullivan was involved in a mid-ocean rescue operation. A New Zealand newspaper issue of Wednesday April 8, 2009, recalled the bravery of Glenarm-born Sullivan, when he helped in the rescue of injured sailors on the night of January 30, 1955.

This incident was the main topic of conversation by a group of old salts known as the 'Vindy Boys' - because they once completed their training on the Merchant Navy's school ship, *VINDICATRIX,* at Sharpness, on the Bristol Channel. They met in the Woolston Club, at Woolston, New Zealand, to recall old times.

Taking centre-stage this time was retired sailor Sullivan, then 77 and a resident of Woolston. His 1955 experience, as a 23-year-old deck hand, unfolded when two seamen on the Panamanian *LIBERATOR* fell down the hatch during rough Atlantic seas, and sustained serious injuries.

Cunard's *QUEEN MARY,* equipped with two hospitals and two surgeons, answered the SOS, and deployed lifeboat crews of volunteers who . . . 'swung into action, and began a daring rescue. Woolston resident Bob Sullivan was one of those men, and was awarded a medal for his courage and devotion to duty by the Shipwreck and Humane Society.'

The story of Sullivan's escapade revealed 1000 passengers aboard the liner *QUEEN MARY* had ringside viewing of the drama from the rails, watching as the lifeboat crew delivered one sailor and one surgeon onto the deck of the *LIBERATOR.* The two injured seamen were then brought across to the *QUEEN MARY* for treatment.

16

A BRIDGE TOO FAR

CAPTAIN Alex Blaney of the Crossroads, Cushendall, lived for many years on a knife-edge, regularly sailing through hostile waters during the Vietnam War. He almost made one run too many, when delivering a cargo of ammunition and other army implements to the American Forces up the Mekong Delta. His ship consumed a heavy hit from a Vietcong rocket.

The nerve-wracking incident cost the life of the ship's Mate. It could have been Captain Alex, but for a fortunate decision to take time out from his customary duty on the ship's bridge, and have a coffee break.

He didn't like to talk too much about it in later years, but explained the harrowing happening to his younger brother Willie, who said: "Many years later, when he was home, we were travelling into Ballymena. He felt I was driving the car too fast, and asked me to slow down. My driving was getting to him, and then he explained why he was a bit uptight. I think the memory of that incident was again back to haunt him.

"Alex said the last time he sailed up the Mekong with supplies for the Americans was a trip he was never able to forget. It was a dreadful experience. He was lucky to come out alive. He was the ship's master, and decided to take time off from the bridge, and leave the Mate in charge.

"He told me he decided to take a rest from duty, and go down below to the galley for a coffee. He was just about to take the coffee when a shell fired by the Vietcong proved a direct hit which blew the bridge to smithereens. Killed was the ship's Mate, whose blood seeped down into the galley.

"It would have been Alex to be killed instantly, but for the decision to go for a mug of coffee. That incident made Alex change work, join a different ship's company, and move away from sailing up the Mekong Delta."

Long before the Vietnam affair, Captain Alex married Ballycastle schoolteacher Margaret Black on November 7, 1972. They lived in Linton Lodge, Cushendun, and later moved to a new home in Ballycastle before he tragically died of a cancer, aged 48, on February 12, 1982.

His widow, Margaret said: "Alex shipped up to Vietnam throughout that war. He was up and down the river with supplies, working in that sea for a very long time. It was an extremely dangerous run. I think he worked for an American company when trading up to Vietnam with supplies for the US troops.

"I'm sure there were some very difficult experiences for him throughout that period. He worked for various shipping companies during his career in the Far East, and changed employers all the time. Alex didn't stay with any one shipping company."

CERTIFICATE OF COMPETENCY

AS

MASTER

OF A FOREIGN-GOING STEAMSHIP

No. 88621

MINISTRY OF TRANSPORT

To Patrick Alexander Blaney

WHEREAS you have been found duly qualified to fulfil the duties of Master of a Foreign-going Steamship in the Merchant Service, the Minister of Transport in exercise of his powers under the Merchant Shipping Acts and of all other powers enabling him in that behalf, hereby grants you this Certificate of Competency.

SIGNED BY AUTHORITY OF THE MINISTER OF TRANSPORT and dated this 24th day of October 1960

Countersigned J. Nicholson Assistant Registrar General

P. Faulkner A Deputy Secretary of the Ministry of Transport

REGISTERED AT THE OFFICE OF THE REGISTRAR GENERAL OF SHIPPING AND SEAMEN.

Patrick Alexander Blaney, born in Ballycastle's Dalriada Hospital on March 11, 1933, received his Master's Certificate of Competence (No 88621) - issued at Liverpool on the 28th of December 1960, after passing the 'Foreign-going steamship' Certificate test on the 10th of October, 1960.

At that time, when 27 years of age, he was the youngest sea captain from the Glens of Antrim, and was very proud of that distinction. For the latter and main part of his sea career he worked out of the Far East, and always there was the high risk included when he sailed up the Saigon River during the ghastly Vietnam War.

The bloody battles, involving Vietnam, Cambodia, Laois, and the US Forces, lasted mainly from November 1955 to April 1975. US military involvement ended in August 1973. The overall death toll from the fierce fighting was astronomical. The carnage including 55,220 US service members.

This gruesome conflict required a constant supply of goods, fuel, and ammunition to the US forces, with the passage of ships through the maze of waterways in the Mekong Delta, along the Saigon River to Ho Chi Mingh City - formerly Saigon City - some 37 miles from the South China Sea. One thousand miles north of Ho Chi Mingh City lay Hanoi, capital of Vietnam.

Captain Alex, who had an all-local Far East crew, worked in this dangerous mix, shipping cargoes of urgent supplies upriver to the US forces. Brother Willie added: "My son John once had a restaurant named 'Chopper's', a bar and grill in Thailand, on an island there named Koh Tao. He found out the small island was once an arms depot for the American forces during the Vietnam War.

"John also discovered his uncle, Captain Alex, ran arms supplies from there to the Mekong Delta during that War. Our Alex also worked on oil tankers bringing petrol fuel up the Mekong for the American aircraft operating in the Vietnam War."

The tiny settlement of Kow Tao ('Turtle Island'), is an idyllic island located on the western shore of the Gulf of Thailand. A popular holiday centre for scuba diving enthusiasts, it covers an area of 21 kilometres, and has a population of around 1,400. The main settlement or village is Ban Mae Hat.

After many years of tense trips into Vietnam, Captain Alex worked throughout the China Seas. Captain Gerry Blaney of the Cushendall seafaring family said he was once mistaken for Alex Blaney, when he went into a Seaman's Club in Hong Kong. Captain Alex's name was listed on a board in the Club.

Willie Blaney said: "Alex continued to work the China Seas, based in Hong Kong, and was in and out of Australia. When his ship would be discharging cargo in Sydney Harbour he would visit our sister Elizabeth. This journey was to become his last route on the seas.

"During those years, his crew generally comprised completely of Chinese seamen. He got along very well with them, and held them in high esteem. They gave him complete respect. He loved those days. Sadly, it was all to end when he began to feel ill. He took the cancer.

"He was married then. Alex and Margaret had also moved from living in Cushendun to Ballycastle. He took seriously ill on his ship, was flown off it to the nearest hospital, and after a cancer was diagnosed it was suggested it would better if he had the operation in a hospital in Australia.

"So, he went to Australia, stayed with Elizabeth, but it was then felt it would be better he had the surgery nearer to his home - for recuperation. Our brother, Dr Sean brought him to London for the operation, but surgery was unable to save him."

Alex Blaney's sea sagas go back to his schoolboy days. He would not be denied his dream of becoming a seaman, twice running away from his home at the foot of the Clough Road. Locked in a college at Newry or working in the family's extensive sheep and cattle farming enterprise were not for the 16-year-old. His father, John Joe Blaney rounded up the auburn-haired Alex, and herded him home after his first bolt from the family home, 'The Bridge', but it was all to no avail.

It was like a chapter out of a Mark Twain yarn as Alex again flew the coop, and for a definitive time. The call of the sea was in young Blaney nostrils, and he successfully negotiated all sorts of barriers before becoming a Master Mariner of deep-sea vessels. His adventures started when he was sent to be a boarding student in St Colman's College, Violet Hill, Newry. He didn't linger there for long. It didn't suit him, so he ran away to sea.

Margaret Blaney often listened to this tale of a young tearaway: "I think he managed to get a job on a Kelly coal boat, sailing out of Drogheda. His father, John Joe, went looking for him. Alex first worked on those coasters, and I remember him telling me he was very, very seasick at the start.

"He stuck to his guns. He was determined to be a seaman, and then stayed with his aunt Brigid in Liverpool. Brigid was John Joe's sister, and was married to James Delargy of Cushendall. I think he was connected to the old Glens of Antrim Hotel.

"Around this period, the story goes that his mother, Lizzie, gave him money to buy books to improve himself, to study all about seafaring. Alex did a lot of studying, and passed the various stages of examinations to progress to First Mate, and then his Master's Ticket."

Alex's brother Willie believes the interest in sea went away back when absorbing tall tales of the oceans from a local shoemaker. "When Alex was a young boy he would often listen to old sea yarns from Dan Campbell, a former sailor who was a shoemaker in Mill Street yard in Cushendall. Dan's brother, Hugh was a herder up the mountain behind us, as was young Hugh Campbell.

"Dan, who I believe was originally from Glenravel, had all sorts of stories. Alex loved that, and this may well have helped to plant the seed for his interest in going to sea. Alex, always curious to hear the spellbinding yarns from the old storytellers, was about 13-years-of-age when he joined old Dan 'Mick' (McAuley), a near neighbour, in securing a white greyhound from Willie Stevenson.

"Alex was always listening to words of advice from Dan 'Mick', and now they joined forces, believing they had a great racing prospect. I remember Alex cycling up and down the Holme field with the greyhound tied to a long rope behind him. This was the training programme, but the dog was a dud, useless.

"The second time he took off for a life at sea he went on a bus to Belfast, under the pretext of going to see Chipperfield's Circus. He had no overnight suitcase, no extra clothes. He cleared off to sea, again - and was not seen for six months. My mother went up to Belfast, and met him coming off the boat. Later on, he stayed with aunt Brigid in Liverpool."

In many respects, it was no surprise Alex Blaney became a sailor. There was sea salt in the veins. In generations past, the family was well represented on the seven seas, especially when three Blaney brothers owned barques - sailing ships of at least three masts.

Alex's first cousin, John Blaney, a retired schoolteacher living at Mullarts, Cushendun, said: "The Blaney brothers of the 19th century were sons of the original Blaney, Neil or Neal, who was born in 1804, and died in 1864. He lived in Glenariffc, where he had a sizeable family. It is believed he married a Brigid Coulter of Glenarm.

"Most of his sons went to sea. Patrick, born 1836, died in 1865 at Demerara. William, born 1838, died 1868, and Denis, born 1844, died on the 9th of December 1867.

"There was also William Blaney, my great, great grandfather, who owned a boat that sailed out of Cushendun beach with cargo of Cushendall ponies for the islands off Scotland. The boat also took limestone cargo from the old pier at Glenariffe across to Scotland. Other cargo included granite, and the boat had a crew of three men and a boy, all from Glenariffe. After using sail, he had the first of the coal-burning steamships, working back and forth out of Belfast to Liverpool.

"Some of those olden-time Blaney's pop up in Kingston, Canada. They first emigrated to a small island on the St Lawrence River, and moved to a place outside Kingston, Ontario, named Kingston Mills. To this day, it is known as 'Little Cushendall'

"Members of that Blaney clan worked on the building of railways, track that came down from Canada to Chicago, stopping at a turnkey, where the trains turn around at a town they named Valparaiso. The workers building the rail track were labourers known as 'Gandy Dancers', because they used a big 'Gandy' shovel. There are Blaneys still in that area. They spell the surname Blainey.

"On a headstone in a graveyard at Kingston Mills the names carved are William Blainey and his wife Elizabeth McElheron of Cushendall, Ireland. The Canadian census of 1851 has William and Elizabeth and five children, and in the census of 1861 it is the same plus 27-year-old John Blainey. The cemetery also displayed a headstone - John McKenty from County Antrim and his wife Mary Ann Blainey, born 1798."

The stylish sailing ship, *LOCH MAREE*, owned by Blaney brothers, was a vessel of 1581 tons, length 255.6 feet, breadth 38.6 feet, and depth 22.96 feet. Built in 1879, she ran from Southampton to South America. Apparently, the *LOCH MAREE* was the last boat of the Blaneys.

Willie Blaney explained: "They had barques, one named *EILEEN*, called after a sister and owned by her. They registered the boats in Liverpool, and often sailed to and from South America, to Demerara, and to the River Plate. Some cargo was Bangor blue Welsh slates, from Swansea to Canada.

"I have a copy painting of the *LOCH MAREE*. The late Peggy O'Neill, a cousin of my father, lived in Glenariffe, where the Hougheys are now. She had the original painting of the boat. The John Blaney of 1822 had a sister Margaret who married in 1859 to a Dan O'Neill from Glenariffe Glen, Peggy O'Neill's grandfather.

"They once ran a B& B or small hotel in Waterfoot, near where the Mariner's Bar is. Margaret died on August 8, 1895. When the house where the hotel was situated was sold by Cushendall auctioneer, Pat McCambridge, he came across an old sign 'Blaney's Hotel'

"Three Blaney brothers all died young men. Patrick died at Demerara aged 29 on the 12th of February, 1865. We don't know the circumstances. His ship was probably taking back a cargo of sugar and rum. Demerara was a Dutch colony region in South America, now known as Guyana, and famous for sugar cane growing and export of sugar - Demerara brown sugar. The main city, situated on a part of the Demerara River, is Georgetown.

"William was born in 1839, and as far as we know did not die at sea in 1868. The family story handed down is that he was at home when killed by a runaway horse. The tragic accident happened shortly after the Blaneys moved, around 1860 - after the Great Famine - from Glenariffe to purchase land at the Crossroads/Bridge area at the bottom of Clough Road.

"It was here a stallion horse belonging to the family bolted. It was yoked to a cart at the time. William tried to subdue the horse, but apparently was struck by a cart shaft and died. Denis, we think, died at sea. Again the circumstances of his early demise are unknown. He was 24, and died in 1867."

An addendum to this Blaney generation is the list of boat registrations in the Port of Belfast in January 1855, which includes the vessel named *BALLOT*, and the joint owners tabled are Bridget, Alex and J Blaney.

Dr Sean Blaney, older brother of Willie, provided valuable additional illumination on the olden-time Blaney seagoings. Some of the wooden barques in the fleet were registered in either Canada, Hull, or in Belfast. He stated: "Three Blaney brothers beame ship's Masters - Alexander (b 1827), William (1838), and Neal (1839)."

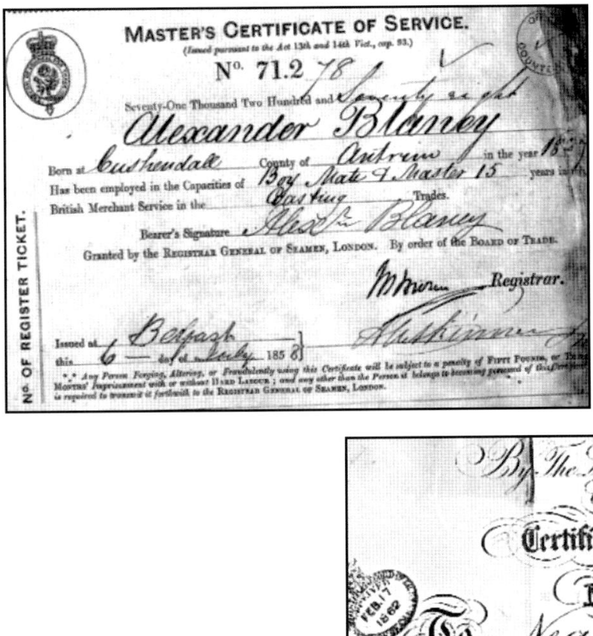
MASTER'S CERTIFICATE OF SERVICE.
(Issued pursuant to the Act 13th and 14th Vict., cap. 93.)
No. 71.278
Seventy-One Thousand Two Hundred and Seventy eight
Alexander Blaney
Born at Cushendall County of Antrim in the year 182[illegible]
Has been employed in the Capacities of Boy, Mate & Master 15 years in the British Merchant Service in the Coasting Trades.
Bearer's Signature Alexr Blaney
Granted by the Registrar General of Seamen, London. By order of the Board of Trade.
Registrar.
Issued at Belfast this 6 day of July 1858
No. OF REGISTER TICKET.

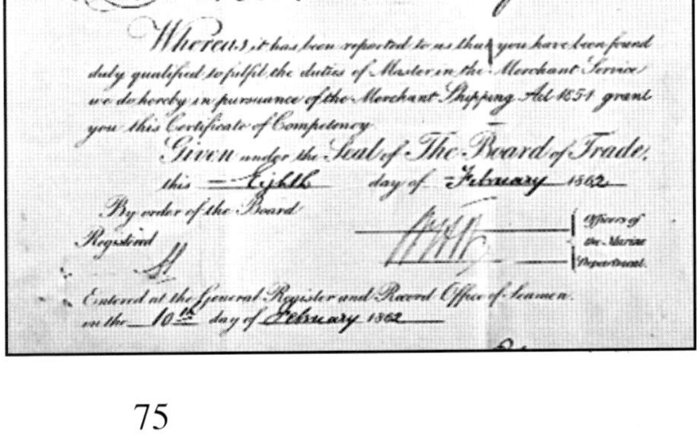
By The Lords of the Committee of Privy Council for Trade.
Certificate of Competency as MASTER.
To Neal Blaney
Whereas, it has been reported to us that you have been found duly qualified to fulfil the duties of Master in the Merchant Service we do hereby in pursuance of the Merchant Shipping Act 1854 grant you this Certificate of Competency.
Given under the Seal of The Board of Trade, this Eighth day of February 1862.
By order of the Board
Registered
Officers of the Marine Department.
Entered at the General Register and Record Office of Seamen on the 10th day of February 1862.

By The Lords of the Committee of Privy Council for Trade.

Certificate of Competency as MASTER.

To William Blaney

Whereas it has been reported to us that you have been found duly qualified to fulfil the duties of Master in the Merchant Service we do hereby in pursuance of the Merchant Shipping Act 1854 grant you this Certificate of Competency

Given under the Seal of The Board of Trade this [illegible] day of December [illegible]

By order of the Board [illegible] Officer of the Marine Department

Registered [illegible]

Entered at the General Register and Record Office of Seamen [illegible]

Vessels named by Sean, who qualified as a doctor in 1959, and began his GP career in Ballycastle, included the *CYRUS, NEVA, LOCH MAREE, NORMANBY, ENCHANTRESS, ELIZA OULTON, KISMET, THE HERTHA,* and the *MINNIE GRAY.* Sadly, records trace the death of Neal Blaney, skipper and owner of *THE HERTHA*, when he was lost at sea off Prince Edward Island, in 1876.

Skippered by a Captain Moncrieff, for the Blaney firm, the *MINNIE GRAY* had to be abandoned on February 10, 1885, when in a sinking condition during a violent storm off the east coast of the United States. The crew of nine survived, rescued by a British ship, the *HUDSON.* The incident was reported in the *New York Times* issue of February 20, 1885, stating the stricken vessel - 'was built in Sunderland in 1867, and owned by Neal Blaney of Hull.'

Dr Sean's cousin, John Blaney of Mullarts also has another sea interest, and, unfortunately, a tearful tale through his mother Anne's family, the 'Johnnie Joe' McCollam pub of Mill Street, Cushendall. He said: "My mother recalled her uncle Denis, who was in the Merchant Navy, was robbed on his boat by a fellow crew member. Apparently, Denis caught the thief in the act, but was killed during a struggle. Denis, born in 1886, was shot to death, murdered near Marseilles on November 6, 1920."

The 34-year-old son of Joseph and Anne McCollam was Second Engineer on the *RIVER TEIGH.* The boat was originally owned by the Denholm Brothers of Glasgow, when it was named *HOLMPSED.* In 1919, she was sold to the Cardiff firm of Merrett Brothers, renamed, and sold in 1926 to a Swedish firm.

PAIN BLAME

JOHN SCOLLAY, from Cushendall, once made television headlines, following a bizarre medical mistake during a stomach operation. After surgery, he was sent home from hospital, yet still in excruciating pain. One of six Scollay brothers who went to sea, he was rushed back to hospital, and a further X-Ray examination revealed the startling sight of a pair of forceps still nestling in his gut!

His daughter Monica, a nurse, remembered the obvious discomfort her father had to endure. "He died shortly after the hospital incident. There was a TV report at the time, to highlight the mistake. It was in 1994. My father retired from sea a long time before that happened. I remember as a young girl when he worked out of Larne, on the Larne-Cairnryan ferry. An AB, he was a deep-sea sailor for a long time, before coming closer to home, to work on the Ferries. It was a lonely life then for my mother, Nora, rearing a family of nine children.

"My husband, Eugene Graffin, is Second Officer on the P&O Larne-Cairnryan Ferries. He is from Larne, and was on deep-sea passages when I started going out with him. At that time, he was working for BP oil tankers, sailing to the Persian Gulf, to Singapore, and was on tankers delivering oil to the Falkland Islands during the time of the war down there. Once we married, he left deep-sea, and got lucky to secure a job on the P&O ferries, on the *EUROPEAN HIGHLANDER*".

John Healy, a nephew of the Scollays, recalled, in January 2013, the horrendous hospital incident. It was the talk of the Glens. "John Scollay's mother and my mother were sisters - McElroys. Following major stomach surgery, he was sent home to recuperate, but still very much unwell. I remember him telling me how much pain he was in when he tried to go for a walk.

"To find out what was wrong, a further X-Ray discovered forceps were in there. It was a shocking story that made local television news. When the radiographers in charge saw the outline they exclaimed:

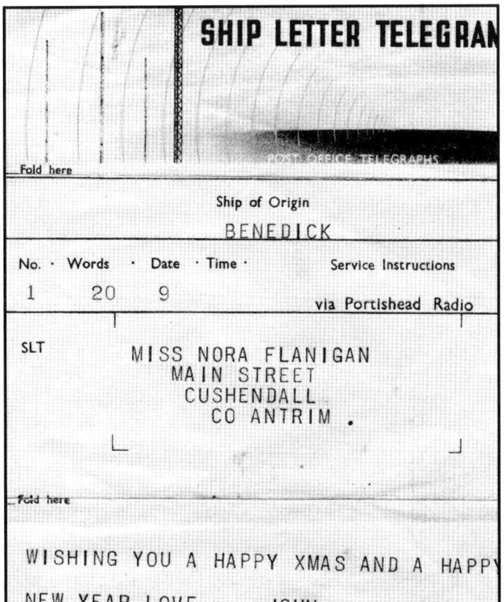
SHIP LETTER TELEGRAM
POST OFFICE TELEGRAPHS
Fold here
Ship of Origin
BENEDICK
No. · Words · Date · Time · Service Instructions
1 20 9 via Portishead Radio
SLT
MISS NORA FLANIGAN
MAIN STREET
CUSHENDALL
CO ANTRIM .
Fold here
WISHING YOU A HAPPY XMAS AND A HAPPY
NEW YEAR LOVE = JOHN +

'How did those get there?' John replied: 'One thing for sure, I didn't eat the forceps'.

"John was a brother of Captain Tommy Scollay, better known as 'Wee Tommy' - as opposed to 'Big Tommy', who was their father. Tommy Scollay Snr was also a seaman. He came down from the Shetland Islands, and in Glasgow met Lilly McElroy, a nurse, and also a sister of my mother.

"They married. 'Big' Tommy, who didn't become a sea captain, would take off on deep-sea trips, and some times not come home for two years. You would rarely see him. One of his sons, Tommy Jnr, became a sea captain. The other sons who went to sea were - John, of course, Jim, who was a stoker, Henning, and Hugh, who were AB's. I think Brendan also went to sea, for a short time. I also believe 'wee' Captain Tommy, who was mostly master of the coaster *CAIRNGORM*, was one of the founder members of the Cushendall Boat Club."

Incidentally, a schoolboy Hugh Scollay had a lucky escape, surviving a road accident outside the village. In 1932, an 11-year-old Scollay was struck by a motorcar while cycling between Cushendall and Waterfoot. The car was reportedly driven by a Mr Alan English of Carnlough. The bicycle was a tangled mess. Fortunately for young Scollay he emerged with merely a few scrapes and cuts.

John Healy's other uncles, Hugh and Jim McElroy went to sea. "The eldest was Hugh, who later became a butcher like his father Hugh in Cushendall's Mill Street - along with a McSparran. That was after his days at sea. He was a long time on the boats, working as a stoker. It was a really exhausting job. He once told me that being a stoker working in the severe heat in the engine room of a ship was - 'pure murder'.

"Jim, whose nickname was 'Killarney', was a seaman most of his life, well over 40 years. He did nothing else. He worked as a ship's cook, and mostly on coasters. Another brother, Jack went to America. The seafaring of the McElroy and the Scollay family circle was also handed on to the Healy's. My father, Frank, who married Dolly (Agnes McElroy), was well known in tracking down foxes. He didn't go to sea, but two of his sons did."

The McElroy connection included the legendary boatman, 'Dixie'. Fisherman Danny McElroy, who didn't go to sea, said: "My mother Anne's brother, John McElroy went to sea when he was a young man, working as a fireman. He was known here as 'Dixie', and was coasting during the Second World War.

"My uncle Dan (McElroy) was also at sea, and was also a fireman. Jim McElroy, a cousin of my mother, was a ship's cook. A lot of fellas from here worked on coasters. Indeed, during the last War there were busloads of young men from along the Antrim Coast travelling to ports such as Belfast and Larne to work on boats.

"My stepfather, John Findlay was a seaman, and later a fisherman at the salmon nets at Cushendun river mouth and at Salmonport. Maurice Findlay, his father, did not go to sea. John was on coasters with the Robertson Company of Glasgow. During the Second World War he was on passage down off the South of Ireland coast, when the weather conditions were, as they say - 'a wild bad night'.

"There were two seaman at the wheel. John and another crew member, such were the awful stormy conditions. Suddenly, at the last minute, John saw another ship loom right in front of them. It was an American vessel. John told me he shouted to his companion to let go of the wheel. Unfortunately, his crew colleague couldn't let go, as a piece of strap became tangled up in the wheel, which spun around fiercely, and caught John in his back.

"John's boat, carrying coal cargo, hit the American ship right amid-ships. He said he saw American sailors jumping to safety. John's boat rammed the American vessel. The thudding impact was fierce. Fortunately, no fatalities were reported, but John was lifted ashore at Cork, where he was taken to hospital. Eventually he was sent home to Cushendall, to recover from his back injury.

"Once he was fit again, he went back to sea, before quitting in 1945. He returned home to do the fishing. The Cushendun net fishing finished for Maurice Findlay in 1962, while I stayed on at the Salmonport net for a few more years. John died. Charlie, Maurice's brother, didn't stay at the fishing while his son Maurice went to sea. Maurice Findlay Jnr married a Dublin girl.

"Incidentally, the weekly wage a deck hand earned during those years of the Second World War was around £3. 10 shillings. I remember my stepfather (John Findlay) sending home weekly money. It arrived in Cushendall by telegram. It was £2.00 for my mother. I was told if you were a ship's cook you could make more money than one of the deck hands. The cook could charge a crew member ten shillings per week for grub, and would be fed free, and also pick up wages for his work.

"Those were dangerous times during the War years. It was a treacherous period at sea, from 1939 to 1945, as far as torpedoes were concerned. The Merchant Navy suffered dreadfully during the Second World War. The little boats such as coasters carried a gun for protection. Two Royal Navy gunners were on board.

"John Findlay, who did not do convoy runs in the Atlantic, once recalled an incident on deck when he was almost shot by one of the boat's members. A gunner was testing the gun, taking in some practice shooting that went accidentally out of control. The gun swivelled, and the wheelhouse was sprayed with bullets. That happened moments after John stepped out of the wheelhouse.

"During that period, we lived at High Street, Cushendall, and later moved to one of the new houses at Dalriada. When I married Ella, I moved down to Shore Street, where I live today, opposite what was the old Cottage Hospital.

"In the days after the War, we resumed the old tradition of staging regatta days at Cushendun, Cushendall, and Glenariffe. The McElroy men were heavily involved as oarsmen in the Regatta races, when they were not at sea. I remember two of the McElroy's winning the Cushendall

Regatta. I also recall the O'Loan's, Danny and Pat, building a special boat for the racing.

"The sea was always a part of our lives. At Cushendun, I recall Scottish folk, maybe half-a-dozen in their open boat, coming in from the wee village of Southend on the tip of the Mull of Kintyre. For years those Scottish people came across the North Channel for the day of the Cushendun Regatta. On one occasion bad weather was coming in fast, and the boatman from the Mull was advised to stay over in Cushendun.

"But, off he went with the rest of his friends in a two-hulled boat, but not heading straight out and across to Southend - instead, he sailed up the coast to near Fair Head, and then cut across the Channel. To keep the rains out of the boat, the people were covered by a large tarpaulin, so that the heavy rains would run off them, and into the sea. They made it. During my time down at the Cushendun nets I helped in a few rescues of people getting into problems in the North Channel."

Back to the McElroy-Healy link, and more young men taking to the waters. John Healy added: "My brother Hugh, presently living in Newcastle-Upon-Tyne, first started work in Elliott's Hotel, Cushendun, at 15 years of age. The Elliott sisters and Bertie Gregg treated him very well down there, but not long after that he moved on. He decided to go to sea - at 16 - around 1956.

"He went to work with his uncle, Captain Tommy Scollay, on the *CAIRNGORM.* I remember Sean Mort going to sea for a first time on the same boat. Hugh worked on Robertson boats, and did a lot of coasting work. He was also away for long spells of over six months at a time, when working on deep-sea runs.

"He was on the first mail boat to leave Belfast. That was in 1960. The boat sailed to London, picked up more mail, and also many passengers, before taking off for South America. He was away for six months on that journey. He married in 1962, and shortly afterwards left the sea. He went to England, lived at Sunderland, where he started an ice cream business.

"Also at sea was my brother Frank, who is one year older than Hugh. He also went with Captain Tommy (Scollay). Frank was later than Hugh when starting. At 14 years of age he joined the St John of God Nursing Order at Stillorgan, Dublin, but came out at 19. He didn't work very long at sea. Frank married in 1963, the same year our mother died when she was only 48. Frank lives in Waterfoot.

"My youngest brother Danny became a schoolteacher, while, once upon a time, I considered going to sea, but instead got a job with Arthur's on Shore Street, and was out on the grocery van run. At that time, Ian Mort, who was at sea with his father, Captain John Mort, told me he would try and get me a job at sea. Ian did just that. He sent me a telegram from Liverpool, to tell me to come over right away. He had a job lined up for me. I took cold feet, and stayed at home."

18

CAPTAIN CHARLIE

CUSHENDUN became a second home for Glenravel-born Captain Charles McQuillan, who brought many young men from the Glens to a career in seafaring. Married to the delightful Brigid McKay, of Ranaghan, Knocknacarry, he spent most of his days on the waves with the Dorey Shipping Company of St Peter Port, Guernsey.

Captain Charlie's love of the sea was part of a family tradition, as his uncle was Captain Mick McCormick of Glenariffe. Mrs Margaret McCausland, one of two daughters, disclosed: "In 1929, my father went to sea, at 16 years of age, with his uncle, Captain Mick, who was my grandmother Maggie Ann's brother. My grandfather was Daniel McQuillan.

"My father started during the period when ships were changing from sail to steam. He was born on March 31, 1913, and was the third in a family of nine. There were six boys - Johnny, Charlie, James, Alex, Mick, and Danny. The girls were Eileen, Kathleen, and Maeve. Five boys went to sea. Johnny stayed at home on the farm.

"Charlie was first to work at sea. He qualified as a Master Mariner in 1941, when he was 28. He sat his examinations in Belfast. In that same year, in June 1941, he married Brigid McKay of Cushendun. During the Second World War he sent many letters home to my mother, but they were heavily censored with large bits cut out of them. My mother never knew where he was, and was surprised on a few occasions when he just 'turned up' at home.

"In July 1942, my late brother Cahal was born at Ranaghan. At that time, my parents lived in the centre house of The Square, Cushendun. It was a first home for my parents. My father was obviously at sea during the Second World War, and worked on the convoys. Cahal was four months old before my father saw him for the first time.

"The family then moved to live at Bonavor, Cushendun, in the house later owned by Bunty McMullan's parents, Alex and Agnes McMullan. I was born when we lived at Bonavor, and on the day War ended in 1945. Cahal, later to become a shipping agent in Belfast, was four and I was a year and a half when we moved to live in Guernsey, because my mother thought we'd see more of my father - if we lived there.

"St Peter Port was his main centre, working for the Dorey Company. We lived for five years at the village of St Sampson, which was not far along the coast from St Peter Port. The big old house we rented had been a convent. The nuns were put out of their home by the Germans, and moved to their mother-house during the War.

"The German invasion meant hardships for the residents on the island.

An awful lot of people in Guernsey were displaced, moved out of their homes by the Germans. After five years there, my mother became very homesick. It was a lonely place for her, as her husband was away most of the time.

"My father was a Continental Ticket holder, which meant he made voyages to various ports in France, Belgium, and Germany. As youngsters, Cahal, me, and my sister Mary (who became Mrs McAllister), were taken with him during our summer holidays. This was in the month of July, and we called at ports such as Rouen. For the month of August my father came home.

"Most of his sea life he worked for Dorey of Guernsey. In his latter years he changed to another company, so that he could be nearer our home, in Belfast. He was not very long into his change of employer when he retired, at 65, so he was 49 years at sea. Two years later, at the age of 67, he died. Ironically, he took ill while doing 'relief captain' for a friend. He is buried in Cushendall Cemetery."

Captain Charlie skippered the *ROCQUAINE*, which was built in 1943 when named the *EMPIRE RIDER* until sold to Onesimus Dorey of St Peter Port, in 1946. It was renamed *LOUGH SWILLY* in 1995, and one year later named *LUNDEN*. Along with Charlie McQuillan, another local man, Captain Dan McFaul of Larne, skippered the *ROCQUAINE* for a spell during the early 1950's.

Captain McQuillan was, for a time, in charge of the 946 gross tons *PORTELET*, built in 1930 as *SANFRY* for J Hargreaves of Leeds, before re-registered in 1940 as *YORKBROOK*. The ship was purchased by Dorey in 1950, and renamed *PORTELET* after the original named ship that was blown up by a mine in February 1940. The second edition was broken up in Dublin, on May 17, 1958.

The McQuillan family sea escapades were many. Charlie was fortunate to survive an accidental explosion on his ship. In 1952, he sustained bad injuries. He could have been killed. He was on a coal cargo run when the lighting of a cigarette touched off escaping gasses coming from the ship's hold.

Margaret McCausland said: "He suffered bad burns on his face and hands. He was very ill, taken to a hospital in Penzance, Cornwall. It was a few months before he recovered, after losing the skin on his hands and face.

"One of his brothers, Captain James McQuillan was a survivor of a North Atlantic convoy that was torpedoed by German U-Boats. Married to Peggy McMullan from Glenravel, he survived the torpedo incident. He was on the last ship in the convoy, the *KENBANE*. All ships were lost. The last ship had four survivors in a liferaft for four days, before they were rescued. James became a Captain some time after that. He was also with Dorey.

"Alex, another brother, was drowned at sea, and in his 20's, while Mick was at sea until he retired. He and wife Gertie moved their young family to Wallasey, near Liverpool. Another brother, Danny was also a Captain.

He had a Master's Ticket, but didn't use it as shortly after qualifying he decided to quit the sea."

Danny returned to Glenravel, where he had a young family that included five boys and one girl. The eldest son, Alex was a former Glenravel Con Magees Club and Antrim gaelic footballer - and once a top Irish League player with Ballymena United.

"Just as Charlie started at sea, with his uncle Mick McCormick, he in turn, took his young cousin Jackie Kiely of Waterfoot to sea. Jackie, who lives in Glengormley, is the grandson of Captain Mick McCormick, and in keeping with the family's seafaring tradition became a Master Mariner," added Margaret.

"Many other young men from the Glens of Antrim went to sea with Captain Charlie, and made a success of their lives. Often, when living in Guernsey, we had people visiting us from time to time, such as my uncle, John McKay from Ranaghan. He was seafaring for a short time with my father, before emigrating to America, to work in New York. He returned home in 1953, to help his brother Henry on the family farm at Ranaghan.

"Also starting at sea with Captain Charlie was a cousin of my mother - Charlie McKay from Gortacreggan, Cushendun. We called him 'Deep-Sea' Charlie. The highlight of those days for us was when Charlie (McKay) paid a visit. He was a lovely man. Once, he brought me a caged canary from one of his deep-sea voyages. He also called to see us in Belfast, when he was in the port."

Charlie McKay was a most interesting and colourful character. He was extremely considerate, yet not a man easily turned. Charlie 'The Sailor' held an impish dimpled grin when he greeted you with a handshake 'grip of steel'. Always a generous individual, he would, when home on leave, bring a round tin of 50 bonded, duty free, 'Ships' Woodbine cigarettes to an ageing maritime mentor, Knocknacarry's Alex O'Hara.

During a lengthy career at sea, the sanguine sailor progressed to become a Quartermaster on both of the famous passenger ships, the *QUEEN MARY* and the *QUEEN ELIZABETH*, yet the strictures attached to such an exacting job did not sit well on him.

The youngest member of that McKay family, Dominic explained why Charlie was ill at ease on Cunard's renowned luxury liners: "Charlie didn't stay too long with the Queen liners, because it was all pressure, no respite. It was too demanding for him. The ship would leave Southampton and stop at Cherbourg to pick up more passengers for New York. In New York harbour passengers were waiting to immediately be taken on board for the return trip. There was no break.

"Along with another quartermaster they had the job of steering the ship. The First Officer would instruct them what they had to do. Always two men would be ordered to take charge of steering at the one time during the voyage across the Atlantic.

"Charlie, who died in 2006, once told me the *QUEEN MARY* liner had a crew of 1,300, whereas a dozen would probably do nowadays on such a big boat, because of all the modern electronic and computer equipment. Working as a quartermaster on a liner proved to be an entirely different style of life for him, than sailing on a cargo boat.

"All deep-sea ships then did not have automatic steering. You had to do shifts of one hour on in the wheelhouse, a long time to maintain relentless concentration. To be a Captain of a Cunard 'Queen' liner you had to have British Navy experience, and I think Charlie told me the name of one of the skippers was Surrell.

"Charlie left the liners, and went to work on oil tankers in the Persian Gulf, shipping oil out of Iraq and Iran. During his time at sea, he had Joe Murphy and Arthur Hamilton working with him. I think on the *TORR HEAD* and *RATHLIN HEAD* ships. He was on Head Line boats then, to North America. I believe he also had spells working on ships skippered by Gerry and Paddy Blaney.

"Charlie started with the Dorey Company, working on coasters at 18 years of age. He went up to Ranaghan, Cushendun, where Captain Charlie McQuillan was then staying, to ask him for a job. Captain McQuillan was Commodore Captain with the Dorey Company, and married to Brigid McKay, a first cousin of our family."

Dominic added: "Through Captain McQuillan our Charlie got a job right away, and off he went to sea for many years. Charlie worked on coasters for some time. I remember when he was with Dorey's he used to send me cigarettes named 'Bucktrout', from Guernsey. It was a brand of cigarette I never saw in any shop here, in County Antrim."

The Bucktrout firm was also involved in producing cigarette cards, a very popular pastime in the 1920's. The 1923 set included photograph images of leading film stars of that silent movie era, such as Mary Pickford, Charlie Chaplin, Mae Marsh, Dorothy Gish, Betty Blythe, Theda Bara, Mabel Normand, Douglas Fairbanks, Harry Carey, and Tom Mix.

The back of the colourful cards included advertisements for three different brands of cigarette - 'Officer's Mess Cigarettes (African Tobacco Company), 'There is always satisfaction in a Guernsey-made cigarette' (Bucktrout), and 'Indo Egyptian Cigarette Company, (Cheribon).'

Charlie's twin brother Danny also tried the seagoing, but for a very short stint. Apparently, in 1947, when a 19-year-old, he made one working trip on water. He died, aged 84 on the 3rd of March, 2012, and was affectionately nicknamed 'Danny Oscar'. He worked most of his adult life as a popular bus conductor and bus driver.

Near neighbour Ian McElheron said: "Danny McKay went to sea for a very short time, a fireman on a cross-channel boat. He worked on a ferryboat owned by British Railways. His brother Charlie, a very decent man, had a grip of steel."

19 TORPEDO TERROR

JAMES McKeegan survived not only one Second World War torpedo incident but two, and all in the same sea trip. From Lubitavish, Glenaan, he possessed the charm of a cat with nine lives. Amazingly, he lived to tell the tale. Ironically, he died many years later during a Coast Road bus journey on the way home, when he decided to retire from seafaring.

The brother of the legendary 'wee' Archie McKeegan - the 'Bard of Glenaan' - James, a merchant seaman, was on a vessel sunk by a German U-boat. He was saved from that attack, and that boat in turn was sent to the bottom of the sea. The ship that saved him came under heavy fire. Once again, James was rescued, this time picked up by a ship named the *MENIN RIDGE* - and landed in Gibraltar. His mother, in Glenaan, received a telegram stating: 'Son on board *MENIN R*IDGE. Safe in Gibraltar.'

McKeegan was fortunate he did not stay on board the *MENIN RIDGE* as it made its way back out into the Mediterranean Sea. On October 24, 1939, and shortly after leaving James and other sailors saved ashore on 'The Rock', the *MENIN RIDGE* was torpedoed. It was a British cargo steamer of 2,700 tons, and heading to Port Talbot with a cargo of 4,200 tons of iron ore. Previously named the *PENTIRION*, she was sunk by German submarine U-37, and 22 members of the crew lost. Built in 1924, the *MENIN RIDGE* became part of a hat-trick of horror as the *LEDBURY* and*TAFNA* also became victims of U-37.

The German submarine's Kapitan was Werner Hartmann. All three British cargo ships went down south west of Gibraltar. An American freighter named *CROWN CITY* rescued *LEDBURY's* entire crew of 33 men, but, sadly. merely five of *MENIN RIDGE's* crew of 27.

Following his wartime great escapes, James McKeegan continued his lucky streak, when he fell into Liverpool docks. A noted good swimmer, he swam around, and sang out, before his voice was heard by a dock security man - a Harbour Policeman. He was rescued yet again. James decided to retire from the sea in the 1960's.

There was a touch of irony in that he didn't make it back to his beloved Glenaan. His homebound voyage this time proved to be his last. He was on an Ulsterbus from Larne. Denis McKillop, connected to the McKeegan-McKillop seagoing fraternity, said: "It was all very sad. James suffered a heart attack on the bus, and right outside the Glenarm doctor's house on the coast road.

"The man in charge of the bus was Danny McKay of Cushendun. He tried to revive James, then lifted him from the bus, and into the doctor's house. Unfortunately, James McKeegan did not recover. He died in the doctor's surgery."

Another Glenaan seaman to ward off German gunfire was John McCambridge, of Milltown, Tavnaghoney. He steered one of the puffers into Dunkirk during the evacuation of troops in the Second World War. He helped with the moving of armed forces, and in the process saved his cousin, Johnny Darragh, a soldier from Scotland, who was trapped in northern France. Darragh survived the War. His mother was Sarah McDonnell.

A Second World War multiple loss of life was the sinking of the *OLIVINE* of William Robertson and Company, Glasgow. The boat was on passage from Glasgow to Sharpness in the Bristol Channel when sunk on March 29, 1941. It is a morbid memory, but should not be overlooked. Those who perished included Donald McLaughlin AB, a relative of the late Tessie McAuley of Knockans, later Mrs Bakewell of the Harbour Bar, Ballycastle.

Other crew members lost in this torpedo incident were - skipper Thomas Ross, Leonard Cornish AB, Alex Dalzeil (fireman), Donald McAuley (OS), John McAuley (Chief engineer), John J McAuley (fireman), Neil McGugan (Mate), Ross Barbour (bo'sun), and George Yendall (second engineer).

On a happier note is the sequence of amazing escapes by Glenarffe's Denis McAllister, who was torpedoed three times in the Atlantic and survived. From Foriff, he was an AB and also Bo'sun, and was working convoys when torpedoed. Denis, who went deep-sea all the time, survived the Second World War to live in Liverpool. During the last of his working days he was on dredgers in the Mersey. He was a brother of famous Glenariffe hurler, Danny McAllister, who featured in the Antrim team that played Cork in the 1943 All-Ireland final.

Liverpool salutes veterans who defied Hitler's U-boats

by John Furbisher

JST like 50 years ago, the en and women were the ars even more than the maines. Spitfire and Swordfish arplanes swooped low over e Mersey in a spectacular 'past, while at sea the ships 16 nations saluted as erseyside put the flags out to mmemorate victory in the attle of the Atlantic.

But the estimated million ople who lined the Mersey d the streets of Liverpool r the spectacle saved their ggest cheers for the 3,000 terans of the battle, some of em in their 80s, who mared through the city. It was highlight of five days of ents to mark the 50th niversary of the victory ainst Hitler's U-boats.

As for many others, it was emotional day for Denis McAlistair, 72, from Huyton, Merseyside. With five decorations, including the Atlantic Star, Pacific Star and Italian Campaign medals adorning his navy blue blazer, he stood ramrod straight and brushed a tear from his eyes as his comrades marched past. "I wanted to be in the parade myself, but with arthritis in my legs I thought it might be a bit too much," he said. "What a proud day. You think people have forgotten what people gave for this country until you see them turn out like this."

McAlistair served 49 years in the merchant fleet, joining in 1937. He was on three ships that were torpedoed. After one ship was sunk, he spent a week adrift in a lifeboat in the North Atlantic. "I lost a lot of good friends," McAlistair said. "Sometimes I thought I would never see the end of the war, let alone a day like this."

For one elderly veteran the mile long march proved too much. He was taken to hospital suffering from a suspected heart attack as he passed the podium in Derby Square where Admiral Sir Benjamin Bathurst, First Sea Lord, was taking the salute.

Along two miles of the Mersey warships and merchant vessels were moored from countries including the United States, Canada, Norway, Denmark, Poland and Iceland. Many were open to the public. A flypast was led by Sea Harriers, Nimrods, Buccaneers and Sea King heli-

In 1995, the citizens of Liverpool, and the surrounding area, celebrated the 50th anniversary of the victory against Hitler's U-boats. Over one million people attended to pay homage to 3,000 survivors of the battles, who were involved in a parade. Unable to take part in the special walk was Denis McAllister. He was then 72, and living at Huyton, Merseyside. He was suffering severely from arthritis in both legs, and stood for the parade.

Interviewed at the time, he wore five medals, including the Atlantic Star, the Pacific Star, and the Italian Campaign. He revealed he spent 49 years as a merchant seaman. He left Glenariffe for a life on the oceans in 1937. Denis worked on three ships that were torpedoed, and after one ship went down he spent a week adrift on a lifeboat. "I lost a lot of good friends. Sometimes, I thought I'd never see the end of the War," he said.

Johnnie O'Boyle of Glenariffe knew of the McAllister torpedo incidents, second hand, and said: "I once worked on the *BALLYRORY* with a fella from Bushmills - Dan Rodgers. He survived German U-boat torpedo attacks in the North Atlantic, and was along with Denis. Dan (Rodgers) told me he worked a long time with Denis, and they survived three torpedo attacks. He said that once, after their ship was torpedoed, he was along with Denis (McAllister) for seven days in a life-raft before they were rescued."

Alex McMullan, a ship's engineer, born in Glendun and married to Agnes Brogan of Glasgow, in 1909, relished recounting his great escapes from German firepower. He was torpedoed three times. Reared in Belfast from four years of age, he attended college and qualified in Engineering. He joined the Royal Engineers as a Lieutenant in the First World War, and served in Mesopotamia (now Iraq). In the Second World conflict he was a Chief Engineer, and served at sea in convoys.

One of the three ships sunk under him happened in the North Sea, and during heavy fog. As the crew members were taking to the lifeboats a U-Boat surfaced. The U-Boat Commander threw down a bottle of brandy into their lifeboat - and also gave them bearings for land. Such incidents were recalled in a special book called the *'Golden Horseshoe'* about the exploits of a famous German U-Boat Commander named Otto Krestchmer.

Later made into a film, the Krestchmer story mentioned that the compassionate German would throw a bottle of brandy, and also give bearings to a lifeboat crew. Krestchmer was eventually captured, on March 17, 1941, and imprisoned near Liverpool, on Aintree Race track. He was later transferred to serve four of the years in the Bowanville POW camp in Canada, before being released in December 1947. Alex McMullan lived, from his sea retirement in 1950, at Barrmean, Cushendun, with his family that included schoolteacher daughter 'Bunty' - later to be Mrs Dan McAuley.

20 BAY of PLENTY

CAPTAIN Mick McCormick was one of the stand-out seafaring characters from along the Antrim Coast. Born in Glenariffe's glen, he lived a good part of his time at the Bridge, Waterfoot, and spent most of his extensive working life on board Dorey of Guernsey boats. He retired in the early 1950's, after a half-century trading on the coastal routes.

In 1928, the enterprising Captain Mick purchased what is fondly known as that haven of warmth, the 'Mariner's Bar' on Waterfoot street. His grandnephew, Hugh McIlwaine eventually became the landlord of the landmark hostelry. McIlwaine said: "He bought the pub from the McIntosh family, from old Archie McIntosh, I think. It became known as Eileen's Bar, named after one of Captain Mick's daughters, Mrs Kiely. Captain Mick had three daughters, Eileen, Annie, and Winnie.

"Her son, Jackie also went to sea with Captain Mick, and eventually became a Master with Kellys. Captain Mick worked a remarkable length of time, 50 years at sea, and sailed on steam ships that had an open bridge. Indeed, the second ship I sailed on - the old *BALLGRAINEY* - started off her life as open bridge, before being converted. A full bridge was built on her deck.

"Mick McCormick, who became Commodore Captain with Dorey, was responsible for helping practically all the seamen from my area get a job. Many progressed, including his nephews - Captain Charlie McQuillan and Captain Jackie Kiely - and also Captain Charlie McAlister. Other locals to join Doreys through Captain Mick included his nephew Neil, and also Patsy McAllister.

"Mick and three of his brothers, Paddy, Johnny, and James went to work at sea. James qualified as a chief engineer, and Paddy and Johnny became engineers. Johnny's son John, better known as 'Count' McCormick became a sea captain with the John Kelly company, while daughter Jeanie married Joe McMullan.

"Tragically, James, who had a Mate's Foreign-going Ticket, was killed in India, when only 24. A letter of James' death was sent to my mother. He wasn't killed at sea, but in harbour, at Calcutta. The official letter, which we still have in the family, explained in language today considered not to be politically correct - 'he was supervising the coolies discharging cargo from his boat when he fell into the hold, and was killed.'

"Years later, there was a further sea fatality in the family, when Captain Mick's son Seamus was killed during a tragic harbour accident in Glasgow. Seamus McCormick, who was a good hurler for Glenariffe in his young days, was an AB. He was married to a Scottish lass, and lived in Glasgow with a young family.

"The older generation McCormick family came from the top of Glenariffe. There were ten members in the family - five boys and five girls. One of the girls, Margaret Ann, married Daniel McQuillan of Glenravel, and one of their sons - Charles McQuillan - started a career at sea with Captain Mick. Of the remaining two boys in that McCormick family, Charlie went to work in New York, while Hugh, stayed at home, to work the farm. Also at home was my mother's aunt Mary. We all lived up the Glen then. Even I helped out as a young boy on the farm.

"I remember Charlie coming home from America, for a visit in the 1950's. He was married to a girl from Glenarm named McKendry, a sister of old Neil Black's wife. My mother, Katherine McCormick, was a niece of Mick. His brother Hugh was my grandfather, my mother's father. Captain Mick's daughter, Annie married soccer legend Jimmy Delaney. Annie and my mother were obviously first cousins."

Waterfoot village, fronted by panoramic Red Bay, the Red Arch, caves, and the Pier, spawned another great seagoing specialist, Captain Charles McAlister. A flamboyant character, affectionately known as 'The Kapitan', his mother was Molly McCormick, a sister of Captain Mick. The 'Kapitan' was a deep-sea mariner, but when skipper he also sailed coasters for the Coast Line - on ships such as the *ULSTER QUEEN* and *ULSTER PRINCE*. He enjoyed a long spell with the Dorey company. A son of Con McAlister, and a cousin of the late Charlie 'The Brock' McAlister, his brothers, Mickey and Patsy also went to work on boats, as AB seamen. Patsy lived in the Channel Islands.

Another genial gent from Waterfoot street was Danny McNaughton, a student at St MacNissi's College when Garron Tower opened in September 1951. His family ran the once immensely popular Glenariffe Inn. He decided on a career at sea. For a period he sailed with the Head Line boats out of Belfast, on the trans-Atlantic run. He was deep-sea for a long time, before ending his working days on the Larne-Cairnryan ferries.

Arguably, the saddest story of a seaman from the village was the murder of retired mariner Dan McVeigh. Ian McElheron of Ballybrack, Glenaan, was a close associate and used to keep regular contact with Dan. He explained the sickening saga: "I knew Dan well - a decent man. Tragically, he was murdered in his own home on Waterfoot street by robbers. The ruffians must have thought he had money in the house. They tied him up, and he died there.

"I remember Dan telling me he was on the coasting boats, and how difficult it was when sailing around the north of Scotland. The old seaman's house in Waterfoot street is presently owned by Dr Alastair McSparran's sister Anne. Way before all that, the house was occupied by people named McGaughey, one of whom married a one-time neighbour of mine, Willie John McGarry of Straid, Cushendun, who once worked in New York, supplying ice blocks for apartments."

The Leech family in the village contributed three sailors in Patrick (better known as 'Pa') an AB, John, an engine-room greaser who married

Annie O'Hara of Bonavor, Cushendun, and Alex - a second engineer. Pa Leech once worked on the *ESSO IPSWICH*. From what I gather, the father of Martin Leech had to take to the air for a first time to join that ship. The story goes he was uneasy about boarding an aeroplane for a flight to Manchester, to report for deck duty. On a Monday morning at Aldergrove (Belfast International Airport), and never before on a 'plane flight, Pa overcame stagefright to reluctantly board the plane.

The hamlet that lies a few sand dunes from the sea has understandably been a natural breeding ground for seafaring folk and fishing enterprises, often index-linked to the hinterland farming community. During the early years of the 1930's, a note in an old Glynn's magazine states a John McAllister of Waterfoot was a regular seaman, while his wife (nee Hennessey) ran a confectionary shop and also a pub in the village.

Amid the bustling street action surfaced such sea-going men as the Leechs and Rowans, part of a closely-knit group. It seemed a natural progression for this clan to go to work at sea, just like their neighbours - the Murrays and the McCormicks. The lapping of the nearby waves indeed proved an irresistible magnet for a 15-year-old Hugh O'Mullan, whose mother was Kate Rowan, but he had to twiddle his thumbs a few more months after being rejected when he first reported for duty.

His Glenariffe Primary School friend, James Murray set up the job. O'Mullan shrugged off the snub to eventually progress to become a ship's skipper, and later Harbour Master at Garston, Liverpool. He recalled: "I was asked my date of birth when I went to join the wee coaster James Murray was on. He was that little bit older than me, and went to sea at 16. He was on a boat that ran coal into Red Bay, the LOCH ETA

"I went to sign on at Larne, but when they asked my age I was turned down. I was only 15. On my way home on the bus I met Jamie Emerson of Cushendall, and he encouraged me not to give up. Many young men, some even younger than me, went to work at sea. Sadly, James Emerson, whose brother Robert also went to sea, was tragically killed after falling into the ship's hold at Spain. Robert was with Jacks of Larne."

O'Mullan, whose cousins include the Leechs and Rowans, was not to be deterred, and through the promptings of Captain Dan Black made it down to the sea and ships. "I was born in September 1938, and was 16 when I started at sea, in 1954. I went to work as a deck boy with the Robertson Company of Glasgow. Captain Black didn't take me to sea, but recommended me to a Captain Davy Millar from Larne.

"I started with Captain Millar on the *AXIMITE*. I joined the boat at Clydebank. We moved coal and stones. I worked on her for seven months, until she was sold, and then I went to work for Kellys, and joined the *CARRODORE*. Charlie 'The Kapitan' McAlister was the ship's Mate. The vessel was one of the old Guinness boats, and ran coal for Davidsons. We mostly sailed to Belfast, and I was on that boat for six weeks. I was now an AB."

Whenever on leave during the summer months he was goalkeeper for Glenariffe's hurling team, and a key player in the '15' that won the 1955 Antrim Junior Championship. "When I was at the old Primary School, I played in the hurling team's midfield with Patsy Black. James Murray was also in that side. James (Murray) was one year at St MacNissi's College, Garron Tower - the year it opened in September 1951 - before going to work at sea.

"James Murray first went coasting, and then deep-sea with Blue Star, before going to America where his brother John lived. John got him United States citizenship, and James continued to work on boats from there. I know he eventually went below - to the engine room - working as a fireman. His brother John was born in America, where the father Archie worked and was an American citizen. Archie married his wife in New York, but then came back to Glenariffe because of the shortage of work during 'The Depression'. Later, John returned to the States."

Of his own sea journeys, O'Mullan added: "I was coasting for eight years. In 1962, I left Kelly boats and went deep-sea with Blue Star, trading down to South America. I moved to join the Head Line boats out of Belfast, and then sat the Second Mate's ticket examination in Belfast. In the middle of the 1960's, when I was studying for the Mate's Ticket, I shared a flat in Belfast with Arthur Hamilton of Cushendun.

"From Head Line I moved to the Hain Shipping Company, out of St Ive's. It was tramping, all over the place, wherever there was cargo business. Often it was from Cardiff to South America. I was on the tramp ships, all with Cornish names such as the *TREMAINE* and the *TREMEADOW*, whenever I sat and took my Master's Ticket, in 1971.

"P&O owned the boat, amalgamating Hain with Norse, owned by Dublin man James Norse. He was a trader in India, and founded a shipping company in the Bay of Bengal. I never did ship's captain. Instead, I left seagoing to work ashore, in harbours, at Garston, Liverpool, and also at Birkenhead. Eventually, I became Harbour Master." With wife Sheila (nee McIvor, Belfast and a sister of Mrs Ann Gore of Cushendall), he settled to live at Wallasey.

Hugh took his cousin, Danny Rowan, a brother of Alistair and Nellie, to sea, and said: "Danny came with me on a Kelly boat named *BALLYMENA*. He progressed from deck hand to engineer, and was a good spell at sea, on and off. It is not easy to go from deck to engineer, and he spent some time at college in Leith, to achieve that."

His uncle, Paddy Rowan, was a sailor, but tragically lost his life at sea, near Cape Town, and is buried in South Africa. Hugh added: "Paddy was an AB, and a great friend of James Emerson. He was also an uncle of Alistair Rowan. In 1955, Pat Connolly of Cushendall got my job on the *CARRODORE*. His brother Con, I believe, brought my neighbour Danny McNaughton of Waterfoot to sea, on the *TOPAZ*."

Alistair Rowan remarked: "My brother Danny worked deep-sea on Esso tankers, and also did coasting on Kelly coal boats. My grandfather was Dan Rowan, who ran a coal delivery service from Red Bay Pier. My aunt, Peggy Rowan was married to Dan McVeigh, and had the wee sweetie and ice cream ship beside the hurling field."

Alistair's sister Nellie (Mrs McKay), added: "My brother Arthur was at Garron Tower when it opened, and then joined the Air Force, while his friend James Murray went to sea. My brother Danny was with Captain Johnny McCormick, on Kelly coal boats. Danny was 15 years of age, when he started out on the *BALLYMENA*, and then moved to the *BALLYEDWARD*, which came into Magheramorne.

"I remember he had to walk home from there until he might manage to hitch a lift. I recall Danny arriving home with his seabag over his shoulder and it was full of green bananas. I didn't know there was such a thing. It was the first time I ever saw green bananas. They came straight off a boat. A considerate Kelly captain managed to encourage our Danny to go to school, to a Sea Training College at Leith, Edinburgh. He was there three years, and did his ticket in engineering. When he came out of College he went on Esso Tankers.

"He was once rescued from a boat that was shipwrecked, after a load of wood shifted on it during a storm, and it sunk. Our house received a telegram with the good news he was safe. All hands were rescued. Danny came home - and never went back to sea again. In March 1971, he went to work in the Michelin factory in Ballymena.

"My father was Alex Rowan. My granda Dan married twice. His second wife was Lizzie Cush, who owned a stevedore business in Belfast, and was able to get in small coal boats to Red Bay. That is how my granda started in the coal delivery trade from the Pier. My father drove the Arthur's delivery lorry for a time. Before all that, my granda was a builder, and built the Robinson Memorial in Ballymoney. So, my father went back to the building trade with Murray and Partners. He was a top stone mason, and built black stonework at Garron Tower."

Hugh O'Mullan recalled other seafolk from the area: "James McCarry, the father of James McCarry, the house painter, was a seaman. I think he was AB, and not only worked on coasters, with Kellys, but also sailed all over the world. I recall he worked a lot to South America, and also to the Mediterranean. He was from up the Glen, and for a time lodged with us in Waterfoot.

"When I was at Garston, boats coming in included skipper Jackie Kiely, one of our longest serving seaman. He went to sea when he was very young, and finished up Commodore Captain of Kelly boats. I sailed with Jackie (Kiely) when he was master of the *BALLYKELLY*, the *BALLYLESSON*, and the *BALLYCASTLE*. Other home folk I met at Garston included Captain John Graham of Cushendun. I came in touch with him a few times, when he was master of the *CRAIGMORE*. It was coal boat owned by Cawoods. I think John was also, for a time, a skipper with Shell tankers.

"Many members of the Leech family went to sea. My grandmother was Leech. Pa, John, and Alex Leech were cousins of my mother. Their father, John Leech, was also a sailor, and worked for a short time on Robertson boats. A twin brother, Alex worked on dredgers in Dublin. Both men were born in this house, on Waterfoot street. My granny and my aunt Peggy Rowan were born here, and so was I. Of the younger generation, Alistair Leech went to sea.

"Also on the street in Waterfoot lived a Larne man named John Kane, a fireman. He was once on a Kelly boat when the boiler blew up. I think one seaman was killed. John suffered burns to his face. Another sailor was Paddy Black, who once lived in the house at Waterfoot bridge, and was Kane's brother-in-law."

Another family, from the Bay area, the 'Dear' McAlister's, provided three sailors, but with one tragically killed on dry land. Paddy and John Eddie followed their father Charlie to sea work. The demise of John Eddie, struck down by a bolt of lightning near his family home at the 'Dog's Nose' landmark of Carrievemurphy, shocked the Glens. He sailed on coasters and deep-sea voyages. He retired, as did his older brother Paddy, to concentrate on helping on the home farm, when the shocking incident happened.

In March, 2013, on a visit to his sisters, Mary, aged 82, and Greta, aged 92, the heart-wrenching tale was laid bare. Retired schoolteacher Mary said: "John Eddie was struck down by a bolt of lightning that killed him on December 18, 1980. His older brother Danny, who did not go to sea, but worked the farm, was with him as they set off up the mountain behind the home house, to check on their flock of sheep."

Greta showed obvious pain when recalling the fateful occasion: "Mary was in Belfast at the time. There was a lot of lightning that morning. We seem to get a lot of lightning in this area, and I think it might have something to do with the old iron ore mines nearby that attract the lightning.

"Later that day, the weather conditions seemed to clear up, and John and Danny decided to go up the mountain. Unfortunately, there was one flash of lightning. Danny was blinded momentarily. When he turned round John was gone, lying there dead. John had a big steel buckle on a belt he once brought back from his sea travels. The belt buckle seemed to have attracted the lightning."

Mary added: "He was 48, killed outright. He was not all that far up the mountain when it happened. He had Wellington boots on, and they were completely burned. There was burning all around him on the ground. Danny had to come down and tell Greta he was dead. It was a nightmare."

In the townland of Druimadraide, the 'Dears' reside in a delightfully appointed bungalow, one that has a stunning and unhindered view across the Sea of Moyle. Mary said: "I remember the day John Eddie decided to go to sea. He started work under Captain John Mort of Cushendall, on the coasting tanker, the *PASS of GLENOGLE*. That was just after my mother died. John had to join the boat outside Limerick. Born in 1932, he was 22 years of age then, and on the boat were the Captain's brother James Mort, and Alistair McKay of Cushendall.

"I remember travelling with him to Belfast, to catch a train. Mrs Sharpe of Glenariffe was with us, going to visit her family in Ballybay, County Monaghan. She got off the train at Dundalk. John went on to what was then Amiens Street Station, then had to cross Dublin city to the south side to catch the train for Limerick. John planned it all well. He was on that boat for a good while, and then he changed to work deep-sea. He joined Head Line boats out of Belfast, for Canada. John also made runs to New Zealand and Australia, and I recall Patsy Black, son of Captain Eneas Black, sailing with him for a time.

"Our father, Charlie, who was born in 1882, and came from the family farm at Carnahaugh, Cushendall, went to sea for a long time. When he was very young, he went to Belfast to work in a bar at the bottom of Divis Street. That area is now all roadways - motorway links. I believe my father took part in some amateur boxing contests, when he worked as a young man in Belfast. It helped when you were working in a city bar.

"He also talked about being in Glasgow, and I believe he worked there for the McSparran's, who were ship's chandlers. He used to talk a lot about that with our GP, Dr Alex McSparran. My father was in Glasgow for a time before he went to sea. Years later, we remember him at sea on the *KERRYMORE*, a Kelly coasting boat. He married Rose O'Boyle of Glenariffe Glen - from where the Forest Park is. My father remained at sea, while mother looked after everything at home."

Greta added: "Father retired from the sea, just before the Second World War started. He had been an AB, and worked for well over 30 years on the boats." Mary said: "Patrick worked for a year for Pat McHugh, who was attached to the Ministry of Agriculture, and also farmed in Cushendun. A cousin of my mine, Mary Catherine O'Boyle, also worked down there for the McHugh family. She later married Henry O'Neill. Patrick eventually went to sea. He started with Kellys, and stayed there for quite a while. Then he worked overseas, sailing to New Zealand and Australia with the Blue Star Line. He was on that Canada run for a period, and used to talk about having to work in freezing conditions at Montreal."

Born on May 19, 1925, Paddy 'Dear's' sea chart includes work as an AB and sometimes Bo'sun on a variety of boats. His Discharge Book (R215292) reveals an AB Certificate achieved in Belfast on August 14, 1953.

Kelly-owned boat coasting included deck work in the mid-1950's on the *BALLYGILBERT, BALLYKIRK,* and then to the *ESSO LONDON.* He sailed out of Grangemouth in 1956 on the *PASS of DRUMOCHTER*, and in December of that year he switched to join Captain John Mort on the *PASS of GLENOGLE.*

This was his first job as a bo'sun, and stayed with Captain Mort until June 1960. He changed to deep-sea sailoring, out of Belfast to Canada on the *CARRIGAN HEAD,* and the *RATHLIN HEAD.* His overseas target swivelled to take in lengthy trips to the Southern Hemisphere, working on the *ENGLISH STAR, WELLINGTON STAR, EMPIRE STAR, SLIEVE BEARNAGH, COLORADO STAR.*

At times, he reverted to coasting on the *BALLYMONEY,* and the *BALLYREAGH.* He returned to trading in New Zealand and Australia, on boats such as *PACIFIC EAST, MARALLA, SPARTAN PRINCE, SANTIANA, SYDNEY BRIDGE,* and an interesting trip out of Singapore in October 1972 on the *HUMILARIA,* trading to the then Republic of Khomain, Iran, and back to Singapore.

Mary McAlister continued: "Daniel stayed on the farm, and died last year, in 2012. He was very young when my father moved in here, at the

'Dog's Nose'. Uncle Jamie and his wife lived at Galbolly, and during IRA troubles Danny, with Greta in his arms, and mammy moved there until the 'trouble' passed."

Mary also related an absorbing family and personal history. "Patrick was friendly with Dan and Teddy McCormick in Cushendun, and often visited them - related to us in some way through the McElhernon's of Layd. My mother's mother was McElhernon of Layd. My grandfather wrote to his people in America, telling them of our uncle Eddie coming round here to live on his own at Ardclinis, above the Monastery. We are not related to the other McAllister family of Carnahaugh. Aunt Mary's farm was there. Closest was the Reid house above where the Murphys lived - James Murphy.

"When I started teaching, I spent one week at Ballyvaddy's old school. It was a very lonely place, I felt, especially being there on your own. I went from there to Riley's Trench, outside Hillsborough, County Down, on the way to Kilwarlin - on the road to Moira. It was an area in the parish of Lisburn. Miss Mary Gormley was the school principal.

"It was a lovely old school, one that had mixed students, with a lot of Protestants living beside the school, and attending it. One big family was the Robinsons, who sold motors and tractors, They were very good and worshipped at the Elim Pentecostal Church. That was around 1952-1953. One member of the Robinson family became a pastor. One of the girls, Margaret, used to come down to Glenariffe to visit me.

"I also remember the children would be allowed two weeks off school in September, to help in the digging of potatoes on the nearby farms. Many youngsters went to help the potato dig on the farm of Billy McGarry. Then I moved to teach at St Annes' School, Dunmurry. It was here I met a new young ginger-haired infants-class pupil, Peter O'Hara, a grandson of Minnie O'Hara in Knocknacarry,"

Mick Graham of the nearby Glen Road was friendly with John Eddie, and said: "Like all members of the McAlister family he was a great reader, always interested in historical fact. When and wherever his ship docked, John Eddie would know where to visit, because he read up about the prominent places of interest in that city. He would visit museums, and so on. He was especially interested in the history of American cities.

"I used to hear stories from John Eddie, about his travels. He worked on oil tankers with another Glenariffe sailor, Dan McVeigh, who once obtained a bucket of herrings from a vessel berthed nearby in a Scottish port. John Eddie told me this yarn about the herring boat skipper giving Dan a bucketful of fresh herrings from his catch. Dan proceeded to gut and clean the herrings. He prepared them for a meal for himself and his crew colleagues.

"Dan set a second bucket, empty, and put the innards of the herrings into it. But, as he was about to take the herrings to the galley, for cooking, he picked up the wrong bucket, pitched and emptied the herrings over the side of the ship and into the water. He was left with a bucketful of fish innards!"

Filtering through the combined memory cells of Mick Graham and enthusiastic former Glenariffe seamen Johnny O'Boyle and Hugh McIlwaine are the names of other past mariners such as 'Paddy Murray, who had a Mate's Ticket. His brother Archie also went to sea. This Murray family was known as 'The Bells', with another family member, Alex, the one-time blacksmith in Waterfoot.

Hugh McIlwaine said: "There was Alex O'Boyle, who suffered burns during an explosion at sea. I'm told it was on a ship loaded with coal when somebody lit a match to check in the hold - and she went up. Paddy Murray, who had just passed his Mate's Ticket examination, was on the same ship, suffered some burns, and never went back to sea after that incident. The Murrays, cousins of my mother, went to sea in the 1950's. Alex and Joe O'Boyle, from near Parkmore, were not only sea-going men but also farmers."

Johnny O'Boyle's list included Mickey Leech, from near the Sawmill. Neil John Delargy, an AB. Johnny McCarry, married to an aunt of Hugh 'The Mariner's' wife Margaret, a McKillop from Glenburn, Cushendall, was also an AB. McIlwaine added: "Malcolm McCollam Snr, was at sea for years - an engineer on coasters. Malcolm Jnr. was an AB, and finished his career working on the Liverpool boat out of Belfast. His brother Tommy was an AB. Johnny McAlister was a brother-in-law of Malcolm Snr, and was also a ship's engineer.

"Another great seaman was Eddie Hyndman, who lived in Ballymena. He came down to visit the Leech family at the Bay. He was a second mate when I sailed with him on the *MAYFAIR SAPPHIRE*. He was a great astronomer. I think there were other Hyndman sailors from Carnlough, also the McVeys. I believe a McVey was drowned at sea."

Jack McBride, who once lived in a cottage situated on the rocky edge of the sea at Garron Point, was a prominent and respected storyteller, Glens of Antrim historian, author, ballad writer, newspaper and radio contributor. He was also a seaman for a period in his early life.

He discloses this in an article published in the *Irish News* issue of June 26, 1944. He had an abiding interest in the seafarers of the Glens, including the feats of local old-time sailing ship skippers Charles McDonnell and Denis Black, and also produced his own interpretation of the puzzle of the 'Fuldiew Stone'. In the 1944 story he includes - 'Years ago, during my seafaring, we were berthed in Sligo, and I went ashore with a shipmate, Malcolm McNeill, a native of Barra in the Outer Hebrides.'

Other Glenariffe sea travellers included Willie Robbin and his half-brother Joe Delargy. John Robbin, a son of Willie and born in 1966, said: "My father was AB on Kelly boats. He went to sea in the 1950's and with him for a time was his half-brother Joe Delargy. I remember my father telling the story about the boat he was on left Glasgow, but ran into a very severe fog near the Isle of Man. The crew couldn't see a thing. The cargo was bound for Douglas, but there was no visibility whatsoever to guide the boat in, yet the skipper used a compass to bring the boat right to the dock at Douglas. He regarded that a brilliant piece of seamanship.

"He also spun the ghost story about a crew member asking the skipper when did the black sailor join the boat. The skipper insisted there was no black seaman in the crew. The crewman insisted when he came off his shift a black man left his bunk to let him have some sleep. The skipper said; 'That sailor died six months go'.

"My father played hurling for Glenariffe. Born in 1919, his first match was in the minor grade in 1938. My uncle, Hugh Delargy also played for the club. My father's first cousin, Alex Robbin was killed when his ship was sunk in Dublin Bay during the First World War. His name is listed on the Bay Memorial."

Sean Mort of Cushendall/Cushendun mentioned: "Old Paddy Reid from up Glenariffe was a bo'sun on Roberston boats. He was married to Mary Moore. Malachy Black married Paddy Reid's wife's sister Mary. I sailed with Malachy and his brother P.J."

A stone's throw from Waterfoot bridge, seamen surfaced such as the legendary 'Red Fella' - Denis O'Boyle, and his brothers Neil, and Jimmy 'Doodles' - who went to work on tankers for a short while. Their cousin, Neil 'Big Nil' O'Boyle was at sea for a spell, before settling to live in Liverpool, where he opened a business. Also from the area emerged Boynaugh's Dan 'of the hill' McAlister, and the Reddington brothers, John and Danny.

Captain Hugh McIlwaine recalled sailing with Danny - "On Esso tankers when he was as an assistant steward and then he went down below to work as a greaser. I sailed with Danny on a couple of ships." Reddington appreciated those days at sea: "Four people shaped my sea career, and gave me a licence to travel the world. I was lucky enough to take part in a way of life that is now gone forever, and never to return.

"Captain Johnny McCormick of Waterfoot started me as a galley boy on Kelly boats. That was on the 14th of August, 1965, and I stayed there until July 15, 1966, when I joined the Head Line Company, Belfast. I was with Head Line for five months, after making three trips to Canada's Great Lakes.

"On February 2, 1967, Captain Paddy Blaney of Cushendall offered me a job as a galley boy on the Esso deep-water tanker *ESSO PORTSMOUTH*, and I was given the assistant steward's job on September 6, 1967 - when I was nearly 18 years of age. I remember receiving a telegram in Waterfoot to join the ship at Portsmouth.

"My first trip was to the Persian Gulf, and on to Japan. Esso, at that time, brought in a work system whereby you were called a steward operator, and you also had to work on the deck, the engine room, and do your own job, too. I liked this for the variety.

"On October 13, 1970, Hugh McIlwaine secured me a job on the coast with Esso. Two years later (14-11-1972) I was promoted to donkey man on the Esso coaster *WOOLSTON*. Previously, I had been an assistant steward with Esso. I was always very interested in working in the engine room, and was lucky that a chief engineer named James Hamilton from Islandmagee got me the greaser's job on the Esso *WOOLSTON*.

"Esso moved me all over the place, working deep-sea and coastal. I was made donkey greaser. It was changed, and I went from Motor Man to Motor Man 1A. During this period, Esso suggested I go to the engineering school in Leith, Scotland. I managed to avoid that, as I was enjoying my job. I liked being moved around wherever they sent me.

"I was made redundant on May 11, 1983, came home on a Tuesday, signed on at the Pool on the Thursday, and on the Sunday morning I started out on a journey to Mexico on a bulk carrier for the Furness Withy Shipping. During that time, I secured a Watch Keeping Certificate, Lifeboat Certificate, and I also did a Fire Fighting Course."

Daniel Francis Reddington added: "I worked for various shipping companies. Along with Furness Withy Shipping, I was with Royal Fleet Auxiliary, Cawoods Shipping, Belfast Steamship Company, Ajax Marine Limited, Sealink, P.O.E.T.S Fleet Management Limited, and P&O European Ferries. For these firms I was a Motor Man 1A, and also Relieving Storekeeper with P&O European Ferries, a company I joined on June 6, 1990. I worked there until June 2, 1993, when I was once again out of work. However, I managed to obtain further sea work until 1997, but eventually became fed up searching for employment at sea, so I reluctantly came ashore for good."

His older brother John quit the sea before Danny began on boats. "John spent ten years as a greaser. He started with Captain Kelly, on the *PASS of DRUMOCHTER*," added Danny, "It was through my father Jim, who had been a coal miner in Scotland until blinded in an accident down a mine, who mentioned to the late Dr Alex McSparran that John was looking for a job at sea. The family's doctor seemed to know Captain Kelly, and John joined the boat on a Christmas Day. He moved from coasting to deep-sea sailing - on passenger liners - and then to work for Blue Star, trading to New Zealand and Australia."

The game of hurling inevitably becomes intertwined in the Glens seafaring landscape, with the link suitably tailor-made to suit the yarns of yesteryear, and doubling as hurler and seaman was Hal Harvey, who played in the Glenariffe Antrim Junior Championship-winning team. A half-uncle of the ever-helpful Artie Harvey, he was an AB on coasters.

Artie (Harvey) revealed: "There is a preserved postcard from Hal Harvey, and probably written when he first went to sea as a very young man. The date on the card is June 3, 1947, and it states he is leaving from Ayr and bound for Glasgow. Hal, who played quite a lot of hurling for the home club, lived on the street at Waterfoot, until he moved to Scotland. He met a girl there, and settled in Ayr, where he worked in a factory."

Another of the Harvey kinfolk who made a distinctive impression was old salt James 'Jamie Barney' Delargy. Artie said: "He was an uncle of my mother, and went to sea during the 1910's. He was one of the founder members of the Glenariffe hurling club, and also played on the first North Antrim hurling team. Also involved in the progress of early Ossian teams were my grandfather, Arthur Harvey and Ned Kane.

"During his sea days, Jamie Barney regularly sent home postcards from almost every port he visited. Before he took to the sea he suffered bad injuries to his legs. On a trip into Ballymena, with his horse and cart, and carrying a load of goods, a leather snapped on the horse. He got down to try and fix it. The horse suddenly moved, and the cart went over him, breaking both his legs. He later went to sea, but eventually had to quit - because the legs gave up on him. For the last 30 years of his life he had to move about on crutches."

From Foriff, Jamie Barney's sea journeys can be traced through the many postcards, starting on March 3, 1914, from Granville Manche, in Normandy. He states in pencil writing - 'Leaving there for Cardiff to load for St Breen.' Sailing on the *BRILLIANT,* he leaves on June 4, 1914, for London. There is a card posted in Galway City on June 17, 1914, and one from St Sampson, the second largest port in Guernsey, on July 27, 1914. 'Loading there for London', he writes.

On September 8, 1914, there is word from Llanelly (and this is the official spelling on the postcard - not Llanelli). 'Leaving there for Cardiff, and loading for Garston'. Eleven days later a postcard arrives in his Glenariffe home from Fleetwood, 'leaving there for London'. During the First World War, he still managed to keep the postman busy, with a card from Poplar, London, on April 8, 1915, 'Leaving there for north of France.'

Eight days later, he posts from Dieppe, but no news of where he was going. He continued involvement in dangerous passage across the U-boat patrolled English Channel. The next scribbling of Jamie Barney was on May 26, 1915, from Newcastle-on-Tyne, and leaving there 'next week for Calais'.

On November 22, 1915, he is on board the *MALVEREN* at Ayr, and suggests he may be paid off. He leaves Glasgow on May 30, 1916, on the *TOMAIRE* - 'I found a ship that morning, and bound for Dublin.' On September 30, 1916, he is working on the *ROSSBANK* out of Le Treport, Picardy - 'and leaving next week for some port in England.'

On October 14, 1916, he is again about to depart Le Treport, on the *ROSSBANK.* He writes, still using a pencil, 'No word of future destination.' There are also a couple of postcards with no date. One is from Dublin, leaving on the *TREMAINE* 'for Westenpoint, to load for the north of Scotland', and the other from Cromarty, Scotland, 'wishing family a Happy Xmas, and a prosperous New Year'.

Johnny O'Boyle listed other seafarers from the vicinity of Waterfoot village, including Johnny McAlister, a brother-in-law of Malcolm McCollam Snr. He was a ship's engineer. Also going to sea in the mid-20th century from the Kilmore townland was Jimmy Gribben, who married a Cornish girl, and lived in Cornwall. The brothers, Johnny and Pat 'Tom' McCormick both went to sea, and from Waterfoot the brothers Neil John and Alistair Delargy. Alistair joined the Royal Navy, and after he stopped going to sea he had a job on the locks of the Manchester Ship Canal.

21 BURMA RUN

PATRICK McKay was the second member of the extended family from Corrymeelagh, Cushendun, to lose his life at sea. Twenty-one years after his uncle Henry drowned in America, the Glasgow-born sailor was yet another victim of the Second World War conflict.

Born in 1927, and with strong connection to Cushendun, not only at Corrymeelagh but also Agolagh House, he was a part of the carnage statistic that followed the cruel sinking of the *KANBE,* after the Glasgow passenger/cargo ship left Rangoon. The vessel was a sitting target for a German U-boat, and all but five crew members, Lascar sailors, perished in the atrocity of May 8, 1943.

His brother Denis, born in 1928, and living in retirement at Agolagh, said: "My father was Patrick McKay of Corrymeelagh. He married Kate McKinley of Ballylaughan. We had a family of eight. My brother Patrick was the one who went to sea, starting at 18 years of age. He began as a Cadet in the Merchant Navy, with the Henderson Line, who ran passenger/cargo ships out of Glasgow.

"He was on a few of their ships before transferring to the *KANBE*, on the Burma run. He was an Officer Cadet when the ship was torpedoed coming out of Rangoon, set on a return journey to Glasgow. The ship was attacked by a German U-Boat. Five Lascar sailors were rescued. Everyone else on the ship did not survive the U-Boat attack.

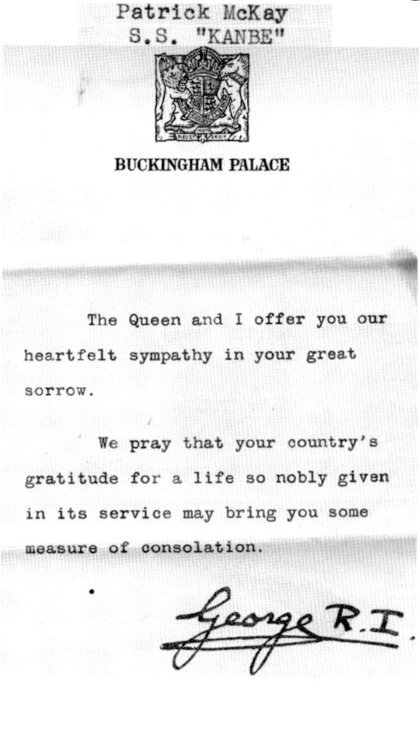

Patrick McKay
S.S. "KANBE"

BUCKINGHAM PALACE

The Queen and I offer you our heartfelt sympathy in your great sorrow.

We pray that your country's gratitude for a life so nobly given in its service may bring you some measure of consolation.

George R.I.

"Following Patrick's death, our family received a letter of condolence from Buckingham Palace. The last local born person to see and have a chat with Patrick was John Joseph Murray, a seaman from Dunurgan, who was then the Harbour Master at Rangoon. John Joseph Murray was the father of Fr John Murray."

The 6,244 gross ton *KANBE*, an armed passenger/cargo ship built at Dumbarton in 1941, was on the way home with general cargo including 3,500 tons of copper when it was attacked 60 miles south of Monrovia, on the west cost of Africa.

Two torpedoes from the merciless German submarine U-123 had the *KANBE* under in two minutes. Lost was the ship's captain, John Frederick Thomas Burke, along with 65 crew members including three gunners. The five survivors were picked up by a Spanish ship. Patrick's name is listed in a Memorial in London.

Denis McKay added: "The tragic death of my brother Patrick followed the loss of uncle Henry McKay, born at Corrymeelagh. He left home to work deep-sea. Born in 1885, he was lost at sea in America, on June 19, 1922. Another member of the McKay family circle also to lose his life at sea, from an accident on his own yacht, was James Francis 'Jeff' McLister, a son of my sister Christine and James McLister of Torr. He was not a seaman, but sailing was Jeff's hobby. It is believed he was struck on the head by the jib of his boat, and was knocked overboard."

Kate McKay, a niece of Denis, outlined a further family extension with seafaring. Two other sons of her aunt Christine secured successful careers in the Royal Navy - Randal and Patrick. Randal is retired. Patrick also, but then he became an independent seaman. He has his Captain's Ticket, and goes on contract work, taking privately-owned boats for millionaires, from the Mediterranean to the Caribbean.

"Randal was in the Fleet Air Arm from 1973 to 1984. He trained as an Air Artificer, and left as a Petty Officer. In 1982, his duties took him into the Falklands War. During his career he was on board the gigantic aircraft carriers *ARK ROYAL, HERMES* and *BULWARK*, and he travelled all over the world. He was involved in various operations, including work in the Mediterranean, South America, North America, South Africa, and Norway. Randal lives in retirement at St Andrews, Scotland."

22

FRIENDLY FOLK

DUNURGAN and the immediate townlands that snake from Straid to Glendun's precise valley produced many distinguished seamen, including those of the Murray families. The father and son of the same name, James Murray, respectively risked their lives during the First and Second World Wars.

Reared in this idyllic corner of Cushendun Parish, the elder James Murray, a grandfather of retired sea captain Murray Brogan, was a Chief Petty Officer in the Royal Navy who specialised in torpedoes. During the First World War, he fought at the Battle of Jutland. This crucial sea conflict took place on May 31 and June 1, 1916, in the North Sea near Jutland, Denmark. The fleet against the German gunships included those of the Royal Navy, the Royal Canadian Navy, and the Royal Australian Navy.

His son, James Murray, was also in the Royal Navy and was involved in the Second World War. He was also a Chief Petty Officer. He was born in Ballycastle, County Antrim, and was a gunnery specialist. He was heavily involved in the Russian supply convoys to Momansk. James Jnr, lived for a time in Cushendall - close to the golf course, and then moved to Belfast, and on to New Zealand.

Both father and son came out of the wars uninjured. Both demobbed. Incidentally, Murray Brogan was a deep-sea master in the Merchant Navy. He attended Knocknacarry Primary School before going to the Sea Training School at Sharpness, around the same time as Arthur Hamilton. He said: "My maternal great grandfather was a coastal captain. He was a Scotsman, from Fife, named Adam Dinsmore, who once lived at Gortacreggan, Cushendun."

Adam Dinsmore, whose death is listed aged 69 in 1901, appears to have started his sea career in his early teens. It seems he was on ships that transported goods and soldiers to the three-year Crimean War, a conflict that took place from 1853 to 1856. The land battles heralded the legendary nurse Florence Nightingale, and involved Russia's empire against the joint forces of the UK, France, and the Ottoman Empire (Turkey). The fighting took place mainly on land around the Crimean Peninsula, and with sea skirmishes in the Black Sea.

Adam and Catherine Dinsmore had seven of a family, when he farmed at Gortacreegan. One daughter, Mary, married Alex Magee, parents of Annie and Jim Magee. Another daughter, Catherine married George Connor of Straid. They lived in Glasgow. Jane, the second youngest, married a McKay, and also livid in Glasgow.

Barbara McLaughlin (nee Gildea) added: "My grandmother, Maggie Anne was the youngest of the Dinsmores, and married James Murray of The Hollies. She died in 1917, during childbirth, and when he was at sea - and unable to come home because of the War." Barbara's mother was Mamie Murray, who married Peter Gildea. The other Murray girl, Rita, married Dan Brogan.

The Dinsmore family also held a short-lived sea connection through Adam's son Johnny. Born in 1863, he ran away to sea as a very young teenager, with his school chum Alexander John McGavock of nearby Dunurgan. They caused consternation when they skipped town, avoiding a search party and eventually obtaining jobs as cabin boys on coasting vessels out of Larne Harbour.

McGavock, born July 1858, worked at sea for two years, and plotted a career on the waves until he was sent to America to work on an aunt's farm. Following his moonlight flit with Johnny Dinsmore, he came home to gain instruction 'in all areas of navigation' by Knocknacarry Boys' School headmaster Joseph Duffy. However, he was enticed by his mother to give up the sea and emigrate to the USA in 1876. Dinsmore also came back home, and appeared to lose interest in sea work. He is registered in the 1881 parish census.

Close to the McGavock farm was another Murray family. From here, Patrick Murray left home at 19 years of age to make a career of seafaring. His adventures have been meticulously logged by his granddaughter, Mrs Deirdre Roberts (nee Murray), in a book named - 'Bound for Valparaiso'. Patrick Joseph Murray was born in March 1872, and died in Partick, Glasgow, aged 84, in 1956. He started as a cabin boy on coasters, and progressed to work as an Ordinary Seaman on tall ships.

He was three times round Cape Horn. It seems his first long distance adventure was to Rio de Janiero on a four-masted full-rigged ship, the *NORMA,* skippered by Captain Dan McDonnell, a relative of the McSparran ship supplier family of Glasgow. The cargo out of Cardiff was coal. At one time his shipmates included the poet 'Dusty Rhodes', the infamous James Stoddard Moore, who died at Coleraine.

Born in what was once an old corn mill at the bottom of Clough Road, Cushendall, Moore claimed his date of birth as Christmas Day, 1844. He also remarked his father was a shoemaker originally from Edinburgh, who married Cushendun girl, Catherine Graham. Dusty stated his parents died of fever at the close of the 'Great Famine', when he was 14.

He went to roam the world, and sailed around Cape Horn. He also worked for two years on a whaling ship expedition. It is said he was in the British Army. Moore returned to Cushendall, and married a Catherine McAlister of Cushendun, who died six years later. His second wife, named Mary Hamill of Carrickfergus, died in 1917.

More information on the Murray family's sea connection was supplied by David McCurdy, a descendent of the Turnamona family: "My research finds Neil Murray, one of seven children, and a younger brother by two years (born 1876) of Patrick, married Rose (Rosetta) McCurdy, my grandfather's sister, on January 4, 1897. They lived in Scotland, where their eldest son John James was born, on April 27, 1899, at Langmuir Rows, Kirkintilloch, Dumbarton.

"Sadly, John James Murray, who became a merchant seaman, was drowned when his ship was sunk during the First World War, in 1916. His death is commemorated on the Tower Hill Memorial, London, and on the family headstone at Carnlough, County Antrim, where his parents came to live out their retirement. Neil Murray died in Carnlough, aged 76, on March 24, 1950. Rosetta, the fourth child of Daniel McCurdy and Rose McCurdy (nee Scally) of Turnamona Bridge, died in Carnlough, aged 91, on November 25, 1962."

Around the corner from Dunurgan lies the townland of Drumnacur, on the main Cushendun-Cushendall highway. Here lived the Martin family, formerly of Calishnaugh. Their house and farmland was adjacent to those of the McGavock-owned 'Jinny's Farm', and also beside George McElheron, whose son Ian said: "Charlie Martin, a bachelor, was at sea for a while, and then worked in America - before coming home to Drumnacur. One of his brothers was Alex, and according to my father, Alex was once in the RIC. When circumstances changed in Ireland - and the police force here became the RUC - he retired, took redundancy, or the likes, and bought the farm at Drumnacur.

"He purchased the property off Johnny McAteer. Before that, the land was owned by the O'Connors. My grandfather's name was O'Connor. Alex Martin was a fairly young man then, and started farming. Not long after that - according to what my father told me - Alex suffered a serious illness.

"Another Martin brother, Hugh, worked as a pilot of harbour craft in New York. Tragically, Hugh's young wife died in childbirth. Apparently, not long afterwards, Hugh also died. Their two children, Mary, who later became Mrs Harry McKay at Carnlough, and Jamie, were brought as toddlers back from America to live at Drumnacur. Their spinster Aunt Lizzie was in charge there. Charlie died in 1962."

Minnie (Mary Ann) McGavock of Dunurgan (later to marry Alex O'Hara of Knocknacarry) once related a tale of idle curiosity that led to a phonetically funny incident involving her and Lizzie Martin. "I was the nosey young neighbour. There was a misunderstanding of the lingo, after I noticed her brother Charlie was again home on a break from sea duties. I asked Lizzie where Charlie had been sailing. She replied: 'Our Charlie was on a ship that brought slippers from Borduck to England.' The cargo was railway sleepers from the French port of Bordeaux."

A next-door neighbour of the McElheron's was another ex-sailor, John Douglas. "Sea work was his trade," Ian McElheron said, "He lived in his retirement at Straid, where Willie Gallagher now resides. He went in there after the McKiernan family left. His brothers, Jamie (known as Justice), Charlie, and Alex lived on a farm up Layd - later purchased by Pat McHugh.

"John the sailor, known as 'By Gum Though', was always perfectly dressed. In those times the men who worked at sea had the money. People at home on the small farms had very little money. I remember, after the Second World War, herding cattle to a Cushendall Fair Day and my father was unable to sell them. There was no money around. I had to herd the cattle home again to Straid. It happened regularly to other farmers.

"Over at Dunurgan was old Alex McGavock, who worked at sea as a very young man. This was known in the valley from the time they were trying to repair the bridge down the Straid path to the Chapel. Before it became a cement bridge, across the River Dun and beside Craigagh graveyard, it was made of wooden planks, and poles. Men were trying to place new poles across the river, and needed to get a rope across.

"Every time one of them threw the rope to the man on the other side the end of the rope failed to reach, and finished up in the water. Along came 'Beat Hell' McGavock, to see what was going on. He gathered the rope into a bundle, and with one throw easily made it land on the opposite bank of the river.

"It was suggested to him he either had been a seaman or worked in the Wild West, because he showed how good he was with ropes. He revealed he had been at sea for a time in his youth, before he went to work in America, mostly in Chicago."

From Dunurgan's other direction, leading up through the splendid Viaduct, lived sailor Charlie McKillop, who died in 1962. Up the Glen resided the Keenan family. Two members, Dan and George, went to sea. George, registered as Ordinary Seaman No 450810, was born on June 29, 1892. He lost his life, drowned at Antwerp. Respected historian, the late Malachy McSparran once stated George's brother Pat, who became an independent cattle breeder in Knocknacarry, also spent some of his young years at sea. Another short-term seaman from up Glendun was farmer Frank McAlister.

23

GRAHAM GRIEF

JAMES GRAHAM, one of three seafaring brothers from Glenariffe, suffered a fatal pier-side accident that obviously left his young family devastated. The heartbreak happened on October 30, 1964, and was another notch on the awful statistic of Glensmen who died from ship and dockside accidents.

Born in 1906, Graham was an AB on the Larne-Stranraer ferry, the *CALEDONIAN PRINCESS*, when he died in Stranraer Harbour. Son Michael said: "My father was killed while working on the ferry, when it was berthed in Stranraer Harbour. He was over the side of the boat, painting, sitting on staging, when it was lowered down over the side of the ship by a couple of ropes.

"One end of a rope gave way. He crashed, and hit his head on the ridge around the middle of the boat. That blow to the head, it was believed, probably killed him before he went into the water. His brother John, also an AB, was also working on the *CALEDONIAN PRINCESS*, the first of the real big ferryboats, a flying machine."

The *CALEDONIAN PRINCESS*, built in 1961 at Dumbarton, was the first roll-on/roll-off stern-loading car ferry on the Larne-Stranraer route. James Graham, after recovering from a leg injury, followed his brother John to work on the new slick ship. The two also sailed together before that, on the Liverpool-Belfast ferryboat, the *ULSTER PRINCE* (2).

Michael Graham added: "My father worked as AB on the *ULSTER PRINCE* for many years, until he suffered a leg injury on the boat. He fell in the luggage hold, and badly damaged tendons, and was out of work for around a year. By the time he was fully recovered, and ready to go back to work, his brother John already moved to join the new *CALEDONIAN PRINCESS.*

"My father managed to get a job on her, and was involved when the boat was doing trials and breaking the speed record for the journey. This happened before it went into service. My father worked on the *CALEDONIAN PRINCESS* until he was killed."

James Graham's introduction to seafaring began when he joined the trans-Atlantic liner, the *ALAUNIA*, the last of six 14,000-ton 'A Class' ships to be built for Cunard in the 1920's. She was launched by the John Brown builders of Glasgow in 1925, and had accommodation for 500 cabin passengers. She made regular passage from Liverpool to Canada, calling at Quebec and Montreal. In 1939, the *ALAUNIA* was requisitioned for service in the Second World War, to work as an armoured Merchant ship. She was scrapped in 1957.

Graham made ten trips to North America on the *ALAUNIA*, the first engagement at Liverpool on April 23, 1926, and ending the link on the 7th of March, 1927. Sometimes, the ship would leave from London. In 1926 and 1927, she switched from passage to Canada to make trips to New York, and it was here he decided to shed the sea, in March 1927, and work in the 'Big Apple'.

Michael added: "After those sea trips to Canada, he joined his sister Annie, who was living in New York. He worked there, and sailed home before the start of the Second World War. He was discharged in Liverpool. He was an American citizen by then. Born at Drum-na-cur, Glenariffe, he was the eldest of the three boys.

"Charlie later lived at Calishnaugh, Cushendun, while John married Maureen Murtagh of Granard, County Longford, and moved from the Glen Road, Glenariffe, to reside at Glengormley. John had a family of four daughters. One of the girls, Marion, married Lawrence Darragh, and lives at the upper end of Glenariffe Glen."

Marion Darragh said: "My father would not retire from sea work, and died on a boat while sitting with his colleagues. He was enjoying a cup of tea when he slumped over, and died of a heart attack. He was 71. I remember when he used to work on a coasting boat that came into Bangor, County Down. Then, for years, he worked on the cross-channel ferryboat, the *ULSTER PRINCE*, on the Belfast to Liverpool run. At that time our family lived in Glengormley.

. "He moved to join the then new roll-on, roll-off ferryboat from Larne to Stranraer. I recall my mother going with him down to Larne Harbour, to join the boat. Working at sea was all he ever wanted to do, and never to quit. The manner of his death at sea was probably the way he would have wanted."

Michael Graham added: "I used to visit my uncle John's family at Glengormley. All three Graham brothers were, I believe, on deep-sea work at one time or another, but uncle Charlie was always working deep-sea. There was a sea-going tradition in the family as my grandfather, Bob Graham, who came from the Braid, and bought a farm at Knockans, Ballyeamon, worked at sea. He married Mary Ann Henry.

"Three of their sons, James, Charlie, and John went to sea, while the other sons Bob, Willie, and Mick did not. The eldest member of the family was Annie, who emigrated to Greenpoint, New York. My father went to America for a time, and lodged with the parents of Henry and Jamie O'Rawe at Greenpoint. The other daughter was Kathleen, who married an 'Arthur' (McAlister's of Shore Street, Cushendall).

"The old Bob Graham married in 1900, and was on sailing ships when he was a very young man. He went back to work at sea as an elderly man, well into his 50's. My uncle Willie told me of the day my uncle Charlie relayed the true story about rejoining his boat in Liverpool docks, and discussing with the captain the need to sign another crew member - only to be told 'Don't worry Charlie, a new man is due any moment, coming in from Belfast'. Just then, he looked down towards the gangplank and there was his father walking up on board, with a gunny-sack slung over his shoulder.

"Incidentally, in the First World War two Graham granduncles from Richhill, County Armagh, were killed in action. I also had two granduncles from Beaghs, Glendun, Mick and Dan McKillop, who survived. The Graham men were my grandfather's brothers." His grandfather copied the natural trend of the early part of the 20th century. He mixed farming with some seafaring.

Michael Graham remarked "He went to work on boats when things were slack on the farm. This was not an uncommon thing during most of the first half of the last century. Uncle Charlie and my father were in America during the 1930's. Both worked on the trams in New York, where my aunt Annie lived most of her life.

"At the start of the Second World War, both my father and Charlie came home from America. Indeed, his return to work at sea was a one-way trip until after the Second World War. The ship that took my father home for New York was the *CRISPIN*, departing New York on November 11, 1939, and arriving in Liverpool on December 8, 1939.

"My father then worked for James 'The Barrister' McSparran, living on the farm at Clady, Cushendun. It was here he met and married Brigid McKillop, who lived at the top of Glendun and was a younger sister of Mary 'Josie' McKillop, later to be manageress of the King's Arms Hotel in Larne. I was born at Clady - so too was my sister Regina, while my brother Brendan was born in Glenariffe."

Then it was back to sea for James Graham, on a John Kelly coaster, the *CROSSGAR*, built in Glasgow in 1936, and renamed the *BALLYGRAINEY* in 1952, and also working Home Trade trips for three months. He checked out of Belfast on October 27, 1947, and signed off this vessel at Belfast on the 23rd of January, 1948. Right away, he switched to another Kelly coaster, the *DONAGHADEE* (re-enlisted the *BALLYGARVEY* in 1952), working from February 4, 1948, until November 4 of the same year.

Thirteen days later he moved from coal-carrying coasters to ferryboat work on the Harland and Wolff built *ULSTER PRINCE* (2), sailing from Liverpool to Belfast on November 17, 1948, until his discharge because of leg damage on February 12, 1952.

He became a crew member of the new *CALEDONIAN PRINCESS* until the harrowing news came through to his wife and family at 5, Lurig View, Glenariffe, of his tragic demise in 1964. During his split sea career he qualified for certificates in EDH and Lifeboatmanship. His wife, Brigid died on September 20, 1983.

His brother Charlie maintained the Graham sea-going trend, and later Charlie's son John, who began his education at Knocknacarry Primary School and progressed to become a sea captain. Married to Caroline McCormick at Calishnaugh, Cushendun, Charlie died, aged 69, on December 31, 1976

Eldest daughter Rita (Mrs Brian Eley) said: "My father was in America for most of my first ten years. He went there in 1931, shortly after I was born, and worked as a tram driver in New York. He was at sea before he married. I was born in September, and he left for America around the following February. He was in America during The Depression years, until 1939. His sister Annie was in Brooklyn before him. She married in America, becoming a Mrs McCarthy. His brother James was there too.

"When he decided to leave America, he worked his passage home on a Greek-owned ship, at the beginning of the Second World War, and here he worked at growing lint and spuds, taking land everywhere. When the War ended, he went back to sea, working mostly on small boats, not going foreign again. He sailed on coasters, coal boats, but never on the ferryboats, like my uncles James and John. Later on, my brother John went to sea."

Rita's sister, Anne (Mrs Alex Sharpe) added: "I believe my brother John went to work at sea when he was 17, and first made foreign trips. He probably went abroad as a deck hand, but then studied to progress through all the Ticket examinations. I remember when John became a captain, passing the Master's Ticket in Belfast.

"He stopped working deep-sea, and was a ship's captain for Shell Mex and BP oil tankers around these waters. On one trip, John was joined on the 1,500-ton oil tanker by his father for a passage around the Scottish coast. My brother John Joseph Graham was born on the 19th October 1933, and died, aged 75, on March 23, 2009."

24

BITTEN by the BUG

ACCOMMODATION on board a small coaster can be cramped, but tolerable, unless you are attacked and bitten nightly by a battalion of bed bugs. This was the unglamorous scenario fledgling seaman Eugene McMullan of Glenarm had to endue.

It brought a new meaning to the old sea saying 'shiver me timbers' as McMullan recalled: "It was not a nice experience. I was on the *INVER*, a Charlie Brown-managed Shamrock Shipping Company (Larne) coaster. It was very unpleasant when you came under attack from bugs once you tried to sleep. There were two Arab crewmen, firemen, next door on that ship. We sprayed our bunks, the blankets, the pillows, everything, with DDT liquid disinfectant.

"The accommodation on the boat was separated by just a partition. There was all that constant loud music from their cabin, but worse was to happen with an invasion of bugs into our cabin every night. All the backs of our hands and arms were bitten. We sprayed the place with everything. We sprayed the beds, the sheets, but still the bugs came back.

"John Burns, a neighbour from Carnlough and a great pal of mine at sea, joined the boat with me at South Shields. We went to Dunkirk for a cargo of pig iron for Swansea. We did two trips, but the boat was not suitable for us, and we moved on."

Before that, 'big' Eugene had his baptism on the waves at 16 years of age, in 1949. There was a time when Glenarm harbour was vibrant, with busy boats constantly coming and going, part of the then very lively limestone trade. "When I was growing up I used to watch the puffers coming into Glenarm Harbour. There would be a queue of young lads watching the boats entering the harbour, but I never really thought about going to sea then.

"My older brother Willie went to work at sea before I did. He was AB, and was on all sorts of boats. He went deep-sea on oil tankers and cargo ships, and became a bo'sun. During the Falklands War Willie made two trips down there on a cargo ship, taking supplies. Still, I wasn't all that keen to also go to sea. However, it was through the harbour scene, in a way, that I went, and with a push from a couple of my old Primary School chums.

"I worked at Glenarm Harbour as a kid, leaving the school two weeks before my 14th birthday. The Harbour was buzzing with business after the Second World War - boats and, of course, railway wagons with lime in them. I was employed when the coal had to be taken out of the ships, using big tubs. I helped to discharge the coal. Two men using pointed shovels had to fill the tubs, which were then swung by rope from the ship's derrick

"A rope was hooked to a horse on the quay, and my job was to release the hook, and the coal would be heaped on to the quay when the tub was emptied. I also worked at packing bags full of lime grit. I had to weigh the bags, and tie them. The limestone went into a long riddle for separation.

"That was in 1946. It was the same for Eddie Laverty, who left school with me. We progressed to the cyndicator, and had to shovel limestone into it. I was dismissed, and that proved to be a good turn as I went to sea, and did what they call a 'Pierhead Jump'. I didn't go through the proper channels, the Pool, to get a job.

"My two Glenarm Primary School classmates, Laverty and James Maguire were working on the ship *ARGENTUM,* belonging to J J North of Liverpool. Maguire and Laverty came home. Maguire said there was a job on the boat for me, as Laverty couldn't stick it. Maguire felt I would be fit to handle it. Laverty said, don't go. I decided to give it a go, and off I went with James Maguire to Preston, to join the *ARGENTUM* - slightly bigger than a Hays puffer that came into Glenarm for limestone."

Born in September 1932, he added: "The boat carried coal and asbestos sheeting from Widnes, sometimes going to Limerick, sometimes also with coal to Newry. I was three months on that wee ship - the worst three months of my life. Maguire didn't tell me I would be working as a fireman - at 16, when you must be 18. Nor did he say that I'd have to go ashore and buy my own food, with a Ration Book needed, and then cook the food. I can still picture me, with my face black as tar from the coal dust, going into a dockside shop looking for eggs to fry.

"My first sea trip turned into a nightmare. The ship had no electricity, just carbine lamps in the engine room, and an oil lamp up forward - where four of us had sleeping quarters. After leaving Widnes on a Thursday, with a cargo of asbestos sheets for Newry, we broke down off the Isle of Man, limped into Ramsey, and were there for three weeks. The shore engineers came on board, but a seafill valve somehow became loose and the boat flooded.

"Eventually, this was solved but by then we had lots of personal gear destroyed, such as my good new sweater - ruined by oil and water. Our chief engineer was Paddy McCloy from Carnlough, whose quarters were better than ours, but were under water at one time, with cabinet drawers floating all over the place. During the delay, I went to see the shipping officer in Ramsey, and he did me a huge favour. He got me into the Seamen's Pool.

"He told me to go down the street, get a couple of photographs taken of myself, and he'd make me legit, and that he would have a Discharge Book waiting for me when we finally arrived in Newry. It was a very kind gesture, and meant I could apply for a seaman's job anywhere. Shortly after that I signed off that boat, got a deck boy's discharge."

Maguire progressed from that disagreeable passage to the top of the sea tree, as Eugene explained: "He worked as Ordinary Seaman then. When we sailed together we shared a cabin. He was on the bottom bunk, and I was up top. All the time he was reading, learning Morse Code, and so on. I came across this Harbour Master's old handbook that explained all about Morse Code. James would be talking to himself, memorising Morse Code . . .A equals such and such, C equals so and so

"I said I knew it from school days. He didn't believe me. He asked me to explain Morse Code, so I did - but I was cheating. I was reading from the handbook - and he didn't know. 'How did you do that?' he asked. It was all a bit of fun. James was very keen to learn, always studying during time off, and he progressed to the top. James Maguire moved to deep-sea, and became a captain on oil tankers, sailing all over the world.

"Later on, I was on a Robertson boat, the *GIRASOLE,* in 1949, with Glenarm firemen Dan Graham and Albert Hegarty, and also Sam Cameron, who worked as donkey man. Albert was a brother of Freddie Hegarty, who moved to live in Carnlough. The skipper was Herbie Houston from Larne, whose sister was noted schoolteacher, Winnie Houston.

"We mainly traded up and down the east coast of England and Scotland. From Penzance we took cargo of stones to the London river - the Thames. I think the stones were used in the making of cement, and then we'd take a cargo of cement from Cliff Wharf to Aberdeen. We'd come down to pick up a coal cargo at South Shields, or Blyth, out of Tyne, or Goole - up the Humber. We'd sail down to discharge at Poole, near Bournemouth, and then return to Penzance to do it all over again.

"I got the job with Robertsons through my sister Kitty, who married another McMullan, Denis McMullan of Clough Road, Cushendall. She knew Davy Kane, a chief engineer with Robertsons who said his skipper was looking for a new crew member, and he arranged it that I was offered the job. I had to travel down to Poole, Dorset, to sign on the *GIRASOLE.*

"My friend, John Burns of Carnlough advised me to go deep-sea. He also suggested not to sign on in Belfast, but go to Liverpool, where I could stay in the Seamens' Mission until I got a boat. Very quickly, I had the choice of going either to Cape Town, on the *WINDSOR CASTLE,* or to New Zealand on the *WAIMERA*. I said I'd try the run to New Zealand. I was back home after 5 months and 17 days.

"Most of the cargo out was that of car casings, and, as we had freezer bays, the cargo back was frozen lamb and cow carcases. We also had 200 passengers. I took a month out, and then returned to sea. I was now AB, and later I became a Quartermaster and also a Bo'sun, when I worked on the Larne-Stranraer boats."

He would make a significant first trip to Australia: "After a period of discharging pig iron and loading coal, John Burns, whose brothers Paddy and Leo resided at Croft Road, Carnlough, with Paddy working deep-sea, agreed with me to leave the *INVER* in Swansea. There was another boat in dry-dock, ready to depart. We asked if there were any jobs available, and signed on the *ASHBURTON*. The ship was supposed to go to Australia, and straight back. This was in the month of August. The passage was for six months, I was first told. I thought this would be great.

"We left Swansea, the ship going up to Liverpool for the last part of cargo. It was there we were warned by one of the ship's stewards the trip looked very likely to last a lot longer than six months. The steward's name was McNabney from Ballymena, whose people ran the Cafe Royal at the corner of Bryan Street. He warned us the ship was going on a long voyage, because he said stores just taken on board were sufficient to last three years!

"He paid off the ship there. I think he said he was sick, and went home. I was only 20 at the time, and went on the trip. John Burns also stayed. We didn't care. We had no ties. On board was Jim Hart from Arklow, County Wicklow. He was about 45 years of age, very experienced in all facets of seamanship - one of the greatest seamen I ever saw. He was once the Master of the *MARY B MITCHELL* in the 1950's.

"Also on board the *ASHBURTON* was a guy named Patterson from Scotland, a good sailor. The crew got on well, the greatest crowd of men I ever worked with. The bo'sun was Tom Cook from Swansea. It was supposed to be a six-month trip, but that fellow McNabney proved to be right. The voyage took us through the Panama Canal. I was through the Panama Canal seven times - and through the Suez Canal on one occasion.

"The *ASHBURTON* was a motor vessel. It had five hatches, and you could have ridden a bicycle around the deck. On top of the hatches there were four chassis for railway carriages on each side - eight on top of each hatch. It took us 54 days sailing from Liverpool to Australia. The ship was slow, just a tramp steamer, and we had no passengers on board, just cargo. On the way we called in at Curacao in the Dutch West Indies for bunkers (fuel), and then on to the Panama Canal.

"Our first port of call in Australia was Sydney. Instead of heading back to England, as I thought, orders changed. Word came through we had to go to the States and Canada. Then I realised how right the Ballymena man was. It took us three months discharging the cargo, because everything was taken off on a sling, and the same for loading wheat in Australia.

"We did stops in the States, in Canada . . . calling at Boston, Philadelphia, St John (New Brunswick), and Halifax (Nova Scotia). We headed back to Australia and New Zealand. While I was in New Zealand with the *ASHBURTON* we finished unloading work at 4.30pm, so I went to the Dockers' Office and managed to get an extra evening job, from 6 to 9 with pay at time-and-a-half. I worked as a docker, driving a winch. Then it was back to the USA. Eventually we sailed for home, after being away for 14 months."

Every sailor accepts there is bound to be a tricky moment in vile weather conditions. McMullan said: "My worst weather experience was in the Bay of Fundy, off the Canadian coast. We were going light ship to St John, New Brunswick. Travelling light can pose problems, especially in bad weather. The sailing conditions became worse, and then we had to go to help two Yankee tankers in gales, and during a snow blizzard.

"The waves were huge. It was frightening. Conditions were so bad you could hardly see the fo'castle head on our ship. Our ship was rolling at 42 degrees. At 45 degrees it can dip over. There was a big cargo hook that came off the hatch, and fortunately hit the ship's railings, and fell in again. It was a desperate situation, very dangerous. Fortunately, nobody was hurt. That was the worst weather ever I had to endure while at sea.

"I travelled through the Bay of Biscay on the same ship, and never experienced anything like that. The rough weather in the Bay of Biscay was upper stern - just big waves - and that was on the way back from Australia through the Suez Canal, and Port Said into the Mediterranean Sea.

"There is always danger when sailing through bad weather. I had an uncle lost at sea, James Donnelly from Glenarm. He was on a passenger ship. Two other uncles who were not at sea, but emigrated to Canada - Alex and John Donnelly. With them was a McGavock man from Glenarm and another man from the Antrim Coast.

"During the train journey in Canada there was a crash when a bridge collapsed. My two uncles were lucky, as they were at the back of a carriage. The other two men were up at the front. The carriage fell into a river. The man McGavock and the other man were killed.

"Looking back at the time we worked extra hours in New Zealand docks while on the *ASHBURTON*, John Burns and me were making more money there than we did at sea. So it crossed our minds we might emigrate to New Zealand. We didn't jump ship, as has been suggested. First off, we tried to get a job in England with a company that was making ships for New Zealand, but we were in a long waiting list. All the jobs were taken.

"We had been out there, to New Zealand, umpteen times before that. So, we decided that was the place for us. We stayed in New Zealand for three and a half years, working on the docks in Wellington. I had to pay back the £86 Immigration Fee. I worked from 8am to 9pm from Monday to Thursday and to 5pm on a Friday.

"Saturday and Sunday were closed down. All the years I was at sea I always looked up the local Irish Club in whatever port of call I was in. You soon found out where the hurling field was. While in Wellington, we went to play hurling every Sunday. There were players from every county involved.

"On one occasion, the President of the Irish Club in Wellington put up a special cup and a set of medals to play for, between two locally selected teams. The first team was packed by all the good players. I recall one of their players, Mick Love from Naas, taunting me in the dressing room before the match - that I wouldn't get a sniff at the cup. That got me well worked up for the game.

"I was full back, because Fr Gleeson decided to switch himself to right back. I was told to stick to the jersey of the opposition's full forward, Cork county player, Fr Joe Kelly. Kelly didn't score. We went home with the medals. We defied the odds, winning by 30 points to four. I also played one match in the famous Sydney Sports Stadium.

"Much later, in 1959, I was in the Antrim team that won the All-Ireland Junior Home championship, Unfortunately, we lost to London in the overall decider. I was injured during the Home semi-final against Wexford, and then played for the second half of the final against Cork. I also started in the game of golf when I was in Wellington. I lived beside a church, where this big Father Gleeson, a 6'4" Tipperary man, had a bag of old rusty golf sticks that John Burns and I borrowed, and went to the local Municipal golf course to hit a few balls.

"I came home to Glenarm for a six-month holiday, and in 1957 married Marie. Hurling in Glenarm was just starting up again, a junior side that won everything in Antrim that year . . . winning every game in the North Antrim League, the Championship, and the all-county. We had to go up to senior level, but that proved to be a bit of a high hurdle at the time."

A Past Captain of Cushendall Golf Club, he stopped the sea work in 1991. "Long before that, I tried to buy Charlie O'Boyle's milk run in Glenarm. It was sold to Ulster Creameries in Ballycarry. My mother wasn't well, so I decided to stay at home. For a spell I had a job as a chauffeur for Lord Antrim, and also fished a dozen creels. Then I received a call to meet a Mrs Pinner in a shop in Altmore Street, who recommended me for a job with the Creamery, on the milk run.

"I was asked to think about it. I went to see Jody McEvoy, who worked for Charlie O'Boyle way back before the Creamery took over. He had an appeal in, but felt that it would not work, and he told me to take the job. I worked for the Creamery for around five years when the manager offered me the chance to buy the run - which I did.

"I had it for 15 years, packed it in, and went back to work at sea. Old Captain James Kelly of Carnlough suggested he could get me a job, and told me to ring the shipping office at Larne Harbour. Inside two weeks I had a job back at sea, as bo'sun on the Larne-Stranaer ferry. Cushendall's Paddy McKeegan, who was on coasters up the north of Scotland, was keen to get a change, and I helped. He became a Second Mate.

"On the boat was Don McGuckian, an AB from Carnlough. Alistair McKay of Cushendall came on board, as relief on the British Railway's *ULIDIA*, a Larne-Stranraer ferry that made four trips a night. The journeys lasted around two hours each. You started at 8 o'clock, and you were 48 hours on and 48 hours off. It was a good job. Hugh 'The Mariner' McIlwaine of Waterfoot also worked then, when I was on the ferryboats. He was a Second Mate."

Archie Gore of Mill Hollow, Lower Gault's Cushendall

Cairns, Cushendall AB 'Red' Jim McKay on the ESSO YORKSHIRE

Danny McNaughton driving 'Arthur's' van in Cushendall

The ASHBURTON

ENGLISH STAR

Bernard McNaughton of Cairns, Cushendall

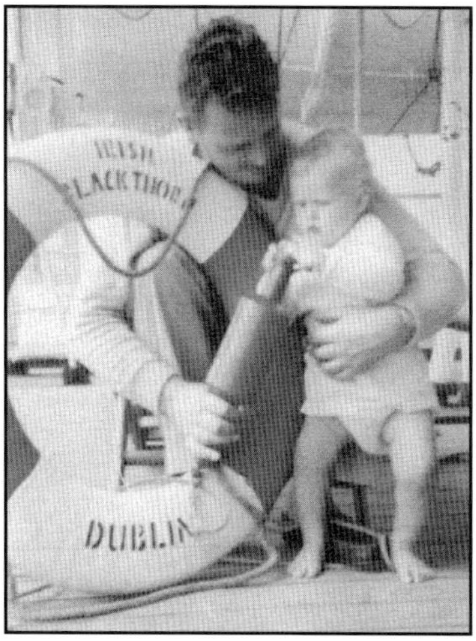

Captain Gerry Blaney with son Gerry on the IRISH BLACKTHORN

Red Bay's Captain Dan Black in Malta

Cushendall skipper Tommy Scollay and wife Maureen

Old Kelly coaster, the BALLYLAGAN

Captain Dan Black and wife Eithne

Cushendall's John Scollay

Cushendun's Denis McVeigh, Master-at-Arms on QUEEN of BERMUDA

Glenarm AB Eugene McMullan, centre, with ASHBURTON *crew colleagues Roy Williams (left) and bo'sun Tom Cook*

PENTIRION *was renamed* MENIN RIDGE, *and sunk by German torpedoes on October 24, 1939,*

Captain John Mort, Cushendall

Captain Paddy McDonnell and wife Mary of Tavnaghan, Cushendall

Hugh McElroy, Cushendall, worked on this tug-assisted boat in the Tay, during WW1

Captain Patsy Connolly, Cushendall

Pat Close, Cushendall AB

Glenariffe brothers Paddy, left, and John Eddie McAlister

Carnlough AB John Burns, right, with Glenarm sea and land colleague Eugene McMullan attend St Patrick's Day races at Wellington, New Zealand

Con Conolly,
Cushendall.

Carnlough-born
Glenariffe-based skipper
Paddy Darragh.

Gault's Road,
Cushendall, seaman
John Darragh

Cushendall sailors, Charles Patrick
'Belturbet' McNaughton (right) and
Johnnie O'Hara

Hugh McElroy gave up sea
work to become a butcher in
Cushendall. He is pictured
lighting 'Twister' tobacco
in his Peterson in front of
brother-in-law Frank Healy's
Standard 8 - RZ 3144

Glenarm ship's fireman Dan Graham, left, and Albert Hegarty

Eugene McMullan, Glenarm, steering the old-time open deck double wheel

Glenarm's Mickey Sullivan on the minesweeper SARDONIC, *December 4, 1939*

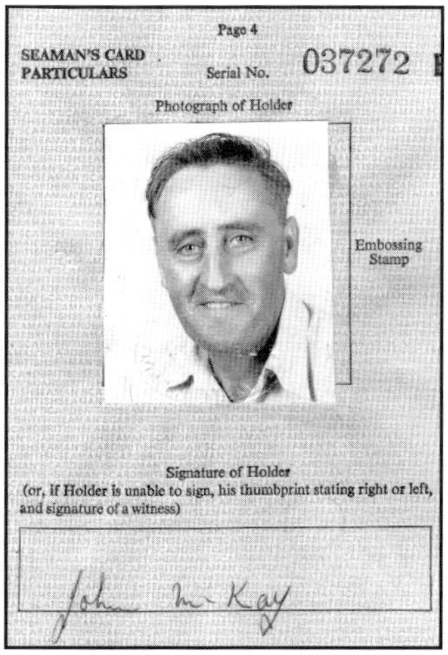

Page 4

SEAMAN'S CARD PARTICULARS

Serial No. 037272

Photograph of Holder

Embossing Stamp

Signature of Holder
(or, if Holder is unable to sign, his thumbprint stating right or left, and signature of a witness)

John McKay

Cushleake, Cushendun, seaman John McKay

John Gore of Gault's Road, Cushendall

Glenaan's Charlie Pat McKeegan

Captain Bill Balmer of Glenarm

Ian Mort with his award-winning pony

Danny McNaughton, Tully, Cushendall

Ship's carpenter and bo'sun Paddy McKeegan of Shore Street, Cushendall

Captain John Small, with granddaughter Clare

Captain Patrick McAuley, Cloughs, Cushendall

Captain Bob Gibson of Jordanstown, right, with his First Mate Brian McEvoy on the Kelly coaster BALLYHAFT

Deck hands on deep-sea work include Cushendall pair, Bernard McNaughton (left) and Colin McNaughton (centre)

Following the First World War, Cushendun's John Leavey and Alex O'Hara had work spells on the WAR HINDOO

Glenariffe-born Orr brothers, Arthur and James, 'snapped' while docked in Malta

Passenger boat, the ULSTER PRINCE

Jack Mitchell's wedding to Mary McLernon. Bridesmaid is Mary McCormick (Mrs Willie Convery), Cushendun, and best man is Jack's brother Jim

Southhampton-born John Leavey with wife Sarah and son Gerald at Cushendun Village

Cushendall's Captain Jack Blaney, left, with Canadian crew during Second World War

Old Cushendun

25 INSPIRED DECISION

A MONUMENTAL career move most certainly saved the life of Jack Mitchell, when he opted to leave the sea for good, and return to raise a family in Glenariffe. One of the three seafaring sons of Captain James Mitchell, he would surely have become a sad statistic of the Second World War, when the last ship he worked on was blown out of the water and sunk with all hands lost.

The *PACIFIC PRESIDENT* proved a sitting duck for merciless U-boat fire in December 1940. Jack's son John related the survival story: "Before deciding to stay at home, not long after he married Mary McLernon of Lower Cloughs and Knocknacarry, Cushendun, his last boat trip was on the *PACIFIC PRESIDENT*. He sailed out of London to the United States and Central America.

"My father worked deep-sea as Mate, and moved from the *IKELA* to join the *PACIFIC PRESIDENT*. It was to be his final voyage. After he left her, to stay at home for good, she was heading out to the States again. She was waiting to join a convoy about to cross the North Atlantic when sunk by a German submarine, with all 52 of a crew lost.

"That was one of many heavy casualties suffered in those convoys. He could have been on that ship, but for making the decision to quit the sea. I believe the ship had guns mounted on her deck, and that was probably why she became a target for a submarine."

Official news of the disaster relates the *PACIFIC PRESIDENT* was a diesel motor vessel of 7,113 gross tons, built in 1928, and owned by the Furness Withy Company. She was en-route in ballast from Leith, Scotland, to New York, but apparently trying to reach a convoy collection point off Rockall, when sunk on December 2, 1940, by U-43.

The incident happened on the morning of the 459th day of the War. She was an armed merchant ship, ironically built at Kiel, Germany, as a ship owed to the British Government, a late reparation vessel to help finalise financial sums still due by Germany to the British Government following the 1914-1918 War. Lost was the skipper James Smith Stuart along with 51 crew members.

John Mitchell added: "My father was very fortunate on another occasion - an escape from certain death. He was washed along the deck, and apparently overboard, during a storm in the Bay of Biscay. He was swept from the fo'castle, and the waves took him right back up again and on to the deck. That was a miracle. He died at home, in 1978, aged 72.

"He went to sea with his father, Captain James Mitchell, on coasters, and stayed a couple of years with his father before going on his own.

Around this time, Dan Black also started to work at sea, and they sailed together on coasters for a while. That was some years before Dan became a Captain.

"I remember my father telling me that during the Second World War he and Dan Black were at Bangor Bay, County Down, doing a salvage job, stripping down a boat. Then my father decided to go deep-sea. We retain a postcard he sent in 1932, from the Panama Canal, to his neighbour, old Dan Monaghan, father of Louis, who lives below us at Foriff, Glenariffe.

"Dan Monaghan had been a sea captain on coasters, and always liked to hear from my father about overseas. My father was on the journey back, and wrote: 'I'll see you in about five weeks, or so, at Foriff.' When he left the sea, he worked for a while with the Murray family of Waterfoot, at the diving and sea salvage business. He handled the oxygen pump, making sure air was getting down to old Alex Murray.

"In all his time at sea I don't think he sailed with any of his two brothers. My father was older than Captain Joe Mitchell. His granda, his mother's father John Henry, was a sea captain, and at one time he ran his own sloop - *THE JOSEPH HOWE* (named after a Canadian politician) - and used to draw coal around the coast, from Derry to the Bay, Waterfoot.

"I believe the sloop carried up to 50 tons of coal, and with some of the cargo destined for Arthur McAlister (Arthur's) of Shore Street, Cushendall. Arthur's, in those days, were also coal merchants. We also had Dan Rowan the coal merchant in Glenariffe in the old days. I believe it was Rowan's pier at Waterfoot."

While John Mitchell and his first cousins are direct descendants of the Mitchell family's seafaring tradition, John has an equally strong link to the sea through his mother's McLernon family of Glendun, Knocknacarry, and Gault's Road, Cushendall. Four McLernon brothers travelled the oceans, three achieving master mariner status, and three of them also surviving varied hair-raising torpedo drama during the First World War.

Captain James, Captain John, Captain Paddy, and the enigmatic Stewart moved from a farm near the old Glendun Primary School to reside and purchase land in Knocknacarry. The Glendun farm was sold, eventually, to the Convery family, who in turn sold it on to the McNeill's of Park. The McLernon men mostly concentrated on seafaring.

The 1881 R.I.C register of Knocknacarry Barracks, diligently researched by the ever-informative Randal McDonnell in his revealing booklet - 'Cushendun and the Glens of Antrim' lists the McLernon family living next door to the Barracks in Knocknacarry. They are registered with Henry, aged 60, a farmer and head of the household. His wife is Anne (46), sons - Henry (30), Patrick (23), James (15), John (12), Stewart (10), and daughter Isabella, then 20 years of age.

The family circumstance changed by the 1901 Cushendun Parish Census, compiled by Malachy McSparran and Denis McKillop (Big Bridge). The men folk appear to be all at sea, with Isabella remaining - now married and living with husband Charles MacCormick, who once staged dances in a barn behind the dwelling house. The main house was occupied by Charles and Bella, parents of Charles and Mary MacCormick, who spent most of their working days in New York. Charlie Jnr was once in the US Army. Generally part of a wider McCormick clan the family headstone at Cregagh is listed as MacCormick.

Across the road in Knocknacarry lived the McKay family, and a young Alex 'Stoots' McKay remembered hearing the music and jollification coming from the barn. He said: "In those days, the old Knocknacarry School was used to stage concerts and plays. Charles and Bella ran the dances in their barn. There were steps leading up to it, on the first floor, and two rooms down below. At one time, Stewart McLernon lived in one of the ground floor rooms."

During the 19th century, the loft was also used as a temporary primary schoolhouse. It is believed this was during spells when the newly-built parish education centre, Knocknacarry National School, opened in 1850, was under renovations. The 'loft' had wooden stairways, both outside and inside. The bottom area became dwelling places.

When the youngest of the brothers, Stewart retired from sea duty, he spent a lot of his time snaring rabbits. One tale from that era is that an impatient Stewart decided to flush out the rabbits on the south slopes above Knocknacarry village, and created such a large fire of whin bushes that it took some considerable time to stamp out.

It is believed the last ship Stewart sailed on was the cargo vessel, *DEWSLAND*, and it appears he survived a torpedo incident during the First World War. The *DEWSLAND*, which was a steam-driven vessel, built in 1883, was sunk on Sunday, June 1, 1916, by German U-boat 39 some 28 miles north east of Cape Carbon, off west north Africa. There were no casualties. The ship was on voyage from Philadelphia to Cardiff with a mixed cargo of lead and a deciduous and evergreen shrub, Shumac.

John Mitchell said: "In his later years, Stewart came up from Knocknacarry to live out his days with us at Foriff. My mother looked after him. I remember being at Dromore Primary School when he died. His brothers, John and Jamie McLernon were both twice torpedoed in the First World War, and survived. I think they were sailing together, probably before one or other progressed to became a ship's master.

"A German U-boat came alongside, and ordered the ship's crew to put out lifeboats. They had to get everyone off very quickly, because they, the Germans, were going to sink the ship. They did. In the second incident they also had to get off their boat pretty quickly, because she was torpedoed without any warning. I think that ship was coming from the United States with cargo.

"I believe the McLernons originally came to Cushendun from the Magilligan area. The eldest of the brothers was at sea during the change over from sail to steam. Captain Paddy's daughter, Mary married my father. A cousin of my mother, living in Knocknacarry, was Annie Ball, whose mother was May McLernon.

"Sadly, my mother's brother John tragically died while working at sea, killed in 1939 when he slipped and fell into the ship's hold, berthed at Birkenhead. He was merely 22 years of age, and was just a short time at sea. I believe he was a deck hand on coasters. John and my mother were

Captain Paddy's family. They lived at Lower Cloughs, Cushendall, and went to Cushendall Primary School.

"Captain John McLernon retired from sea work, and like his brother Stewart remained a bachelor. Captain Paddy sailed deep-sea, and made many passages down to South America. His wife, my grandmother, was Catherine Gore, a sister of old John Gore. She was an aunt of the Gore family that included wee Denis, and John - who was killed at sea. A sister of Catherine was the mother of John Joe Blaney.

"Captain Jamie McLernon gave up the sea to study, and become a schoolteacher. After he died, on December 16, 1931, his wife Nora sold the farmlands at Glendun and around Knocknacarry, and purchased a house in Ballymena - Number 12, Market Road. Jamie's family included two nurses, Mary and Brigid, a nun - Anne - and two sons, Henry and Patrick.

"Captain Jamie was first a teacher in an old primary school up the Glen Road, Glenariffe, near Drum-na-cur where Willie Graham lived . . . where James and Charlie Graham were born and reared. Bob Graham was a cousin of my father. My granny, my daddy's mother, was Rosie Henry, who married Captain James Mitchell, while her sister Mary Ann Henry married Bob Graham. Mary Ann was Kathleen (Arthur's) McAlister's mother. Captain Jamie later became a teacher in the Bay Public Elementary School at the bottom of the Glen Road."

26

MERCY MISSION

ALISTAIR McKay of Cushendall was once in the centre of a high-seas rescue drama. The medical mercy mission happened towards the closing weeks of 1956, in the Indian Ocean. The ship-to-ship doctor's call enjoyed a successful outcome, despite having to cope with huge waves. The incident made media headlines.

"I was on the *FREMANTLE STAR* when that rescue happened. We took a doctor, who was on our ship, across in the lifeboat to the other ship. The *FREMANTLE STAR* was on a run from London to Australia with general cargo, and also 14 passengers, fortunately including the doctor.

"We sailed through the Suez Canal, the Red Sea, and were on course for our destination when the S.O.S happened. The doctor had been studying in England, where he had his wife and young family with him. They were returning to their home in Australia

"I joined the 18,000-ton *FREMANTLE STAR* on November 15, 1956, and we left from KG5 dock in London. We were three weeks out when our ship received the radio call, in the Indian Ocean, from the *TREWORLAS*. They urgently needed medical help, and wondered if, by any chance, we had a doctor on board."

Born on June 26, 1936, and sailing on the oceans since he was a 17-year-old, he sent home a copy of a report of the incident in a Perth, western Australia, newspaper. The headline heralds the occasion . . .'LIFE SAVED IN OCEAN DRAMA' - and the picture/article included photographs of the transfer from ship to ship, and of some of the main players.

The picture-caption report is: 'This is the scene in mid-Indian Ocean ten days ago, when a ship's doctor made a dangerous half-mile lifeboat dash through 12-feet waves to save the life of a man on another vessel. He is Dr A. W. Sonia of Moe (Victoria), who returned to his ship, the *FREMANTLE STAR*, at Fremantle, after a 9,500-mile international journey by plane.

'Dr Sonia is pictured with the chief officer of his ship, Mr. G. J. Stanley, who piloted the lifeboat on its dangerous journey. Their ship crossed the path of the outward bound wheat ship, *TREWORLAS*, during a violent storm.

'The *TREWORLAS* skipper pleaded for medical aid for their chief steward, who was seriously ill with an internal complaint. The *FREMANTLE STAR* answered by lowering a 29ft-powered lifeboat into the heaving sea with the doctor, the chief officer, the bo'sun (Mr. C. Farrell), and an eight-man crew.

"Oil was poured from both freighters to stop spray whipping from the

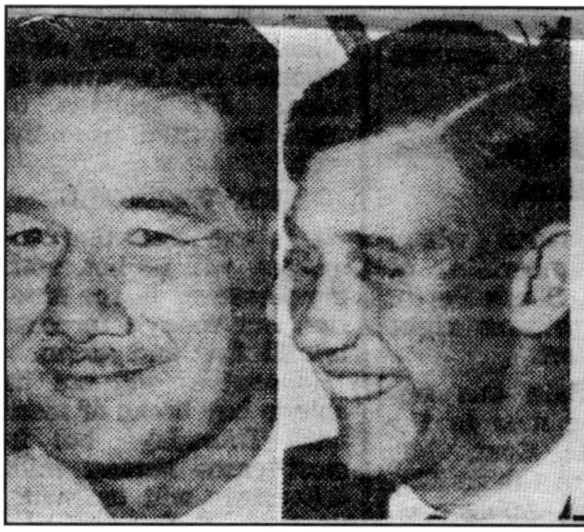

This was the scene in mid-Indian Ocean ten days ago when a ship's doctor made a dangerous half-mile lifeboat dash through 12ft. waves to save the life of a man on another vessel.

He is Dr. A. W. Sonia, of Moe (Victoria), who returned to his ship, the Fremantle Star, at Fremantle yesterday after a 9,500-mile international journey by plane.

• *Dr. Sonia is pictured left, with the chief officer of his ship, Mr. G. J. Stanley, who piloted the lifeboat on its dangerous journey.*

Their ship crossed the path of the outward-bound wheat ship, Treworlas, during a violent storm.

The

waves, but the lifeboat men were drenched by the time the chief officer made the almost impossible manoeuvre of bringing the boat alongside the *TREWORLAS* without smashing it.

"On the way back, the lifeboat's engine broke down, and the crew rowed frantically against the waves. When they reached the *FREMANTLE STAR*, wet and exhausted, Dr Sonia was already treating his patient on the *TREWORLAS*.

"In the next five days he had only four hours' sleep, standing by the patient day and night, until he could be sent to a hospital in Mauritius. Waiting for the doctor, when he returned to the *FREMANTLE STAR,* were his wife and two little girls. Dr Sonia is returning from study in Britain.'

Alistair McKay completed the happy-ending story: "After the incident, our ship, from the Blue Star Line, went into Fremantle, discharged our cargo, and then loaded a cargo of lamb into our freezers. We worked around the Australian ports, and after six months I was back home."

Affectionately nicknamed 'Tony Curtis' - and for a very obvious likeness reason - McKay used family seafaring connections to start his life on the waves in July, 1953. "Overall, I spent 42 years at sea, and I kept three Discharge Books of my journeys, quitting on June 29, 1995. It all began when I approached my uncle, Captain John Mort for a job. He gave me one, and off I went on the 4th of July 1953.

"My mother, Molly was ill at the time, and receiving treatment in the Waveney Hospital, Ballymena. She didn't know I was on my way to work as a sailor. I was away a week before she was told. I sent her a note from England. My mother never wanted me to go, although she knew I was trying to get a job at sea. My father, Alex, knew I was sailing with my mother's brother, Captain John Mort and his brother, James Mort.

"John (Mort) was Master of the *PASS of GLENOGLE*, an 800-ton oil tanker. Uncle James worked in the engine room. Also from Cushendall was Pat McKeegan of Shore Street. He was the bo'sun. We mostly sailed on the east coast of England, up north, and also the odd run into Larne. I spent three years and eight months on the *PASS of GLENOGLE.*

"I was an Ordinary Seaman, and then EDH (Efficient Deck Hand). I didn't sit the First Mate ticket examination, because I never settled to the studies. My brother Jim, who is five years younger, sat and passed all the examinations, and became a sea captain. He worked in the Far East."

On June 26, 1957, he came close to quitting the sea, and jumping ship in New Zealand. With him was Pat Connolly of Cushendall. "Of all the places I visited the one I nearly ended up staying in was Wellington, New Zealand. I was on a trip with the *FORT MacQUARIE* of the Port Line, and so was Pat Connolly. Our first call with general cargo was Wellington, and it was there I celebrated my 21st birthday Pat (Connolly) went ashore with me, and in a pub we met two fellows from Ireland.

"One said he was from Bellaghy. They asked us if we wanted jobs in Wellington, as they could fix us up. We could jump ship, and obtain work in an ice-making factory. It was tempting. Anyone nailed for jumping ship then would serve six weeks in jail, but after that you could stay in New Zealand, and also have no trouble in getting work there. It was a period when New Zealand business people were crying out for workers.

"Pat Connolly started at sea with Doreys of Guernsey, and was deep-sea on Blue Star boats, including the *FREMANTLE STAR*. He was an AB, and once worked under Captain Jim McGonnell. Pat quit the sea shortly after he married Moira McCambridge of Ballymena."

McKay occasionally switched from coasting to deep-sea employment, such as the run from London to Australia. "Often I would get a telegram at home from different shipping companies to inform me there was a boat available. So, off I'd go again. After that trip on the *FREMANTLE STAR*, I sailed on the *AUSTRALIAN STAR*. This was a similar run, including 14 passengers. On this one we had a 'Crossing the Line' ceremony, when passing the equator - Neptune and all that - a custom from olden times once you cross the equator.

"Our ship's captain came down to what was a make-up swimming pool on the ship. He was dressed to the nines, displaying all his finery, and decided to say a few words beside the pool. In fun, one of the lady passengers gave him a push, and he fell into the pool, which had water in it that wasn't all that clean. Captain Happee, believe it or not that was his surname and from England, had his clothes all soiled. He was not amused. I don't think he saw the funny side, was not a happy man. As it was a passenger who pushed him he couldn't say anything.

"It was again a six-month passage, there and back, and then I joined the *VACUUM PIONEER*, a tanker belonging to the Mobil Oil Company. I was with Cushendall neighbours, Jim Blaney and old Pat McKeegan on this ship. Jim was the Mate, and Pat was the Bo'sun.

"The *VACUUM PIONEER* traded along the UK coast, to ports such as Birkenhead. We also made a trip or two to the Baltic - to deliver oil from Corrytown in London to Copenhagen. We called in at Rotterdam, coming back light, with ballast only. That was in 1959. I was one year with that ship.

"I moved to join the *AMBER*, one of Robertson's boats, and went to Copenhagen for a cargo of phosphate, bound for Derry. Then it was light to Llandulos in north Wales, to load up with stone. This is a place where you ran the boat up onto the beach during low tide, filled up the cargo, and let the boat go out on the incoming tide that floated our boat.

"The cargo was for Odda in Norway, a port at the top end of the Hyardangorfjord. The stones had to do with the making of glass. From there we took back paper pulp to England. Also on the *AMBER* we ran cargo of Blue Circle cement from London to Belfast. I always looked forward to that, as you had three or four days in Belfast. I was on the *AMBER* for one year. I also worked on two other ships belonging to Robertsons of Glasgow - the *CAMEO,* and the *PEARL.*

"I gave the deep-sea trips a break, working along the coasts here instead, I wanted to be near home for a time - especially in the summer. It was easier, naturally, to be in Cushendall for some of the summer when you sailed on coasters. If you joined up in London for deep-sea work you were never sure when you would get back home.

"However, I decided to return to the long voyages. I joined the *BRITISH CORMORANT*, a crude oil carrying tanker, and one of eight British oil tankers I worked on. The passage was supposed to be for three months, and I figured I would be in Cushendall for the summer. Instead, the trip lasted ten months. The passage took me through the Suez, to Singapore, Ceylon, and to South America.

"At one stage, we ran up to Vietnam with fuel for American war planes. It was during the Vietnam War years. We docked and unloaded at Satraam, near Hanoi. We could hear the US planes taking off in the mornings. We made three trips, and then our oil company was threatened by the Viet Cong, that they would place limpet mines on our ship, blow it up, if we continued to bring in oil for the American forces."

McKay often worked side by side with another long-serving seaman, John Murphy of Cairns, Cushendall. "It was always good to have somebody from the Glens with you on a voyage. Often that was not the case, but generally you would meet up with somebody who worked with you on other ships. One of my great companions was John Murphy, who was with me a lot during my days at sea.

"John was a greaser, down in the engine room. He went to work at sea slightly before me, and started on Kelly boats. We met up at home, and then went to London's KG5 docks to sign on for deep-sea work. There you had an opportunity to pick where you wanted to go. You could see where the ships were going - the Far East, South America, and runs to Australia, and also to New Zealand.

"One of the strange things John did was to have a different toothbrush for every day of the week. Those teeth of Murphy's were cleaned three times-a-day. Ironically, despite those precautions, he suffered cancer in his throat. However, he was a very heavy smoker.

"Overall, John was with me for about 30 years at sea, going all over the place, the Australia run and so on. We had to fly out of Belfast a lot in those days, to join ships, especially when working for the Texaco Oil Company. Their ships sailed out of different places - indeed, once on the *TEXACO GENT* out of San Fernando in the West Indies, near Trinidad.

"How could I forget this trip? We joined the ship in San Fernando, left the harbour, and ten minutes out the engine broke down. We were there for a month, and had a good time. It was like a holiday in the sun, although during the day we would do chores on the ship - cleaning, painting, freshening things up, and then on the town at night.

"Once, when on the Australia run, we managed to get extra dock work when discharging another ship in an Australian port. I remember the mate of another ship coming on board to seek permission to use us as help in the evenings with his discharging. Once we finished our day's work on our own ship some of us went to work on the other ship, discharging cargo - and at Australian wages. We worked up to four or five hours at night. It was good extra money

"There were also tricky jobs, such as the one, along with my great friend Murphy, when we joined the *LAPAMPA* in London on September 10, 1960. Our cargo was oil pipes for Kerim Shah in the Persian Gulf, above Abadan. It took us six weeks to discharge the cargo, because of the intense heat that prevented the dockers there from working through the afternoons.

"From there, we sailed to Goa, India, for a cargo of iron ore for Odda. Murphy and me paid off the *LAPAMPA* on the Humber, on the 9th of February, 1961. Next we joined the *GRAND* out of London, with general cargo for Bodwood Port in Canada, and there we loaded paper pulp for England. I also made one trip through the Panama Canal, going to New Zealand, after coming out of Savannah in South America."

The most demanding sea journey was easy for Alistair to recall: "The worst weather conditions I experienced were when going through the Pentland Firth on the *ABBOTSFORD*, a tanker carrying ammonia. Immingham was one of our ports. We came out from near Elsmere Port, and later passed Duncan's Bay Head lighthouse in north Scotland, and when going through the Pentland Firth we hit really bad weather when facing the Atlantic.

"We came down along the west coast of Scotland, and it took us four days. We had to put in at Lough Swilly, County Donegal, because something was wrong with the ship's engine - probably because of the pounding and battering the boat had to take during that storm, ploughing through huge waves. Our ship was around 3,000 tons.

"Of all my travels this was the scariest experience. I never had any trouble in the Bay of Biscay, nor during the one occasion I went round Cape Horn. We half-circled the world on that trip around the Horn. It was a big oil tanker. The *GULF DAN* was from the Persian Gulf, bound for San Francisco.

"That was an unforgettable adventure, to be anchored just off the famous prison in the Bay, Alcatraz Island. We had some time ashore in San Francisco's harbour front. On other trips to North America and Canada I visited Norfolk (Virginia), New York, St John (New Brunswick), Quebec, Montreal, and up the Great Lakes. At the close of my time at sea I worked on the ferry out of Larne, on the *BISON*, a Pandora boat."

More about John Murphy from his brother Danny: "Our John started at sea with Captain James Kelly. Before that, he worked for Willie Graham at the quarry, where he damaged an ankle. He had to stop for a while, and then went back again, after resting the ankle. However, the ankle ballooned up again, and he couldn't get a boot on the foot. The doctor couldn't find anything seriously wrong.

"Still, John quit the quarry work, and went to work for 'Arthur's', out on the delivery lorry with our great Antrim and Ulster hurling goalkeeper Mick McKeown, who also went to sea for a short time - as did old Mick McKeown. John moved to work in the Glens of Antrim Hotel, lighting up the boiler and stacking the bar.

"At that time, a retired man named Becker lived opposite the Glens, and must have been a physiotherapist. He cured a bad back ailment for Kathleen 'The Rock' McNeill, and when John told him of his ankle problem he had a look, and found a bone was out of place. He pressed it back in, bandaged the foot, and John never had further pain in the ankle..

"My mother had a chat with Captain John Mort, who then also lived at Cairns. John Mort helped to set up a work opportunity for my brother John, with Captain Kelly on the *PASS of DRUMOCHTER*. John worked as a greaser for Captain Kelly, and was a long time there before he teamed up with Alastair McKay, to go deep-sea.

"Other sea interests in our family circle are those of my father, Daniel and his brother Robert, father of John Murphy of near Tavnaghan. There was another brother, James Murphy. My father was at sea for a short while, before emigrating to work in New York harbour on the barges. A cousin, Archie Murphy was out there for a while, working on the docks. I was born there, and so too was my late brother John. My mother was Teenie McKillop, related to Francis and Michael, and was born at the corner of the Turn, Cushendun.

"We came back from the USA when I was three, and lived at Drumfaskey, Glendun, for a time. My sister Ann was born there. In later years, she went to California, a nun in the St Louis Order. We moved to Carnahaugh, Cushendall, and lived beside the 'Dears' (McAlisters). Up there, lived Mrs Reid, a sister of my father.

"My uncle Robert died on September 18, 1934, after an accident at sea. He was in his bunk when another ship crashed into his. He was badly injured. His right leg was severely broken. Robert was taken to hospital in France, but at the third attempt in the operating theatre the surgeons failed to save the leg, and he died there, in hospital.

"He was an Ordinary Seaman, a fireman. His son John was 12 when Robert died. Robert's daughter Ita, older than John, was a teacher who married an Englishman, a banker. Because she was educated at Ballymena Academy, and did not have Religious Studies, she couldn't find a job in a local Catholic school. That is why she went to teach in England. She also worked out foreign."

27 FAMILY AFFAIR

SEAN MORT looked back with justifiable pride at being a part of a Cushendall family unit devoted to seafaring. He became a link in the chain of that great Glens of Antrim network of sailor men. It was almost a predictable annual exodus from the small villages and hill farms, until the ways of trading over the waves became no longer a profitable exercise for many great fleet owners of small, medium, and tanker-sized craft.

There was a time when the shipping lanes of the Irish Sea and the North Channel would be choc-a-bloc with craft of all sizes, from little trawlers, small coasters, to big container-loaded vessels, majestic liners, and generally at least one mariner from the Glens working on board. For a period you didn't have to look too far to find a member of the Mort bloodline, one that included the McKay's

Of all the old 'sea dogs' I interviewed none was more enthusiastic about talking of the past than Sean Mort, who lives with wife Marie (nee Leavey) in Cushendun. With great gusto, during a lengthy interview in December 2012, he sailed proudly down memory lanes that took me on a time-travel experience all over the globe.

Born in the Spring of 1939, he spent 19 years working as an AB. and of all the places visited the one spot that always brings back happy memories is New Zealand. He retained a special warmth for the Kiwi country. "If I had a choice to go back to sea again I would take the New Zealand run," he insisted, "I was down there nine times, unloading and loading cargo in ports such as Dunedin, Nelson, Wellington, Bluff, Auckland.

"One of the more memorable cargoes was a shipment of champagne. We picked up crates of the expensive bubbly in Italy. It was part cargo bound for New Zealand. I was on the *SOUTH AFRICA STAR* that had fridge hatches, and in New Zealand we picked up carcases of chilled lamb from ports such as Auckland - the City of Sails - and back to London. We also had cargo of bales of wool."

Before those deep-sea passages, he started on jaunts of a more modest scale. "My first job was on a wee coaster loaded with cement from Magheramorne, outside Larne, and bound for Creetown in Scotland. The skipper of the *CAIRNGORM* was none other than Tommy Scollay from Cushendall. Also on board was Hugh Healy, who later went to live in England.

"I asked Tommy Scollay for a job, when he was home for a short break. He said he was looking for one man to help. So, I got the job, and travelled with Tommy in a car to Magheramorne, where we boarded the boat. I was on about five of those Robertson vessels. I once worked on a William Robertson boat that ran out of Glasgow, when Charles 'Belturbet' McNaughton was on her, as were the Black brothers from up Glenariffe Glen - P.J. and Malachy. I also sailed with big Paddy Leech."

Sean journeyed extensively with Red Bay-born Captain Dan Black, who then lived 'round the shore' near Garron Point. "I was with Captain Dan on three different ships, and I was on them four different times, and with him - on the *OLOPHINE*, the *EMERALD,* and the *AGATE.*"

As was so often the case, family traditions proved an irresistible magnet for some teenagers. Sean was no exception, and followed older brother Roy to an early life on the oceans. For a short spell, before going deep-sea, he joined older members of the Mort family circle that was steeped in seamanship. He joined his uncles, John and Jim Mort of Cushendall on the *PASS of GLENOGLE.*

"That was in 1959. My uncle John was skipper of the coastal tanker. My uncle James Mort was a fireman in the engine room. My father, Bob Mort did not go to sea. He was well known in the Glens for breeding greyhounds, and at one time had 18. In the very old days, as a young man, he helped his father haul goods with horses and a big cart down from Retreat Railway Station to Cushendall."

Sean stayed eight months under the guidance of Captain John Mort: "Also on that ship was Dan McVeigh of Glenariffe. He was what is known as a 'donkey man' in the engine room, a greaser. Sadly, Dan, who was owner or part owner, as far as I know, of the wee shop near the Glenariffe hurling field, was murdered during a robbery in his house at Waterfoot.

"On the *PASS of GLENOGLE* were the two McAlister brothers from round the shore, near the old pier - John Eddie and Paddy 'Dear' McAlister. Paddy was bo'sun. Tragically, in later years, John Eddie was killed by a bolt of lightning while crossing a stream on the mountain behind his home.

"For all the size of that ship, it was a four-on and four-off watch, and also in the crew was a cousin of mine from Cobh, County Cork - Denis McElhernon. I was a deck hand, and stayed on the 'PASS' for eight months. Alex McElhernon Snr was a ship's officer, living at Cobh. His sons Alex Jnr and Denis were AB's. I visited Denis's home in Cobh, when we were berthed there."

The Mort connection with County Cork was through Alex McElhernon, who married Ann O'Hanrohan of Cobh. Their family was Mary, Betty, Denis, Johnny, and Alex Jnr. Sean's aunt Rosa's family tree research also disclosed a brother of Alex Snr. He was Johnny, who married May Belle McAuley in Paisley, and was a ship's officer for the Burns-Laird company sailing the ferry route between Glasgow and Belfast. In the late 1930's, his boat was in collision with a vessel belonging to Cammel Laird in the North Channel.

He was badly injured, and never fully recovered. Marie Mort said: "As a result of the accident, his health deteriorated, and he went to live with his sister Anne Jane (Nancy) in Shrewsbury, where he died in hospital. His eldest sister, Mary Catherine married Robert Mort. Mrs Annie Spiers was a McElhernon from Layd before she married Dan McCormick. She and my Granny, Sarah Leavey were related."

"According to aunt Rosa (McQuillan), her grandfather, a great grandfather of Bob Mort, came on a ship with old James Speers. It was then he met Rosetta Speers, old Jim's sister, and married her. That is how the Mort's came to the Glens. Bob Mort's aunt Rosa's full name was Rosetta.

"My husband's great grandfather married Ann Jane McElhernon, and their family included Bob Mort, and also Captain John, Molly, James, and Elma - whose proper name was Elizabeth Margaret. Jim Speers Jnr then married the widow Annie McCormick."

Back to Sean Mort's career. Now well groomed in the ways of the waves, he decided to extend his ambitions, and move on from coasting to seek distant horizons as a deep-sea mariner. "The Blue Star company ran ships to New Zealand, Australia, South America, and they left from London. You had the pick of different ships and different sea routes with Blue Star. You went to New Zealand via the Panama Canal. I also did the South American run to the River Plate, Buenos Aires. You went to Australia around South Africa, and via the Cape of Good Hope or the Suez Canal

"I worked the Persian Gulf, and that generally meant going through the Suez. At Port Said, you just had to be patient and sit there, in the Bitter Lakes. There could be up to a dozen ships waiting to get through, and you would be stuck in a queue, half-way through. Ships couldn't pass in the Suez Canal, because there was not enough room,

"Once we went to Hobard, Tasmania, to pick up crates of apples and pears to take back to England. On those runs we always had cargo going and cargo coming back. I did the run to New Zealand, Tasmania, and Australia on the *ENGLISH STAR.* Often, you would stop off at every port in New Zealand.

"Working as an AB deck hand we had shifts of four hours on and eight hours off. You had to try and sleep. I wasn't much of a reader. During time off some of the crew would gather in the room, and yarn. Sometimes you could watch television, but it was out of vision, out of reach in mid-ocean. You could always pick up radio stations.

"I was on the early day shift that started at 6.30am on deck when going to New Zealand on ships that always carried, along with part cargo, a small number of passengers - around a dozen. You had to scrub the decks clean. It was called 'Holy Stone' the decks, have them washed down, and the deck chairs out in time for the passengers. Sometimes, you had to do a bit of painting, or washing down the paintwork.

"I took 'Pay Off', and then rejoined the Blue Star line. I was with them for four years. I took on runs to the River Plate. I remember getting a telegram, when on a one-month leave. A message to the Post Office in Cushendall stated: 'Rejoin the ship in London.' I was in a lot of different places, including up the Great Canadian Seaway. On those occasions I was on a tramp ship for Dehholms, sailing up the St Lawrence, and then we'd branch off into the Great Lakes. We moved up to Detroit City and Cleveland, to take on a load of America-made motorcars - mostly big Buicks.

"We shipped the cars to various places, generally to South America, calling in at Montevideo in Uruguay, and on to the Argentine as well. We not only carried big loads of cars but also loads of car tyres. I was on a Denholm boat that was bought over by Shamrock Shipping when I joined her.

"I was also on the Jacks of Larne ship, *MOYLE*, a vessel that regularly transported cargoes of potash fertiliser from Casablanca to Dublin or Cork. On another journey, this time back across the Atlantic, I was on one trip up the Mississippi, to New Orleans, on the tanker *BEECHWOOD JACOB*, which was loaded with grain."

Few sailors have ever managed to avoid the dreaded massive storm. It goes with the job, and Mort said: "The worst experience I had was during a very severe storm in the north Atlantic. The waves were so severe they washed all the wire reels off the fo'castle head. They crashed into the accommodation area, and bent all the steel parts. We had to 'heave to' for three days, before the storm passed. I was fortunate never to suffer from seasickness, but that was one of the toughest times.

"Working on a light ship in the north Atlantic was also no fun. I had another nasty experience when we had a cargo that kept shifting on the *AGATE* during a storm. The coaster was carrying steel rails for Durban, the rails to be used for trains to run on. During bad weather the rails kept moving. When I was working on the coasters, wife Marie listened into the trawler-band radio frequency, the RT Radio. She would often hear the chat between the boats, and knew where I was. My brother Roy once took ill on a boat off the coast of Norway. Marie heard about that incident on the waveband."

James Hugh McNaughton of Cloughs, an AB on the GEM *when killed on Christmas Day 1914*

Captain John Henry 'Jack' Blaney, Cushendall

1920's Gault's Road schoolboy John McLernon, later to die at sea, in 1939

James McKillop of Cloughs, Cushendall

ESSO TENBY

Hugh McIlwaine's first sea voyage was on the BALLYMONEY

Miaflores Locks, Panama Canal.

The PERIDOT *foundered off Islandmagee in November 1905.*

Captain Neal Blaney, Master and owner of THE HERTHA, *was lost at sea off Prince Edward Island in 1876.*

Captain James Kelly, O.B.E

Three Cushendun sailors pictured in a Glasgow studio during the 1920's - John Lewis, left, Alex O'Hara (sitting) and Hugh McCormick

James McKeegan of Glenaan, Captain of the ill-fated GEM, *who was killed at sea off Scarborough in December 1914*

28

PERILS of PENZANCE

FOUR Cushendun sailors survived a scary experience when shipwrecked off the Cornwall coast in late September 1920. A 22-year-old Alex O'Hara of Knocknacarry, Charlie McLarnon, Pat McKendry - an uncle of the same named who lived at Cushendun bridge - and the infamous Dan 'The Duck' Hernon were part of the crew rescued from raging seas.

During what was then described as 'The Great Gale of 1920', many ships were wrecked along the Cornwall coast. Hernon, O'Hara, McKendry, and McLarnon were on board the 6,483 gross tons *ANSGIR*, a diesel steam driven cargo ship that foundered on the rocks near Land's End. She ran aground at Mounts Bay, Penzance, during gale-force conditions, and was wrecked. All crew members were saved.

The ship left Dartmouth on September 29, 1920, on a trans-Atlantic journey, but never made it. It was Alex O'Hara's second trip on this boat, once built and owned in Germany, and annexed from the War. It became a case of out of the frying pan and into the briny. The dramatic Penzance episode for O'Hara was in his second job back, after the debilitating experience of an illness suffered in Colon, Panama. While sailing on the *VOLGA*, he took seriously ill. At first, it was felt he was ailing from the dreaded Yellow Fever, and rushed to hospital at Colon, on November 29, 1919.

He recovered three weeks later. Even though in a physically weak condition he managed to secure a working passage on the *TRIDENT* from Panama. On December 31, 1919, he sailed via Hamburg to arrive at London's Victoria Dock in early March 1920. Incidentally, the *TRIDENT*, often taking grain cargo from Montreal, was sunk during a German air raid on August 2, 1941, at the mouth of the River Tyne.

On August 12, 1920, Alex O'Hara resumed work on the *ANSGIR*, sailing out of Leith for overseas passage, and returning to Portsmouth on September 2, 1920. The *ANSGIR* then took off on another intended foreign trip, the ill-fated passage.

O'Hara's wife Minnie (nee McGavock of Dunurgan, Cushendun) once explained: "After the Great War, he was on a ship which had been taken from the defeated Germans and was shipwrecked off the coast of Cornwall. Himself, Charles McLarnon, Dan Hernon, and Pat McKendry were rescued by Breeches Buoy - a harness deployed to complete single person transfer from ship to ship, or from ship to shore. He told me many ships taken from the Germans suffered a similar fate."

Charlie McLarnon later developed a very successful bakery at High Street, Cushendall. His brother Pat farmed at Ballyteerim, next door to Shane's Cairn on the Torr Road, while Pat McKendry was an uncle of hurling men Pat and Harry McKendry. Dan Hernon would become a self-made personality at seaside Cushendun, when known as Dan 'The Duck'

It would appear 'The Duck' decided to leave the water for land. According to historian Randal McDonnell, he went west to the New World. "Dan left the sea and was in America, working in New York, during Prohibition. He returned home in 1931, and worked around my grandmother's pub, McBride's in Cushendun, for the rest of his life. He became a high-profile person, because he was at the pub, and visitors met him.

"He was a carpenter to trade. A handy man, he was proud of the tools of his trade, and always kept them in perfect working order, saws and so forth. The farming community used to come to him regularly to have sheep shears properly sharpened. His brothers, Jack and Tom were, I believe, also at sea for a short period before they settled in New York. Jack used to restore furniture after he came back from the United States. He probably was a carpenter as well as the 'Duck'.

"Tom Hernon once had 'a notion' of my aunt, Nora McBride, and bought her an engagement ring. Unfortunately she died, and my grandmother, who never had an engagement ring, put it on her finger and wore it for the rest of her days."

'The Duck' was born in 1890, at Edenderry, County Offaly, and died in Cushendun in 1967. He was, for many years, general factotum at McBride's Pub. His people were carpenters and blacksmiths. "His mother was a McKillop of Barrmean, Cushendun, while his father died when the sixth child was born in County Offaly," added Randal McDonnell. "The widow Hernon took the children to Cushendun, to the Duck's grandmother, a McAllister of Tyban. Five of the children went to the USA, and one to Scotland.

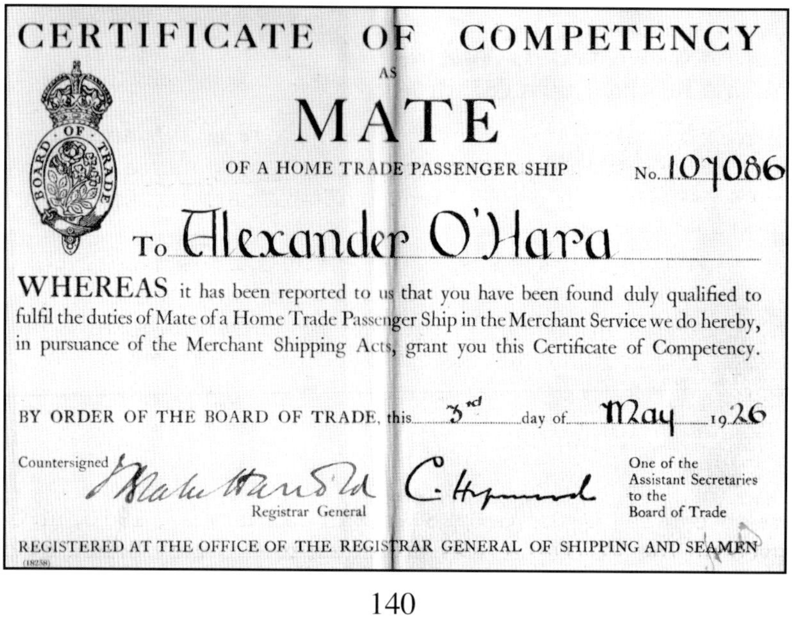
CERTIFICATE OF COMPETENCY

AS

MATE

OF A HOME TRADE PASSENGER SHIP No. 107086

To Alexander O'Hara

WHEREAS it has been reported to us that you have been found duly qualified to fulfil the duties of Mate of a Home Trade Passenger Ship in the Merchant Service we do hereby, in pursuance of the Merchant Shipping Acts, grant you this Certificate of Competency.

BY ORDER OF THE BOARD OF TRADE, this 3rd day of May 1926

Countersigned

Registrar General

One of the Assistant Secretaries to the Board of Trade

REGISTERED AT THE OFFICE OF THE REGISTRAR GENERAL OF SHIPPING AND SEAMEN

"The 'Duck', apparently, once swam Cushendun Bay for a bet, and hence his nickname. Tom and Jack became riggers and sail makers. The sisters were Nellie, Annie, May, and Kate. I was told the 'Duck', after being in America for a time, returned to rejoin his mother in 1931, and with £900 in savings. Tom and Jack worked in New York for many years, before retiring to Cushendun."

Meanwhile, as the Hernon men shipped out to the States, O'Hara continued his sea passages. He took time out to study for his First Mate's Ticket in Dublin, staying with his then bachelor cousin, Nelson Brogan,

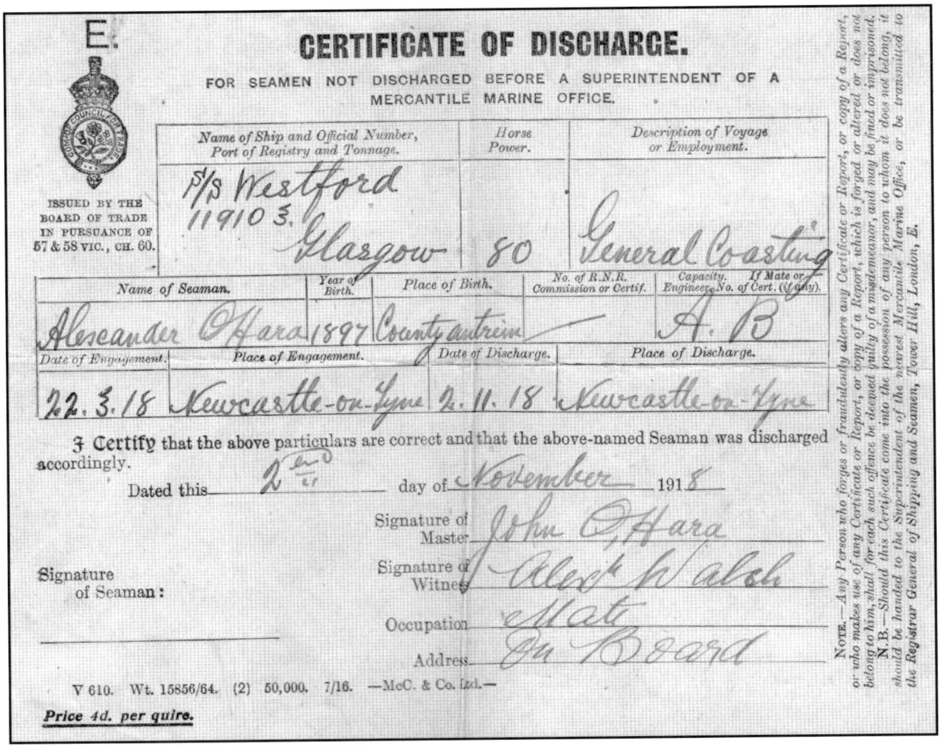

E.

CERTIFICATE OF DISCHARGE.

FOR SEAMEN NOT DISCHARGED BEFORE A SUPERINTENDENT OF A MERCANTILE MARINE OFFICE.

ISSUED BY THE BOARD OF TRADE IN PURSUANCE OF 57 & 58 VIC., CH. 60.

Name of Ship and Official Number, Port of Registry and Tonnage.	Horse Power.	Description of Voyage or Employment.
S/S Westford 119103 Glasgow	80	General Coasting

Name of Seaman.	Year of Birth.	Place of Birth.	No. of R.N.R. Commission or Certif.	Capacity. If Mate or Engineer, No. of Cert. (if any).
Alexander O'Hara	1897	County Antrim	—	A. B

Date of Engagement.	Place of Engagement.	Date of Discharge.	Place of Discharge.
22.3.18	Newcastle-on-Tyne	2.11.18	Newcastle-on-Tyne

I Certify that the above particulars are correct and that the above-named Seaman was discharged accordingly.

Dated this 2nd day of November 1918

Signature of Master John O'Hara

Signature of Witness Alex Walsh

Occupation Mate

Address On Board

Signature of Seaman:

V 610. Wt. 15856/64. (2) 50,000. 7/16. —McC. & Co. Ltd.—

Price 4d. per quire.

NOTE.—Any Person who forges or fraudulently alters any Certificate or Report, or copy of a Report, or who makes use of any Certificate or Report, or copy of a Report, which is forged or altered or does not belong to him, shall for each such offence be deemed guilty of a misdemeanor, and may be fined or imprisoned.
N.B.—Should this Certificate come into the possession of any person to whom it does not belong, it should be handed to the Superintendent of the nearest Mercantile Marine Office, or be transmitted to the Registrar General of Shipping and Seamen, Tower Hill, London, E.

who operated a butcher's shop in Parnell Street with another cousin, Johnny McVeigh. The O'Hara seaman's study lasted three months before he passed the examination, overseen by Tom Casement, brother of Roger Casement.

Born on October 17, 1897, Alex O'Hara died of a cancer on September 11, 1955, aged 57. His Certificate of Discharge record number was 842395, an official black-bound booklet that disclosed he was merely four days light of his 18th birthday when he started his sea career on October 13, 1915. Through the help of his Glasgow-based uncle, and ship supplier, John Brogan he found work as an assistant steward on the *VERDALA*.

The ship, sailing from Newport, south Wales, was on 'Trooping' duty, and his first discharge date for war cargo assignments of transporting soldiers to combat in the Great War was January 27, 1916, at Cardiff. He stayed on the *VERDALA*, was promoted to Ordinary Sailor, made one voyage to the United States, and discharged after a trip to India for the Admiralty, leaving from Barry in south Wales during mid-December 1916, and signing off this ship at Newcastle-Upon-Tyne, on April 19, 1917.

His next outing was on the 6,293 gross tons passenger/cargo liner *HERSCHEL* from Cardiff on June 17, 1917, again for the Admiralty, until September 18, 1917. From January 1918, he went on further foreign trips, on the Maryland USA-built 3,107 tons converted tanker *VOLGA*, later lost through fire, on January 12, 1921, on voyage back from Abadan to Italy.

In between the long hauls, he fitted in two short coastal passages to and from Newcastle-Upon-Tyne, the first from March until July 7, 1918, on the 80-horse power *WESTFORD*. He is listed as AB. The skipper was ironically John O'Hara, and the First Mate Alex Walsh. He was away again on the *VOLGA*, and back to home port at Poplar, London, on August 17, 1918, and out again and across the Atlantic, leaving on the 18th of October from Glasgow.

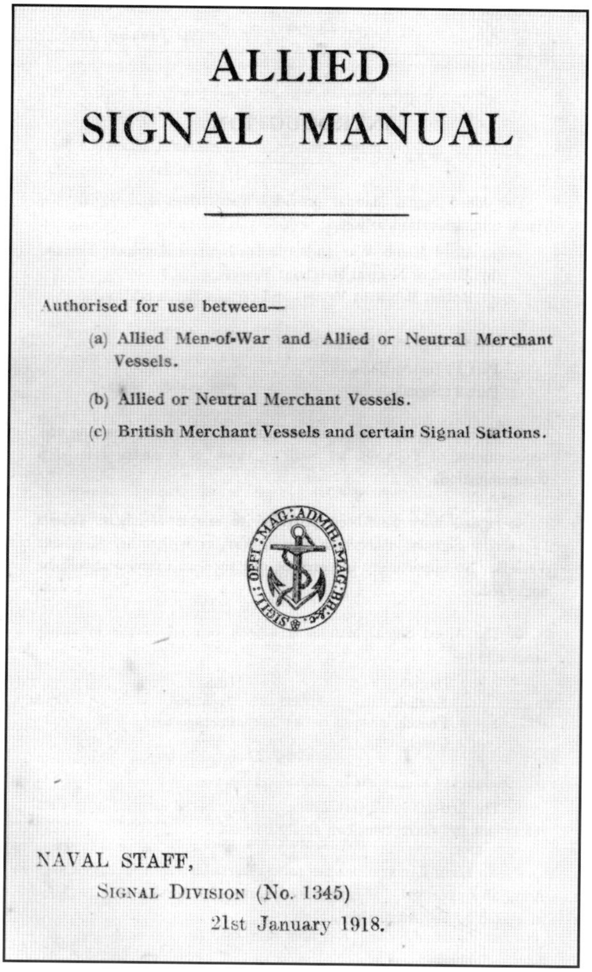

ALLIED SIGNAL MANUAL

Authorised for use between—

(a) Allied Men-of-War and Allied or Neutral Merchant Vessels.

(b) Allied or Neutral Merchant Vessels.

(c) British Merchant Vessels and certain Signal Stations.

NAVAL STAFF,
SIGNAL DIVISION (No. 1345)
21st January 1918.

On return, he was re-united with Captain John O'Hara on the coaster *WESTFORD*, signing off on November 2, before going back on the *VOLGA* for one of the most uncomfortable experiences of his seafaring - the pain in Panama. Following the First World War, Alex O'Hara was recommended, in 1919, for British War and Mercantile Marine War Medals, although these were not processed until October 1925.

By early August 1920, he was off again, this time on the ill-fated *ANSGIR*, completing one overseas trip, out of Leith and back to Dartmouth, and fortunate to survive the sea wreck in December. After the Penzance drama, he did not return to the seas until May 23, 1921, leaving Portsmouth on the 5,585 gross ton tanker, *WAR HINDOO* for foreign admiralty work, and returning to dock at Glasgow on July 3, 1921. This was the same boat old John Leavey of Southampton and Cushendun worked on, after it was launched in September 1919. The ship was scrapped in May 1958.

O'Hara continued to make foreign passage on the *WAR HINDOO,* until April 1923. He switched ships, joining the *BRITISH LIGHT* out of Glasgow on Admiralty foreign passage, and signing off at Plymouth on the 20th of March 1923. Then it was coastal work on the *BARON AILSA 11* out of Glasgow, Grangemouth, and Ganton, until October 30, 1923. On February 20, 1941, and now known as *JEANNIE 11*, she was shelled and sunk by German guns.

He moved back to deep-sea work, on board the *ATALANTA*, out of Glasgow in April 1924, and back on June 18, 1924. He joined the *VOREDA* as bo'sun for trans-Atlantic voyages from Leith to Galveston, Texas. After this, it was coastal work on the *DUNMORE HEAD* out of Belfast, from February 17, 1925 to November 3, 1925.

Overseas work for numerous trips as bo'sun on the Gow-Harrison's Greenock-built 5,528 tons VESTALIA resumed from September 8, 1926 to the United States and also down to Brazil. This lasted until May 14, 1927. This ship was lost in the Second World War, sunk during a German air raid at Suda Bay.

At the close of the 1920's he gave up seafaring, and switched full attention to farming, and married schoolteacher Minnie McGavock His son Daniel recalled occasional sea chat in the home: "In later life, he still remembered how to signal in Morse Code, and used to recite about taking precautions on the seas, to avoid collision (Article 18)- 'Green to green, Red to red, Hard to starboard, Straight ahead.'"

Alex O'Hara never lost his love of the waves, and enjoyed many hours chin-wagging over those faraway places of strange sounding names with neighbouring farmer and ex-seaman George McElheron, who also returned from the ships to work a small farm at Straid, Cushendun..

Ian McElheron said: "My father George went to sea for a while. I don't think he sailed with his friend Alex O'Hara, who was a long time at sea. My father was an Ordinary Seaman, and one of his journeys was on board the *LONDON IMPORTER*, a ship that belonged to a firm called Furness Withy.

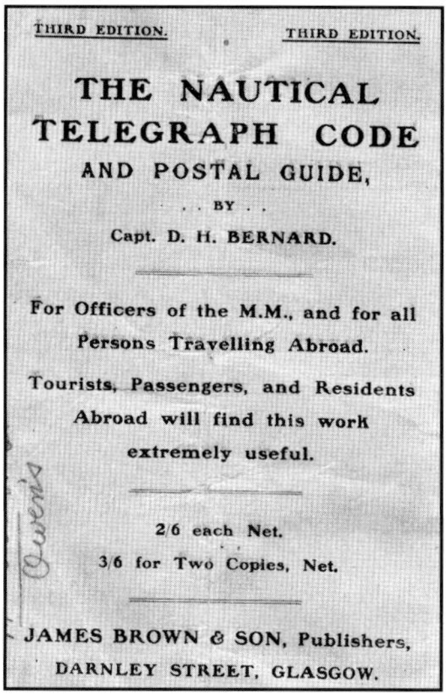

THIRD EDITION. THIRD EDITION.

THE NAUTICAL TELEGRAPH CODE AND POSTAL GUIDE,

. . BY . .

Capt. D. H. BERNARD.

For Officers of the M.M., and for all Persons Travelling Abroad.

Tourists, Passengers, and Residents Abroad will find this work extremely useful.

2/6 each Net.

3/6 for Two Copies, Net.

JAMES BROWN & SON, Publishers, DARNLEY STREET, GLASGOW.

"The ship sailed through the Panama Canal with general cargo, and made stops up the west coast of north America and Canada, at Seattle and Vancouver. The ship then took general cargo back to Europe. I think this was around the late 1920's. I remember him saying the crew members were told to be on alert at all times going through the Caribbean waters, especially when you saw small boats with fishermen on board, maybe shark fishing.

"There was always a fear of pirates getting on board, and the crew members had to keep watch over the sides of the ship, to make sure nobody was trying to slip on board. He also said the ship never stopped when moving straight at the wee boats. Up ahead might be an innocent-looking fishing vessel, but with pirates hoping to get close enough to throw grappling irons onto the ship, and board her. She just sailed on. It was up to the wee boats to move out of the way.

"I think that ship was a 12,000 tonner, and all members of the crew had to stand along the rails when sailing through parts of the Caribbean and the Gulf of Mexico. Apparently, the order then was that no ship must stop in those waters, not be lulled into thinking it was a genuine distress call."

Long before George McElheron took to the deep waters, piracy on the high seas was supposed to be over and done with. Not so. Indeed, it is a plague very much alive in the 21st century, mainly in the Indian Ocean, The original piracy plundering area was known as the 'Spanish Main'. It corralled all the Caribbean islands, the northern coastline of South America, the Gulf of Mexico, the Isthmus of Panama, along the west Texas coastline, to also most of what is today the US State of Florida, and the natural pirate sanctuary of the Florida Keys.

The antics of pirates in the 'Spanish Main' helped to inspire writers such as the wonderful imagination of Edinburgh-born novelist Robert Louis Stevenson, and his most colourful production - *'Treasure Island'*, featuring such fascinating and sometimes frightening figures in the tall tale as the one-legged seaman with the obligatory chittering parrot on his shoulder - Long John Silver - Blind Pew, Ben Gunn, and young Jim Hawkins.

The swashbuckling buccaneers took off from England in search of buried treasure on a tropical island in the Spanish Main, on board the fictional schooner *HISPANIOLA*. During schoolboy times I was carried away by this novel, with its the perceived romance of the pirate's paradise.

Flights of fancy had me sifting through bucket loads of silver pieces of eight and gold treasure. That seemingly glamorous world of adventure and danger came in a splendid technicolour film, *THE SPANISH MAIN*, with a cast that included Maureen O'Hara.

Sorry if I became carried away, indulging in recalling one of the first books I ever read, to be followed by master wordsmith Stevenson's *KIDNAPPED*. To later witness both spellbinding yarns become 'reality' on the silver screen remain with me forever. However, I'm sure George McElheron and the many sailors from the Glens were far removed in mind and spirit from fantasy land when ordered to beware of pirates.

By the by, the *LONDON IMPORTER* was built in 1923 by the Furness Company. The large cargo ship was sold in 1949 to the East & West Steamship Company in Pakistan. and renamed *FIRDAUSA*. It was owned by the Cowasjee, who changed the ship's name in 1957 to *MINOCHER COWASJEE*. In April 1963, the ship was broken up in Karachi.

Before going to experience sea spray in his face, George McElheron worked in Glasgow for O'Hara's uncle, John Brogan. His son Ian explained: "The Brogan's then were ships' chandlers, and he helped to deliver supplies from their premises to the ships docked on the River Clyde. This led to making a decision to go to sea. I think it was through the Brogan family he got a job at sea, and then worked on the *LONDON IMPORTER*.

"He liked that run, but was not a professional seaman like his friend Alex O'Hara. I remember Alex (O'Hara) when he farmed beside us, after he quit the sea. On a daily basis he would be up at Straid, and talking on the wee bridge with my father and Willie John McGarry, who smoked tobacco from a very big pipe. Life held a slow and easy-going pace in those days. They did a lot of talking. People had time, and took time to talk.

"My father married Kate Murray in 1930, and stayed at home. Kate's sister was Mary Ann Murray. Minnie O'Hara's grandfather, Hugh McGavock was married to a McAlister of Carnahaugh, a 'Dear'. My grandmother's mother was a 'Dear'- a McAlister of Carnahaugh.".

Another regular then making memory trips with Alex O'Hara, was James 'Bach' McMullan of Knocknacarry. One of the inimitable personalities of the Glens, McMullan once recalled accidentally meeting O'Hara after docking at Rouen, a city in north east France situated at the mouth of the River Seine. Rouen boasts the magnificent Notre Dame Cathedral, although almost 50 per cent of the city was destroyed in June 1940 by German artillery.

'Bach', who was in the French port during the 1920's, quirkily referred the local police as 'jondy-arms'. He made voyages to South America, once sailing up the River Plate. He docked in New York, and recalled; "When I went for a break from the ship, I walked up one of the most dangerous streets in New York, and didn't know it. It was an area known as Hell's Kitchen. Afterwards, I was told the street I wandered into was where Senegal's World Light-heavyweight champion boxer Battling Siki was murdered."

'Bach's' father, of the same name, was a sea captain born in Glenariffe, but killed off the Scottish coastline during the First World War. "My grandfather, Jim McMullan went from the Terraces, at The Bay, Glenariffe, to Scotland, and joined a boat when only 16. He also worked in Scotland for a while," said Rosemary McKay of Knocknacarry.

"Later, he married Rose McKay from Ballylaughan, Torr. They lived in Glasgow. Uncle Jim was born in Scotland. My mother Mary, who was a couple of years older than uncle Jim, was born there too, and baptised in St Mary's Church, Glasgow.

"My mother, who died on January 20, 1979, married Jack (John) McKay, who died on May 14, 1968, His brothers were Sandy, who lived at Tully, Cushendall, and Charlie of Gortacreggen, father of seaman Charlie McKay. There were three in the McMullan family. A sister Margaret died of meningitis at seven years of age in Scotland, and is buried in Glenariffe. My sister Peggy is called for her.

"Sadly, my granda McMullan was drowned at sea. His remains were brought back to Glenariffe. Apparently, he lost his footing when going aboard his vessel, slipped, and fell between the boat and the dockside. He is listed in our headstone at Craigagh, but is buried in The Bay Cemetery.

"The McMullan family returned from Scotland. Alex 'Stoots' McKay's father, John McKay, who came back from Australia, and his sister, my granny McMullan, bought what is now Scally's farm. John McKay then married Annie McKillop, and consequently my grandma couldn't keep it, the farm, on her own. I believe a Polly Hamilton bought the property.

"My grandmother came to Knocknacarry, after buying the house and farm from the Stewart's. (In the 1881 census Daniel Stewart of Knocknacarry is listed as 'farmer'. His wife's name is Anne). Keenan's of Glendun provide the connection, making the Stewarts relatives of the McMullan's. James Stewart, whose brother owned the farm next door - later to be Brogan's farm - married a Rose McBride of Glenshesk.

"He was a sea Captain, before moving to Killyleagh, County Down, where he bought a pub, and subsequently got married. Their sons are Fr John Stewart and schoolteacher James, both relatives of mine. When they had the farm at Knocknacarry, a Cushendun Parish curate, Fr Small, stayed in the house."

Also in the marine chat mix of the Tilley Lamp era was the local postman, James 'Fisty' McAlister. It was a cruel nickname given to a man with one arm. Ian McElheron said: "I recall my father telling me how Fisty lost an arm, in an accident at sea, and doing what he was told. He was working in the engine room of a ship when the engineer dropped a wrench into a tank filled with oil, to keep the pistons working freely.

"Fisty was instructed to retrieve the wrench, put his arm into the drum. At the same moment the piston came down and smashed the arm. Steam would filter into the piston, and when the pressure was right it would suddenly begin to work. It was unfortunate for Fisty." McAlister is listed in the 1901 Census as related to the MacCormick/McLernon family in Knocknacarry. Born in 1877, he later married Annie Goyer, who was connected to the Loveday Cochrane family, according to John Mitchell of Glenariffe.

Mitchell said: "Fisty's widow, Annie was taken from the cottages at Knocknacarry to our house at Foriff, because she was unable to look after herself. My mother (Mary McLernon) looked after her, and said Annie was a Goyer from Cushendun, and late in life suffered blindness in both eyes. She died with us, and was buried at Cregagh."

29 TERRIBLE WASTE

SECRETS of the deep remain just that, in most cases. The wonder of what happened to the tons of nuclear waste allegedly dumped into the oceans continues to create controversy. Whatever the outcome of such reported toxic waste disposal generally remains a mystery. Many Irish seaman dutifully obeyed instructions to roll unidentified barrels over the side of a ship, and watch them slip silently under the waves on a journey to the seabed.

Ian Mort of Cushendall remembered being involved in such an assignment. "Once I sailed to South America, and on the deck of the ship we had a cargo of barrels, securely tied down. I had no idea, until afterwards, what was going on, what was inside the barrels. The other crew members were like me, kept in the dark, not told what it was all about.

"When we were well out into the Atlantic, and the ship reached a certain point, we were told to dump the barrels over the side, and into the ocean. We tipped the barrels over, as instructed, There were hundreds of barrels, apparently full of nuclear waste stuff. Some of the barrels had a steel band around them. Some barrels were covered in lead, and were very heavy."

To this day, it seems there is no infallible solution to the problem of making radioactive waste disappear. From the time when it was discovered nuclear waste was being dumped in the oceans there has been a constant furore, and a steady search to find and build secure undersoil storage sites.

Wikipedia reveals the ocean disposal of radioactive waste involved 15 countries worldwide, and indulging in this unhealthy exercise from as far back as 1946, and then through to 1993. Nuclear/radio-active waste material included liquids and solids housed in various containers, as well as reactor vessels, with and without spent or damaged nuclear fuel.

Since 1993, ocean disposal has been banned by international treaties. It was believed some dumping only diluted the waste with surface water or containers that imploded at depth. Even containers that survived the pressure physically decay over time. From 1948 to 1982, it would seem the UK had 15 sites in the North East Atlantic, and 18 dumping sites off the coastal line of the British Isles. Low-level waste was solidified with cement or bitumen, and packaged in metal containers.

Born in 1944, Ian Mort added: "Obviously, ours was not the only ship dumping barrels in the Atlantic. I was on the *ROMNEY* then. On the side of the ship a door opened, and it wasn't hard to move the barrels out through it, and into the sea. We were never told, officially, what was packed inside the barrels, nor given protective clothing, no gloves. We could only go on what was said, before and after the journey.

"At that time, I cannot think of anything else other than nuclear waste we were dumping. Why sail so far out into the middle of the north Atlantic? Those barrels were heavy. They were 45-gallon size, and made of steel. I believe this dumping was happening quite a lot with deck cargo on the Atlantic run. That was in the 1960's. I was also led to believe a lot of munitions, and stuff like that, were dumped in the North Channel."

The barrel-tipping mission completed, Mort's ship sailed south to Buenos Aires and up the River Plate to Rosario. "This was quite a place," he said, "Rosario's pubs reminded me of the old Wild West. There were hitchin' rails for horses outside the batwing doors, sawdust on the floor, and young gauchos on horseback galloping up and down the street.

"When we arrived there our ship just pulled in and tied up to a side of the port that was a big high clay bank in the river. We loaded a lot of wet cattle leather hides, and on the way back to Liverpool we called in at the Canary Islands, where we took potatoes on board. That trip finished around the end of January, so potatoes were needed here at that time of year.

"I was also on a run to Cape Town, and one to the Persian Gulf for a cargo of oil. We never got to see much while we were loading the oil, because we were tied up at a very long jetty, and that was it - that was all we saw of that country. It was turn around, and straight back to the UK. After that run to the Persian Gulf I went back to coasting."

One of two sons of skipper John Mort (his brother Hugh did not go to sea), Ian's ten-year adventure started on his father's boat. "I joined him on the *PASS of GLENOGLE* when I was 18. I stayed coasting with him for one year, and decided it was time to try deep-sea work. I went to the Pool in Belfast, and managed to get overseas work. I sailed out of there, but never on a Head Line boat.

"Captain John brought an awful lot of people from the Glens to sea. When I was with him, the crew included John Eddie McAlister and his brother Paddy. Before my father went to sea, he worked as a young lad in 'Arthur's' shop on Shore Street, Cushendall, going out in the van with Mannix McAlister. He left there, and at 18 years of age went to sea - working on coasters belonging to Robertson's of Glasgow.

"He stayed with Robertson's for a while. He worked for the Bulk Oil Steamship Company, which was later named-changed to that of Corry's of London. The boat funnels were painted white, purple, and white. I recall when I was very young, probably around three-years-of-age, when my father practised for examinations. He was working on improving his Morse Code, by doing it at night - flashing a light on and off to get a reflection off a window in our house.

"I think he did all his ticket examinations in Glasgow. During the Second World War, he was on a Robertson boat that took people off the beach at Dunkirk. It was when he became captain of the *PASS of GLENOGLE*, he brought a lot of local people to sea.

"A number of the captains from the Glens did great work for an area that had no employment. There was no work. You had Captain Charlie McQuillan from Glenravel, Captain Dan Black from Garron Point, Captain James Kelly from Carnlough, to name but a few.

"My father took my cousins, the three McElheron brothers from Cobh, Cork, to sea. When Johnny, Alex, and Denis were youngsters, down at Cobh, Captain John, now and again in the summer time, would call in, and then take them for a sail on his boat - when he sometimes docked in Cork.

"When they became older, he took them to work. He sent them a telegram from Cushendall offering them work at sea. Annie, a sister of my granny, married Alex McElheron. They had three boys and two girls. at Cobh. My uncle, James Mort also sailed with my da. Sadly, Captain John took the 'Big C' when he quit sailing in 1972. Coming into retirement he took ill. He did not have a long retirement, and died in 1973, when 61.

"When I quit the sea, I came home to work with John Healy on a Ministry piling-drilling, job, doing Site Investigation all over the place. I also had a fishing boat, and went trawling every Friday evening and Saturday. I took the fish to Ballintoy Harbour, and sold them there."

Ian also developed a strong interest in Connemara ponies and Irish draught horses, and once proudly claimed the rosette for this class at the Gymkhana in Willie Blaney's Holme field at the Crossroads, Cushendall. "The judge was the late Patsy McGarry of Straid, Cushendun, and Ballycastle, whose father Willie John once bought the last Cushendall pony - the only one I ever saw. He bought it from Barney McKeegan at Lisbane. It is a breed of pony that has died out.

"That pure 'Cushendall Pony' I believe that was the last seen in these parts. I bought the Connemara pony, with foal at foot, from Alex Boyle of Loughguile. I also went to Clifden, Connemara, to buy ponies. I bred them in a field at Cairns, and also up Glenaan."

Back to Mort sea memories. Captain John's crew once included two of his wife Sadie's nephews, Danny and Alex McAteer from Tully. However, their careers were short-lived. I believe Danny lasted a month on board, and then younger brother Alex followed, determined to give it a go. He tried his luck, stayed three weeks on the *PASS of GLENOGLE*, and returned forever to dry land!

Spare a thought for Alex, who became a first-rate motor mechanic. Many young men from the Glens will resonate with his experience. Numerous sailors, keen to try the life at sea, had to endure the retching that came from energy-draining bouts of the dreaded sea sickness. Alex was such a person, floored by the terrible tummy torment.

"Many seaman persevered, and eventually overcame the problem, and never had it again. Once I set for home I started to rue not sticking with it for a few more weeks, and overcoming the sickness," recalled Alex, "I don't think Captain John was too pleased when I quit. After all, I pestered him to get a job. My uncle by marriage, Captain John Mort was married to Sadie McAlister, a sister of my mother, Mary, and when I left school I kept at him, to bring me to sea.

"I had him tormented. I wanted to be a seaman. Some time before all that, our Danny went with him, but stayed only around a month. In the meantime, I started work as an apprentice motor mechanic with Pat Fyfe, in his garage, which was then beside what was the old Cushendall Hotel, Patrick's. I was about 15 at the time. Then this telegram arrived from Captain Mort telling me to report to his boat at Sunderland. I decided to go, take up the offer. It was around 1955.

Born in December 1939, Alex had never been further afield than one trip to Ballymena. "I don't believe I was ever at Larne, until I took the bus to there, in order to get the boat to Stranraer. All I had with me was this big case with only a few duds in it. I was on my own. It was quite an experience for such a young cub. It was onto the train for Newcastle-Upon-Tyne, where I would change to another train down to Sunderland..

"On the train to Newcastle, I met two men who were wearing hard hats and carrying wee cases. They had sandwiches in their cases, and shared them with me. They asked me where I was going. They told me they owned factories in Newcastle, and had been to Belfast on business. They thought I was a bit young to be going to sea. They gave me a business card to call, should I not like being at sea, and they could set me up with a job

"The two men also helped me find the railway station platform for the train bound for Sunderland. They told me I'd find an all-night cafe at that early hour of the morning. On that platform, walking in a different direction, was this man with a big hat. I realised it was a Waterfoot seaman, Pa Leech, who seemed to be heading to join his boat.

"When I got to Sunderland, I had to walk down this long cobble-stoned street from the train station, and across a swinging bridge to the boat. I was welcomed aboard the *PASS of GLENOGLE* by Captain Mort, but from then on I suffered very severely from sea sickness. After a fortnight, and sick all the time, Captain Mort put me on the wheel.

"Strangely enough, when working the wheel I did not feel sick. I recall once we were in very stormy conditions, huge waves. You'd think Lurig Mountain was coming at you, and washing all over the boat. I was at the wheel, with the boat plunging down and up, yet never rolling I was not seasick then. I think the concentration needed while working on the wheel helped, but when not on the wheel I was again very sick.

"And when in the bunk I couldn't sleep. I felt I was going to die. I tried to keep down some toast. Still, the problem remained, and when I heard the boat was heading for Carrickfergus, I told Captain Mort I was quitting, He was not happy I was giving up the job. Later on, I regretted I didn't stay on the *GLENOGLE*. I was told once you overcome sea-sickness it never returns. Other sailors never suffer from the problem.

"Heading home on a bus down the shore, after leaving the boat, I remember beginning to rue the decision. The money then was very good. Off the bus, and walking home from Cushendall village, I passed Pat Fyfe's garage. He saw me, asked where had I disappeared to, and then offered to take me back to the garage - which is where I went."

Alex's granduncle, Johnny McAteer of Glenaan was an engineer on on sailing ships. "My granny was a McAteer from Glenaan, originally the Derry crowd, and not the same as my father's McAteer family. My granduncle Johnny lived to be 103, and was one of the first folk from around here to have a motor-car. Old Johnny had a farm up Glenaan, and also once owned a farm near Dunurgan, at Drumnacur, Cushendun. That farm was later bought by the Martin family, and then by Hugh McKay of The Turn, and his son Barney, who lives there now."

Gerry McAteer, who appeared to have a clandestine connection with the American CIA, was a nephew of the old Johnny McAteer, and born at Falmacrilly, Glenaan. "He was a captain of American tugboats," said Ian Mort, "He was captured by Fidel Castro's soldiers during the Bay of Pigs battle in Cuba, was imprisoned for a year, and severely tortured. He had many bones broken in his body. Gerry was related to my late mother Sadie, who made representation to the Irish Embassy to try and have him released in Cuba. Gerry came back to live in England, where he died.

"There is a grey area as far as Gerry's involvement in the Bay of Pigs skirmish was concerned. As far as we were told, he was working for the C.I.A. He may have been in charge of an American boat during the incident in Cuba. My granda, Hugh McAlister was a chief engineer at sea. His wife was a McAteer. He left the sea, and became a foreman in a shipbuilding yard on the Clyde."

Alex McAteer added: "Gerry McAteer's father was another Hugh McAteer, a brother of Johnny, who went to America. The story goes he worked way out into the wilds. The last time he was seen was when bringing in a load of furs to a trading station, and leaving with a lot of money to go back into the hills. He was never seen again. That is what I was told. I think Gerry tried to find out what happened to his father."

30

CLOSE CALLS

HAPPY CHRISTMAS melodies tend to stir nostalgic recall, but not for Cushendall-born Pat Close. And no wonder. On two occasions during his sea career the pencil-slim Close spent Yuletide in hospital beds on the Continent of America. He was fortunate to survive the incidents.

He had to undergo an emergency appendectomy in a Buenos Aires hospital in December 1960, and a year later was floored by a near-crippling ankle injury, and treated in a New York hospital. "For the first time to be hospitalized, I was AB on a Shell tanker, the *HALIA*. It was late December 1960. We were taking a cargo of oil from Curacao down to Brazil, but I became very unwell. I had this grumbling appendix bothering me for quite a while. Suddenly it erupted.

"We were near Buenos Aires. I managed to hold on, until we docked, and the skipper had me rushed to hospital for surgery. The *HALIA* discharged, and left for Cape Town and Durban. I was detained a week in hospital, and just out before Christmas Day. I then had to stay in the Seamen's Mission until a ship became available.

"Shell had a big office in Buenos Aires, and their representative looked after my welfare very well while I was marooned, waiting for a ship. He came from a big Irish contingent there, and kindly took me to his mother's home for Christmas dinner. The lady of the house told me she had relatives who were on the board of the once famous Belfast tobacconist shop of Leahy, Kelly, and Leahy that was situated near Corn Market

"All those folk in Buenos Aires were very good to me, including the late Fr Owen O'Kane of Carnlough. I first met him when he was running the Seamen's Mission. Also down there was a Fr O'Leary from New York, who had Irish family connections. Fr O'Kane arranged with some of the Irish community there to invite me to their homes during that Christmas period. Before he came to South America, Fr O'Kane was once held in cramped conditions in a China prison for 18 months.

"He was a big man. He stood 6' 3", yet the prison cell height was less than 5' 10"! That was an awful experience for him. Later on, he came home to Carnlough. The last time I saw him was when my wife Veronica and I visited him at Ballymun, in north Dublin. He looked after me well when I was stuck in Buenos Aires, as my way out of there was delayed until early New Year, when I managed to get work on a tramp steamer that had to go to Antwerp, and then to dry-dock at Cardiff."

At the end of that year, Close was in the pain pen yet again, when he sustained nasty ankle damage. It was a career-threatening setback for a young man once rated a very talented sprinter. During the recovery years after the Second World War, when a sense of 'normal' life came back to the Glens, one of the most enjoyable annual community occasions was the Parish Summer Sports Day, with the variety of attractions to suit all ages.

Before metres overtook yards in the school books, reliable young fun runners from Cushendall were the Close brothers, Pat and Tom. The latter was the loping long-distance man. Pat was the expert over 100 yards. How sad it was when he suffered horrific injuries to his left ankle. Following an accident on board his boat, while moored in New York harbour, he was again rushed to a hospital.

"Damage to my ankle was very, very severe, and almost finished me completely from working at sea. I was out of the business for ten years," revealed Close, who lives at Carnlough, but never lost touch with what happens in his native Cushendall. His son, Francis is headmaster of Glenaan Primary School.

The man with the distinctive flat peak cap, who went to sea at 17 years of age, had his ankle crushed. "We were taking oil up from Curacao, during December 1961. Weather conditions on the trip to New York were very bad. It was one of the worst journeys I was ever on, and during the passage the lifeboat was wrecked. The storm moved it right over the ship's bridge.

"We had to pick up a new lifeboat in New York, but the smashed one was still jammed on the boat - up on the bridge. We reached New York harbour, where a new lifeboat was waiting for us, but how to get it on board was the puzzle. It was Christmas Day when a number of us tried but failed to shift the wrecked lifeboat. Some of the crew took a break. I stayed with this other fellow, and kept looking at the problem, trying to figure it out.

"I felt if we tried to slacken the cable around the two davits she would move. I got a spike up on the davit, to try and loosen the shackle. I got to the end of it when she suddenly snapped. I had to think quickly. I had to let go. I couldn't hold on, and fell down with the lifeboat - all of 30 feet. I landed on my left ankle, on wood, and took all the weight on it.

"I was rushed to a hospital attached to Yale University, and found out I totally shattered the ball joint in my heel. The doctor told me he never saw anything like the damage, and that the ball joint was smashed into pieces. What a way to celebrate Christmas Day. I was kept for a fortnight in the New York hospital, then flown back by the shipping company to Dublin, where a taxi was laid on to take me to Carnlough. I was just settling down to live in Carnlough, after being married earlier in 1961.

"That accident completely wrecked me. It almost finished me off as far as sea-going was concerned, but not quite. I was crippled for a long time, unable to walk. It took me four years to really get back to walking properly. I was 10 years away from the sea when I went to the Pool in Belfast. In my mind I felt I would be fit to work on the ferries, but first there was a medical examination to be passed. If I could overcome that test then I would go back to sea. A Dr Caldwell represented the Pool, for the medical inspection in Belfast.

"He told me right away he could not allow me to go deep-sea again. The good news was that he would permit me to work on the coast. So, I got back to sea, working AB on the Larne-Stranraer ferry, and for 10 years. Things then changed. Sealink took over. I got out in 1994."

Canny Close first reached water's edge on the way to maritime adventures through a next-door neighbour. "I was taken to sea by Captain Thomas Scollay. He lived beside us at High Street, Cushendall. He was skipper of the *CAIRNGORM* then. It was one of the Robertson's of Glasgow fleet. It was a small ship of 300 tons, and delivered cargo around the coasts here, coal or stone, and the odd cargo of grain. It was often taking cargo of stone from Llandulus, in north Wales, to Norway, up a fjord to Odda, and then back down light to do it all over again.

"We also took coal from Ayr to Dundalk, and coal from the Manchester Canal to Dublin. I was eight months with the *CAIRNGORM*, and came home for a break. Then I got to talking on a Cushendall street with McKay (Alistair), whose ship - skippered by his uncle John Mort - was in dry-dock. I knew Captain John, who also lived next door to us after he was married. I think he came there after Tommy Scollay moved to live on the Barrack Brae, Cushendall. It is not often you can say you had two successive sea captains living next door.

"So, I sailed with Captain Mort for ten months, on the oil tanker - the *PASS of GLENOGLE*. Also on the ship were McKay (Alistair), John Eddie 'Dear' McAlister of Glenariffe, Pat McKeegan from Shore Street, Cushendall, who was the bo'sun, and down below in the engine room was Jim Mort. I believe it was John Eddie starting out at sea. He was a very nice man. In my early days at sea I thought it was brilliant to make a trip as far away as Rotterdam.

"Things then changed for me. I started to sail foreign. I was home for a summer break when I had a chat with Paddy Blaney. I knew his brother Mick well. Paddy was sitting and qualifying for his Foreign Mate's ticket. Up to that stage I had not joined the Pool, and Paddy suggested I should do that right away. I would have a chance to get to work deep-sea. Paddy put me right. He'd been on the Head Line run to Canada.

"I managed to get a job, and joined him on the *FANAD HEAD*, running light across the north Atlantic to St John, New Brunswick, and coming back loaded with a cargo of timber and grain from Canada. We discharged part of the cargo in Liverpool docks, then sailed across to Dublin, and finally up to Belfast to discharge the remainder of the cargo. That journey took about one month."

Born in 1936, he added: "I was on my own a lot, but not worried. I just went to whatever job came up. Then it was back to coasting for a spell, on the *VACUUM PIONEER*, on which the First Mate was Paddy Blaney's brother Jim. He also had his Captain's Ticket at the time.

"I was always on the move, and went back to deep-sea sailing. I was in and out of the Head Line boats, on the Canadian run. Paddy Blaney was third mate then, the other Glensman on the ship.

"On the way back from Canada, Paddy Blaney took me aside to let me know the old lumbering ship had been sold to a Chinese company. I was out of a job once the journey ended. However, I soon found other work, and on a Shell oil tanker, sailing from Liverpool to Curacao."

Glendun, Cushendun yachtsman Barry McCartin

Young skipper Hugh McIlwaine, Waterfoot, working in the Persian Gulf

Captain Patrick McKeegan (Cushendall), Coleraine's Harbour Master

Ballyeamon's Colin McNaughton with sister Kate

Holywood icon Liam Neeson meets Cushendall's Alistair 'Tony Curtis' McKay

Alex McKillop of Gault's Road, Cushendall, displays the painting of the EGLANTINE *and gold topped cane presented to his great, great grandfather, Captain Alexander McKillop.*

Silver service presented to Captain Charles McDonnell

Ship's engineer Gerry Blaney Jnr, (third left) of Cushendall celebrates New Year's Day, 2006, with HASTULA *crew colleagues at Colombia*

Red Bay yachtsman Gareth Rowan and GEORGE *crew colleague Justin Rowe of Melbourne*

Vindy boys remember daring rescue

Emma Dinwiddie

Every other Wednesday the "Vindy boys"- ex-sailors who completed their training aboard the TS Vindicatrix at Sharpness in England - get together for lunch at The Woolston Club to reminisce about their time at sea.

One such tale began in the middle of the night on January 30, 1955, when two sailors aboard the Panamanian S.S. "Liberator" fell down the hatch in rough Atlantic seas and sustained serious injuries.

Cunard's RMS Queen Mary, equipped with two hospitals and several surgeons, answered the SOS and deployed lifeboat crews of volunteers who swung into action and began a daring rescue that would remain a legend for many years to come.

Woolston resident Robert Sullivan was one of those men who, at just 23 years of age, was awarded a medal for his courage and devotion to duty by the Shipwreck and Humane Society.

"I was never scared. All my life I was brought up on small boats," said Bob, now 77.

Originally from Glenarm in Northern Ireland, Bob recalled the treacherous rescue mission in his thick Irish accent and said it was all part of a sailor's duty to look after one another. "If he's a sailor and he needs help, you do it."

"Vindy boy" Bob Sullivan with a replica of the RMS Queen Mary at the Lyttelton Museum. *Photo: Gilbert Wealleans*

The Queen Mary's 1000 passengers lined the rails as their crew safely delivered one sailor and a surgeon onto the Liberator's deck. The injured sailors were then brought over to the Queen Mary for treatment.

On their return Bob said the rescuers were immediately rewarded for their efforts. "The captain called us into his cabin and said whatever we wanted from the Queen Mary we could have it."

In true sailor fashion he asked for a glass of "Nelson's blood" (seaman speak for rum) and waited for the rest of his mates to get back.

If you're a Vindy boy who has lost touch with your fellow sailors, get in contact with Terry Knight on 03 384 2057 or Dave Spice on 03 383 7152.

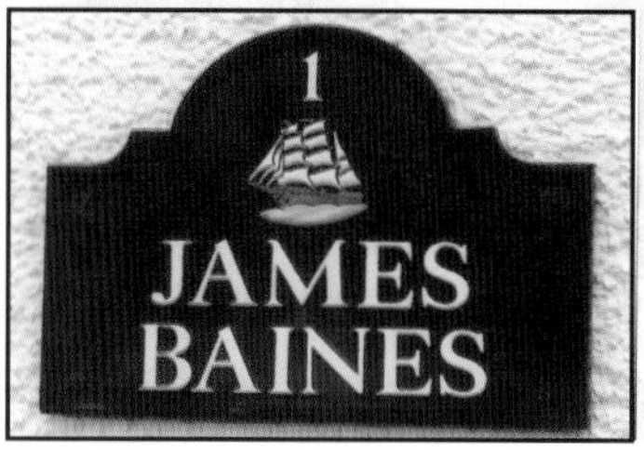

Tribute tablet to the JAMES BAINES *on Hugh McIlwaine's bungalow*

A New Zealand newspaper issue of April 2009 recalls the 1956 sea rescue heroics of Glenarm-born Bobby Sullivan

Teenage yachtsman Barry McCartin with his Cushendun parents, Catriona and Gerry, after winning Moyle Council's 'Sportsperson of the Year.

Golf fun at Cairndhu - Captain Brian McEvoy (left), Eugene McMullan, and Davy Magill, eldest son of former Irish Cruiserweight and Heavyweight boxing champion, Dave Magill of Cairncastle

John O'Hara, Tromra, Cushendun, the Chief Pipe-Laying Officer on the DEEP BLUE

Cushendall seaman Alistair McKay with his cousin Hugh Mort

Florida-born Jim McLaughlin of Cushendun

Chief Engineer Charlie McAuley, Cushendall

November 7, 1972. Wedding Day portrait of Captain Alex Blaney, Cushendall, and Ballycastle schoolteacher Margaret Black

Ballycastle-born ferryboat bo'sun John O'Neill

Glenarm Harbour

The Mariner's Bar, Waterfoot, a haven where you can list to starboard.

Gerry Blaney,
Chief Engineer, Cushendall

Cushendall's Jim McKay skippered the chemical cargo vessel,
PASS of DRUMCHTER *(2).*

Legendary Glenariffe mariner,
Captain Charles McDonnell

New Zealand-based Glenarm seamen, Brain McEvoy Jnr, and (right) Tom McMullan

Cunard's QUEEN MARY

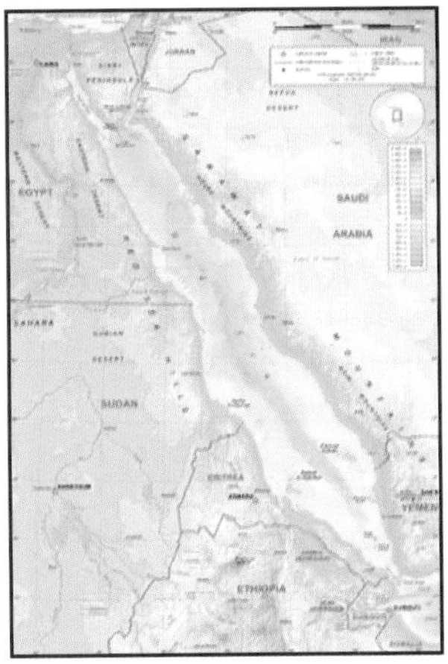

Suez Canal-Red Sea

Glendun-born Mary McAuley (nee McNeill), is surrounded by family circle during the 'Fuldue' Seat launch at Cushendun

Cushendall-born Ballycastle-based John Higgins

Captain Joe Mitchell, Glenariffe, and wife Mary

Willie Blaney of Gault's Road, Cushendall, with painting of LOCH MAREE

Paddy McCormick of Dunurgan, Cushendun, displays the Maurice Wilks portrait of his uncle Paddy 'Tom' McCormick

Painting of the JAMES BAINES *sailing ship presented to Captain Charles McDonnell*

Captain Joe Mitchell of Glenariffe working in Aruba

Cushendun-born Alistair Scally, became a New Zealander

Glenariffe Captain James Mitchell, detained in a German World War One prison camp

Captain Kieran McNeill, Cushendun

Iconic Cushendall Captain Gerry Blaney displays a painting of his grandfather's sailing ship - LOCH TORRIDON

Painting of the BALLYGARVEY

Captain Jim McKay,
Cushendall

The Isle of Man-based STORINGTON, *one of Paddy McNeill's assignments*

The sea history of Red Bay,
Waterfoot.

Old Custom House, Cushendun

Carnlough-born Patsy Black (left), who sailed with Captain James Kelly, is seen with Cushendall wife wife Ann (right), and brother-in-law Cathal McCann and his wife Mary

The jumbo tanker P&O NEDLLOYD SOUTHAMPTON *was Cushendall Chief Engineer Charlie McAuley's last assignment.*

Carnlough's Harbour history...

Caribbean luxury liner OCEAN MONARCH.

Cushendun's young yachtsman Barry McCartin in action.

The BALLYGRAINEY.

Cushendall skipper Paddy Blaney

31 OIL SLICKS

PERSIAN GULF oil games of the unexpected once caused some anxiety and soul-searching for Glenariffe's Hugh McIlwaine. During a time of enforced misdemeanours, he confessed he walked a tightrope in the Gulf, where he literally had to go with the flow in what was an open-secret scam.

The man known as the 'Wee Mariner' was Master of the *AL SHAHEEM,* a tanker that made regular deliveries of clean oil from the Abadan refinery, near the coast of the Persian Gulf, to Muscat, the capital city of Oman, a port on the Arabian Sea. "I had an all-Iranian crew," recalled McIlwaine, "I did not know there was a scam going on with the oil deliveries until I joined. It was then I had to play the game, or else I could find trouble with my crew.

"After we loaded at Abadan, and headed down the Gulf, the clandestine oil arrangement started. On the port head side on the way out of the Gulf there are two small islands, and it was here we dropped anchor. As soon as that happened, up to half-a-dozen dhows came out, and the owners bought oil off our ship.

"We had a special wee pump to put the fuel into their tanks or drums.
" "On the *AL SHAHEEM,* I recall one member of the crew who would have nothing to do with the scam. He was the chief engineer, and a strict Muslim. A very nice man he was, but he wanted no part of it. He wouldn't take any of the money. But he didn't mind us doing it.

"It was the done thing, and was happening long before I joined the ship, as Captain. I suppose you could say I was half a pirate for a while. The skipper I relieved on the *Al SHAHEEM* was an Englishman. He showed me all the ropes, and told me I had to do it. I could not get out of doing it. I was strongly advised I had to go along with the system, otherwise the crew members would mutiny.

"As far as I know, I believe all Iranian ships there were operating the same system. I was told one ship had an Arab master, and it was reckoned he became one of the richest men in Bahrain. Every ship in the fleet did the wee bit of private oil trading. It happened all the time, and on every trip. The ship's mate, organising watch-keeping officer, did all the business. There was also oil left over in the ship at Muscat. All I had to do was put the ship into port, into the meeting places on the way back up the Gulf.

"We sold the oil, after setting anchor in a lovely bay on the other side of the Persian Gulf - this time on the way in. As soon as we dropped anchor, out came the dhows. I remember one serious incident, and when I was asleep in the middle of the night as this transfer of oil to the dhows was taking place. The crew members were working away when one of the dhows went on fire. Fortunately, the crew managed to douse the fire, otherwise the whole lot would have gone up in smoke - including the *AL SHAHEEM*.

"I worked on that ship for six months, and then went to the company's sister ship, as master of the larger, *PACIFIC MARINER*, which was 2,500 tons. I was making the same trips up and down the Persian Gulf for a further six months, and the same business with the sale of oil on the side continued. When the deals were done with the owners of the dhows we went to the money-changers in Bahrain. Mind you, I was in fear of my life something would go wrong.

"In our home port of Bahrain, as soon as you docked some members of the crew walked ashore carrying big bags on their shoulders. This intrigued me at first, so I asked one of the crew what was going on, and what was he carrying in the bag. It was another smuggling enterprise. The bags held contraband cigarettes. I was also informed they often sold their cigarettes to customs officials, and doubled their money. The Shah of Persia was in power then." Because of the mammoth wealth so suddenly created by the gushing of oil wells the inhabitants of Bahrain did not have to pay taxes.

Another McIlwaine adventure had him close to real money, mouth-watering bars of gold bullion. He said: "I made this one trip on the mail ship, the *EDINBURGH CASTLE*, which traded down to South Africa and back to Southampton. I joined her on the 28th of August 1963. We had a bit of cargo and some passengers, and called at East London, Port Elizabeth, Durban, Cape Town. On the trip we also made calls at Madeira, Las Palmas, Ascension Island, and St Helena.

"We came back to England with the gold bars stored in a special hold, and sealed in the ship. All we did was open the hatch for the people who loaded and unloaded the gold bullion. I would guess there were 50 tons of gold bars on her. We loaded at Cape Town, and docked at Southampton, where there were also lots of security people to take the gold bullion off the ship.

"I imagine the gold was then taken to London. The security was very strict at both ends of the journey. The officers of the *EDINBURGH CASTLE*, which was run like a naval craft, had to wear uniform at all times. No one on the ship was allowed near the movement of the gold. It was all done by specialist people.

"I believe on one occasion, from one of those Union Castle ships, a Belfast man managed to nick a gold bar or two, but was later caught. I can understand the temptation to try and pinch a gold bar. I could see the gold going on board, and a gold bar reminded me of the size of a pan loaf. What would that be worth!

"I had no responsibility on that ship. I was an EDH (Efficient Deck Hand). I can claim I was once very close to a huge amount of money. I could have been another gold-finger. I could see into the hold. All around were massive security men. The peculiar thing about the loading and unloading of the gold cargo was that there wasn't a black man in sight. Not one black man was involved in that work, all white workers belonging to the owners of the gold shipment. On the ship it was black men who cleaned down the wooden deck, using massive brushes.

"The gold was stacked by dockside men. On the way back from South Africa there was further excitement involving other bars, not gold bars - but prison bars. We had to call at the island of St Helena, to pick up three prisoners. Any convicted criminal on St Helena had to go to gaol in the UK. The prisoners were locked in on the ship, and taken off at Southampton to serve their prison time in England. The *EDINBURGH CASTLE* was a beautiful ship, later to have a mast cut down a bit. I remember painting the masts when they were 132 feet high.

"Some Belfast seamen were with me in the crew, but not one would go up the masts, and paint them. I volunteered, and also did the stays, homeward bound, with white lead and tallow. Using a bo'sun's chair, with a rope around a block and tackle, I did the stays with just an old cloth. The bo'sun's mate was below on deck, and he'd lower me down bit by bit.

"Normally, you would have a system to lower yourself down, but not in this case. It was a precarious perch, and obviously a bit of danger involved. Thankfully, I never suffered from a fear of heights, no vertigo. I had to go out and do the yardarms as well, and that wasn't easy. I was given bonus money for doing all that."

The Union-Castle liner fleet consisted of large mail ships and 'intermediate' size vessels offering a 'Round-Africa' service. The *EDINBURGH CASTLE* and the *PRETORIA CASTLE* were the heavyweights. They carried 214 customers in 1st Class and 541 in Tourist. By the mid-1970's the Union-Castle liner runs were losing money. While all of the pre-war liners had been retired, there was a joint effort with the South African Corporation (Safmarine Lines) to continue the service, but there was further decline. In 1975-76, the *EDINBURGH CASTLE* and, what had become the *SA ORANJE* (ex-*PRETORIA CASTLE*), were retired, and sold to breakers in the Far East.

McIlwaine followed his father and uncles to seafaring, starting in 1959 on the *BALLYMONEY* as a 16-year-old deck boy, and quitting to run the family pub in Waterfoot when he was 41 years of age. "Before deciding to go to sea," he said, "I was a student at Garron Tower for a spell, didn't like it, left and returned to St Aloysius Secondary School, Cushendall. I left there to work as an apprentice butcher for Harry McMahon Snr, the father of Harry and Owen. Harry Snr's wife was Roisin O'Kane - a sister of Fergus Kelly's wife in Waterfoot.

"I was out in the butcher's van at 14. The butcher's shop in Waterfoot was sold, and my mother bought it. I was put into it, but didn't like the job. I always had a longing to go to work at sea, probably because there were so many members of my family circle who were seamen, so many McCormick's. I went to the telephone box on Waterfoot street, and put in a call to Kelly's Shipping, looking for a job

"I managed to get employment. My first boat was the *BALLYMONEY,* and joined her at the West Power Station in Belfast. That was on a Monday morning, working on this 1,600-ton steamer that burned oil. We had a cargo of coal trading across the Irish Sea, to and from Garston, to Ayr, and so on. We sailed into Ballylumford Power Station, and also to the West Power Station.

"I worked on the *BALLYMONEY* for six months, and was transferred to the *BALLYGRAINEY,* which was only a 600-ton coal burner. I sailed with a man named Dan McLaughlin, who lived in Glenarm. He also had a wee shop in the village of Glenarm, which was run by his wife. He was a brother of Barney McLaughlin, who came from Tully, Cushendall. Dan was a lamp trimmer on the *BALLYGRAINEY,* one of Kelly's coal boats that travelled to and from ports such as Garston, Blyth, Ayr, and so on. Dan's job was like that of a second mate, and could take charge of a watch.

"By this time I was spitting coal dust. There was no shower facility on this ship. You washed out of a bucket under the forecastle, where we lived. I managed to obtain a transfer to the *BALLYLOUGH,* which was a 1,000-tonner, but again a coal burner. I soon became browned off with breathing in coal dust, but at the same time I studied for the 'ticket' examinations. I sat all my examinations in Belfast, progressing at first from Ordinary Seaman to an EDH - an efficient deck hand.

"After one year on coasters I had the EDH certificate, just a step below Able Bodied seaman - and decided to make a move. I went to the Shipping Federation in Belfast, and they transferred a crowd of us to London. In May 1961, I went to Victoria Docks, London, and got a transfer to a ship named the *GRETAFIELD.* She was 6,000 tons, and left for the US Naval Base at Norfolk, West Virginia. What was our cargo? Coal! This time the coal was not so dusty. It was a cargo for Japan, via the Panama Canal.

"The *GRETAFIELD* had absolutely nothing by way of modern equipment - no automatic steering, no radar, no navigational equipment, whatsoever. She was an old tramp steamer, and very slow. It took us 31 days to travel from Panama to Japan, unloading at Yawata and Tabata. We couldn't get a load in Japan, so we travelled light to Long Beach, California, and loaded a cargo of potash, fertiliser for sugar cane plantations in Australia.

"We sailed to Cairns and Townsville, and it took 26 days to discharge, yet merely 10 hours loading at Long Beach, because we used our own derricks. There were not so many cranes or conveyor belts. Then it was off to Brisbane, for a part cargo of wheat, and topped off our cargo with more grain outside Melbourne, at the grain station there, in the wee port of Boogay.

"We took that cargo to Bombay, now called Mumbai. We went to Goa, India, and the port of Mormagoa, and loaded a cargo of iron ore for Japan, unloading at Yokohama, the second largest city in Japan after Tokyo. It was light ship back to Australia, calling at Newcastle and Port Melba. Here we loaded up with a cargo of steel for the Argentine port of Rosario on the River Plate, which also has Port Asalla.

"From there, we went to Bahia Blanco, and loaded with grain for Shanghai, China. It was light ship down to Australia, loading up again with steel for the same trip all over again - to Argentina. We again loaded with grain at Bahia Blanco, and this time we sailed for Germany, unloading at Emden, near Hamburg.

"I went home after the ship sailed empty to dry-dock at Newcastle-upon-Tyne for a service. I was paid off, after completing one year at sea, non stop, from May 14, 1961 to May 14 1962. With me was a Carnlough seaman, Paddy McMullan. We were a good many days at sea on the first trip before I knew who he was, and that he came from up the Antrim Coast. He was a very quiet fellow.

"Paddy, who was a DHU (Deck Hand Uncertified), shipped out again on anther boat, and I heard later he jumped ship in South America - before arriving home in Carnlough over a year later. Indeed, I almost did the same as Paddy. In Australia, I was tempted to jump ship at Cairns, but changed my mind.

"A lot of seamen jumped ship from time to time. John Rowan of Waterfoot did it. I was home until September 22, 1962, when I joined the 18,000 tons *HYALA*, a Shell tanker, trading mostly to the West Indies, to Curacao, staying for one year before being paid off in 1963."

During the Autumn of that year, at Southampton docks, he bumped into his father, Patrick McIlwaine. "He worked mostly for Kellys, and was an engineer, down below. My father started off seafaring as a fireman, and worked his way up to be second engineer on Kelly coal boats. I remember him telling me he once worked alongside big Paddy O'Boyle from up Glenariffe. My father was not tall, 5'6", while Paddy stood 6'7", and they worked in the engine room of a ship called the *CORTEEN*

"Namesakes of Paddy O'Boyle, the brothers Alex and Joe from near Parkmore were sea-going men, and also farmers. They were cousins of my mother. Unfortunately, Alex was badly burned during an explosion at sea. He was on a ship loaded with coal when somebody lit a match to check in the hold, and she went up. Paddy Murray, who had just passed his Mate's Ticket examination, was on the same ship, and suffered some burns. This was during the 1950's. Paddy Murray never went back to sea after that incident.

"My father became fed up on the coasters, and sailed deep-sea on the famous *CANBERRA*, making up to half-a-dozen trips across the Atlantic. He was a greaser there. I remember meeting him in Southampton, when I arrived there on the cargo mail ship *EDINBURGH CASTLE* from South Africa. He had just arrived on the *CANBERRA*, from the States. It was on October 1, 1963.

"I went down to the *CANBERRA*, to get on board and see my father, but the security guard wouldn't let me board until my father appeared, and sorted it out. I had a good look over her. The *CANBERRA* was a lovely ship, painted green on the side. Later, I had an evening ashore with my father, who went to sea after he was married. He was taken to sea by my uncle Neil McCormick, my mother's brother. Neil was an AB on coasters.

"Neil McCormick also worked for Dorey, and with Joe O'Boyle, who was a cousin of my mother and was with Dorey boats all his sea life. Later Joe bought the Toberwine House and farm, near the Glenariffe Tea-rooms.

Generally, my father went to sea during the winter months, and was at home to work on the small family farm during the summer. He finished at sea in 1978, when he was 60. He was still at sea when we were in the pub at Waterfoot."

The 'Wee Mariner' made quick progress up the ladder. He passed his Mate's Ticket, in 1966. "Odd things happened in those days, as I often sailed with First Mates who did not have a First Mate's ticket, and I sailed with qualified Captains who worked as First Mates, and didn't use their Master's ticket. Once I worked on the *St COLMAN* as Second Mate when I had a First Mate's ticket, yet the seaman acting as First Mate on that boat had no First Mate's ticket. He was an AB, but he was a very experienced seaman, extremely good at his job.

"On January 13, 1969, in Belfast, I passed the examination for my skipper's Certificate. It is a Certificate of Competence for a Home Trading Masters' Ticket. It qualified me to work as a sea captain throughout these isles, and also from the Elbe in Germany to Brest in northern France. You could, however, get endorsements that would permit you to be a skipper further afield - to the Azores, for example."

During his career, he experienced varied adventures, including a time when a fellow Glenariffe native saved his life. "That was a scary incident, and one I'll never forget. I'm lucky to be still around to tell the tale. In 1976, I was skipper of the *WHITONIA,* a small tanker. We had to dock at Oban in the north of Scotland, because of a severe storm.

"With me on the boat was Alistair Leech, an AB. Alistair, who also worked with me on the *ESSO LYNDHART*, is the son of Alex Leech, and his mother - a Murray of Waterfoot. At Oban, we were light ship when caught in the storm. We were on the way from Stornaway to Belfast, to load with oil. I decided to shelter in Oban Harbour for the night. We just couldn't make it to Belfast in those conditions.

"After we docked, Alistair and me went ashore. Because of the high waves, the big rise and fall of the tide, we couldn't set out a gangplank, and a long extension ladder was used. Coming back to the ship, I slipped on the ladder. Alistair grabbed me by the back of my neck, and prevented me from crashing onto the deck. I could have been killed. Alistair Leech definitely saved my life. I have retained my two discharge books, but one was damaged by seawater during that storm, and it also reminds me how close a shave I had,

"Another narrow escape was when shipping oil to the island of Tiree. On that same wee ship, the *WHITONIA*, and when I was master of her, we were trading from Belfast to the Western Isles. I received orders for part cargo to Scarinish, the main village and port of Tiree, where they were taking oil and petrol. Tiree is the most westerly of the islands in the Inner Hebrides.

"It was my first time to go there. I looked up my sailing directions for Scarinish, and headed there. Fortunately it was in daylight. I was going into the port, as I thought, when I saw people on the harbour frantically waving to us to stop. They were making signals for us to circle clear. I immediately stopped her, and put her astern. The tanker I had was too big to go into the harbour. I was in the wrong place, as there was a quiet port just around the corner to facilitate the discharging of oil.

"During another period, I worked out of Nigeria for four years. I sailed on a Nigerian vessel, the *BENIGN CREEK*, that carried a Nigerian flag but was owned by the British Land and Marine Company. It was a big tug, taking oil tankers from off shore to Forcadas, a small port 100 miles east of Lagos. I was the only white man on board, the skipper, and I got on all right with a full Nigerian crew. I was also captain of the *VERCADAS RIVER*."

On a holiday break from working in Nigeria, big-hearted McIlwaine's generosity led to a short overnight stop in a Manchester calaboose. He was minding his own business, relaxing at home when a seaman entered his family pub, the Mariner's Bar, seeking help. The sailor reported a problem aboard his boat. Captain Bertie Rea of Glenarm took ill on the coaster that was delivering a cargo of coal to Red Bay Pier.

McIlwaine said: "It turned out a never-to-be forgotten experience, after I volunteered to help. Bertie Rea was skipper of the *MANTRA*, a coaster out of Garston with a cargo of coal. This was around the early 1970's, during 'The Troubles'. The boat's Mate, who was from County Donegal, came into our bar after the *MANTRA* discharged the cargo at the Bay Pier. He was looking for me. Somehow, he heard I was home from Nigeria.

"He told me Bertie was unwell, and unable to take the *MANTRA* back to Runcorn. The Mate said he would not feel too confident of bringing the ship up the Manchester Canal. He asked me if I would come along and help. Meanwhile, Bertie, a man with a Foreign Master's Ticket, was taken to his home at Glenarm. The Mate wanted me to take charge of the boat. I reluctantly agreed, and his office was informed.

"On the way to the boat I met Martin Leech at Waterfoot bridge, and asked if he'd like a wee boat trip to Manchester. Martin, a fisherman, agreed to come along. The only problem we had on the journey was to hit fog off the south of the Isle of Man, at the Chickens' Lighthouse. We had no radar. Incidentally, I often passed the Lighthouse at the north end of the Isle of Man, known as the Point of Ayre, where the old Caroline Radio Ship used to be anchored.

"Anyhow, we safely reached Runcorn with the *MANTRA*, got her docked, and the owners sent Malachy and me back home via aeroplane from Manchester Airport. Then the problems began, in the Manchester Airport Departure Lounge. Security forces thought we were IRA terrorists from Northern Ireland. They wouldn't listen to reason. Martin and me were arrested, handcuffed to each other, and taken away to be questioned by Special Branch detectives, who came up from London - and also over from Belfast.

"We were held 28 hours in the cells, and without any grub offered to us, before it was all sorted out. What a carry on, in the slammer all that time. My mother and the Leech family members were all very worried - the folks back home praying for our release. As soon as we were released we headed for a nearby Chinese restaurant"

32 CATTLE CROSSING

CAPTAIN PADDY Blaney, of the Cushendall seafaring clan, was glad he had Glenariffe man Malcolm McCollam on board to help solve an unexpected veterinarian-style problem in mid-Atlantic. The ship's cargo included pedigree cattle bound for Canada, when all of a sudden one of the animals in the hold started to give birth.

On the Head Line, Belfast, ship was Able Seaman McCollam, who knew a bit about farm husbandry during his younger days at home, and he solved the calving mini-crisis. It was an episode in his sea-going career Paddy, who died in 1997, loved to relate.

Wife Margaret (nee McKeegan) said: "I recall him telling of that tricky voyage to Canada. The main cargo in the boat was cattle, and I think all pedigree animals. Malcolm McCollam sailed with him for quite a while. I believe Paddy might have known a wee bit about cows and calving, but was certainly relieved Malcolm was with him as one of the crew. I think there was more than one cow ready to produce a calf on that voyage. Paddy also told me that from here to Canada it was also not easy keeping the cattle from moving about too much."

It was no surprise when a teenage Blaney decided to go with the flow, and take up a career at sea. Margaret, who lives near Ossian's Grave, Glenaan, added: "Paddy was born on the 16th of December, 1931. He arrived in the morning, and Malachy Skelton was born in the evening. It was Turkey Market Day in Cushendall. He liked to relate that story of his birth. When Paddy left school at 16, he went to work at the salmon fishing for Maurice Findlay. A year later he went to sea, in 1948, and worked on a Head Line boat out of Belfast."

Another passage, and this time with wife Margaret on board, proved to be extremely demanding and dangerous. She said: "I was with him when sailing from Rotterdam to the Shetland Isles in the north of Scotland, to Sullum Voe. Weather conditions were very bad. I never saw a storm like it. I had been on other trips with Paddy, mostly up to Sweden, but never to North America, which I would have liked.

"It didn't happen, sailing to Canada, because I was at home then, raising a family. However, that run to the Shetlands, on a Texaco oil tanker, I'll never forget. It was not a good one, because the conditions were so awful. We sailed on the *TEXACO GLOUCESTER*. It was the last time I was with Paddy on a boat trip.

"Around the end of March-early April, I flew to Amsterdam, and from there to the boat. I decided not to come back with Paddy, but it took a variety of ways to return home. I could have been to America and back for the length of time it took, before flying to Edinburgh, from Aberdeen, and before that from a very small airport in that north part of Scotland. Eventually, I made it to Belfast. It took around three different flights to get me home."

In the Shetland Isles - an archipelago off the north west coast of mainland Scotland - lies in an inlet the oil terminal of Sullum Voe, It has been there since 1976, when oil and gas was discovered in those seas. It subsequently became one of the largest oil terminals in Europe. Nearby is the small airport of Scatata, 20 miles north of Lerwick, where Loganair flights went to Aberdeen.

Launched in 1959, the *TEXACO GLOUCESTER* was firstly named *FIVE LAKES* and then *REGENT EAGLE.* First owned by the Regent Petroleum Tankership Co Ltd of London, from 1959 to 1969, until registered in London by Texaco Overseas Tankerships. The ship was sold in 1981, to Fuego Shipping of Panama.

"Paddy sailed on oil tankers all over the world, apart from going to Russia. He preferred to work on tankers. Once he was in the Far East working supply trips into Vietnam, during that war there," added Margaret. Her husband did not enjoy a long retirement. He quit the sea at 65 years of age, but suddenly took ill, and died, also at 65, in 1997.

33

AMERICAN DREAMS

THREE brothers from the McMullan family of Cushendall sailed the oceans around the same time, before Jack (John) decided, in 1922, to leave the village, turn his back on the sea, and settle in Greenpoint, New York. He was one of four sons of Dan McMullan of High Street, a noted hurler of his day, and founder member of the Cushendall Club.

The other sons were Jim, Danny and Chris. Nephew and former Antrim and Ulster hurler of note, Chris Barrett, whose mother Josephine was a daughter of Danny, said: “Jack worked deep-sea. He went away with Captain Dan O’Hara of Shore Street, and worked for a number of years at sea. He used to bring home mementoes from the different countries he visited, such as whalebone. I remember a letter opener with an ivory handle, and also a leaf turner with an ivory handle.

“There was the yarn about uncle Jack visiting Naples, and told by his skipper to take a good look. It was the old saying - ‘See Naples and Die’. Jack replied he’d rather see Red Bay, Glenariffe, any day. After some years at sea, Jack jumped ship in New York, and worked there. He lived the rest of his life in America. He was a Long Boatman on barges in New York Harbour. He also played for and skippered an ‘Antrim’ hurling team in New York.

“Jack met up with another Cushendall man who was in New York then - Dan McKeown, whose brother died in a motorbike accident at the Turn, Cushendun. Jack and Dan (McKeown) married two sisters named O’Malley, whose people came from County Mayo. Jack’s son, Jackie Jnr, became a top American footballer, starting with Notre Dame University, and then professionally for a New York team. Another son, Danny became a policeman in New York, and later was the head barman in the New York Giants’ Stadium.

“My two other uncles went to sea, Jim and Danny. Uncle Chris stayed at home, yet was brilliant at showing young seaman how to make reef knots, and help them as they were studying to sit sea ticket examinations. Jim and Danny McMullan stuck to working on coasters. Danny, father of MLA Oliver, once sailed on a coaster named the *HAWTHORN*. He decided to quit the ship, but left a jacket behind on it. The *HAWTHORN*, while on a journey from Belfast to Derry, ran aground near Cushendun.

“He was fortunate not to be on it. Amazingly, his jacket, with some personal belongings, was washed ashore. Danny retired from seafaring. Jim played hurling for the Glenariffe team that won the Antrim Championship in the 1930’s.”

Oliver McMullan added: "I believe my father, Danny went to sea when he was a very young man. He was no more than 16, and worked on coasters. There was nothing else here, by way of obtaining a job, for teenagers like him. Nearly every family in the Glens had someone working at sea. My father stopped seafaring when well into his 20's.

"For a time, he was employed by Maurice Findlay at the salmon fishing nets in Cushendun, and then went to England, where he worked at pressure piling. My uncle Jim also worked on coasters, while Jack left conventional seawork, jumped ship, and became a longshoreman in New York".

Four other Antrim Coast seamen also found New York an intriguing place, but with hidden treasure the magnet. It is hard to resist the temptation to go treasure hunting, always a fascinating and exciting pastime, but more so when the prize is massive financial reward. This was the bait that attracted the Antrim men, when a Captain Harry L Bowdom decided to try and find sunken treasure off the USA's Virginia coast in 1932.

Captain Bowdom believed he had the specialist diving equipment and suits to bring up over $2 million in gold, silver and jewellery from the wreck of the *MERIDA*, which sank on May 12, 1911. The tantalising tale unfolds when the wide-eyed mariners and specialist divers sailed out of New York Harbour. Apparently, the crew of 32 aboard the *SALVOR* included - 'a Mr Hyndman of Red Bay, James McKeegan of Glenaan, and the brothers Charles and Malcolm McCambridge, sons of Mr Malcolm McCambridge of High Street, Cushendall.'

As far as I can ascertain, the ambitious expedition was unsuccessful, as was another attempt by a salvage firm 50 years later. The secrets of the 6,207-ton passenger-freight *MERIDA* appear to remain 210 feet down, silently lying on the ocean bed off Virginia Capes She was on passage from Vera Cruz, Mexico, via Havana, to New York, when she collided in heavy fog 80 miles east of Virginia Beach.

She was, apparently, accidentally rammed amidships by the *ADMIRAL FERRAGO*, which also became hopelessly disabled. The *HAMILTON* came to the rescue of both sets of crew members and passengers. Initially, the *MERIDA's* cargo was taken on board by well-heeled Mexican nobility, who were in a hurry to escape the Revolution in their country, and were absconding with the late Emperor Maximillian's hoard of gold, silver copper, and jewels.

The site of the wreck of the *MERIDA* was found in 1924. Some estimates at the overall value of the cargo were placed close to $5 million, so there was a lot at stake for the crew of the *SALVOR*, an ocean-going tug built and registered in Liverpool in 1909.

Cushendall McCambridge men of another generation took to the boats - Sean and Mally McCambridge. I'm told they first lived at Cairns, and then moved down from the hill to reside with an uncle, Johnny McCambridge in Mill Street. Their brother Gerry and mother Kathleen emigrated to Australia.

Another High Street resident who was a seafaring man was Arthur Dowling, while the Stewart brothers, John and James also worked on the boats. Their father John went to sea. John Jnr of Knockans married Kathleen 'Gatha' Faulkner of Cushendall's once-named Thornlea Hotel. He sailed with Captain John Mort on the *PASS of GLENOGLE*. James Stewart was an AB, who once worked alongside Hugh O'Mullan of Waterfoot on Kelly coasters.

Captain Mort and a member of the McGaughey clan once survived fire drama in an English harbour. The McGaughey in question was reluctant sailor Willie, who lives with wife Teresa on the fringes of Waterfoot. Willie was as good as waving goodbye to the seawork from almost the moment he stepped aboard a Mort-skippered boat.

He had no intention of taking to the oceans, and when his father found him a job his first thought was to quit the sea. Expected to carry on the family tradition, he lasted two years as an AB. When a teenager, living opposite the old Cottage Hospital, down Shore Street, Cushendall, he was suddenly presented no choice in the matter of job selection.

"My father, Owen made the decision," recalled Willie, "I doubt if I had any intention of going to work at sea, but there was not much employment about in those times. No work available. One evening my da insisted I go to sea, and instructed me to report to Captain John Mort. He said: 'You are to meet John Mort at Grangemouth'.

"I asked. 'What for?' 'For a job', he replied. 'Now off you go, and report at Grangemouth.' That was my introduction to the seafaring. You didn't argue with your father. I was 17-and-a-half at the time, and off I went to join John Mort's boat. I had no idea where Grangemouth was situated. In fact, I'd not been to Belfast. The furthest I ever travelled up to that point was when making two trips to Ballymena.

"For my debut at sea, I went to Ballymena, and round to the train station where I purchased a ticket that booked a passage right through . . . rail to Belfast, and then crossing over to Scotland on the ferry. I joined Captain Mort's boat, the *PASS of KINTAIL*, a 903 gross tons oil tanker owned by the Bulk Oil of London. I was a deck hand with her for two years, doing coastal cargo work, and making many runs to the Continent, mainly over to Holland.

"Even though I was a relatively short spell at sea it was a period not without incident. On one occasion we were in Teesport when there was a fire accident on board ship. We were berthed at Middlesbrough, at a big wooden jetty. It was a huge old place, and there were men cutting part of it away. That was about a quarter of a mile from us. However, we had some fuel spilling and running over the deck.

"We had our lids open, ready for inspectors to take sample of our cargo, when a spark from the workers touched the fuel in the water that had leaked down through the scuppers. The whole thing caught fire. The flames shot up out of the water, and raced across the deck to the wheelhouse. The front of the wheelhouse was badly burned, right to the metal, and also there was fire along the deck. Fuel was running right through her.

"At that time only four of us were on board . . . me, Captain Mort, the chief engineer, and the bo'sun. Captain Mort shouted to the engineer to get the engine started. I worked furiously to put the lids back on the hatches. The bo'sun ran for the fire hatchet, and cut all ropes, to let us move away from the pier, and out into the bay.

"Quick thinking Captain Mort took the wheel, and he ran her out into the middle of the Tyne. That move by Captain Mort prevented a possible catastrophe. Out in the bay we anchored, and then steamhosed the decks, and all over, to completely put out the fire. That ended the emergency. Nobody was hurt, thankfully."

Outside of that drama, Willie was not enamoured by his burgeoning career: "When I first went to sea it was in the middle of winter. For the first two months I never stood on dry land. It was into port, discharge the cargo, and out again. Very soon, I felt there were other things to do rather than be at sea all the time. When I first went I did not have a Union card, but signed up at Aberdeen. Instead of moving on I quit, and went to work on building sites in England."

His father (Owen) was at sea 'all his working life', and mostly on coasters.' Willie added: "In those times a lot of the boys from here did coasting, and took off a couple of months from the seawork in the summer months to do a bit of farming, save the hay, cut the turf. My uncle Jamie, a brother of my father, was also all his life at sea. He was a bo'sun on coasters - and a grandfather of Brendan and Jude.

"My grandfather was Willie McGaughey, and he also worked at sea all his life. His son was Captain Neil McGaughey, who died in 1953. I think Neil was with the Robertson company for a while, but most of his years with Dorey of Guernsey. My cousin Angus was Neil's son, and also a skipper. He retired a couple of years ago, to live at Crumlin, County Antrim. His last sea job was that of skipper of the Liverpool-Belfast ferry. Before that, he was a long time working deep-sea."

Willie's cousin, 'Big' Brendan McGaughey recalled his uncle Neilly suffering nasty injuries from a fall into a ship's hold. "Uncle Neilly sustained some facial damage, but was left with a very bad shoulder injury for the rest of his life. He was married to Rose McAuley, and they lived at Mill Street, Cushendall. Old Owen McGaughey lived up Glenariffe, and came down from there to reside in Cushendall.

"Neilly's brothers were Willie (Willie 'Pat' is named after him) and my father James, who did not go to sea. James worked in England. Lilly McGaughey and my father were twins. Three generations ago there was Captain Neil McGaughey. A headstone in the Bay Cemetery states he died on the 6th of March 1953, and wife Grace died on the 15th of January, 1994. I was three years old when he died. He was a captain of Dorey boats."

Mick Graham of Glen Road, Glenariffe, added to the McGaughey sea going chart: "When I was a very young boy, I recall Captain Neil coming to Lurig View, to visit my then next-door neighbour, Captain Paddy Darragh, Lawrence's father. I also remember his son, Angus McGaughey and a sister coming down to Glenariffe from Rathfern, Abbott's Cross,

Newtownabbey." Lawrence Darragh added: "My parents were very friendly with the McGaughey's. Captain Neil and his wife Grace, who was a sister of Jim McKendry from up Glenariffe Glen, would make regular visits down from Abbott's Cross."

Incidentally, Willie 'Pat' McGaughey's wife, Teresa also claimed salt water in her veins: "Very much so," she said, "My grandfather was John McCormick of Glenariffe, a ship's engineer. His brother was Captain Mick McCormick of Waterfoot. Also, there was James McCormick, who was killed in India. Patrick also went to sea." Teresa's father was Joe McMullan, who married Jeanie McCormick, a daughter of Johnny McCormick, and a sister of Captain John 'Count' McCormick.

More bits and pieces of sea news include the McKillop brothers of Cushendall. Seamus McKillop, an avid member of the Glens of Antrim Historical Society and prominent amateur golfer at the Cushendall Club, revealed his father, Danny worked for a time as a merchant seaman during the Second World War. "My uncle Archie was also at sea, and I believe he was a steward on the Larne -Stranraer ferry. He lived at Stranraer," McKillop said.

Retired college lecturer Colm Thompson, a nephew of seaman Paddy Mooney, recalled a sea-going man named Dan Connolly, who was one of the first residents of the then new houses down Dalriada Avenue, Cushendall. "He was not related to the Cushendall Connolly family. He was married to Freda Henley, a sister of Dean Henley, who was Parish Priest of St Paul's, Belfast."

Thompson's brother Alex also remarked that a young Barney Humphreys of Layd fell into a ship's hold, and was injured so severely he had to leave working at sea. He added that Bobby McFetridge, who once operated a garage and petrol pump facility in Mill Street, Cushendall, served in the Royal Navy. It is believed Robert Stewart, who lived in the famous and historically preserved Cushendall Tower, was also in the Navy, and suffered a near crippling leg injury in the process.

Risking life and limb on the convoy duty during the Second World War were seamen such as Tom Newe and Terry McCann, the latter a great friend of Captain Gerry Blaney. McCann, an engineer on oil tankers, came to live in the Glens in a roundabout fashion, from Ballymoney to Belfast, to Glenariffe, and finally to Cushendall.

Tom Newe's sea saga stalled, and all because of a vision problem. His son Paul explained: "My father worked deep-sea, and also survived Merchant Fleet convoy duty during the Second World War. He had high hopes of achieving top qualification, but was turned down. He was sitting his Mate's ticket when it was discovered he was colour blind. That ruled him out of any promotion or progress, so he quit sea work."

A regular summer visitor to Cushendall was Captain Frank Davey from Belfast. He was a captain on Head Line boats for many years. Davey was renowned for being the first skipper to take his vessel up the Great Lakes in Canada after the winter freeze.

A John McNaughton, born at Cushendall, worked as a deck hand on coasters, and his traced discharge is that of October 6, 1927, from the *ENID DUNFORD* at Cardiff. Able Seaman Alexander O'Hara, registered RS2 No 331 672, was born in Cushendall on October 15, 1891.

34

TAX RELIEF

A PERSISTENT tax collector unwittingly saved the life of Glenariffe seaman Louie Monaghan. In late 1957, when living outside Dublin, Monaghan was under heavy pressure from an irritatingly insistent Inland Revenue representative, after returning from a stressful journey in the White Sea to dock at Preston.

Little Louie was two days into the unloading of timber from the ill-fated *NARVA* when the tax collector's detective work paid dividends, or so the civil servant thought. Alarmed at the sight of a bill for £109, for alleged overdue taxes, a substantial amount for the 1950's, the quick-thinking deck hand stalled his tracker, and then did a flit to County Meath.

Monaghan's decision not to remain for a third trip on the *NARVA* to the Baltic, and instead do a runner from the Revenue man, saved his life. Weeks later, the *NARVA* went down in the North Sea, with the loss of all on board. It was a dreadful disaster, and a tragedy forever embedded into the Monaghan memory bank. But for the intervention of a Taxman he would not be around to tell so many spellbinding tales of seafaring.

"I was on timber-run boats for Glen's of Glasgow," he recalled, "The Glen group did the north Scandinavian trip. I was on the Baltic timber trade when we brought out a load of barrels of something to Archangel, the main port on the White Sea, on the north west coast of Russia. I was on the *NARVA*, for my second trip.

"We got the barrels off, and the timber on - but managed to get stuck three times in the ice. The boat had a new skipper on board, after the *NARVA* completed the first timber journey - discharging, in Dublin, and then it was turnaround for the Baltic, to pick up another load. It was Captain Parrish's first command.

"I remember when we were sailing past Rathlin Sound he asked why the bells on the sides of the wheelhouse were wrapped up. The *NARVA* was an old ship. The bells, once used to sound watch, had been stuffed with canvas - and the gongs tied up tight to keep them quiet. They were no longer needed, and now just ornaments.

"Still, he made us take the canvas off the bells, have them all cleaned out and shined up. We did that, and I tell you there was some ringing of bells as we hit stormy weather when rounding the north of Scotland. To get to the Baltic from Dublin we had to go up and around the top of Scotland.

"We ran into freezing conditions in the Baltic. To get us out of there, we had to send for the ice-breaker, who goes around you in a circle breaking up the ice, and then moves in front of you. He had only left us when we were stuck again, and one more time after that - completely jammed.

"The ice-breaker skipper came back for the third time, when we were into our fifth day stuck there. He pulled alongside, and asked to speak with our engineer. He said he could not come back any more, and told the engineer if he wanted to get out of there to 'put the boot to the floorboards' and follow him. The wheel was really shaking and shuddering as we went full throttle, and made it out.

"By then, we were running out of bunkers, and had to go to Copenhagen to refuel. The drama didn't end there on this eventful journey, as half way across the North Sea the foredeck went. We lost timber - enough to help build the half of the houses in Glenariffe. The after-hatches were all right, but with the fore-hatches bursting open we lost 50% of it.

"We got into Sinclair Bay, near Caithness on the east coast of Scotland, to get the remainder of the timber tied on. We sailed to near Manchester again. Two days after we docked at Preston, and as the unloading was going on I was taking a rest in my bunk when this man, a total stranger, came on board and asked to see me. He said he was from the Tax Department. The Inland Revenue wanted money from me. He said I was behind with my taxes.

"He said I owed £109, which was a huge amount in those days. He disputed any of my claims. He challenged any allowance claims I made. When you are on the move so much at sea you just don't think about the taxman. I said I couldn't give him any money until I got my pay. I had no money right then to pay him, but hoped to receive my wages the next day.

"I knew the ship was going back to the Baltic for another load of timber, and I would be back in time to get home for Christmas. But, when the man came looking for £109 I felt I'd have no money to bring home for Christmas. At that time I was living in a different jurisdiction, near Ashbourne outside Dublin, and close to the airport.

"So, before the taxman returned, I decided to hand in my notice there and then, picked up pay that was due to me, and took off for Dublin. The *NARVA* left for the Baltic, and I wasn't on board. She never came back. I was fortunate not to be on her. She went down in a storm in the North Sea. All hands were lost. It was a lucky escape for me. That taxman, who wanted the £109 there and then, but never got it, did me a huge favour. Unwittingly, he saved my life!"

The *NARVA* was built at Gavle, Sweden, in 1943, and named the *ALETTA NOOT*. The name changed to *EMPIRE CONFERENCE* in 1945, and two years later this 2,000 tonner was named *NARVA*, and owned by the Scottish Navigation Company, and managed by Glen and Co Ltd. She foundered on December 22, 1957, during heavy weather, and apparently after attempting to help another ship in distress - the London coaster *BOSWORTH*, which was later towed to safety by Hull trawler *FARADAY*.

The *NARVA* was on voyage from Hudiksvall, Sweden, with a cargo of wood pulp bound for Aberdeen and Grangemouth. Her crew of 28 perished. Norwegian passenger ship *LEDA* tried to help *NARVA*, by sending a lifeboat of seven crew and one officer, but couldn't get alongside without the risk of smashing the lifeboat to bits. The lifeboat sailors cried out to *NARVA* crew to jump into the sea, but no one did. Nobody in the stern abandoned ship.

The *NARVA* bows were already heavily down, completely awash, and her propeller high in the air. Significantly, no lifeboats on the *NARVA* were lowered. A Ministry of Transport enquiry, held later in Glasgow, could not state what caused the loss of the *NARVA*, and the lives of the complete crew.

A small, wiry man recovering from a hip replacement operation, Louis Monaghan shuddered at what his fate might have been but for a quick decision to dodge an overdue bill. He had many other illuminating recollections to share with me on a wet Saturday afternoon in January 2013.

"I'm 86 now, and lucky to be still here," said Monaghan, after looking down the list of the 28 men who lost their lives in the *NARVA* tragedy. He became understandably pensive, noting the names of Captain Reginald Parrish of County Durham, and First Mate Samuel Dunwoody of Dublin. The crew also included Radio Officer Denis Kiely of Innishannon, County Cork, Bo'sun George McDowell of Bangor, County Down, and Belfast AB's - Stewart Nelson, of Rathcoole, and Frederick Gawley, of Hamma Street.

Monaghan returned from County Meath to the family home at Foriff, alongside the main road heading towards Ballymena, half-a-mile from Waterfoot Bridge, following the deaths of his brother Charlie and sister Margaret. This proud adventurer, who survived many treacherous moments on the oceans, added: "In the old days there were not many families in the Glens who didn't have somebody working at sea.

"My father was Dan Monaghan, and he went to sea. He took seriously ill, and died in a Belfast hospital. Also going to sea was a Captain John Monaghan, on sailing ships during the 18th century. In 1807, Captain Monaghan was buried in the old graveyard at the Broken Bridge, Ardclinis. Other members of my family are buried in the Bay Cemetery. I believe the Monaghan family originally came to the Glens from the Derry area, to work as coastal watchers.

"The headstone names a young John Monaghan. He was, I believe, a son of Captain John. The Captain is a great, great granduncle of mine. After the change from sail to steam there was an old sea saying. 'God be with the days when we had iron men and wooden ships. Now we have iron ships and wooden men.'

"When my father went to sea, he worked for the Robertson Company of Glasgow. Fifty years later I worked for the same firm. I was on coastal oil tankers. In the early 1900's my father came home from working at sea to farm at Glenariffe. Living here was his father Charlie, then in his early 70's, and his sister Brigid.

"Home before the First World War started, my father married Margaret McCormick from Glendun. I think down there they were known as the 'Casey's'. Her brother, my uncle, was Pat McCormick. I believe he was known in Cushendun as 'Parliament Pat'. I was born in 1926, and after going to the old primary school up the Glen, and working on the farm for a while, I went to sea with the John Kelly boats, in 1948.

"The man who helped me get my first job was Archie Murray of Waterfoot, not of the Murray 'Diver' family. I was pretty friendly with him.

I felt I was wasting my time working on a small farm. Obviously we were self-sufficient on the farm, but I was never able to put any money behind me. There were no wages at home. You were just getting by. I felt it was time to move.

"I told the man Murray if a job came up would he put in a word for me. Then I received a telegram to report to a ship berthed in Belfast. I went on the 'bus, and onwards to the docks there. I didn't know the name of the ship I was to start work on, but knew if the man Murray was on deck I'd have the answer. He was there.

"I worked as a stoker. It was difficult when starting out. You had to quickly get used to the sway of the boat on the sea, the shift-work, the change of food, and not feeling too good for a bit. I did not have a lot of bother with sea-sickness, once I settled to the new routines. I was on the *KERRYMORE* for a year, and then she went into drydock. I worked on other Kelly boats.

"My job, in the engine room, had its advantages. You wouldn't be on the deck all night. You were warm, and it was less sway down there, more comfortable than up above. But I moved. One day the First Mate told me there was a job going on deck. He said: 'How would you like to earn a couple of pounds more by going on deck. There is a job coming up in a few weeks time." I went for it, and got the job on deck, where I worked the rest of my time at sea. That was in 1948/1949 - and £2 extra was a lot of money then.

"The deck crowd was also getting overtime, whereas in the stoke hold it was a flat rate. This was a much different life for me. At home you were working for nothing. At sea I started off earning a wage in the region of £6.50-a-week, after money was taken out for your grub. The coal boats took money out for your food, but that was not the case when you were deep-sea. I was on coal boats for up to three years, and then I left Kellys. I got a job with B & I boats for a while, Dublin to Liverpool, but not on the passenger boat. I worked on the general cargo boat. I stayed on that job for six months."

Monaghan, if proof was needed, was one of the multitude of mariners from the Glens who were part of a transient, almost fickle, workforce. The seamen migrated from ship to ship, from coasters to deep-sea, from oil tankers to bulk carriers and often back to coasting, to be nearer their home folks. He added: "In 1951 I went to Robertson of Glasgow, following half-a-century later in the footsteps of my father. I was on their second edition of the *GEM*, and not all that far away from the disaster on the night the *PRINCESS VICTORIA* went down. We took cement out of London to Belfast.

"I was on the *GEM* when we took her, as brand new, out of Troon dockyard. That run from London, the time of the dreadful *VICTORIA* disaster, was not easy, because of the poor weather. Normally it took two and a half days in ordinary weather. On that occasion it took five days, down the English Channel and up the Irish Sea. After discharging our cargo of coal, we left Belfast on the evening before the *VICTORIA* went down.

"We were light, and going to north Wales to pick up a cargo of stone for London. By now the weather was really bad. We couldn't get near the quarries at Llandulus. We had to turn round, and coast up and down, from about 5.00am until daylight arrived shortly after 7.00am. We pulled up in the Menai Strait, and had to keep the engine ticking over. We were there for a time, as we still couldn't get to the quarries.

"I know it was around half past seven the next morning when we heard the bad news on our radio transmitter. We were still light ship, and no point in trying to go anywhere, to try and help anyone in trouble. We couldn't believe it was a passenger ship that went down. I think we were stuck in the Menai for over 24 hours, before the weather improved, and we moved out of shelter to load up at Llandulus. I did the Canadian run on the *GEM.* The captain was Tom Barry. We also did northern Russia."

Monaghan claimed he diced with danger on one curiously uncertain voyage to Canada: "Around 1951, we had a strange cargo on board. We took some sort of special chemical from London to Canada. The cargo consisted of little shiny black balls - the size of a hen egg. Looking back, they were possibly dangerous, maybe with radioactive content, or something like that.

"All we knew on the boat was that the black balls were some sort of chemical, and they lay loose in the hold. We were told nothing. However, the first indication that this was something different was when watching the dockers in London loading the cargo. The workers at dockside there had some sort of cream all over their hands and faces.

"The dust coming off the black balls could cause some burning of the skin. We were not given anything to protect ourselves, no pair of gloves in those days. At the time, we thought little about it, hosed down the decks and away we went to Canada. We were sure our cargo was something special, when we took it to a remote factory building on the side of a river on the St Lawrence.

"The big building was near nowhere. This was a pretty bleak place. The back of beyond. I reckon the nearest houses were three miles away. When we got there, and docked, the first thing we noticed was that workers there were all wearing gasmasks. The employees in the factory were nearly all foreigners - mostly Hungarian people.

"I'm sure other ships took similar cargo to that place. Some time after that trip we heard cargo for that factory in Canada was for making explosives. Anyhow, we put the cargo off, the black balls taken out loose through the use of grabs, and then we sailed further along the St Lawrence before we went up a river to load timber.

"We moved past a place called O'Brien's Bridge. I think it was in the late days of March or early April when we were up there - and a wind was blowing when we tried to load the timber. The dockers refused to load, because of this black dust, the residue from unloading the black balls, was burning their faces. Strangely enough, we seemed used to it. This very fine black dust was blowing about the deck, and was affecting the Canadian workers.

"We washed the decks, hosed down the ship from top to bottom, to get rid of the dust, and then the Canadian dockers came back and loaded the timber. It was a deck cargo, and when you are on the north Atlantic it rolls. She was really rolling badly. The bulwarks burst, but the ropes held the timber on, before we reached open sea. At the mouth of the river we slowed down. The skipper put her head into the wind, and we went out and tightened the load. We never lost a plank, and took the cargo to Manchester.

"For a spell, I also worked for Jacks of Larne. They had trampers on the Portuguese-northern Spain run, trucking iron ore to south Wales. We went up the White Sea for timber cargo. We would go up there light ship, and take timber back to England. Then I came home, as some of the children were born. I went to live outside Dublin, where my wife was from. We were out in the country, and eventually started a shop. But once you go to sea that is the one place where you feel at home. You get used to going to sea, and you don't want to do anything else.

"I went back to sea for a couple more years, working this time once again with Robertson's. I also worked on oil tankers, coasting for Everards, but by then home trade had dried up. I was on the long runs. I went down to Spain, up the Baltic, and made another run to Canada for timber. I also worked for the Tanker Company of London, which I believe was owned by the British Government, and made one run on a big tanker, the *BRITISH RELIANCE* through the Suez Canal to the Persian Gulf to load up with oil.

"I didn't like it, really. You saw nothing of Persia. All we witnessed was a wooden jetty beside the desert. The massive tanks of oil were nearby, and after twelve hours we were loaded. We had a cargo of around 48,000 tons of oil, and took it to a British-owned oil refinery in Saudi Arabia. We went from there back to the Gulf, reloaded, and sailed for home.

"I joined that ship at Port Talbot in Wales, and discharged half cargo in Dublin. We had trouble getting into Dublin Harbour, because she was drawing that much water. She needed a minimum of 29 feet, so we had to wait a day on the water, until the tide and water levels were right. From there we took the remaining half cargo of oil to the north of Scotland, and it then went into dry-dock. I was paid off.

"I quit the sea in 1960, and returned to work in the shop. I look back and feel my greatest day ever was when going to sea for the first time. When my brother Charlie and my sister Kathleen died I came back to the home place in Glenariffe."

Another sister, Mary also worked at sea, as a stewardess. "She was away from home at 16 years of age. I rarely met her until late in her life, as I was at sea when she was at sea," said Louis, "I know she became friendly with the Leavey girl, Kathleen (Dalla), who worked on the Cunard liners out of Southampton.

"Mary worked on liners that mostly made the run from Southampton down to South Africa, and later met and married a man from Rhodesia. She was in her late 30's then, and gave up sea work. After her husband died, she came home. Three years later she took ill, and died in the Ballymena hospital, aged 73."

35

NUCLEAR NERVES

ACCEPTING the risky assignment of helping to transport the always controversial cargo of nuclear fuel from England to Japan proved quite a challenge for Captain Paddy McNeill of Cushendun. The task required nerves of steel. This type of work was far removed from the customary oil tanker or bulk container ship cargo delivery demands he had been used to.

This was specialist work. But needs must, and Paddy, who spent his latter days down in the chilly climes of the south Atlantic, sailing in and out of the myriad of small delivery stops among the Falkland Islands, signed up for the tricky trips to the Far East.

Known along the Antrim Coast as Paddy 'The Rock', he explained the move to tackle a pretty spooky task: "It was during a period of change in the seafaring business. The Pool system of obtaining work was different, almost over. It was not like the old days. Now it was agents who were setting up the jobs.

"A man named Hamilton in Belfast telephoned me from his agency, and offered me a job as Second Mate on nuclear transporting ships. The money they were paying was exceptionally good. So, I joined the Pacific Nuclear Transport Company, to take nuclear fuel to Japan from Barrow-on-Furness. The fuel came down by rail from Sellafield, in Cumbria, to the ship,

"I did two trips on the *SANDPIPER* to Japan. Often, their ships would do one trip a year, and some times ships sat for two years at Barrow-on-Furness, fully manned, and ready to sail at a moment's notice. It was boring when not sailing, but I learned a lot then on ships that were exceptionally well run.

"The jaunts to Japan meant sailing through the Panama Canal. Security was tight. Off the territorial waters of Panama we were met by security vessels. We were taken through the Canal at night, with a helicopter hovering overhead at all times. We had four security boats beside us, two forard and two aft. Also, a dozen armed guards came on board.

"We made our way to Japan, and discharged the fuel for Reactor Plants at small towns such as Toki and Ogawa. We had two tons of nuclear fuel to the big jar, and four jars overall. The fuel in the flasks had to be kept cool, and were immersed in a big tank that had a refrigeration system.

"We took a couple of empty flasks back to England. The depleted flasks were quite hot to touch. We had 30 of a crew, and used a Geiger counter around the flasks to check them from time to time. It was a very dangerous job, because the fuel is invisible. We never detected any emissions. Nuclear

Waste had to be dealt with too. We did trips with cargo and trips with waste.

"On the way back home from Japan, we stopped for four days in Panama City, and held 'Open Days' on the ship. It was a good PR exercise. Then 9-11 happened, and it was decided there would be no more cargos of nuclear fuel for two years. And so, I decided I would move on rather than do nothing as the ships lay waiting. Luckily for me, two of the ships were decommissioned, and I was able to leave with some redundancy."

Born on December 5, 1943, he decided to follow his father, John in mixing salmon fishing with ocean travel. The McNeill family 'of the rocks' - at Rockport, Cushendun - is inextricably linked to the rhythm of the oceans. Many of the male members became slaves to the sea. They could not resist the magnetic pull of the salt water, and took to the boats as local fishermen, working on coastal trawlers and cargo ships, or as deep-sea sailors.

Paddy McNeill said: "My grandfather was the original John McNeill, and he worked on a barge-schooner on the St Lawrence Seaway, and on the Great Lakes, Canada. This was in the days of sailing ships, and in the 1890's. I believe he sailed with old Captain Arthur Hamilton of Ballindam, Cushendun.

"He came home to marry Rosetta McCurry of Ballyeamon, a relation of the brothers, Charlie and James McCurry of Clough Road, and their cousins - the brothers Dick and John McCurry. He worked a few acres of land, crofting more or less, and fishing.

"My father, John of the Rocks, first worked for Dorey of Guernsey. The Dorey company was small then, with no more than three or four ships. They carried coal mainly, and any other cargo they could find. Just like his father, he went to sea as a young man, and left it when he got married. In 1950, he decided to go back to sea. I remember him working on Kelly boats."

Paddy's older brother Sean said: "When he returned to the sea dad was mostly on a Kelly boat named the *BALLYGARVEY*. On the night the *PRINCESS VICTORIA* went down, the boat he was on was ten miles off the area where the ferry sank. I think he was sailing from Liverpool. I remember him saying the weather was bad whenever they heard this other ship was in distress. But, the information was not quite accurate, the wrong position of the *PRINCESS VICTORIA* given, and eventually on dad's boat they decided to take shelter in Ramsey Bay, Isle of Man."

Sean added: "The family of grandfather John McNeill and Rosetta McCurry included Kate, Dan, Randal, Paddy, Rosetta, John, Mary, and Maggie. Mary married Makie McNeill of nearby Brablagh, and Maggie became Mrs Bonner, married to a Donegal man, She ran a B & B in Dublin. Kate married a sea captain McAuley, when apparently she was 18 and he was 50.

"Captain McAuley owned a small farm at Tromra. They lived in the wee house that has decayed, the roof falling in not so long ago. The wallstead remains at the head of the lane leading to John McKillop's bungalow. I think the farm later belonged to the Daly's. Captain McKillop was lost at sea. There was no young family

"Aunt Kate then had a window cleaning business in Glasgow - and later emigrated to Canada. She remarried, and moved to live in Chicago. My dad married Kathleen O'Hara of Knocknacraw. Her brother Alex worked at sea for quite a while, I think he was a stoker on coasters."

It was a fresh-faced Paddy McNeill who took the plunge to work at sea. "I thoroughly enjoyed getting out on the ocean - a new horizon every day. Before my first job, I went to the Sea College at Sharpness, a year after Joe Murphy was there. I was nine weeks at the school, training on a sailing ship named the *VINDICATRIX*, which was moored up at the top end of the Bristol Channel. The course, run by the Merchant Navy, was for catering and deck ratings."

He started work as a deck boy on the 15th of April, 1961. He was 17. The ship, the *PACIFIC UNITY,* was owned by Furness Withy. "For my maiden voyage, I set off from Glasgow across the Atlantic, with a cargo of 10,000 tons of Scotch whisky for ports in north America. We sailed through the Panama Canal, and then up the west coast to Los Angeles. From California, we progressed to Vancouver. The whisky came in cases, built on pallets.

"I'll never forget watching the loading of that ship in Glasgow, where I saw a Glasgow docker taken out of the hold totally intoxicated. It was easy pickings down there, to nick a bottle of Scotch. On my second day at Princess Dock I met a man from Glendun. He was 'Archie Archie' McNeill, and he worked as a docker in Glasgow.

"Before that, I also recall going to Glasgow on the Belfast ferryboat. There was an elderly steward on board on this frosty April morning in 1961. He saw my sailor's bag. We had a chat. I asked him where the Pool was situated in Glasgow. He informed me it would not open until nine o'clock in the morning. He gave me a bit of advise on how to avoid sea sickness. Drink plenty of milk, he said. He also added I was not picking a good day to start my career at sea, as it was the anniversary of the sinking of the *TITANIC.*

"My first trip proved a brilliant experience. There was no container used in those days, and it took two weeks to unload the cargo. I did three trips on the *PACIFIC UNITY,* bringing back timber from Vancouver to the UK. On the second journey we again had a cargo of whisky, and also some machinery and 12 passengers - who brought their cars with them as they emigrated to America. Part of my job was to scrub the wooden decks, starting at six o'clock in the morning. It is called Holy Stoning."

He moved to the oil tanker *LUCERNA*, taking cargo from Curacao to Dakar, and sailed to Bonny River in Nigeria, where an oil pipe was attached to a buoy near the mouth of the river. Oil was pumped into the ship from a large hose tied to the buoy. "Outside the mouth of the river lay a large Shell tanker that topped you up with oil once you came over the sand bars. We had 25,000 tons of oil that was taken to Hamburg. After that one trip I joined the William Robertson of Glasgow's *BRILLIANT.*

"We were involved in an incident in Oslofjord with the *BRILLIANT*. Our captain decided to let the pilot leave early, as he felt he knew the waters and could get us out to sea. But, we went around the wrong side of a buoy marker, and ripped the bottom of the boat. We were not in danger of sinking. The boat was double bottomed, and we made our way home to dry-dock in Troon, Scotland. We were there for six weeks.

"I was an Ordinary Seaman now, and I made a summer trip on the *TOPAZ* of Robertsons, up around Sweden, Norway, the Baltic. We picked up timber at Archangel in Russia. We also loaded paper pulp at North Statland, in the northern part of the Arctic Circle. My brother Seamus was with me on the *TOPAZ.* We were both AB's."

Paddy sat and passed the EDH (Efficient Deck Hand) examination in Belfast, and after he and brother Seamus were paid off the *TOPAZ* they went to London docks to seek fresh work. With them went near-neighbour Joe Murphy, but all three couldn't secure employment on the same ship. "Seamus took a job on the *MEDIA CARGO* for Cunard to New York. Joe and me joined the *MARCHON ENTERPRISE,* running to Casablanca. Charlie Graham of Calishnagh also worked on the Marchon-named ships, but I didn't meet him.

"As folk say, you always remember where you were on the day and time US President John F Kennedy was shot and killed in Dallas, the motorcade murder by Lee Harvey Oswald on November 22, 1963. I do. It was on the way out of Casablanca Harbour, with a load of phosphate, when we heard the news on the ship's radio.

"With Joe (Murphy) I also went deep-sea out of KG5 docks in London. We got jobs on the *SCOTTISH STAR,* and left to sail down to Tenerife in the Canary Islands, where we stopped for bunker (refuel), and then on to Cape Town, before heading across to Australia. The cargo included cars and farm machinery from the UK. In South Africa, we also loaded copper ingots, and transported the ingots to a big foundry at Geelong, near Melbourne.

"I remember calling at Durban, Lorenqo Marques, and Bira. Joe Murphy met some of his family's friends in Durban. They were people from Cushleake, who were related to the John McKinley family that owned a pub in Princes Street, Glasgow, and one at Campbeltown. We also took 12 passengers, along with cargo of clothes and shoes, to Australia - as well as surface mail. For the return journey, we loaded up with frozen lamb and fruit. On one trip we went to Tasmania to load with apples.

"Joe now stayed at home, as it was the lambing season, so Seamus joined me on the *SCOTTISH STAR* for four trips to Australia and New Zealand. After that, I sailed on the *FREMANTLE STAR* to Australia and New Zealand, out through the Panama Canal and home via the Suez Canal. The trip lasted four months.

"After this, in 1965, I took time away from the sea for five months, to study for a Second Mate's ticket, at Blyth Street school in Sandy Row, Belfast. I also did a lot of studying on the boats, on my own bat, and in my free time. I had to get sea time before I could sit for First Mate, and finally, in 1970, the Master's Ticket. I had a very good tutor in Captain

Sam Pollock. Nowadays it is a Limited or Unlimited Master's Ticket, and has to be revalidated every five years. Mine is up to 2017. It is Unlimited, and that used to be called Foreign Going. Limited used to be known as Home Trade.

"The *GEM* was my first captaincy, in 1982, when trading around the Baltic, Norway, and the Scandinavian coastline. Robertson's of Glasgow named all their ships after precious stones - gem, jade, emerald, topaz, sapphire. Robertson boats were sold to Stevenson Clark of Newcastle-Upon-Tyne. I worked for them for a number of years.

"I also worked on an intriguing old ship that had a lot of history, the *CLIFF QUAY*. It was built in 1950, and used by the British Electricity Authority to take coal cargo to London's Power Plant Station on the River Thames. It had been a steam ship converted to oil. The engine area was famous in that the engine room was used to shoot scenes for the first great film about the sinking of the *TITANIC* . . . *'A Night to Remember'*. The cast in the movie, made in 1958, included Kenneth More, Honor Blackman, Kenneth Griffith, Joseph Tomelty, Richard Hayward, Harold Goldblatt, and a deck hand part for a young Sean Connery.

"I was ashore for a couple of years, in the early part of the 1990's, and then Mate on the *STORINGTON*, working out of the Hook of Holland, and down to La Corunna in Spain. The *STORINGTON* was registered at Douglas, Isle of Man. We shipped a load of steel from Lithuania to north Spain. Once I took part with the rest of the crew in a nine-a-side fun soccer match against Russian opposition at Gdansk."

He decided to drift away from long voyages, purchased a trawler, and returned to his first love, sea fishing. He proudly sailed out of Cushendun Bay on the *MOYUNA*. "I spent four years at home, fishing, but went back to sea, and put a skipper on board the *MOYUNA*. I eventually sold her to two men from Greencastle, County Donegal. The boat later ended up in Kilkeel.

"The Common Market was stepping in with all sorts of rules and regulations about fishing, and that is why I sold the boat - because of all the European restrictions on fishing. It became financially not viable. I remember fishing off the Isle of Man, at the Douglas banks, when we had to stop on the 30th of September.

"We were not allowed to fish any longer, yet the foreign boats were fishing away in our waters, including Spanish trawlers fishing for herring. It was more than a farce as far as I was concerned - it was a disgrace. We were very restricted. On the *MOYUNA*, my older brother Sean was with me for a couple of spells, during winter months; also Davy Smyth of Carnlough. The rest of the five-man crew came from around Ardglass."

Paddy McNeill's sea travels often included heavy helpings of danger. Like the nuclear fuel trips, he highlighted other 'interesting' passages. "I did a delivery job, taking the *BAGHERA*, once a ferry at Piraeus, Greece, to Sierra Leone. I spent up to four weeks in Greece getting the ship into shape and ready for the voyage. I joined her as Mate. Then a strange thing happened. We had to sail to Gibraltar, where the crew was paid off, except the chief engineer and me. We stayed there for three weeks.

"The British Government was supplying her to the Sierra Leone Government. After arriving in Gibraltar, on December 4, 1999, the British Government decided to keep the boat in dry-dock for six weeks. I was allowed to come home for Christmas. I was working for the Portland Towage firm, and during the lull they asked me to go as skipper of a tug, the *SANDSPOOL CASTLE* at Falmouth, and take her to the old part of Stockholm.

"The tug was used as a restaurant accommodation in the heart of the Swedish city. Once known as the *MARTHA*, it was originally a small German passenger ship. We did that job, and we were then flown back to Gibraltar. I went down to Freetown, Sierra Leone, as master of the *BAGHERA*. On the way down I received a Fax from my company, and was asked to stay three more months in Freetown - to train the native seamen on the running of the ship.

"But, we didn't complete the job, because war erupted there, and we were evacuated out of Freetown. There was quite a nasty war in Sierra Leone. Freetown was a pretty grim place then. I remember seeing young kids running about the streets with only one hand or arm, as the other limb had been chopped off.

"My chief engineer was a Scotsman, John James Nicholl, who once worked in the Clyde Shipyard with the 'Big Yin' - Glasgow comedian Billy Connolly. Because of the unrest, we were told to remain locked indoors for 48 hours, and stay well away from the ship. The British Army came in. We stayed in our accommodation, a small bungalow in the hotel grounds.

"What we were not told, until afterwards, was that information came through to the police that the rebels planned to kidnap us. Along with other people, we were evacuated out of there by Chinook helicopter, from our accommodation to Freetown's Lungi Airport, and then by Hercules aircraft to Dakar. From there, we flew to Paris, London, and Belfast, and back home to Cushendun. It was quite an experience. It could have been a lot worse,

"I was captain for two weeks - on the *SEABUNK HARRIER* - a tug that was converted for salvage work off the coast of Iraq, during the Iraq War. I joined her in Bahrain, and we sat ten miles off the coast of Iraq for the duration of the second Iraq War. We saw a lot of activity, lots of noise - with shells and missiles flashing off to targets.

"We salvaged two helicopters that crashed in mid air, after taking off from their aircraft carrier. They were British helicopters, and all crew members were killed - ten British and one American. I was one month there. I went as Mate, but the Captain had to go back early. We were stood down at this stage.

"I moved to join the *CIROLANA*, a Fishery Research Boat that trawled mostly off the west coast of Ireland. We would do ten tows with the same type of net as used twenty years before, to compare the catch. I did another on the double-hulled *CORYSTES*, and was Mate on both.

"One of the trips was up to the Dogger Bank, a large sandbank 60 miles off the east of England where the Danes were fishing sand eels - and using them for industrial purposes. Sand eels provide the cod diet, and the cod fields were diminishing. We were checking on the demise of the sand eels. We would take samples. We also found evidence that tiny cod were taken from the sea bed, destroyed, and that was also contributing to wiping out the cod stocks."

How McNeill ended up in the Falkland Islands came about when once again the Belfast agent, Mr Hamilton of the International Marine Company, made him an offer of a job near the frozen Antarctic. "The job was on the *TAMAR*, owned by the Falkland Government. Gardiners of Glasgow also had the *St BRANDON* there, and were looking for crew. I went as Captain, reluctantly, because I did not know that territory. It was a new part of the oceans for me. I started on the 12th of July 2003. It was a complete change of scenery for me.

"In the Falklands, there are many Irish people, and from the Maghera area. A man I got to know very well is Danny Donnelly from Maghera. Also Dan Bonner. There are around a thousand islands. The big islands are the East and the West, with sheep farming the main industry. Strangely enough, for an island race the people have nothing to do with the sea, don't do any fishing, but leave that to the Spaniards, Japanese, and Taiwanese.

"The natives have a tradition with the land, mainly rearing sheep and some cattle. It is a bleak place. I once described the Falkland Islands as Orra Mountain, at the head of Glendun, without the trees. Some of the farmers might breed up to 10,000 sheep, some others up to 20,000 sheep. Wool is a big business. However, an abattoir was recently installed, to cull the sheep, and export the carcases back to the UK.

"It is mainly the Marino breed of sheep reared, because of high wool return. They are now breeding fatter lambs, to gain better meat along with the wool. My base is at Port Stanley, and I describe the *TAMAR* as a floating grocery shop. We go around the islands, delivering stores, farm machinery such as tractors, moving sheep or cattle from one island to another, and collecting wool.

"The weather is very windy. It can be grim at times. Storms can come up in half an hour. In recent years we welcolmed a better and more accurate idea of the weather, from computers that give a clear forecasting system. When I went there this was not so. I went to Chile once, for a load of beer, wines and spirits, and the boat was caught up, on the way back, in a very nasty storm that came up from Cape Horn.

"We had to 'hove-to' for 36 hours. The sea was breaking over the ship, and we had some cargo damaged, but not too much. That was probably the worst storm I was ever in. Negotiating around the islands is tricky, because it is poorly chartered, and with merely two lighthouses in total throughout the islands. I had some basic local information to start with, took it from there, and learned as we went along.

"One of the ways you can carefully and slowly guide the boat around the islands is by watching the kelp beds. You can watch the seaweed coming up, and that is where the reefs are - even well away from the shoreline, in places. I probably had to go back to my roots, as a young boy at Rockport, where I had a bit of knowledge of seaweed and danger spots.

It is also very tight going to negotiate the boat into and out of some of the small ports.

"You have to be very alert, but under no commercial pressure during two trips a month. You can complete the two in 20 days, providing weather conditions are not too bad. Some days you have to lie waiting in shelter, in Tamar Pass. It is very narrow there. It is a bit like the Pentland Firth, and you have to wait until the tides suit you. You have to be on your toes, and take nothing for granted.

"In May 2011, the *TAMAR* was sold to a lady from Oban, Scotland, named Heather Chaplin. Bought was a new ship, the *CONCORDIA BAY*, a drive-on, drive-off vessel. The*TAMAR* was destined for northern Scotland, to work around the western isles. Heather Chaplin asked me to take it there. I agreed, but after calling into Montevideo, Uruguay, where the new owner tried and failed to get cargo, I was told the owner was now bankrupt.

"She owed me and the crew two months pay. We eventually got our money. I had help from home in getting the back pay for myself and the crew, and also pay to fly me and the crew members home from Montevideo. The *TAMAR* sat for a year, before she was bought and renamed the *ST TERESA* to trade around Samoa, Tonga, and New Zealand. Meanwhile, the new ferryboat owners down in the Falklands had two captains, and one wanted to come back to the UK to take up further studies for an Unlimited Ticket. I was asked would I deputise. I agreed."

36

LUXURY LINE-UPS

SAILING blissfully through calm and balmy Caribbean seas is a dream way to spend a holiday, providing you have a healthy bank balance. The romance of posh passage, amid the paradise of tropical islands, was initially a speciality target for the super rich.

Having to work as a deck hand or such likes in a strict regime demanded by the shipping companies was not such a glamorous occupation, and soon lost appeal. No doubt, there were occasional compensations, when docked in an azure blue harbour to let the well-heeled voyagers time on shore, but John McKay of Corrymeelagh was much more content when he returned to basic seafaring.

At one time, three Cushendun men worked on the *QUEEN of BERMUDA*, sailing out of New York harbour to meander through the West Indies. One member of the crew was McKay, and the other two Glensmen were the McVeigh brothers, Johnny and Denis, both born at Ballindam, overlooking Cushendun Bay.

McKay wearied of this life. It was not all that it was cracked up to be, he felt. His widow Kathleen (nee Laverty, Glenariffe), said: "John was with Denis McVeigh a long time at sea, but always felt the voyages meant being away too long from home. He worked on liners *OCEAN MONARCH* and *QUEEN of BERMUDA*, and became Master at Arms. I think Denis (McVeigh) was responsible for helping John get the jobs. I used to hear him talk highly of Denis. I remember Denis attending our wedding, in 1967.

"The cruising from New York went around the islands of the Caribbean. He was also on runs to New Zealand and Australia. He was three years overall on this long-voyage work. Denis McVeigh worked as Sergeant at Arms on the *QUEEN of BERMUDA*, and John was alongside him. John's aunt Kate lived in New York, and we still have letters from her, one dated 1961 when John was on the liners. His brother Pat also worked on the liners with him, as a steward.

"Pat left the seas, to settle and work in New York. It would seem John also stopped off to work in New York, but only for a short spell. I think Pat, after he left sea work, had a job looking after a boiler. Pat, a twin of the late Alex, who died in Glasgow, aged 65, lived for many years in Long Island, and then moved out west to Gilbert, not far from Phoenix, Arizona.

"John left New York to go back to work at sea. He stopped those long voyages before I knew him, and changed to work on Head Line ships out of Belfast, passages to Canada. He also did some sailing in the

Mediterranean, including trips to Greece, and also other parts of the Continent, and on different ships."

Long before John McKay sailed on the proud, majestic liners, he managed to escape the often unrewarding drudgery of working for various local farmers. It is believed his first paid job was that of assistant gardener at Glenmona House, Cushendun, when four gardeners were employed on the estate. He was 14. John was a late starter at seafaring, going on boats for a first time in 1952. I found his fractured sea career most interesting. Born in 1927, he died aged 84, on November 11, 2011. John did not take to the sway of the sea until 25 years of age, and mostly due to exasperation.

Wife Kathleen explained: "When he left school, there was not much work to be had locally. He did jobs here and there for local farmers. There was not a great deal of money in that. He then drove a tractor and baler for Duggie Kenny, who came from Ballygarvey near Rathkenny, and did contract threshing and baling throughout the Glens. That lasted until Duggie decided to emigrate to Canada.

"John worked for Glenariffe sheepman Jim McHenry. I believe Jim was at sea for a very short time. During that period, while working for Jim McHenry, John was in conversation with Paddy 'The Mariner' McIlwaine, who said he'd find out if there was a job going that would get John started at sea. Paddy did just that. John received a telegram to report for work. He had to travel to Swansea to join the boat. He told me then he didn't know where Swansea was. Anyhow, he managed to get there. I remember him telling me he started as a fireman on a coal burner. It was hard and dirty work."

During his overall career on the water, John Anthony McKay attained his Seamen's Certificate on June 10, 1953, while on the *BELGRAVE.* The skipper was Thomas Mitchell. McKay was then an Ordinary Seaman, and 13 months later took the EDH (Efficient Deck Hand) Certificate at Swansea. On November 1, 1956, he earned his AB and Lifeboatman Certificates, and on May 31, 1984, the Navigational Watch Rating Certificate.

"When we married, in 1967, he stopped the sea work," added Kathleen, "I had a cousin who worked for Hughes Bakery in Belfast, and John decided to quit the sea to became a breadman. It wasn't a good time. He was not atall happy in that job. 'The Troubles' started. He tried to get back to work at sea, and found it very difficult. He was unable to return to the work he did before he married, at deep-sea sailing, but eventually he found work on container ferryboats. One of the last boats he worked on was the *BISON*, the ferry to Fleetwood. He also worked on the Dublin to Liverpool ferry."

McKay joined the 3,452 gross ton *BISON*, on the 15th of September 1975, and also acted as relief bo'sun for a long time, along with a man McLaughlin from the Inishowen Peninsula. It was one week on, and one week off. He was also on the *BUFFALO*, setting off from his home by bus and train to join the boat in Dublin.

He moved to work on the *BUFFALO* on November 21, 1980, as Chief Petty Officer, until March 19, 1981, and then back to the *BISON*, out of Liverpool on March 31, 1981. The Master signature was that of N.C. McGaughey for both *BUFFALO* and *BISON*, and by Danny McNaughton in 1984. He signed off the *BISON* for the last time, on February 11, 1988.

Kathleen McKay's own family circle had strong association with seafaring. "Brian Black of Carrivemurphy, Glenariffe, went to sea. He was an uncle of my father, Francis Laverty - a brother of my father's mother who was Ann Black. My mother was a McVeigh." Her mother's brother was the ill-fated, long-serving seaman Daniel 'Dingle' McVeigh from Carrivemurphy near the 'Dog's Nose' who was murdered in his house in Waterfoot.

Back to those balmy days of sophisticated sailing on liners. By contrast to John McKay, the McVeigh's and Dalla (Kathleen) Leavey relished the life of comfort cruising. The whiff of seaweed was never far the nostrils of the McVeigh brothers. It is believed their forefathers traded on schooners from Cushendun to Dunaverty, on the Mull of Kintyre. Also Daniel Brogan, an uncle of the McVeigh men, was a long-distance seaman. Tragically, he died of the yellow fever in Bombay, in 1918.

The sons of Daniel McVeigh and Anne Brogan were born and reared above the Milltown, Cushendun. It appears Daniel (McVeigh) spent time at sea. Two of his offspring followed, and eventually joined forces as crew members on the 'millionaire's' cruise ships. Denis was first in security services in the Far East. Johnny, born in 1893, moved from his job as a butcher with his cousin, Thomas Nelson Brogan, at Parnell Street, Dublin, to become a Master Butcher in the cruise ship business.

He was appointed Head Butcher of the *OCEAN MONARCH*, a sister ship of the *QUEEN of BERMUDA*, that also belonged to the Furness-Bermuda Line. Denis, who married Annie McCormick of Bonavor, was appointed Sergeant-at-Arms and worked alongside his brother on the *QUEEN of BERMUDA*.

Johnny married in America, and lived at Aladdin Avenue, New Jersey. Incidentally, he had a son, who also became a butcher, but moonlighted in a mortuary. Johnny once joked, during a visit in the early 1950's to his cousin in Knocknacarry, Alex O'Hara: "My boy decided to go to evening classes, and study at our local High School to become a mortician. So, he must be unique in New Jersey - a butcher by day and a mortician by night."

The two luxury liners, built in the 1930's at Tyne, England, and featuring three funnels, were among the elite vessels of the lucrative trade. During the 1930's the passage between New York and Bermuda took merely 40 hours in each direction, with four days to be spent on holiday on the island.

Both ships were requisitioned for war duty during the Second World War, and afterwards the QUEEN of BERMUDA returned to cruise service in 1947. It appears around this time the McVeigh brothers teamed up on the restored run from New York to Hamilton Harbour, Bermuda. Sadly, the MONARCH was unable to rejoin the old luxury trail, gutted by fire while under refitting after the War. She was salvaged by the Ministry of Transport, and converted into an emigrant liner.

As a young impressionable youngster at the old Knocknacarry Primary School, a two-room establishment divided by a wooden concertina-style partition, and a place that doubled as a parish centre for concerts and plays, I was hypnotised by the tales of Johnny McVeigh. He was in our kitchen, paying a flying, and, I believe, final visit to Cushendun. I wanted to go to sea with him. My imagination ran riot. I could live out my fantasies of visiting all those magical foreign places,

Johnny recalled times of working as a butcher in Dublin, and then converting his skills to sea travel, following in the wake of his cousin, Alex O'Hara. He said he'd come back one day, when I was out of short pants, and take me with him. I never saw him again. Anyhow, other interests took over. My younger brother, Daniel also 'nearly' made the sea, taking advise from Denis McVeigh to become a purser on the *QUEEN of BERMUDA*. Just as Daniel Vincent was about to pack a gunny sack full of 'quells', and take off over the horizon, the liner went out of business.

Daniel said: "The notion to go to sea happened after having chats with Denis (McVeigh). That was in 1966, when involved in accountancy examinations. I believed I'd like to work on ships as a purser. I even had Arthur Hamilton purchase a Merchant Navy badge for me. I think the liner was due to arrive in Belfast when she was decommissioned. That put an end to my plans to go to sea."

The luxury living on board liners also suited Dalla (Kathleen) Leavey of Cushendun Village, sailing on both of the fabled Cunard ships, *QUEEN MARY* and *QUEEN ELIZABETH*. The Southampton connection remained firm. It was from here her father was born. He married Sarah McAfee of Cushendun. Dalla's niece Marie (Mrs Sean Mort) said: "Dalla worked, mostly as purser on the two great luxury liners, travelling first class to New York and back to Southampton for over 40 years. She was able to visit her brother Jack in the United States, where he became a janitor at a school in New York."

"Dalla was 80 when she died in 1990. During her years at sea, she met many famous people. She was born in Cushendun, and later became Mrs Smith. She settled close to the trans-Atlantic luxury liner base at Southampton, and during some glittering voyages secured the autographs of famous folk. She spent many years working on the *QUEEN MARY*, until this majestic vessel was taken out of service, and is now at Long Beach, California. She was also employed on other well-known liners, mainly the *QUEEN ELIZABETH*.

The *QUEEN MARY*, with the significant three black and red funnels, and 12 decks, completed her maiden voyage on May 27, 1936. She had passenger capacity of 1,957, and a crew of 1,174. Constructed by John Brown and Co Ltd of Clydebank, she was 81,237 gross tons, and had a cruising speed of 28.5 knots. Used as a troop ship, from March 1940 to September 1946, she was back into service, but retired from passenger duty and was then purchased by the City of Long Beach, California, in December, 1967.

Incidentally, the autographs garnered by Dalla Leavey included the then husband and wife partnership of Mel Ferrer and Audrey Hepburn,

Victor Mature's signature, the 1956 signing by flamboyant American pianist Liberace, of Glasgow-born actress Deborah Kerr of *'The King and I'* and *'From Here to Eternity'* film fame.

On September 29, 1962, Dalla collected the wacky squiggly signature of inimitable comedian/actor Bob Hope. Also listed in a special booklet is a further array of matinee idols of the 'Golden era of Movies' and the sophisticated period of sea travel - New Yorker Van Johnson, Chicago-born silent movie and early 'talkie' actress Gloria Swanson, Brooklyn-born Jeff Chandler - fabled for his depiction of North American native warrior, Cochise in *'Broken Arrow'*, and American actress/singer Sophie Tucker.

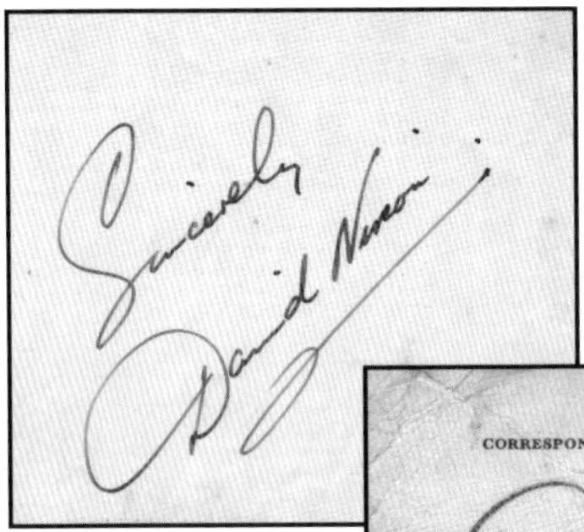

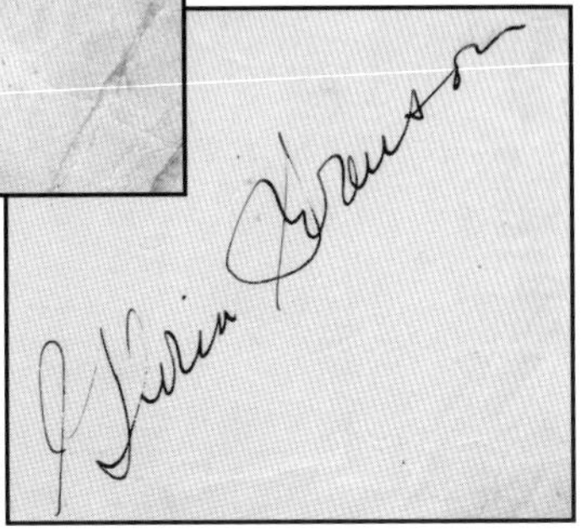

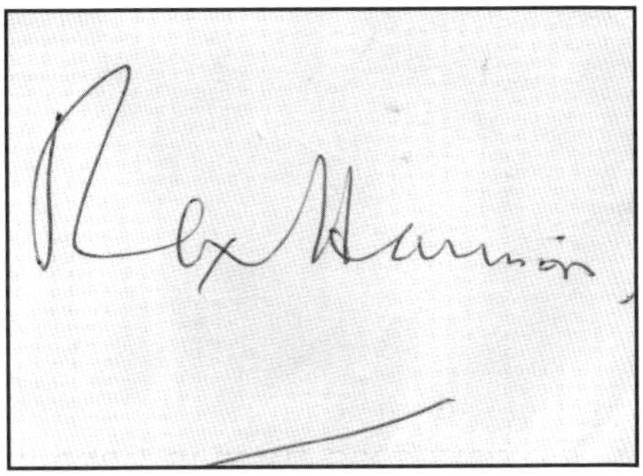

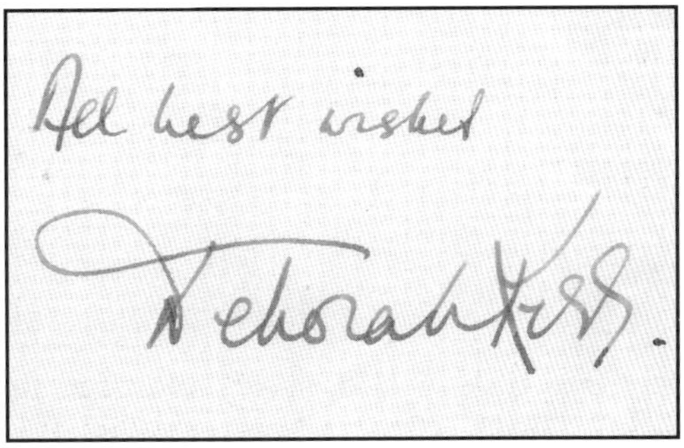

In the book of fame also are the names of Rochdale-born singer and comedy actress Gracie Fields, English big band singer Dorothy Squires, Australian-born actor Ron Randell, and his pin-up actress wife, Laya Raki, English magician David Nixon, English actresses Joyce Grenfell and Anne Todd, American actress Rosalind Russell, and the then husband and wife pairing of Rex Harrison and Kay Kendall.

Marie Mort retains the tartan-covered autograph book, featuring the outline of the *QUEEN MARY.* She added: "By far, the *QUEEN MARY* was the most popular and famous of the Cunard liners. As a purser, aunt Dalla was in the ideal position to meet and greet all the famous personalities. The names of the Queen ships suggested an air of romance, style, and luxury - and they were used by the elite of society.

"I was delighted to be given her autograph book. The signatures create priceless memories from a magical time when films provided fabulous entertainment after the Second World War. One of my favourites in the book list is Victor Mature. How could you forget those big eyebrows, and that smile." The broad-chested Mature was born in New York City in 1913, and died in 1999. One of Hollywood's most popular male actors after the Second World War, he featured prominently in *'My Darling Clementine'*, and biblical epics such as *'Samson and Delilah'*.

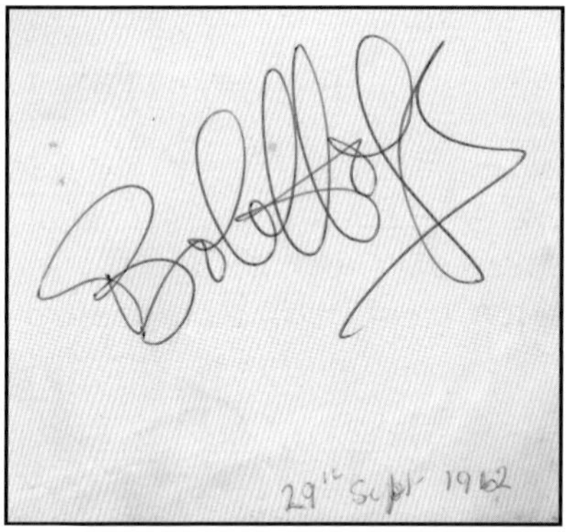

Other locals to work on the *QUEEN MARY* and *QUEEN ELIZABETH* liners included Charlie McKay of Gortacreggan, Cushendun, and Barney McLaughlin of Tully, who lived at The Bay, Glenariffe,

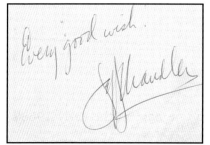

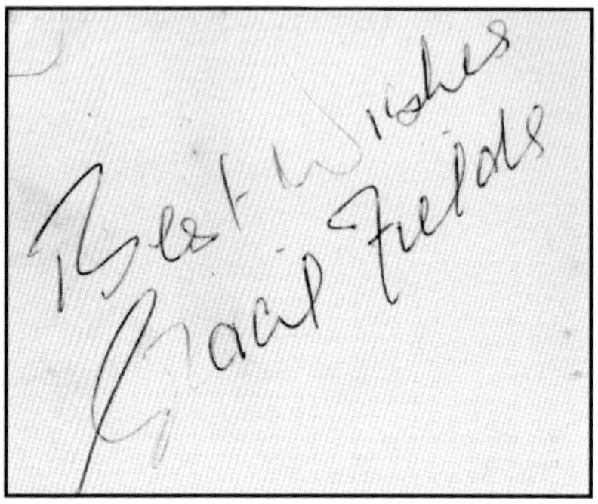

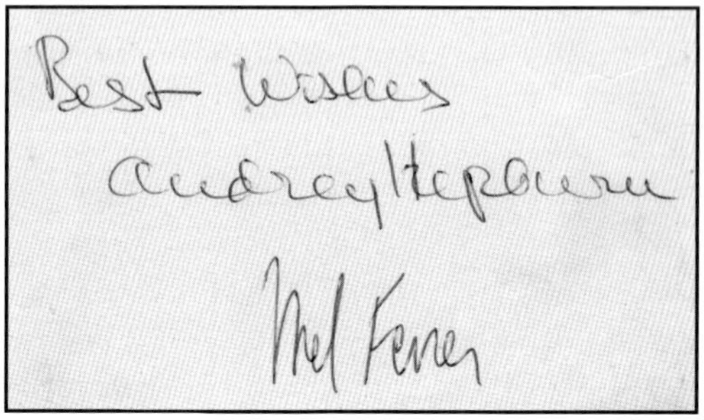

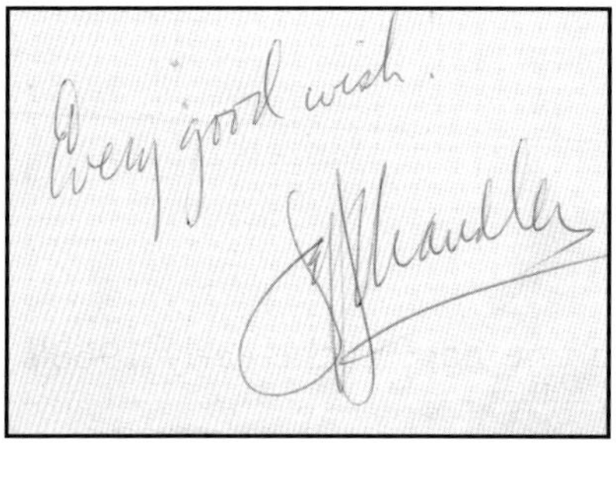

37

CURRY FAVOURED

CULINARY delights were not expected on small coastal trading vessels. A good wholesome fry was more the menu, in keeping with the occupation, yet the late Captain Danny McNaughton, of Tully, Cushendall, used to relish recalling the greatest meals served during his lengthy career at sea were concocted by a one-armed cook.

It is mind-boggling to contemplate how this physically-hampered chef could keep his balance when the Dorey boat and stomachs were heftily heaving during an unrelenting storm, and make and serve a meal in the cramped galley conditions. Hot curry was this eccentric cook's speciality. "The best curry I ever ate, He was a remarkable cook," McNaughton would declare.

This was one of many fascinating sagas that filled close on 30 years of seafaring for Captain Danny. Before he took to the boats it was literally a case of switching from tea chest to sea chest. He was employed by the Shore Street, Cushendall, grocery firm of McAlister's, still affectionately known as 'Arthur's'. One of his early tasks was to help in the tea blending and tea packaging process.

His widow Margaret said: "Danny went to sea at 17, after working for 'Arthur's', from the day he left primary school, at 14 years of age. I remember the loose tea from McAlister's. It arrived in a big square box. The empty wooden tea chest came in for a lot of uses."

Born on November 11, 1939, Danny helped in sorting out various blends of tea from chests imported from overseas. He progressed to making deliveries in Arthur's grocery van. He worked alongside Malachy Skelton and Betty Spence, the latter to marry Jackie Carson, and down the line their son John Carson would, in turn, marry Danny's daughter Marion. That was an easy-going era, when 'Arthur's' patented their own distinctive tea-brew blend in the Glens.

Andrew McAlister, part of the family-run business, recalled: "I remember our tea-blending enterprise, and having to mix the teas, weigh, and fill our own blend into firm white paper bags featuring the McAlister logo. It used to be three separate types of tea in chests that were supplied to us by S. D. Bell of Belfast. The packed wooden tea chests were shipped into Belfast from India.

"My father, Danny, showed me how to mix the teas, to make it our special flavour. The early system was to take a scoop of tea from each of the three types, and mix them together in one bag. In the early 1960's, James 'Jimmy' McNeill of the Rocks, a very handy man, invented this very functional weighing system for our tea-packing. At that time, he worked at our salmon-fishing net, and also did all sorts of jobs for us.

"He had a great pair of hands, and invented this contraption that could exactly weigh one quarter pound of tea or one half pound of loose tea, to pour into the bags. It was a perfectly reliable and accurate weighing machine. Jimmy's weighing system helped to speed up packaging - and when it broke down he would repair it right away.

"That was Arthur's tea. Later, I believe it came down to two types of blend mixed into one bag, for the customers. It was a good tea. Unique. Towards the end of the interest in our tea, in the late 1960's, due to changing tastes and probably the introduction of perforated tea bags, the firm of S. D. Bell mixed it for us. It was never quite like our own homespun blend.

"Empty tea chests, by the way, were in 'wild' demand in those days when the tea was very popular in the Glens. The chests would be used for a lot of things, such as the first type of a children's playpen, but mostly used for housing new-born chicks, and also lambs. Of course, we delivered the tea bags and other goods throughout the Glens in a big van

"My uncle, Mannix used to drive the delivery van. I also remember Mick McKeown driving it, then followed by Mick Quinn, and finally Seamus Murphy. My father (Danny) occasionally went out in the van to deliver goods. Way back in the 1930's 'Arthur's' also delivered coal around the Glens, and had coal cargo imported into Red Bay Pier, before giving up the trade. It was taken over by the Murphy family."

When blending and packaging loose tea, and some times out on the delivery van, Danny McNaughton become hypnotised when listening to tales told by some of the local seafarers. The man who most influenced the teenager was Captain Jim McGonnell, and this was to eventually lead to a very successful career on the local sea lanes.

Job opportunities before and after the Second World War were far from plentiful in the valleys . . . working on farms, the road repairs or quarries. 'Arthur's' was part of the limited outlets. The main opening was out on the oceans, and Danny decided on fresh horizons. He moved from McAlister's shop to seize the golden opportunity of a life at sea.

It appears he first approached Shore Street skipper Jim McGonnell, and from there the sea career took off. Less than four years of working for Arthur McAlister's, McNaughton took off on the great adventure, and worked his way through the grades, to qualify as a Home Trade captain. A willing worker, he spent the opening twelve years with the Dorey Company of Guernsey.

McNaughton's widow, Margaret (nee O'Neill of the old Pheasant Inn, a one-time popular roadside hostelry in Glenravel) added: "I was only 12 years of age when Danny went to sea. Two of his brothers, George and Charlie had short spells at sea. Charlie was away for merely a week or so, while George stayed at sea for a couple of months."

Married in 1968, she kept Captain Danny's record of sea travels. Daniel Joseph McNaughton's chart was registered R 674221. He completed the EDH Certificate on May 29, 1958, the Mate's Home Trade ticket on July

CERTIFICATE OF COMPETENCY

AS

MASTER

OF A HOME TRADE PASSENGER SHIP No. 112326

'In this document wherever the expressions "Minister of Transport" or "Ministry of Transport" occur they are to be read as if the expressions had been "Board of Trade".'

To Daniel Joseph McNaughton

WHEREAS you have been found duly qualified to fulfil the duties of Master of a Home Trade Passenger Ship, in the Merchant Service, the Minister of Transport in exercise of his powers under the Merchant Shipping Acts and of all other powers enabling him in that behalf, hereby grants you this Certificate of Competency.

SIGNED BY AUTHORITY OF THE MINISTER OF TRANSPORT and dated this 25th day of March 1966

Countersigned

Registrar General

An Under ~~A Deputy~~ Secretary of the Ministry of Transport

REGISTERED AT THE OFFICE OF THE REGISTRAR GENERAL OF SHIPPING AND SEAMEN

21, 1964, the Certificate of Competence in Radiotelephony on February 18, 1965, and the Captain Home Trade Certificate on March 31, 1966.

His Discharge Book discloses he started with Dorey's on March 31, 1957, and sailed out of Swansea for Goole on the *PERELEE*. He signed off from Dorey in November 1969, leaving from the *PORTELET*. He quit the sea on December 31, 1987, leaving the ferryboat *NORSKY*, at Ipswich, and sadly died of a cancer on October 16, 2012.

His brother Archie stated: "Danny was one of nine of a family. Sadie was the eldest. George, the third member of the family and the eldest boy, went to sea for a short period as a stoker on Kelly coal boats, and then went to live in Oxford. Next in the pecking order was Danny, then Charlie (deceased) - who also had a brief spell at sea. I am the third youngest, followed by Pat, and then the youngest is Alex (Big Al).

"Danny went to sea with the Dorey Company, with Captain Jim McGonnell, and was based in Guernsey. He did coastal trips, and also to Rouen and up the Baltic. He then joined Captain Charlie McQuillan, and the trips included runs down to Casablanca. I remember Danny studying in Belfast for his Captain's Ticket, in the middle 1960's. I was still at school then. He had to take time off work, on block release from Dorey's, to do it. He obviously did the Mate tickets before that. When he was sitting his Captain's Ticket examination, he stayed in digs at Newington Avenue, off Belfast's Antrim Road, in 1966, and I stayed in the same digs, in 1967.

"After he passed his test for Captain he didn't get a ship of his own, and was First or Second mate, and did not have a captaincy of his own. He stayed with Doreys until moving to the ferryboats. He followed a family trend in taking to the sea. My father, Charlie, had three brothers, John, Alex, and Archie, who went to Canada. Of the three, uncle John, the eldest, I believe sailed deep-sea for a time, and then became Harbour

Master at Vancouver. The three brothers went to Vancouver when my father was four years old. Alex and Archie, who married Rosie Gore, also settled in the Vancouver area."

Harriet McKay (nee Quinn), a first cousin of Captain Danny, also included the tragic death at sea of a young James McNaughton, Danny's uncle. She said: "James was killed, drowned at sea. He was on the *GEM* when it struck German mines on Christmas Day, 1914. I was told James wanted, first of all, to go to Canada, to join his three older brothers there, but his mother, my granny, was against it. She didn't want him to go, insisting he was too young to emigrate with his brothers.

"I think James was probably about 17 at the time. So, instead, he went to work at sea with Captain James McKeegan. Five years later, aged 22, he was dead. There was nothing much else in the way of work in those days, locally, and going to sea was a way of making money. After that Christmas Day tragedy, my granny said she would never again stop anybody in the family from going wherever.

"She was Mary McDonnell, married to Alexander McNaughton at Lubitavish. I always felt it was also very sad that because Sarah McNaughton was born long after the eldest member of the family - John - went to Canada, she never met him until she was 48 years of age. That was when John came here on a holiday."

Adding to the McNaughton sea connection information are valuable contributions by Captain Danny's brother-in-law James (Jimmy) Docherty, married to Ellie McNaughton, and living at Bishopbriggs, Glasgow. Historian Docherty traced McNaughton seamen to the 19th century, including a Thomas McNaughton, born in Cushendun on June 18, 1799, and taking to the ships at 16 years of age.

Docherty stated: "He had a ticket registration number, 60142, issued at Cork on June 30, 1845. He was based at Cobh. Then we had James McNaughton, listed as seaman/cook, and born in Cushendall in 1827. His ticket registration was at Belfast on June 30, 1849. He was the son of Alexander McNaughton and Ally Murphy from Torr. James, a great grandfather of Captain Danny, married Anne Martin around 1860, and died at Tieveragh, Cushendall, in 1901.

"Another son was Charles, who was born in 1828, and went to sea at 21-years-of-age. He registered in Belfast, and was an Able Seaman. There was also the eldest son, Daniel, born at Layd around 1820. It is believed he was first in the Dublin Metropolitan Police, and listed a Daniel 'McNattan'. He left there in 1845, returning home to go to sea. He died in 1887, aged 67. Uncles of Captain Danny who went to sea were John and James, the latter killed on board the *GEM* in 1914."

Docherty also maintained John, before going to Vancouver, left Cushendall in 1911 and started a sea career out of Glasgow. "The McSparran's of Knocknacarry had a shop in Glasgow, and, at times, gave accommodation to seamen from the Glens. I understand John McNaughton stayed with them. John and his brothers Archie, Patrick and Alexander went to Canada. At a later date Patrick returned home.

"When John came back to Ireland, in the early 1960's, Ellie and I were at home in Tully. Charlie and his sister Rosie (Harriet McKay's mother), travelled to either Louth or Meath to see John, who was staying at his wife's home. I remember Charlie coming back that evening very excited after seeing his brother, who had left home when Charlie was four years of age."

Back to the Captain Danny story. Three years after his start at sea, he was promoted to Second Mate on the *PERELLE,* on July 23, 1960. That vessel was scrapped on July 3, 1962. In 1964, he was a First Mate. Coastal trips, and with Guernsey his base, took in ports such as Goole, Swansea, Blyth, North Shields, Cardiff. He sailed mostly with Captain McGonnell or Captain J. D. McFaul, and also worked on the *AMBER*, out of Swansea, and the *AMETHYST*, out of Sunderland.

He joined the *PORTELET* at Amsterdam on October 24, 1961, and was back on the *PERELEE,* under Jim McGonnell. He also sailed under Captain Charlie McQuillan. He was with McGonnell on the *BELVEDERE,* also switching back and forward to the *PORTELET.* He had shifts on the *PUTNEY* and *HAVELET*, and was First Mate on the *PORTELET* during 1967 and 1968. Some of the journeys took in New Ross, Belfast, Sharpness, Goole, Barry, and he signed off the *PORTELET* as First Mate on November 3, 1969.

Captain Danny decided to take a break from seafaring, following the birth of his first born, Marion. He returned to the sea, but in a career switch - to work on channel ferryboats. He was with the Belfast Steamship Company vessels *ULSTER PRINCE, BISON*, and *ULSTER SPORTSMAN.* The *BISON* trips were out of Larne, and for a long period.

Wife Margaret said: "He used to take me and the children on the P&O ferries. By the way, his mother Annie Harvey was born in Scotland, and as a youngster was sent to be reared by her granny and grandfather up Glenariffe Glen. She married Charlie McNaughton. Her brother Johnnie was held prisoner by the Japanese in the Second World War."

Ports visited on the ferryboats also included Dublin, Hamburg, and Belfast, and he was either Second Officer or Relieving Chief Officer. During March 1981, he was on the *BUFFALO,* and again on the *ULSTER PRINCE,* on the Liverpool-Belfast run, as Relieving Chief Officer. There was a period when he switched from working on the *BUFFALO* to the *POINTER*, then to the *BISON,* and back to the *POINTER.*

In December 1983, he was Chief Officer of the *POINTER,* out of Belfast, and on February 2, 1984, was Chief Officer on the P&O Ferries *PUMA*, from Larne to Fleetwood. Danny moved back to the *BISON* on March 26, 1986, and was either Relieving Chief Officer or Second Officer. Working for P.O.E.T.S Fleet Management Limited, he quit the sea on December 31, 1987, leaving the *NORSKY* at Ipswich.

From the early days of working in Arthur's, there was pleasing irony when his daughter Marion married John Carson, the son of his former work colleague Betty Carson (nee Spence). There was also a short sea link between the families. Betty's husband Jackie Carson went to sea.

John Carson said: “My father was at sea from 1949 to 1954. He sailed for a period with Captain James Kelly of Carnlough, on the *PASS of DRUMOCHTER*. He also worked in London, and with him was Willie Graham of Glenariffe. The Carson family came from the lower Ormeau Road, and my dad’s father had a butcher’s shop where we lived in Joy Street, in the Markets area. My father served his time in the nearby slaughterhouse, and then joined the family butcher’s shop.

“He went to the St Malachy’s Primary School, in the Markets. My brother Oliver and sister Margaret were born in Belfast. We had a shop in May Street, but it was burned out in 1968, at the beginning of ‘The Troubles’. My father was keen on boxing, and in his youth was an active member of the old St John Bosco Club, at Sailortown, Belfast. He also played club Gaelic football in Belfast, and in later years helped to start a Gaelic football team in Cushendall. He died aged 77.

“My grandfather once planted trees in Joy Street, and they are still there. The family lived in Joy Street. My grandmother was Margaret McAuley, a ‘Henegan’ from Glenariffe. She was a seamstress. After she married my grandfather, she opened a seamster business above the butcher’s shop in Joy Street. My father was once sent down from Belfast to help work on the McAuley farm, and that is when he met Betty Spence.

“He was, for a long time, a driver for Citybus, and once drove a busload of bandsmen during the 12th of July parades, taking them to and from the ‘field’. At the same time, on the same day, our house was burned out at May Street. So, we came to live in Cushendall, where Dane McKillop now lives - before we moved around the back. For a while, my father had a butcher’s shop on Mill Street. I think before that McIlroy and McSparran ran a butcher’s shop there. He packed that in, and went to work at sea.”

Glenaan seaman John McKillop, left, with seated concertina-playing colleague at Liverpool docks

James McKillop of Glenaan

Patrick McKillop, Glenaan, has his 'likeness' taken in an Ostend studio

The HADRIANA, *Bombay*

Old Pier, The Bay, Glenariffe

The oil tanker BRITISH GULL

April 1943 - A young Gerry Blaney with his mother Mary

Glenariffe-born Charlie Graham of Calishnaugh, Cushendun

Captain John Graham, Cushendun, with his sister Winnie

Cushendall AB Sean Mort

The SCOTTISH STAR

Cushendall skipper Jim McGonnell

Paddy McCormick of Dunurgan, Cushendun

War hero shooting star Johnnie O'Hara, Cushendall

Cushendall Mort brothers, Bob (left) and James

Submariner Alex McDonald skippered this submarine

On passage to Australia - Cushleake's Joe Murphy (centre), Cushendun colleague Paddy McNeill and (left) Dubliner Paddy Meehan

Captain James McQuillan with wife Peggy

Captain. John O'Hara, Shore Street, Cushendall

Commander McDonald's ST. KITTS, *moored off Cannes, May 1956*

Cushendun's Paddy McNeill, second left, and crew colleagues

Cushendun's Francis McQuillan

Commander Alexander Smith McDonald and wife Betty when receiving the O.B.E.

Charlie 'The Sailor' McKay of Cushendun makes a 1949 visit to meet his cousin Mrs Brigid McQuillan (nee McKay) and his neice Margaret McQuillan in Guernsey. Right is Kathleen McQuillan - sister of Captain Charlie

Three amigos - teenage Cushendall sailors Alistair McKay, Roy Mort, and Pat Connolly

Wedding day of George McElheron, Straid, Cushendun, and Kate Murray

June 1941 wedding day of Captain Charlie McQuillan and Brigid McKay of Cushendun

Old-time Glenariffe sailor Jamie 'Barney' Delargy

John McKay of Ranaghan, Cushendun, with his nephew and niece, Cathal and Margaret McQuillan in Guernsey

Award-winning Cushendall seaman Pat Connolly

Cushendall seaman and blacksmith Joe McElroy

Coasting sailor Johnnie O'Boyle, Glenariffe

Future sea skipper Hugh O'Mullan, Waterfoot

DOREY'S PORTELET

38

ISLE of CALM

RAMSEY BAY, at the north tip of the Isle of Man, has often been a sanctuary of shelter for ships during the vilest of weather conditions. Running 18 kilometres, from the Point of Ayre to Maughold Head, the large bay was a welcome sight for many small craft during ferocious storms that lashed these islands at the end of January 1953.

In that frightening challenge, Johnnie O'Boyle of Glenariffe was glad of respite from a vicious torrent of high winds and mountainous waves that claimed one of the biggest sea disasters in these isles. On January 31, 1953, the remorseless seas took many lives in the shocking sinking of the *PRINCESS VICTORIA*.

O'Boyle had to use all his strength to help his Islandmagee-born skipper Bobby Ross turn the wheel and head the *BALLYGARVEY* out of the eye of the storm, and nudge into the calmer waters of Ramsey Bay. "That was the scariest incident of my days at sea. It is easy to remember the date, as it was during the *PRINCESS VICTORIA* calamity," he recalled,

"The skipper of the *BALLYGARVEY*, Captain Ross remained very cool in that crisis. Also on board was young Archie Murray of Parkmore, a deck boy, and John McNeill of Cushendun, who was AB - and better known as John the Rock.

"It was a wild morning on the Irish Sea, when we heard on the ship's radio about the *PRINCESS VICTORIA*. We were taking a cargo of coal from Garston to Belfast, but the weather was so severe we had to turn her, and pull in for shelter at Ramsey Bay. It wasn't an easy manoeuvre. Both the skipper and me were on the wheel to turn her round.

"The skipper was very calm. He told a deck hand aft to inform the chief engineer we were going to turn her around. It was a dangerous procedure in such ferocious conditions, huge waves, and screeching winds. I'd like to believe we got a wee break with a bit of calm. The danger was when you would put her broadside on. Thankfully, she came round all right, and we made it into Ramsey Bay.

"I was Lamp Trimmer and not Second Mate on her, but took watch. I did a Second Mate's job nonetheless, because she was not the tonnage for a second mate. She was 750 tons, whereas when I was on the *BALLYRORY* she was 2,000 tons and I was used as Second Mate. I was on the *BALLYGARVEY* for around nine years. I joined her in Belfast on January the 13th, 1953, and worked on her right through to discharge in Belfast on November 17, 1960." He once spent a year before that drama on the same boat, when it was known as the *DONAGHADEE*.

Back to the beginnings of a lengthy career at sea for this quiet sheep farmer, who came from a hillside near the head of Glenariffe Glen - close to the Laragh Lodge restaurant, and the nearby magnetic attraction of the famous waterfalls.

It is a peaceful place, with a distinctive backdrop of pine forests. Ahead lie the stunning views across the Sea of Moyle, but in a bygone time a difficult setting for survival on small hill farms. Born in 1929, there was sea mist in O'Boyle's vision, as both his father and uncle went to work on ships. and also his older brother Neil.

He said: "In my young days, there was hardly a house in Glenariffe that didn't have at least one man working at sea. Nowadays all the young people are off to find work in Australia. My father, John O'Boyle went to sea. His brother Paddy tragically drowned in Guernsey, during the Second World War blackout. That happened in 1940. The War was only starting. It appears, as far as we were ever able to find out, that a member of the ship's crew fell overboard into the harbour.

"Paddy jumped in to try and save him, and both were drowned. His daughter is Rosemary Carey, widow of Vincent Carey of Glenravel, and his son is Neil of JNK. Rosemary was only two-years-of-age when her father died. Paddy, who was born in 1900, is buried in Guernsey. I barely remember my father coming home from sea. He was at it a good while. He sailed deep-sea, as well as on coasters. Then my brother Neil, who was two years older than me, went to sea - and I was hell to get away as well. Neil was a long time coasting - over 30 years - firstly, on Kelly boats out of Belfast, and then he went to join Robertson's of Glasgow.

"He was a lengthy spell on the *St CONAN*, before moving to Gardiner's of Glasgow, and then back to Kelly's. He suddenly took ill, and was only 53 when he died of a cancer, collapsing one day at his car in Waterfoot. His eldest son, Sean was at Garron Tower at the time of his death. Neil left five of a family, three girls and two boys. 'Ginger' Pat is the other son - the motor mechanic. One girl is married to David Burns of Cushendall. At the time of Neil's death I was finished at sea, and was working with local builders, Murray and Partners."

Sean O'Boyle said: "My father was an engineer on Kelly boats. I never saw a lot of him, He would be home a couple of weeks, but mostly away at sea. I was 14 when he died suddenly, in 1978." His uncle Johnnie's Certificate of Discharge Book (No R 336241) lists his date of birth as August 19, 1929, and from Barrahilly, Glenariffe, with next of kin his mother Mrs Margaret O' Boyle. His A.B Certificate was issued at Guernsey, on the 8th of May 1950 (No 002252).

Behind the statistics, the list of boats he served on lies the fact a near neighbour and cousin, Eneas Black, helped Johnnie take to the oceans. "I was 19 when I went to sea. I hurled a bit for Glenariffe, but when the right age to play the game I was at sea. It was through Eneas Black I went to work on boats, and joined Dorey of Guernsey. Eneas and my mother were first cousins. He became a Dorey Relieving Captain, and had a farm just down the road from where I live."

Black was an experienced skipper, and lived at St. Samson, Guernsey. In his youth, he was an exceptional hurler for Glenariffe. He was in teams as far back as 1932, when the Ossian's eliminated the defending Antrim champions, Cushendun Emmets, in the North Antrim semi-final, at Ballycastle. Eneas was also in the Glenariffe teams that won the Antrim Championships of 1935 and 1937. His sons, Patsy and Eneas Jnr, also became superb hurlers. Patsy worked as AB on deep-sea Esso tankers for around ten years.

Johnnie O'Boyle added: "Young Eneas Black was a brilliant hurler, very quick. The oldest boy, Patsy was a very stylish hurler. I recall Patsy sailing to the Persian Gulf on a tanker to pick up oil cargo. I also believe he started off at sea on a small oil tanker, the *PASS of GLENOGLE.* under Captain John Mort of Cushendall.

"I worked on the *SARNIA,* when I first went to sea, in 1948. I sailed on her with Charlie McKay of Gortacreggan, Cushendun. I stayed one year on the *SARNIA*, and went to the *PORTELET* on May 9, 1952 at Guernsey, where I was signed in by the ship's master, Eneas Black. I discharged at Swansea on May 20, 1952, but remained on the same boat to work under Ryan T Alexander, and then for a short time under Jim McGonnell. Also on that boat then were the two McGaughey's from Cushendall - Neil and Willie.

"I joined the *ROCQUAINE,* under Captain Charlie McQuillan, and stayed a couple of years. Joe O'Boyle of Garron Point also worked for Captain McQuillan. Joe, whose sister Mary married Paddy McQuaige of Cushendun, was from the Rockhead, at the top of Glenariffe Glen. The other townland name of that place is Legrenagh.

"He married and lived at Garron Point, until he left sea to take up farming, when he bought a farm near Laragh Lodge, at Toberwine. Joe's brother, Alex was also at sea, for a while. Unfortunately, he suffered injuries. He was on a boat when there was an explosion, and he got his hands badly burned."

In October 2013, the late Joe O'Boyle's son, Joe revealed his father was taken to sea by Paddy O'Boyle of Parkmore, who was also an uncle of Johnnie O'Boyle. "My dad was from Parkmore, and 17 years of age at the time he went to sea. Born in 1917, he spent 38 years working on boats for the Dorey firm of Guernsey. He sailed mostly on the *LAND CREST*, the *SARNIA*, and the second *PORTELET*.

"He worked under Captain Charlie McQuillan, and a Larne skipper named McCullough. His last boat was the *PORTELET*, and with Captain McQuillan. My dad was First Mate when he suffered a heart attack in 1955, at Swansea. He came home to retire from sea work, and then bought the farm at Toberwine, and we live in the house beside the Laragh Lodge car park.

"At that time, when married to Margaret O'Kane of Garron Point, he moved from there to the farm. I was 17 when we went to Toberwine, where my mother still lives, fresh and well at 95. Daddy died aged 77 in 1996. I married Patricia McKendry, daughter of Jim, who was married to Shebbie McAllister, a sister of Mannix and Danny 'Arthur' of Cushendall.

We are also related to other sea going folk, Captain Angus McGaughey, a deep-sea man who retired to live at Crumlin. His father was Captain Neil McGaughey." Incidentally, Joe's mother Maggie celebrated her 96th birthday on Sunday, March 23, 2014.

. Johnnie O'Boyle, who has different spellings for his home patch - the townland of Barraghill, nowadays called Barrahooley, added: "When I was with Captain McQuillan, I also sailed with John McKay of Ranaghan, Cushendun, on the *ROCQUAINE*. John left the sea to work for a while in America.

"I was once in the McQuillan family home at St. Samson, Guernsey. I remember working as a deck hand on the *ROCQUAINE* when Captain Charlie brought his young son Cathal on board for a trip. The boy was always keen to get at the ship's wheel, and steer her. He'd ask his father: 'Can I drive her?'

"We would be carrying a cargo of gypsum, a chalk-like mineral used to make plaster of Paris and also plasterboard for ceilings, from up the River Thames to Rouen, France. I also recall taking cargo of cement from Antwerp to Derry. That was a four-day journey.

"After that, I came home for a bit, and then joined Kelly's in Belfast, for no particular reason, other than probably it was handier to home. I joined the *CARRICKMACROSS*, a ship's name that stayed for a bit during a period when Kelly's bought over ships from Corry and Sons. I was AB on her for a couple of months, until she went into dry-dock, and I went then for one year to the *DONAGHADEE*, a coal coaster.

"I signed on with the *BALLYHILL* as Second Mate, on November 17, 1960, at Derry, again working under Bobby Ross, and stayed until January 11, 1963. I was sent to join the *BALLYRORY* in Aberdeen, as Second Mate, and I was again reunited with Captain Ross. It was the month of January, and very cold. I had a touch of the 'flu, and a pain in my back. But for the letter asking me to report I probably would have stayed home, in bed.

"I headed up to Belfast, to go on the Glasgow boat, and for a first and only time I travelled first class. The ticket and travel costs were paid for by the company. I had a first-class cabin, turned in but couldn't sleep nor lie down, because of the pain in my back. I paced the deck all night long. Imagine having a first-class cabin and not being able to use it. I managed to get to Aberdeen. The pain went away, eventually.

"The *BALLYRORY* was a brand new coal cargo ship. On her first voyage, starting on January 16, 1963, we picked up cargo at Blyth, and sailed around the north of Scotland and down to Belfast, arriving on the 26th of January. Shortly afterwards, I had one outing on the *BALLYRUSH*, before returning to the *BALLYRORY,* on November 6, 1963, working until January 1965."

O'Boyle, a member of Glenariffe's 1955 team that won the Antrim Junior Hurling Championship, added: "I returned to work for Dorey's, on the *PORTELET*. Jim McGonnell was the Master, and I sailed with him for 18 months. I remember coming home in time for Christmas, when I received a letter from Captain Ross, asking if I would return to Kelly's. I decided I would, and went back to the *DONAGHADEE*, which was now renamed the *BALLYGARVEY*.

"I stayed over nine years on that ship. I took a break of 18 months, and returned to sea on October 18, 1966. It was after the National Union of Seamen's (NUS) strike of 1966. At first, they wouldn't let me sail, not sign on, but after the dust settled I got a job on another Kelly coal boat, the *BALLYMENA*. I was AB for two trips, running from Belfast to Ayr, and ending my days at sea in Belfast, on January 19, 1967."

O'Boyle, a mine of information on things Glenariffe, and seafaring, is related to some other O'Boyle's yet not directly related to others. As he explained "Quite a number of O'Boyle's live in the Glen, just like the Black's, McCormick's, Leech's, McNaughton's, the Murray families, and so forth. I'm not related to the O'Boyle's who were well known in hurling. They were called 'The Targers'. The one who was very well known was Alex 'Goshie'. 'Red' Denis O'Boyle, another strong hurler who went to sea, and Alex were cousins.

"From the top end of Glenariffe, we also had old Paddy Murray of Parkmore, who was at sea. His son, Paddy was also a sailor, but not for long. He went to the National Seaman's School, and qualified for a Mate's Ticket, but never used it, as he did not return to sea. He worked on the land from then on. Paddy Jnr was also a student at the Christian Brothers, when the Hardinge Street students came down to live in Cushendun during the Second World War, with the classes held in the Cushendun Hotel.

"Some others who went to sea included Jimmy Gribben of Kilmore. He married a Cornish girl, and lived in Cornwall. The brothers, Johnny and Pat 'Tom' McCormick both went to sea. From Tamlaugh, Pat and Joe Delargy went to sea. Joe was not that long on the boats, because he took ill, with a heart condition.

"From Drum-na-cur there was Willie Robbin, an AB There was a Captain Eddie Hyndman, but I don't really know where he came from. He lived about the Bay area for a time, and later went to live in Ballymena. From Boynaugh, above Waterfoot, there was Dan 'of the hill' McAlister, who worked at sea for a long time. He had three brothers, Charlie, Alex, and Willie, and I have a notion Charlie also went to sea for a while. Over at The Bay, an uncle of mine, Frank O'Boyle, was at sea for a good long spell, before he married Kate McCart of the Bay."

39

LEAP of FAITH

JUMPING ship has been a side product of long-haul ocean travel, ever since intrepid explorers discovered new and sometimes exotic locations to drop anchor, and begin a new life challenge in another country. The tale of the mutiny on the *BOUNTY*, and the Pitcairn Island hideaway, is perhaps the most colourful example of sailors leaving ship for a fresh shore.

In more modern times it was not as dramatic as that, no cat o' nine tails, even though naturally frowned upon as an irritation by ship captains and ship owners. The magnetic appeal of settling roots in a new surround often became too great to ignore, and I have a few examples of Glensmen who found far-off fields rewardingly green.

New Zealand became the favoured destination for young seaman such as Cushendun's Alistair Scally and Paddy McKendry, and from Cairns, Cushendall, the brothers McNaughton, Bernard and P.J 'Patsy'. Colin McNaughton, of Clough, Cushendall, made Australia his adopted base.

The natural outlet then to a career at sea was through the Training Schools. Alistair Scally's sister Eileen explained: "After he left St Aloysius's Intermediate School in Cushendall, Alistair joined the Sea Training School in England. He started working deep-sea, and on Port Line vessels to Australia and New Zealand."

Her husband, Eric McCullough added: "He went to the School at Sheerness at around 16 years age. The course was for ship's stewards and deck boys. When he came out of the School he managed to quickly get a job as a deck boy on cargo ships. He made a few of journeys from England to New Zealand and Australia, before deciding to leave his ship when it berthed in New Zealand,

"Alistair did not go back to his ship. Instead, he gave himself up to the local authorities, and was placed in a detention centre for a few weeks. That is what happened then. You had to serve a penalty, but for a short time. Workers were welcomed in New Zealand then, and after he was released he was allowed to remain there. He became a citizen of New Zealand. He took up seafaring jobs again, and worked for a New Zealand shipping company. The sea journeys were mainly to Australia and up to Taiwan.

"He lived in Auckland for a time. Alistair married a local girl, Margaret, who sadly died in 2011. They reared a family of two girls, and a boy, the youngest of the family is named Shane. They settled in Papakura, a town on the North Island. It is situated in the south side of Menokoa Harbour, on the opposite end of the bay from Auckland."

Moving to live in the Antipodes was a must for Patsy McNaughton. He had good reason to seek a change of lifestyle, after testing his nerves to the limit while sailing up the Mekong Delta during the Vietnam War. Anywhere in the vicinity of Saigon City proved to be an extremely high-risk occupation. During such hazardous trips in the Mekong, a young McNaughton decided it was time to switch to a less stressful occupation.

He was working for an American shipping company, taking supplies to the US forces in Vietnam. It was a lucrative job, yet never too far removed from the actual bloodbaths of that horrible conflict. He was soon to find that out, and when it became too much to stomach Patsy jumped ship in New Zealand, and worked there ever since.

A brother of prominent Cushendall and ex-Derry county hurling and camogie coach Kevin 'Mogey' McNaughton, he and brother Bernard, nicknamed 'Bunny', decided to follow their father Pat to a life on the waves, Patsy started on coasters from Belfast. He began as a galley boy. Like Bernard, he became an AB, and moved from coasters to work on deep-sea tankers.

Kevin McNaughton said: "For a time, he worked for an American shipping firm, making very dangerous journeys into Vietnam. That was during the war there. His ship brought in oil and petrol supplies for the American Forces. He once told me he saw dead bodies floating downstream as his ship was travelling up the river. I think that finished him with sea work.

"Patsy had enough of the Vietnam run, and when the ship eventually berthed in New Zealand he decided to stay on dry land. He jumped ship, and has since worked on the railways in New Zealand. He lives at Napier. He keeps himself very fit, running for miles - and also loves to do a lot of swimming. He's like a walrus in the water. When he was home on a holiday, he swam from Limerick Point to the old salmon net, and then back across Cushendall Bay.

"Bernard also jumped ship in New Zealand, but remained a seaman. Now 67 (in early 2013), he is still working on coasters around New Zealand. Throughout his working life he never left the boats. He married in New Zealand, and raised a family of three. Sadly, one of the children was killed in a crash in 2008.

"Bernard went, at 16 years of age, to the Sea Training School in the Bristol Channel. I remember food parcels being sent from home to him. After that, he went to work deep-sea, and was an AB most of his days. A big mate of Bernard's out there in New Zealand is Paddy McKendry, a son of the late Pat McKendry of Cushendun Village, and an older brother of Kevin 'Brass' McKendry.

"Paddy (McKendry) was at sea, and also jumped ship to live in New Zealand. Before making the move to stay there, Bernard and Paddy McKendry were on Blue Star Line ships, sailing from London to travel all over the world. The main trips were to the Far East, Australia, and New Zealand. Paddy and our Bernard live pretty close to one another in Auckland. Around 300 miles south lives Patsy, who is known out there as

'Chris'. They put that nickname on him, because they thought the name, Patsy a derogatory one, a soft touch."

Johnny O'Hara of Tromra, Cushendun, once bumped into McKendry and Scally while berthed in Auckland. "It was there I met Alistair, and I think it was in 1974," O'Hara said, "Everyone at dockside knew him as 'Paddy' Scally. After they jumped ship, Alistair and Paddy (McKendry) continued to work at sea, with New Zealand shipping companies on the Trans-Tasman route."

Kevin McNaughton resumed his family's sea-going stories: "My father Patrick worked on Kelly coasters. He went to sea in his early 20's. Born in 1914, he started work around 1934, and remained a seaman until he retired at 65 years of age. He worked as a fireman in the early days, when boats were coal-driven. When the change was made to oil-driven engines he became an engineer. His brother Charlie also went to sea for a very short time. The last place Charlie lived was in Sunderland."

Another McNaughton, the late Colin, worked alongside namesake Bernard at sea. He too jumped ship, and in this instance it was to live in Australia. A son of another old sailor - Patrick Charles McNaughton, better known as 'Belturbet', he died in 2000 of cancer - following return from 'Down Under' to his native Cushendall. He purchased the house beside the (Thornlea) Glens Hotel.

His brother Fergus, a former Antrim Hurling Board chairman, said: "Colin went to Ballymena Technical school, and then directly at 16 to the Merchant Navy's Sea Training School in south Wales. Born in 1946, he was one year younger than me. He went straight to work with the Blue Line, at deep-sea, and was quite a while going back and forth to Australia and New Zealand. I believe he jumped ship in Australia when around 21 years of age. He didn't return to boats after that.

"Colin set up a steel-erecting business in Melbourne, and supplied materials and the workforce in the building of the Gaelic Park, Melbourne. With him working on that project were Charlie McAuley of Altmore, and Harry McCurry, a brother of James and Charlie of Gault's Road. Colin was also President of the GAA in the Melbourne area, and also followed the Hawthorns football team in the Australian Rules."

Fergus, who was Antrim Hurling Board Chairman during the county team's stirring run to the 1989 All-Ireland Senior Championship final, explained how the family became known as 'Belturbet': "My father took the Belturbet nickname because there were other Charlie or Pat McNaughton men in the Glens. He was born and reared in Belturbet, County Cavan, before coming to live on the home farm at Ballyeamon, Cushendall, when he was eleven years of age.

"At the farm then were an old aunt Mary and uncle Paddy, both unmarried. This was where my grandfather was born. My grandfather and the grandfather of Captain Danny McNaughton and Big Al were brothers. My grandfather was Alexander McNaughton, who went to St Malachy's College, Belfast, and later opened a chemist shop on the Newtownards Road. Unfortunately, his shop was burned out during 'troubles' there, in the 1930's, the problem known as the Pogroms. Alexander left there, and went to live in Belturbet."

Fergus, whose younger brother is the famous Antrim and Ulster player and All Star, Terence 'Sambo' McNaughton, added: "My father Charlie also played hurling, but in a Cushendall team that was of a very poor standard then. He also played Gaelic football for Glenravel. He went to sea at 17 years of age, and was coasting for a while with Captain Dan Black. He talked about sailing with a number of Antrim coast men, including a McGavock from Glenarm."

Also with him as crew colleagues on the *OLIVINE* and *EMERALD*, skippered by Dan Black, were Sean Mort, P. J. and Mally Black. Fergus said: "He was very pally with Johnnie O'Hara of Shore Street, Cushendall. He spent close on 40 years at sea, including a time deep-sea. From the information in his Discharge Book, he sailed on 48 different ships." It would appear the Cloughs, Ballyeamon, sea veteran, born on January 22, 1914, started on boats when joining the coaster *TOPAZ* at Dublin, on May 31, 1941. The trip was to Glasgow. He is listed as a fireman, and later an AB.

Towards the end of his career he was often rated as ship's Bo'sun, and took the EDH examination in Belfast, in 1953. His Registration number was 240027, and among the many other vessels he worked on were the *PORTAVOGIE, PEARL, CORNWOOD, SCOTTISH MONARCH, KYLE BUTE, BALLYDUGAN, BRITISH CROWN, CALDYFIELD, WESTFIELD, PARAGUAY, BALLYKERN, BENGOR HEAD, CAMEO,* and in mid-summer 1961 he was on board the fabled *PASS* of *DRUMOCHTER*. In late 1963, he had a stint on the *ULSTER PRINCE,* and followed with AB work on the *LOCH LINNIE* - up to October 30, 1964.

Fergus added: "He was twice shipwrecked, including one time on a boat torpedoed by a German submarine. During the Second World War he was on cargo ships in convoy on the north Atlantic. He received medals for those experiences. He quit the sea in the early 1960's, and died in 1980, aged 66. My mother was Mary McGrath, born and bred in Ballyeamon. Her father was from Omagh, and her family owned farmland next to ours up Ballyeamon. While my father was at sea my mother ran the farms."

RABBIT RUN

JOE MURPHY knew how to snare rabbits, and sell the skins. As a schoolboy scampering along the steep braes around his home at Aughnasillagh, Cushleake - a headland north of Cushendun Bay - he made pocket money from this early-morning enterprise. Years later, he was in for a huge surprise when he watched 300 tons of rabbit carcases being loaded into the freezer hold of the ship he worked on as an Able Seaman.

Born in September 1941, Murphy was trading in the Antipodes, on the Blue Star Line's *ENGLISH STAR*. Also swaying on the ship was a near neighbour and another young seaman, Paddy 'The Rock' McNeill. "For the passage back from Australia we took on a part cargo of fruit at Hobart, Tasmania. Then we sailed to Brisbane, and loaded the 300-ton cargo of frozen rabbit carcases," said Murphy.

"It reminded me of my young days, when I snared rabbits, and sold the carcases to Barney Devlin and Dan Brogan. Barney, who lived in a small bungalow at Rockport, and for a time at Bonavor, had a little lorry. He collected the rabbit carcases, and took them to Larne, where they were shipped out to England. When you were paid 2/6 (two shillings and sixpence) a rabbit skin it was brilliant money in the 1950's."

Like Joe, I remember this little 'cottage' industry after the Second World War, when up at dawn to check snares that were carefully placed the evening before along the hillside above Knocknacarry, and right up to Jinny's farm at The Turn. Those were exciting times, working with the always enterprising Patsy McGarry of Straid, who owned two sharp-toothed ferrets.

I could understand Murphy's wonderment at such a huge amount of dead rabbits filtering into the hold of the ship. "The *ENGLISH STAR* was a fridge ship, able to handle perishable cargo. We also loaded bales of wool for England. The rabbit carcases were unloaded at Hamburg, and the fruit at Hull. It took us 28 days to come home from Australia, through the Suez Canal.

"On the way out, from Glasgow, we moved down to Liverpool, and went light ship to Hamburg, where we loaded cement for South Africa. We had stops at Durban, Port Elizabeth, Cape Town, and at Lorenco Marques, the capital and largest port of Mozambique." The port city of Lorenco Marques on the Indian Ocean is now known as Maputo, after the country secured independence from Portugal in June 1975.

Murphy added: "We loaded copper in South Africa, and from there we went to Melbourne, Sydney, and Brisbane, This sea passage takes longer when going round the Cape of Good Hope. I made the Cape journey on that one occasion, but was never round Cape Horn, nor through the Panama Canal. The weather at the Cape of Good Hope was fine when I was there, but I know it can be a treacherous place during storms. I believe a Glenariffe man, Captain Angus McGaughey was shipwrecked at the Cape of Good Hope."

Murphy's first sample of the demands and hazards of sea life happened when he was 14 years of age. From the front door of his home, he witnessed the early morning shipwreck of the *SAINT RONAIG*, the coaster crunching against the shoreline rocks at the foot of his father's farm. On December 14, 1955, the *SAINT RONAIG* ran aground during a storm. The vessel was on her way from Garston to Westport, County Mayo, with a cargo of coal and salt.

Joe alerted his father, Archie. At the same time a radio message from the stricken ship was picked up by Portrush and Ballycastle Lifeboats. The smashed boat's crew of 10, including Captain Smith, was taken safely ashore by Breeches Buoy. "Unfortunately," said Murphy, "the *SAINT RONAIG*, belonging to Gardiners of Glasgow, was wrecked. I saw the rescue operation. The skipper was Bill Smith from Liverpool."

Mrs Mary McCollam, a sister of Joe, added: "I was not at home then, but at school. I remember my mother telling me the crew members were brought to our house where she made them fries." The incident did not deter her brother from taking to the waves. "I went to sea at 17 years of age, in 1958. I attended the Sea School at Sharpness. It was the only way to get a job at sea in those days. Before that, if you knew somebody to speak on your behalf you could get help to join Kellys when a job became vacant," added Joe.

"I found out about the School from Arthur Hamilton, who was over there a year before me. I stayed ten weeks at the School, and came out a deck boy. I was sent to the Pool at Waring Street, Belfast, and from there got my first job at sea. I joined the *BARDIC* ferry, working between Larne and Preston. Also on that run was the *IONIC*. They were known as old LST boats, once used as landing craft during the Second World War.

"Also with me was Arthur Hamilton. We were on that trip for six months when the *BARDIC* moved to Tilbury Docks in London - and then we worked the ferry run from Tilbury to Antwerp. I felt we were now moving so far from home that it seemed almost like being overseas. Arthur Hamilton agreed, so we looked for a job on a deep-sea boat.

"We managed to get work with Head Line of Belfast. The Pool sent Arthur and me on the *RATHLIN HEAD*, a ship Charlie McKay of Gortacreegan (Cushendun) had been working on for quite a while. A very decent man, he was with Head Line for some years, and right away helped me. When I was signed on it was as a deck boy. Charlie went to the skipper, and asked him to make me an AB seaman. Yes, Charlie did me a good turn, as the ship's master agreed, put me up to AB, and that meant a good rise in pay.

"The *RATHLIN HEAD*, a 10,000-tonner, often ran up the Lakes in Canada. For that trip, the boat left from Belfast, where most of the Head Line boats were from - and built by Harland and Wolff. We loaded Ford cars from Dagenham, bound for Canada, and called at two ports, St John New Brunswick and Dalhousie. When Charlie left the *RATHLIN HEAD* I left, too. Arthur Hamilton stayed on.

"During the years I was at sea I would be home for a while, and then take off again to sea. Paddy 'The Rock' McNeill and me sailed together for a while. We were on a coaster running from Whitehaven to Casablanca, where we'd load a cargo of phosphate and take it back to England. I moved to the Blue Star line, for deep-sea trading down to Rio de Janeiro. It was me and Arthur Hamilton on the *ENGLISH STAR*, while Paddy McNeill joined the *SCOTTISH STAR*.

. "I switched from deep-sea to join Captain Charlie McQuillan on the Dorey boat, the *PORTELET*, a coal coaster out of St Peter Port, Guernsey. Danny McNaughton (Captain Danny) of Cushendall was also on that boat. We worked a lot up the east coast of Scotland, calling in at ports such as Methel. I stayed with the *PORTELET* for over six months, until I heard a farm beside my home was for sale. I took a flight back home, bought the farm, and that ended my days at sea. That was around 1963.

"My uncle, John Murphy was a sailor. He started on the puffers, the coal boat coasters. Then he went deep-sea, and one time was paid off a boat at Sierra Leone, in West Africa, along with John McBride of Crook. They were stranded at Freetown, the third largest natural harbour in the world. They survived by living on a beach there, while waiting on a ship to come in.

"When a chance to get a job happened the ship concerned had the one vacancy only. My uncle and McBride tossed for it. McBride won. Uncle John had to rough it for a few more weeks - I think six weeks - before another work opportunity on a boat came along.

"He got work on a ship, and was home in front of McBride. I think uncle John quit the seafaring then. My uncle Charlie was also at sea for a spell, before my father, Archie, took him to work in America, in New York. Unfortunately, after merely three months there, uncle Charlie suffered from meningitis, died, and was buried in New York."

Another seaman of Joe Murphy's era, and from that craggy coastline, is Joe McAfee. He lived further north, along the roller-coaster road, at Torr Head, and spent eight years at sea. Like Murphy, he started out by attending the Sea Training School at Sheerness. Born in April 1939, he left home at 16 and a half years to join the School. He spent twelve weeks there, and joined the Glen Shipping Company of Glasgow, working as a deck boy.

It proved to be a far-from-glamorous start, toiling on a ship that caused many problems. "She was the *JURA*, and she was underpowered. The ship had been built in the United States for one purpose, to bring American troops across the Atlantic to join the action in the Second World War. It couldn't operate very well in bad weather conditions. The Glen company bought a number of those American boats after the War ended."

They were known as American 'jeep ships'. The *JURA* was previously listed as the *CARA META TIRCUMA*, built in the USA. She did 10 knots. Some of these ships were built on the Great Lakes, to help the American effort in the European war theatre. The Glen firm bought other boats - *TUNA* and *SHUNA*. The Head Line firm also purchased 'Jeep' ships, three vessels that were renamed *DUNMORE HEAD, KINSALE HEAD*, and *MALIN HEAD*.

McAfee added: "The one I was on was a poor ship, a coal burner; The *JURA* sailed out of Belfast, on a run to Scandinavia, where we brought back timber. My introduction to seafaring first meant calling at Troon for bunker, loading up with coal for the engine before going to the Baltic.

"We even had to throw timber into the engine to help get up pressure. Because it hadn't enough power to cope with full cargo in difficult conditions we couldn't go around by Scapa Flow. I made two trips on her. Obviously, I had to start work as a deck boy, which meant you got all the rubbish jobs to do. I progressed to work as Ordinary Seaman, then passed the Efficient Deck Hand test, and was promoted to Able Seaman

"I decided to leave the *JURA*, and move to deep-sea work. I went to Liverpool, and joined the Blue Star Line Company, on ships making passage to Australia and New Zealand. I did a fair number of those trips, and on different ships, bringing back frozen lamb and/or apples. It was tough going at times, but I liked to go on foreign trips in the winter months, to warmer climates such as South America, New Zealand, and Australia.

"I went on the *STENTOP* (Blue Star Line), then the *DELPHIC* (Shaw, Savill and Albion Line), on the *CARNATIC* (Shaw, Savill and Albion Line) to Australia . . .taking back frozen lamb. Next outings were on the *BRINA*, a Royal Mail ship. We went to Buenos Aires, taking three weeks out and three weeks back. We returned with a cargo of chilled, not completely frozen, Argentine beef. I did three trips there. Unfortunately, in my next change of ship I suffered an injury.

"I was on the *LOCH LYALL*, for a journey through the Panama Canal, and up the American west coast to San Francisco. We left San Francisco, and I was finished on the wheel, and coming down the steps, when I slipped. I thought at first I had a twisted left ankle. But, next morning it was badly swollen, up like a balloon. I was taken into a Vancouver hospital. I had it X-Rayed. The ankle was broken, so I was paid off there, because I was unfit to work.

"I came home on the ship to Southampton, and eventually arrived back in Ballycastle. That put me out of work for a while, before I was able to go back to sea. I joined the Blue Star Line again. I was with the *SYDNEY STAR*, a 11,095 gross tons refrigerated cargo liner, and also worked on the *BRASIL STAR*, doing runs to Australia, and with the capacity for 53 first-class passengers and six refrigerated hatches. She was launched in 1947, and scrapped in 1972. I liked those runs.

"Of all the places I visited, New Zealand was the best. I can understand people emigrating to live there. I think it also helps to have a climate much like ours, but generally that little bit better - warmer. Also, there is a strong Irish and Scottish connection to make you feel at home.

"I finished up working on a coal coaster, the *BALLYLAGAN*, taking coal cargo from Ayr to Ballylumford Power Station. This Kelly boat was built in 1955, and in 1970 sold to the Shamrock Shipping Company. I then married Margaret McKendry, a daughter of Harry from Cushendun, and quit the sea. Unfortunately, Margaret died a few years past."

Also from the Torr Head area to take to seamanship was Sean Bonner, who once sailed with Sean Mort on the *EMPIRE STAR* to New Zealand. Uncles of Dan O'Neill of Cushleake left there during the late 19th century, to sail the seven seas on high-masted wooden ships.

Denis O'Neill, born in 1863 according to an 1881 register, survived the pitfalls of long-distance passage to eventually settle and live in Australia. "From what I was told," Dan said, "Denis sailed a lot out of Liverpool on long voyages all over the world, and then left the seas. He never married, and died on dry land in Australia.

"Two other uncles, John (born 1857) and Hugh (born 1865) both died of injuries suffered while working at sea. We believe John, and a neighbour, Henry McKay, an uncle of Denis McKay of Agolagh, Cushendun, died from damage suffered during a shipping disaster in the Azores. John was brought home alive, but had been in the water so long he suffered from the Bends and died here in hospital. Hugh died when he fell from the crow's nest, in 1922. His ship was sailing around the Cape of Good Hope, when he was killed. I also had two grandfathers who went to sea - Dan McBride, and Duncan O'Neill."

At Turnamona lived members of the McCurdy family, one of whom left the area to work at sea. The 1881 register features, in the townland of (R.I.C spelling) 'Turnamoney', the family of Alexander McCurdy (48), his sister Elizabeth (40), sons - Patrick (22) and Denis (20), and daughter Mary (18). The 1901 census of the same family reveals Patrick McCurdy (43). Died 1926. Wife Anne (34) (nee Magee). Died 1923. Daughter Mary (9). Later married John 'The Burns' McKendry and died in 1986. Son Alexander (80) later married Maggie McQuaige.

Through the generous help of David McCurdy, who lives at Grantham, Lincolnshire, he refers to the brothers Daniel and Patrick. Daniel is his direct descendent, while Patrick links down to Paddy McCurdy of Turnomna, and also Sandy and Nan McCurdy and Mrs Mary McQuillan. David said: "Born on June 3, 1877, my grandfather, Alexander McCurdy was the youngest son of Daniel McCurdy and Rose Scally. He left Turnamona with the entire family, and he went to sea, aged 15.

"He later married Mary O'Neill, of Campbeltown, in Edinburgh, in 1905. Mary O'Neill's parents were from Ballyteerim, Cushendun. They went to live on the Mull of Kintyre. Alexander seemed to give up sea work, to emigrate to Australia in 1906. He moved to New Zealand's North Island, before returning to Edinburgh with wife and three children, embarking from Wellington on December 29, 1911, on board the *CORINTHIC*. Alexander must have kept in touch with seafaring, as he worked his passage back as a deck hand, and paid for his family to travel Third Class. The ship's voyage was via Montevideo, to Plymouth, and then London, arriving there on April 11, 1912. Alexander McCurdy died in Edinburgh in 1921."

41

GOOD SAMARITAN

WITNESSING a ship break into three parts during a violent storm in the north Atlantic remains a vivid memory for Captain Seamus McNeill of Cushendun. A man of quiet resolve, from the noted 'Rock' sea-going family, he was an AB on board a Cunard cargo boat, the *MEDIA,* when called to help the stricken *ANZIA*.

"No lives were lost, I'm glad to report, but the *ANZIA* became a complete loss," recalled Seamus, "In such a terrible storm, the *ANZIA*, which was as big again as our boat, broke in three. She was so long and large the problem happened when she was sitting on the crests of three different huge waves at the same time.

"Under such enormous strain like that something had to give. She buckled, and broke up. Everyone on board was saved. We took her crew off. The *ANZIA* had no cargo, was on ballast, and was heading for the Great Lakes. The US Navy sent out a vessel that sunk what was left of the *ANZIA*."

Another unforgettable occasion was when he sailed aboard the *MEDIA*: "We were in New York on the day John F. Kennedy was shot. People were crying in the streets. Then we went down from New York to Baltimore, near Washington, and were there the day President Kennedy was buried. Our ship was general cargo to New York and Baltimore.

"We had cargo of containers, and quite a lot of machinery. Then it was containers back to Liverpool, and also more machinery. What was in those sealed containers I don't know. I was on that run for 18 months, working as an AB. It was a monthly tour.

"Our best sailing time from Glasgow to New York's Statue of Liberty, in good weather, was five days and six hours. We'd make the same time coming back. But, on one particular journey it took us 18 days, because the weather conditions were so bad. At one stage of that trip we were off the Azores, and with nowhere to hide. We hove to, and did zig-zag for three days. That was one of my more difficult trips across the Atlantic."

McNeill first went to sea in late 1958. "My brother Paddy was already ahead of me. I got a job as a deck boy with Robertsons of Glasgow. I was on the *PHRASE*, an oil burner, and trading along the Irish coast, taking coal cargo to ports such as Dundalk. I stayed on her for one year. After sea time I decided to sit the AB examination at Corporation Street, Belfast. I went to the Navigation School at Sandy Row, Belfast.

"I was still with Robertson boats, going up the Baltic on the timber run. We also went to the White Sea. You signed up for six months at a time. I remember once at Archangel being pulled in by two tugs. We were loaded with big containers. Again, I don't know what was in those containers. They were sealed. It took us a fortnight to unload them, and then load up with more containers.

"This was during the early 1960's, the 'Cold War' years, and a time of high security there. There were soldiers with sten guns, everywhere. Yet it was a desolate place. We had to have our cameras and such like sealed. We were not allowed to take photographs, probably because the people there did not want the outside world to see how deserted and wild this place was then.

"I spent one and a half years with Cunard, and then joined my brother Paddy on the *SCOTTISH STAR*, running to New Zealand. I enjoyed New Zealand, the climate so much like we are used to. On one of the trips, we took out horses from England to Auckland, and brought back frozen lamb. Sometimes we took machinery out to New Zealand."

In 1966, he decided to try and improve his standing: "I returned to the Navigation School, Belfast, and sat my Mate's Ticket. I went back to Robertsons as First Mate on the *SPINEL*. I was back on the Baltic timber run. Sometimes, we took limestone blocks out to Odda, and also to Trollhatten, at Gothenburg.

"The shipping company then backed me when I decided to sit the Master's Ticket. They paid my wages for three months, while I was ashore doing the studies in Belfast. I sat the examination in April, and passed first time. I felt then I should stay working as First Mate for a little longer, I said so - but they (Robertsons) insisted I should be captain of one of their boats right away.

"They gave me a push, and I was appointed skipper of the *BRILLIANT*, working in the Baltic and White Sea. Sometimes, we were down in the Bay of Biscay, to Bilbao in northern Spain. At this stage we had a new owner, Stevenson Clark of London. On one occasion they asked me to bring a ship to be scrapped at Bilbao. The ship also had a cargo of scrap.

"Because of the friction of the scrap she went on fire near Bilbao. I was directed to steer her onto sand, to beach her - run her up a bank at full steam, I had to go in guided by tractor lights. It was a tricky process. I thought I was going into a cave. It was a relief when we came upon lights.

"The local pilot didn't come to help. He said: 'I'm not going on board. Give her full steam.' We landed on sand. We had a skeleton crew of seven, in total. Nobody was hurt. It was a strange request, but we got the job done. I stayed with Stevenson Clark, and was skipper up to 1991. My last ship was the *BEEDING*.

"At times, I had some local men with me, including the late Paddy Walsh of Cushendall, who also worked for my brother Paddy during the trawling days of the *MOYUNA*. Paddy Walsh was a great character. He used to tell the rest of the crew that the country singer Philomena Begley was his sister.

"Paddy was with me for six months, doing runs to the Baltic and down to Casablanca, to Spain, Portugal, and also across the Mediterranean, to Italy, to take paper pulp from Norway and Sweden down to Alcona. I also had Conor McQuaid's brother, John with me for three months, and the late Mickey McGaughey of Torr for three months."

42

HAPPY WANDERER

FOUR YEARS into his career, swashbucklng seaman Roy Mort survived a jolting setback. He suffered a perforated ulcer while on board a BP oil tanker. “It was a bolt from the blue. I didn’t feel ill before the severe pain happened,” recalled Roy, a member of the prominent Cushendall sea-going family circle.

During an emergency, off the Norwegian coast, the then 21-year-old was rushed by lifeboat and followed by a 30-miles ambulance dash to hospital in Oslo. He added: “I suffered an awful pain in my stomach. I was operated on, and detained for one month in hospital. I had to go home to recuperate, and travelled back to Cushendall by ship from Oslo to London, and then by boat from Liverpool to Belfast. I was away from work for a long time.”

Mort celebrated his 76th birthday on December 27, 2013, and was still missing the sea. I had the feeling he would love to be able to turn back the clock. “I got out around 1968, after 15 years. I had great times at sea. Often, I look back, and realise they were the happiest days of my life.”

Unlike his younger brother Sean, and first cousin Alistair McKay, he surprisingly did not cut his sea teeth with a Cushendall skipper. Instead, he started out on the great adventure with the legendary Captain James Kelly of Carnlough. It was through Jackie Carson of Cushendall he secured a place on the *PASS of DRUMOCHTER*.

“Jackie Carson worked on that ship, and told me he could get me a job - that there was a vacancy. He knew I was interested in making a career of seafaring. I was always talking about the life at sea, and chatting with some of the older seamen when they came home.

“I was 17 when I left home. I joined the *PASS of DRUMOCHTER* in Cork. That was in 1954, about 18 months after Captain Kelly was involved in saving the lives of some passengers during the *PRINCESS VICTORIA* ferry disaster of January, 1953. Captain Kelly’s ship was a wee old oil tanker.

“I’d never before been out of the Glens. How to get to Cork, and join the boat, was my problem. My mother, Mary, was not happy about me going to sea. It was breaking her heart. Nonetheless, she gave me a note with written instructions on how to get to Cork - take the bus to Ballymena, then the train to Belfast, and the train journey to Dublin, and take yet another train to Cork. It was a long trek.

“Jackie Carson was on the boat with me. My first job was in the engine room. I didn’t like it, and eventually got up on deck. I didn’t stay too long with the *PASS of DRUMOCHTER*, about four months. I was not all that interested in coasting. I wanted to go deep-sea, and see the world.

"In those days you served your time at sea. Later on you couldn't get a job without going through one of the Sea Training Schools. When I went you served an apprenticeship on the boat. I also had to go on the Lifeboat Ticket examination in Belfast Lough. I was AB, but later on in my career I became a Quartermaster."

Mort, who lives in Ballymena, added: "To get work deep-sea I went to London, to KG5 dock, and out of there I worked for a number of shipping companies - Blue Line, Port Line, Palm Line. I was with Head Line out of Belfast, and I worked on old tramp steamers.

"I worked for Palm Line boats in Sierra Leone, where you took local crew boys on to go up the fresh-water creeks, where the blacks unloaded the cargo. We did the same up in Ghana, in places where the names are no longer the same. We would have cargo of machinery, including farm machinery, and would load up for the return journey to England with heavy logs.

"I was also on trips down to Australia, with cargo of machinery, and returned with frozen lamb. That was with the Blue Star line. I was also on ships that loaded cargo of fruit at Hobart, Tasmania. I was on the North American run that included up to the Great Lakes in Canada, and trading down the coast to Tampa, Florida - all around the east coast of north America."

During his north American odyssey, the intrepid Mort was joined by another enigmatic character from Cushendall, Francie McGinty. The colourful duo ran foul of the law on a couple of occasions. Nothing serious, though. Perhaps the most audacious episode in the antics of the sometimes-maverick mariners happened in Miami, where they temporarily lost touch with their ship. They almost lost their jobs, but for a kind-hearted Scottish skipper.

"It happened when we were trading down the Yankee coast. After discharging paper pulp from Canada, McGinty and another seaman, from Scotland, were ashore in Miami, having a night out on the town. Our boat was about to depart for Tampa, but no sign of the two boys," recalled Mort, "What happened was, the bo'son then sent me ashore to search for the two, and bring them back. Anyhow, I found them, but also lost track of time.

"With the jukeboxes in the bars, and a drink or two, I soon forgot about going back to the boat myself. Then I figured it was about time we returned to the ship. When the three of us finally arrived back at the dock our ship was not there - gone. We were stranded. I ran out of cash, just a couple of dollars left. From the Discharge Book, the people in a bar knew what happened. Somebody rang the authorities. All of a sudden, these security guys burst through the bar door, as if looking for Al Capone. They put us up against a wall, and questioned us.

"We were adrift for three days in Miami, and at one stage we got split up, separated. The authorities realised we were marooned, had lost our ship, but soon they found out it was down the coast, at the Everglades, at Tampa. So, they put us on a Greyhound bus for Tampa, where we were able to rejoin the ship. Thankfully, the old Scottish captain was lenient, very understanding, otherwise he could have put a bad discharge for us. He did us a favour, and that was the end of the incident."

The Canadian run was also remembered for other incidents. Maybe it was the cold winter climate, but once again the lively lads landed in hot water, unwittingly. They were nicked for swigging alcohol in a 'dry' town. It was probably a Sunday shutdown. "McGinty and me had some sessions during our time together. We ran into a tricky situation in Canada, while sitting in a cinema. It must have been a dry town in a dry State we were in.

"I had this bottle with some whisky in it. I was taking a drink while watching a film, but somebody in the audience must have reported us to the law. The next thing is - there is a tap on my shoulder by a member of the Canadian Mounted Police. We were taken out of the cinema by the Mounties, and we were kept locked up in jail overnight. Next day, our ship's captain came up to the police station, paid a fine, and bailed McGinty and me out.

"While we were shipping up in Canada I also experienced the worst days of my 15 years at sea. Obviously you will have to make some difficult journeys. I was through lots of tough weather conditions. You got a lot of bad weather, even in the tropics, but there was nothing to match the trips up to Canada, around Quebec, where you had an ice-breaker ahead of you.

"You followed the ice-breaker, but still had to do look-out on the foredeck. I remember having to do watch, and I was wearing a very heavy jacket, and also a muffler to cover my mouth. The cold was dreadful. Even the muffler became totally frozen. Your breath was freezing. That was my most uncomfortable experience at sea.

"I was on ships a long while before McGinty. I remember we sailed together under a Captain Davey of Carrickfergus. I did a trip on a Head Line boat, but then decided not to go out of Belfast again. I didn't like it. I preferred to avoid an all-Irish crew, and instead felt it was better to sail out of London.

"When I started I was with local seaman. After that, apart from Head Line runs out of Belfast, I sailed mostly from KG5 dock in London, where nobody cared who or what you were. Some of the overseas trips went through the Suez Canal. I was also through the Panama Canal many times, an unbelievable place - just like going through a jungle.

"There is Frenchman's Creek. The French first started to make the Canal, and then the Americans took over. They moved it in a different direction, and blasted through rocks. At the Canal, there is a special plaque, with all the names of people, including seamen, who lost their lives there because of the Yellow Fever."

The 48-mile international waterway, to allow ships to pass from the Atlantic to the Pacific Oceans, is a technological marvel. Opened on October 10, 1913, the Canal, built by the United States, offered a safe and quick route from one ocean to another, and thus avoided sailors having to risk life and limb while attempting to round Cape Horn.

. In 1966, Roy Mort had to do his one-hour stint on the picket line in Belfast, during the Seamen's Strike. It was nigh impossible to survive on the £2.00-a-week Union money. He said: "During the Seamen's Strike it was difficult for any of us to find another job during the Strike. People did not want to know you. Many folk felt we were doing the wrong thing, hampering trade, industry, business, and so forth.

"Still, I managed to pick up work with a construction company, in Newtownards. The job was knocking down old houses. I hopped on a bus in Smithfield early in the morning, and back again in the evening. I also did my one hour on the picket line.

"I went to live in Belfast around 1968, after I was married. Shortly after that, I was urged to quit working at sea. I lived at Sailortown, and then moved into a maisonette near Divis Flats. The 'Troubles' began.

"We moved to a very nice home in Rathcoole, where, at first, we had no bother, until 'The Troubles' became worse, and we were put out of there. Fortunately, a job offer came up in Michelin, Ballymena, and I moved to work there."

Mort's sea travels were, for a time, in conjunction with the great McGinty. Joined at the hip, they, nonethless, didn't share the same interests in sport. Roy did not have any great relish for the game of hurling, yet his buddy retained an unwavering devotion to the game. Renowned in the Glens more for his instinctive skills as a hurler for Cushendall Ruairi Og and Antrim teams than a much-travelled seafarer, McGinty managed to combine both work and play.

Born in 1938, he retired to live in Ballycastle, County Antrim. "When I worked at sea I always tried, whenever possible, to get home for a few weeks in the summer so that I could play hurling for the Ruairi Og," declared McGinty.

"Most of the young sea-going guys from the Glens, who were keen on playing hurling, all tried to get home during summer time. When you could manage it you took a 'wheen' of weeks away from the sea. Mind you, it was not always possible. I was 18 years of age when taking the plunge to go to sea. Before that, I worked on a farm for the Kinney family, up Layd, and starting at 13 years of age in October 1951. I finished there in April 1956.

"My first experience of sea was only for a short spell of around four months. Alistair McKay helped me get a job with his uncle, Captain John Mort on the *PASS of GLENOGLE*, a coastal oil tanker. I quit the sea to work on land, in England, but suffered a bout of pneumonia. Whenever I recovered I went back to work at sea for a second period.

"I was now 22 years of age, and remained at sea, an AB, until over 50 years of age. When I returned to the sea it was under Captain Mick Blaney, on the *SHELL FITTER*, another oil tanker working around these coasts. I worked on that ship for seven months, and then decided to try deep-sea. I went to the Shipping Pool in Belfast to get a job, and joined a Welsh company to work on their oil tanker, the *KEYSOM* - taking oil from the Persian Gulf to England and Holland.

"In the early 1960's, I was on Head Line boats, working under Captain Davey of Carrickfergus. We would take a cargo of Scotch whisky to the

United States and Canada, and load a cargo of grain for the home trip. Our ship, the *ISAAC CARTON*, went to the Great Lakes, calling at Quebec, Chicago, Cleveland. Roy Mort was with me as an AB.

"We were taking paper pulp rolls down from Canada to ports along the North America's east coast, mostly to Miami, Florida. When we were up in Canada, for the paper roll cargo, it often meant having an ice-breaker in front of us. It was freezing cold. You would be foundering up there, on the St Lawrence in winter.

"Usually it was to Three Rivers, past Quebec, where we went to collect the paper pulp. I think we were on that run for six months. Roy (Mort) and my brother Mally (Malachy) were at sea together for a short period of time - on the *PASS of DRUMOCHTER*. In 1966, we had the seamen's strike, one that lasted around seven weeks.

"I remember doing picket duty in Belfast. After the strike, I returned to the Head Line. I also went shipping out of Tilbury, London, on tankers. I worked on BP oil tankers. I also worked on the Head Line boats with Charlie McKay of Cushendun and Jim Blaney. I was with them for a six-month spell, in 1967.

"I made many long journeys all over the world, to Japan, New Zealand, Australia, South America, I was once with a Scottish shipping company, working on an old tramp ship, the *BARON BELHAVEN*, which was registered in Glasgow. I joined her in London, and went to South Africa with general cargo, and then took iron ore out of there to Japan. I was also on a Palm Line run out of Liverpool, to West Africa, up fresh-water creeks at Sierra Leone.

"Roy (Mort) was also working on those boats, but I wasn't with him then. However, on another occasion I sailed with Roy to South Africa, where we were involved in an incident on a public transport bus in Cape Town. We went ashore, boarded a bus, and sat at the back where the coloured passengers were.

"We were told by the bus driver we were at the wrong end, and ordered us to go to the front of the bus, where the white folk sat. I said the coloureds were as good as us. This was during the height of apartheid. At that time I believe blacks were not allowed on buses, at all."

McGinty sailed alongside many other men from the Glens, including John McQuaige from Cushendun. "He was a quiet man. I was with him for a few months on the *PASS of GLENOGLE*. I was there with Captain Mort when he had nearly half-a-dozen seamen from the Glens at the one time on the ship.

"The area was noted for having many mariners in my time, including Alex Murray, 'Red' Denis O'Boyle, Danny Connolly, Pat Connolly, Con Connolly, James and Robert Emerson. My brothers, Malachy and Seamus were at sea, but not for long.

"Yes, a lot of guys left to work at sea, including the Scollay brothers - Tommy, John, Jim, Brendan, and Henning, Also Alistair and Jim McKay, Pat Close, and Kevin McKillop of Mill Street - who gave up the sea to set up a business in England. I was 34 years in total at it, finishing up after 15 years on the Larne-Cairnryan ferry. On it, I worked with a veteran seaman from Glenarm, Willie McMullam."

43 SMALL WONDERS

WEDDING BELLS rang out the changes for Captain John Small of Jarrow and Ita Clarke of Belfast, when they met for a first time, in Cushendall. They were attending the nuptial ceremony of Captain Gerry Blaney and Ita's sister Eithne.

"John and Gerry Blaney are related, and it was through Gerry I met John. I recall chatting with Gerry outside Lynn's ice cream shop in Cushendall when he told me of this John Small, who was coming over from England to attend Gerry's wedding. I remember Gerry saying: 'John will suit you down to the ground'. Gerry was right," said Ita Small.

"My late husband went to sea when he was 18 years of age. He started at Newcastle-upon-Tyne, and did all the examinations to become a sea captain. He worked mostly on deep-sea voyages. In those early days of his sea career he lived at Jarrow. That was where he was reared, although he was born in Cushendall.

"He was a first cousin of Captain Gerry (Blaney). John's mother was Ellen O'Hara, of Shore Street, Cushendall, who was married to a man named Joe Small. A sister of Ellen was married to a Blaney. So, there was a strong connection with seafaring, through the O'Haras and Blaneys.

"After John moved up the grades, he was a ship's master for 30 years. I estimate he worked for 41 years. He started off on coasters out of Newcastle-Upon-Tyne, and then changed to work most of his life at deep-sea. He spent many years as master of boats owned by the Irish Shipping Company of Dublin.

"All of their boats were named after trees. He was skipper of such vessels as the *IRISH OAK, IRISH ASH, IRISH ELM, IRISH CEDAR,* and the *IRISH MAYPOLE.* Most of the ships worked overseas. The smaller boats did coastal work, and occasionally John worked a bit of coasting for the Irish Shipping Company.

"Many times he was able to take me with him, We travelled all over the place . . . to the United States, New Zealand, Australia. I remember the ship, which had part refrigeration holds, took back boxes of fruit from Australia. Irish Shipping Limited was an Irish State-owned enterprise for global trade, launched in 1941, and ended in liquidation in 1984.

"I well remember my first time at sea, my first overseas trip with John. It was to Philadelphia. Outside of being in a rowing boat in Cushendall Bay I was never at sea. When I was a youngster, my mother took us, the Clarke family, down from Belfast to Cushendall for our annual summer holiday. We stayed in Miss Kearney's house. My family had a strong connection with Cushendall, as my mother's mother was a McAlister of Knockmoy.

"Sometimes, on our school holiday, we would be taken out in rowing boats, a treat, but a far cry for what was in store for me when I went on my first trip with John. I don't think I was ever as sick in my entire life. The ship left Dublin. I was suffering sea-sickness right away. An hour later, I asked John were we anywhere near Philadelphia?

"He replied: 'We are not even past Wexford' I was sick for nearly the complete trip out, but okay on the way back, docking in Belfast. In Philadelphia, we spent some great days before making the return journey. Out there, I wanted to visit a Drug Store, to get something to overcome the sickness. What a surprise when John took me into one. It was a restaurant, a cafe, an ice cream parlour - certainly not a chemist shop that I needed to find.

"My brother was waiting to pick me up at the quay in Belfast, and just as I was walking down the gangplank the Chief Steward shouted after me. 'You have forgotten something'. I asked: 'What? He joked: 'The basin you used so often during the voyage.' Not funny.

"Still, I got over the sea sickness. After that first trip I never had further problems at sea. I made a lot of journeys to New Zealand and Australia. I recall three voyages down to Auckland, where a cousin lives. There were never any passengers on the boats. The crew members on the ships were always very good to me, often making me a small pool on the deck where I could paddle and cool my feet. It was a wonderful time. John did me proud."

Sadly, Captain John Small died suddenly, aged 59, shortly after leaving his ship in 1985. "He was coming home for Christmas, after docking his boat at a port in the south of England. It was on a Sunday. We had a telephone call from a Church Minister living in Carnlough, to say John died while coming off the ship. I think the Minister was contacted by the Seamen's Mission."

44 VILLAGE PEOPLE

FLORIDA-born Jim McLaughlin provides an intriguing addition to the traditional cosmopolitan trend that has been the make-up of Cushendun village, and the surrounding area, for over a century. The sturdy Yank, when on leave from long-haul sea projects, resides in The Square with driving-instructor wife Deborah, daughter of Danny and Pearl McQuillan.

In 2001, he met 'Debbie' at a party, while visiting friends in Ballintoy, County Antrim, and since then has learned to say 'Aye' - just like his wife. They settled into the distinctive Cornish-style heavily roof-tiled house once used by other seafaring folk many years ago, the McCleery family.

Home for a break during late 2013, before he sat pre-Masters examinations in Florida, and then rejoined his ship for another six-month sojourn, the seasoned sailor provided an absorbing interview. McLaughlin revealed his roots are in County Donegal: "My grandfather was John McLaughlin of Donegal Town. Along with two sisters, he emigrated to Chicago, and later to Gary, Indiana, where he became Chief of Police and Detectives. His sisters also moved to Gary, where they all lived within a mile of each other. They never returned to Donegal.

"I have sea connection through my maternal grandfather, Brady Thompson, who was in the US Navy, a sailor on battleships during the Second World War. He came out okay from the War, and returned to his job of electrician for the rest of his days."

In a rich, crisply delivered drawl, he disclosed he was recently working as a civilian seaman on US Government ships delivering petrol to Buson, South Korea's second largest city. He is Officer-in-Charge of an assisting boat, the *FAST TEMPO*, when the intricate pipe-discharging operation with a hose off the stern is undertaken from the mother ship, which anchors eight miles off the Korean coast.

Born in 1962 at Fort Lauderdale, a city on the Atlantic Ocean 23 miles north of Miami and - known as the 'Venice of America' - because of a myriad of canals, he left home in 1979 to join the US Navy. Merely 17-years-of-age, he joined the submarine division based at San Diego, California, and soon passed an examination to be a Quartermaster.

"I spent four years on submarine duty, mostly on the USS *BARB*," he said, "I moved to work on many sea jobs, including an enjoyable six months on a fishing boat. I worked on a torpedo-testing assignment, on the *RANGE MASTER*, at Andros Island, 30 miles south of Nassau in the Bahamas. The boat was a torpedo retriever, used in sea trials of torpedoes. We would retrieve 14 torpedoes, bring them back to base to be reloaded, and do it all over again. I was down there at the time of the Grenada kick-off. Hotel Charlie was the US land base.

"I was years working on delivering sailing boats. It was a hoot, delivering charter boats. I loved being on board the brigantines, but the pay was not all that good. So, I moved on yet again, after discharge at Cadiz.

"I was also six years involved in sea cable laying, a job Kieran McNeill of Cushendun has been on. I had a different employer - Tyco SubCon, an American company - and sailed on the *RESPONDER*. Kieran's work is with Cable and Wireless. Once our ships were docked in the same harbour, and it wasn't until afterwards I heard he was there."

He was also involved in an anxious storm-tossed dilemma, when working off the coast of Taiwan. He was Second Mate and Navigator when trying to retrieve a yellow spar buoy and extensive length of cable that broke away from his ship.

McLaughlin called the buoy a 'buuey' or 'booey'. It is the American saying. "We certainly would not be heard using the term 'boy' for a buoy. Our way of saying buuey is best. Anyhow, this buuey that broke clear in the storm was spotted sitting on a Chinese fishing boat. We got the cable back, but not the buuey. The Chinese refused to hand it over. Our skipper then decided to pull out of there, forget the incident."

His cable-laying commitments also featured a high-risk factor during violent storms off Iceland. "Aye, it was one of the scariest jobs I was ever on," he declared. "It was during vile weather conditions off Reykjavik. It was a project for DanIce. Using a 42-ton underwater plough. It was towed astern when suddenly the weather conditions dramatically deteriorated, in late October.

"The work we had to do in Iceland was pretty bad, because of the weather. It became a dangerous job, but I also have one happy memory of Iceland. I remember swimming in the hot waters of the geysers up there, the 'Golden Circle', yet outside the water my wet hair was turning to ice. That was an amazing experience. I was on cable-laying projects up to 2010, laying fibre optic armoured cable mainly around India, west and east Africa, the Red Sea, the Jeddah area, and when it finished the ship went back to Baltimore docks."

Like so many of the mesmerising yarns of the mariners, McLaughlin's assorted escapades also later created subliminal cuts in my mind. His description of passage had me right at the scene. One of the tales was his time working on a car transporter ship, the *INTEGRITY*, from the United States to Europe. I still cannot believe BMW two-door coupes were built in the USA, and taken across the Atlantic to be sold in Germany.

"Those cars, loaded at Baltimore, and made in the United States, should have been named AMW, not BMW," he insisted: "The cargo also had farm machinery, including tractors - delivered to LeHavre, and then on to Antwerp, Bruges, and Bremerhaven. When we docked at Bremerhaven we unloaded the BMW's, and also cars specially for American military personnel working in Germany. On the way back we carried Lamborghini cars to Bayonne, New Jersey. We also took cargo of locomotive shells back to the States, for discharge at Baltimore."

McLaughlin's target is to qualify as a ship's Master. "I'm a First Mate at the moment. I sat all previous sea exams in Miami, and also did a small firearms efficiency course in Alabama. I had to get a firearms certificate. I'm sitting more tests, something I should have done six years ago. Because of so many new rules constantly coming in, it is very difficult to upgrade. I'm a 16-ton Master, but not an Unlimited Master. You also need top security clearance at all times."

Debbie's father, Danny disclosed additional family interest in seafaring. His brother Francis McQuillan left Knocknacarry in March 1951 to work on Dorey coasters. "Francis was one of the triplets - born on the 24th of September 1929 along with Colm and Harry. Colm and the 'old man' - my dad James - both had short spells working at sea," Danny said.

Francis started as an Ordinary Seaman on the *BELGRAVE*, sailing out of Goole on March 23, 1951, under Captain Thomas Mitchell. The first trip was to Avonmouth. Later, he progressed to be an AB, switched to the *FERMAIN*, taking in coasting jobs from Guernsey to Cork. He also worked under the command of other noted Dorey skippers such as David McWilliams, and Glenariffe's Neil McGaughey.

"Captain Charlie McQuillan of Glenravel helped to get Francis sarted at sea. After a few years Francis quit the sea to join his brother James at pressure-piling work in England, and later had a public house in Salford, in Greater Manchester. It was named the 'Old Shears' at Greengate.

"At the same time, he worked as an overhead crane driver for the Metal Vick Company. Unfortunately, he pushed himself too hard. The pressure took a toll, and he suffered a heart attack. He was confined to a wheelchair for some time before he died.

"Our family is related to the seafaring McQuillan family of Glenravel. My father and Henry McQuillan were second cousins. My grandfather, John McQuillan, lived near Dungonnell Dam. As a young single man, along with a neighbour named Higgins, they sold out their farms to buy arable land near Rasharkin. John McQuillan married down there. My father, James and his brother Frank, who became a pub manager for Mooney's at Cornmarket, Belfast, were born there."

A strong sea link in the Village is that of the Leavey family, with the beginnings in Southampton. John Leavey was an olden-time sailor of the early 20th century. He came from the south coast of England to marry Glens of Antrim girl, Sarah McAfee, who was listed a ten-year-old in the 1881 census. She was the daughter of John and Sarah McAfee of Drumnasmear. Also in the family were Mary (14), John (9), and Dan (7).

Marie Mort said: "My grandfather, John Leavey, was a ship's cook. Because he was from Southampton, I believe that is how and why his daughter, Kathleen (Dalla) became interested in sea work. Through her father's connections there, she went to Southampton, to work as a ship's purser. John Leavey had a brother who was a fireman in Southampton. In 2012, I met his brother's grandchildren, two sisters, for the first time, when they visited Cushendun.

"My granny, Sarah McAfee, worked in Belfast, and that is where she met John Leavey. It is likely he arrived there while working on a ship.

They married, and came down to live in Cushendun village where they opened a bakery. John Leavey was a pastry cook specialist. Up to 1955, the shop/restaurant was known as 'Hiker's Rest'

"It was run for a time by Aunt Dalla. John Leavey died on the 15th of January 1943. My granny (Sarah) died on June 20, 1969. My father was Gerald, who was in the RAF for spell, while my two uncles, John and Charlie Leavey both died on June 18, 1974.

"My grandmother's brother Johnny, a twin of Dan McAfee, went to sea - perhaps a hundred years ago, or more - and was never heard of again. We could only guess he may have been lost at sea. There is no trace. My grandfather (John Leavey) once worked on the Guinness boats, taking cargo out of Dublin to ports such as London, Southampton, Belfast, Glasgow, and Liverpool."

Marie's sister Kathleen (Mrs Oliver) unearthed the old man's seafaring chart. Born on May 3, 1878, in Southampton, he was registered as chef/ cook from 1918 to 1930. Listed are the following sailing details - Card type: CR10 Discharge number: 728088, Identity certificate No 807292, Series BT350. *WAR HINDOO* - 143458 - London 1919 Steam, *LORD ANTRIM* - 113518 - Belfast 1902 Steam, S*CONFELS* - 144408 - London 1920 Steam, and *BENHOLM* - 149690 - Liverpool 1928 Steam. *CARRIGAN HEAD* 21 Feb 1919 to 5 May 1921 *BENIUCA*. Date of Engagement Greenock 17 May 1925 -*ILLWASTON* - 15 Jan 1930.

Other dates of engagement on ships include 28-12-1921 19-9-22, 15-1-24, and 5-9-28. Knocknacarry neighbour Alex O'Hara also sailed on the *WAR HINDOO* in the early 1920's. The ship was launched on September 30, 1919, for Gow Harrison, was built in Port Glasgow, was a 5,585 gross tons tanker, and was scrapped in May 1958.

Another John Leavey, son of the old man, went to sea for a short spell, in the United States. John Joseph 'Jack' Leavey spent most of his life as a school janitor in New York City, but also had two years working as a seaman, from 1937 through 1938.

Marie Mort revealed: "Granny Leavey had a sister Mary, who married and lived in New York. Jack was sent there as a young boy. In his latter years he came home to Cushendun every summer. Sadly, when he was making his final journey here, to retire in 1974, he took ill. He collapsed and died in Dublin, when coming off the 'plane, following a flight from New York. He was 66. On the same day, Jack's brother Charlie died in Cushendun. I also had a cousin who served in the Royal Navy - my uncle, Danny Leavey's son John William, better known to us as Billy."

Jack Leavey became an American citizen in December, 1937. On the 30th of that month, Leavey, born April 20, 1907, in Cushendun, was awarded a US Department of Commerce 'Seamen's Certificate of Identification' in the Port of New York by a Frank C Cogan, an Irish-American official. The Certificate stated Jack Leavey 'having taken the oath required, qualified to work on board American vessels of 100 tons and upward in the 'Steward's' Department, in a rating of 'Messroom-Foodhandler'

Another seagoing family from the Village was the O'Drain's. According to the 1901 Parish census, both Archie O'Drain and later his son Archie worked at sea. They lived in The Square, near the McCleery brothers. Also at sea was Stephen Cochrane, whose niece Anona Robertson said: "I think the McCleery family came from the upper Ormeau Road area of Belfast. Three of the brothers went to sea. The eldest, Hector didn't, but emigrated to America. My mother, Loveday, was once engaged to Hector.

Form 718
SERIAL NUMBER Z70945
UNITED STATES DEPARTMENT OF COMMERCE
BUREAU OF MARINE INSPECTION AND NAVIGATION
SEAMAN'S CERTIFICATE OF IDENTIFICATION
(TO BE RETAINED BY THE SEAMAN)
Port of NEW YORK
DEC 30 1937 19
The bearer: John Joseph Leavey (Name of seaman, in full)
whose home address is 1234 Morris Ave. Bronx, New York, born in Ireland (State or Country)
on April 20, 1907 (Date of birth), is a citizen of Ireland
If naturalized – year ___ if 1st papers – year ___ if alien – date of head tax, if any ___
Statement of personal description: Height 5 ft 5½ inches, Color of hair Brown Color of eyes Gray, Complexion
Frank Hogan (Signature of issuing officer)
Seaman's Thumb Print
John Joseph Leavey (Signature of seaman)

"She was very young, probably 17. I think that was in 1920. There was quite a gap in age difference. My grandparents were not too happy about the situation, and sent her to Belfast to attend the Commerce College. That got her out of the way. The romance petered out. Hector went to North America, yet my mother wore that engagement ring until the day she died.

"The ring is now worn by my sister, Rhoda. I remember hearing of Jack, Bill, and Jim McCleery all going to sea, in the 1940's and into the 1950's. I think they were all in the merchant navy. Bill may also have been in America for a few years. As a very young girl, I used to be regularly in and out of their house in The Square, Cushendun, where their sister Maisie looked after things, kept house.

"I have some bone-handled knives that came from Bill McCleery. He got them on board ship when was on his travels. Jack was the elder of the three. Bill would relate his journeys oveseas, boast of his travels abroad, of all the countries he visited. The McCleery's were very generous, kind people. I remember being in their house when Jack crossed my palm with a half-crown, when he heard I passed the 11-Plus examination. That was really great money then.

"Jim and Bill were quite alike. Bill was the youngest, and died in the 1960's. They had a boatshed at the back of McBride's pub, where they stored and preserved their rowing boats. They gave the shed to John Carey. When the McCleery's gave up the boats two were bought by Gerald Leavey - the 'Marie' and the heavier 'Jolly Sailor'.

"When my father, Jim, visited Cushendun he always joined the McCleery's for a yarn in the boatshed. I would come down with my father from Belfast, and spend a lot of time in the McCleery house. I don't think Hector married. Certainly the McCleery's who lived in Cushendun never married. Hector came home once, around the time my brother Roger died, in 1945. My mother was in Cushendun during most of the Second World War. With her were Rhoda and Walter, who was just a baby then.

"My uncle, Stephen Cochrane was a merchant seaman. He went to school in Cushendun, and also played hurling here. He helped to start and train the Cushendun camogie team. During the Second World War, he was on convoys. He was born in 1905, and worked at sea when well into his 50's. Uncle Stephen led a chequered life, and died in the early 1970's. His sister was Loveday Cochrane, my mother, The Loveday name is prominent in Cornwall, and my mother got it from the Bolitho-McNeill's. My granny and Maud McNeill were sisters." Captain Walter William Beasant, related to the McCreery family, was lost at sea.

My brother, Daniel O'Hara believed Stephen Cochrane helped in the building of Cushendun's one-time Bay Hotel - Elliott's. Cochrane was a skilful forward when the Emmets defended the Antrim SHC title in the summer of 1932. The team lost by 5-5 to 3-2 in the North Antrim semi-final against Glenariffe Ossians at Ballycastle. Also in the side was another Cushendun sailor, James 'Bach' McMullan. Both did not participate in the 1931 Championship victory. Glenariffe seamen in the Ossians side included Eneas Black.

A Cushendun resident who spent time on boats before settling in the Vllaga, was Johnny McNeill, a maternal grandfather of Rosemary, Seamus, and Gerry McNeill. "He came from Templepatrick," explained Seamus, "My grandfather worked as an able seaman. It was said by Mary Brogan that after he retired from the sea he used to read the newspapers in Leavey's 'Reading Room' for any locals who were unable to do so. From those olden times, my mother used to mention a sea-going man named William Chard, who lived in Cushendun, and once was in the Royal Navy.

"My maternal grandfather, Johnny McNeill, married Rose McBride of the Tops, Cushendun. Their daughter Mary was my mother. She married a different McNeill, Johnny from Glendun, who once worked in America, digging tunnels during the early 1930's in the New York area. My mother's brother was also named Johnny McNeill, who was the Cushendun and Antrim hurling team goalkeeper, but tragically died a very young man from heart failure, while cycling up to Cairns, Cushendall - from the Crossroads."

The player who took over from the ill-fated Johnny McNeill in the Cushendun team was James 'The Bear' McDonnell, a hurling hero of the 1931 Antrim title-winning team. James and his wife Barbara of Kennedy's Row, Knocknacarry, left the Glens to open a B&B (aptly named 'Cushendun') in Dundee. Their son John - and also daughter Rosemary, the eldest child, attended the Primary School in Knocknacarry. John later went to sea, but suffered a head injury, and had to quit.

Cushendun's area also produced Captain John McCambridge (died 28th March, 1923), Captain John Black, Captain Dan O'Hara (died August 30, 1867), Captain Pat McMullan (died November 2, 1926), Captain James Hamilton (died July 4, 1907) and 27-year-old William McIlreavey, son of William Robert and Mary McIlreavey, Knocknacarry, who was lost at sea in 1901.

The village once became home from home for a teenage Antrim Town-based Paddy O'Neill. Returning to family roots always proved a magnet.

His mother was Brigid McAuley, a sister of celebrated Glens of Antrim landscape artist Charles McAuley. With a grounding of Gruig (Glenaan), and Glenravel blood flowing through his veins, he followed a well-trodden path of Glensfolk to the sea. However, his was a rare outlet, as he decided to become a ship's Radio Officer. He is the sole radio man I managed to trace from this area.

O'Neill, who lives in retirement at Plymouth, retains links with the Glens, where he met his wife, Frances (nee Morris). He said: "I spent a lot of summer time around Cushendun, the Blue Room, and all that." He keeps in touch with the Leavey family. It was through Kathleen Oliver (nee Leavey) and her sister, Marie Mort, and also a cousin, Mrs Mary McFadden, I managed to track him down.

The Leavey clan, dedicated gatherers of nostalgia - photographs and records - unearthed an old postcard sent by Paddy, on August 10, 1973, from Curacao. O'Neill, whose brothers Desmond, Noel, and Donagh also studied at St MacNissi's College, Garron Tower, sent a card that depicts the ship he was working on at that time. It was the oil tanker *SERENIA*. He was First Radio Officer. The card postage was 25 cents - signed by Paddy and his wife Frances.

"I remember sailing on Shell oil tankers to and from Curacao. It was near the end of my career at sea," added O'Neill, "I enjoyed my time on ships, almost twelve years, from 1963 to 1975. When I left Garron Tower, I went to the Radio College, then based in Hardcastle Street, and a part of the old Belfast Technical College.

"The Radio College had a strong connection with the Marconi Company. I was there nearly two years. You could leave after 18 months, with a P.M.G. (Post Master General) Radio Certificate. Like most of the students, I stayed on for a further four months, in order to complete the Radar Maintenance Course. I joined the Marconi Marine Corporation, and my first ship assignment was on the *PERSIC*.

"It was a cargo vessel, and the trip lasted four months. It was a very enjoyable experience, as I saw most of the world in one fell swoop. The ship left Liverpool, went through the Suez Canal, and then around Australia, before moving on to New Zealand, After that, it was across the Pacific to go through the Panama Canal, and back to the UK, to London.

"From there, I moved to work for the sugar company, Tate and Lyle, on their ship, *CRYSTAL JEWEL*. After that, and towards the end of my days at sea, I worked on tankers for Shell Oil. The ships included the *SERENIA*, trading out of Curacao."

The inability to achieve advancement in this side of the seafaring business eventually proved too great a frustration for Paddy, who added: "I enjoyed my career at sea, but after almost twelve years I decided to quit, in 1975. There was no progress to be made. As a Radio Officer you came out almost the same way you went into the job.

"My last ship was the *MILO*, an oil tanker working from the Persian Gulf to Italy. We would go light ship through the Suez Canal. After loading in the Persian Gulf, we were unable to go back via the Suez Canal, and had take the long way home - sailing around the Cape of Good Hope, in order to take the cargo to Italy."

45

CULTURE CLASH

GERRY BLANEY Jnr's introduction to life on the oceans proved to be grippingly gruesome and deeply uncomfortable for a 22-year-old. In a jolting clash of cultures, he was forced to watch the punishment of a criminal having a hand chopped off in the centre of the Saudi Arabian port of Jeddah.

A member of the acclaimed sea-serving dynasty from the Glens, the raw rookie went to work on the waves on December 10, 1981. Before witnessing the bloodletting, the setting for his first step on board could not have been more colourful, as he recalled: "It was a very exciting moment for me as I joined my first ship in Casablanca, where I was appointed fifth engineer for the Sasmarine Shipping Company of South Africa.

"What an experience that turned out, the ship taking a cargo of oranges from Morocco to Jeddah. I'll never forget spending Christmas Day in Jeddah, and witnessing a horrific incident - forced to observe a man having his hand chopped off! We were made to watch this gut-churning happening, because we were foreigners.

"Along with two other members of the crew I was off the ship and sightseeing in the city square when religious policemen arrived in their land rovers to hold the punishment of a prisoner, who was all wrapped up and seemed to be drugged. That is the way it looked.

"We tried to leave the square, but the policemen stopped us. We were forced to stay. The religious police not only blocked our way out but also made us go to the front of the crowd, right beside the punishment incident. The crowd went wild with delight, cheered, when they saw the hand being chopped off. Very quickly we made our way back to the ship. That incident certainly put me off my Christmas dinner. It was a blood-curdling experience."

Later in his career he didn't bargain for another disagreeable episode, when having to face, and subdue, a meat cleaver-toting total madman on board a vessel in the Far East! Fortunately, he survived the nightmare scenario, in what was one of the most frightening experiences of his life. This was above and beyond having to combat the elements on the oceans, but a conflict with a crew member who was completely off his trolley.

It was like a chapter from one of those fascinating adventure novelettes - 'Rip roaring yarns from the South Seas'. There is nothing in the 'How to survive at Sea' manual about what to do when facing down a crazed crewman who comes racing and screaming across deck, wielding and waving two meat cleavers. What do you do to curb a madman who is threatening to maim or kill you? An instinctively fortuitous reaction by big Gerry was to grab a nearby fire extinguisher, and thump the assailant.

"The extinguisher was completely effective, but, for a few seconds it was a pretty scary incident," recalled the burly son of Captain Gerry Blaney, who advanced his sea career to become a Chief Engineer. He revealed this terrifying true tale of the unexpected was like a scene from a horror movie. The spaced-out sailor was a Filipino AB.

"This crew member went totally mad, completely out of it. He wanted the ship to turn around, and take him back to the Philippines. It was a close shave when the Filipino AB went bananas, and came charging at me. He nearly got me. He also threw paint thinner on the deck, and threatened to burn the ship. That could have been very dangerous.

"He wanted off the ship, and was told we couldn't accommodate him. He was out of his mind, insisting the ship must turn back, and leave him in the Philippines. We were out at sea, having left the port of Batangus in the Philippines. I was joined by another member of the crew, and to subdue the madman we hit him on the head with a fire extinguisher. That sorted him out. We turned the ship around, returned to Batangus where he was arrested by the police, and charged with a bundle of offences."

Before that rowdy rumpus, and after the Jeddah affair, he enjoyed traversing many horizons. "The good part about my maiden trip experience at Jeddah was that the ship sailed for Cape Town, and remained a few weeks there in dry-dock. At that time I considered emigrating there, but things were starting to erupt in South Africa. That was in January 1982. So, I took in a different scene, travelling to Brazil where I spent one month there.

"We collected a cargo of chickens and 50 million eggs for Aquaba, the only port in Jordan. I believe this cargo was eventually for Iraq, during the Iran-Iraq war. Shortly after that, I made my first trip to England, when loading a cargo of apples and pears for Sheerness. I was fifth engineer for two trips.

"I joined a container ship, the *LANGEBURG,* sailing from South Africa to Europe. Once we took gold bullion to Italy, docking at La Verno. I never managed to get my hands on a gold bar. The security, as you would expect for that cargo, was intense.

"After that, I spent seven years with the oldest shipping company in the world, the Jardines of Hong Kong, and progressed with that firm from fourth engineer to second engineer. We worked runs to Canada and Alaska, to bring paper products such as pulp, timber logs, and paper rolls to Japan.

"I switched to sign with Shell, as second engineer, and was then appointed Chief Engineer. I joined the Shell company in 1990. Shell has been my employer ever since, and I've been based at Bonny Island, Nigeria. The trading involves runs to Mexico, Europe, and Persian Gulf. The cargo is gas, or as we know it - LNG - liquid natural gas. Because of the epidemic of sea piracy along the African coastline there is always danger. West Africa is called HRA, a High Risk Area.

"Once I was on Shell oil tankers taking cargo out of Curacao, a small island with an oil refinery off the coast of Venezuela. That was a good run. But, the trips with the gas cargo became very strict, crew members not allowed to go ashore. Unlike the old days, you cannot leave the ship when it docks. From the moment I get on the ship I cannot get off, until I am on leave to go home to Cushendall.

"Trips are faster, lasting around two months. Also, the ship is dry, a new rule of no alcohol allowed on board. The job is not so glamorous now, and I suspect young people would not put up with the restrictions. We've had one or two skirmishes with pirates on some of Shell's other ships. Armed security experts, military-type personnel, are expected to come on board with the guns to protect the ships."

Born on July 15, 1959, he lived childhood days with his family in Belfast, and travelled worldwide on his father's ship. "Along with my younger brother Brian and sister Patricia, we went with my father and mother on his ship. I was too young then to go to primary school. I am the oldest of the family. I was a little late starting out at school, about five years old when I went to the Holy Child Primary in Belfast.

"My mother, Eithne, was a schoolteacher there. My last year at the Holy Child School was spent in Casement Park, where four classes were held in temporary accommodation, because of renovations going on at Holy Child. I went to St Malachy's College for five years, and then spent a further two years at St MacNissi's College, Garron Tower. I moved to study naval architecture and shipbuilding at Jordanstown. I qualified from UUJ, where I was sponsored by Harland and Wolff. I worked for H&W for three years, and then decided it was time to move an, and to go to work at sea."

All sailors have to endure passages of stormy-weather conditions. Gerry Blaney Jnr was no exception, as he remembered: "I was through plenty of bad storms at sea. However, the most demanding weather experience was my first trip around Cape Horn. We came out of the Persian Gulf with a cargo of gas for Chile. We made round the Cape of Good Hope, and headed for the Horn. We were obviously sailing east to west, but we couldn't get a pilot to take us through the Straits of Magellan.

"We were told we'd would have to wait a couple of days before a pilot became available, so we decided to head on down to the bottom, and to go directly around the Horn. There was a massive storm, and to make matters worse for us the ship broke down, and we nearly ran aground, right on Cape Horn. The exhaust valve fell off the main engine.

"We had to open up the engine to get the valve out and a new one in. All the while the ship had no power, and was heading for rocks. It was a very tense and dramatic situation. It took 24 people to help put the new valve in, and just in time to avoid smashing onto rocks. It was fate that helped have the engine restarted, and we steered the ship clear of danger. I did the Cape Horn trip another time, and with no problems. Chalk and cheese. It was flat calm then, and very scenic."

During his early career he improved his education under the supervision of Captain Mick Blaney, the youngest of his Blaney uncles. "In 1983, I sailed with him on the *OLIVE*, an 1,100 tons coaster that was initially built for Newry Canal. It was a round-bottom boat owned by the Head Line Company out of Belfast.

"It once carried cargo of tapioca feed from Holland to London, and we also took a cargo of stones from Arklow, County Wicklow, to London. The boat was involved in taking china clay from the south of England to Spain. I was with uncle Mick on the *OLIVE* for six months."

The game of golf provides a suitably soothing escape for Gerry, when he is home on leave. He has also enjoyed swinging clubs on a few exotic locations such as in Chile. "Perhaps the most stunning golf course I ever played on was at Vina del Mar in Chile. The Grand Adello Country Club was something special, a very old and established golf club. It was situated quite high up, and overlooking the city of Vina del Mar.

"It was one of the most beautiful places I have ever seen. Quite breathtaking. I discovered the Club's first captains were catholic priests from Ireland. I also spent a few days playing golf in Australia, and at Port Alico in Canada, where you had to watch out for brown bears wandering all over the course."

He played golf in unusual circumstances on the Solomon Islands, and on another visit there was relieved to get away from the place. "I had the good fortune to explore one of the most picturesque but most novel of golf courses I ever played on. The course was on the Solomon Islands. It was a wonderful experience.

"I was able to hire golf clubs to play on a course that had good fairways, green enough, but oil-sanded greens. There was a big heavy rake to make a path from the hole to where your ball was. You couldn't miss, as the hole in the green was about a foot in diameter.

"However, I have less happy recall of another visit to the Solomon Islands, after taking a flight from Brisbane to Honiari Airport on the Solomon Islands, to link up with my ship. It was in 1999, during a time when there was a local 'war' going on.

"With me on the 'plane were three journalists from New Zealand, who were going to the islands to report on the disturbances. Just as we were arriving in taxis from the airport, there was a roadblock. The journalists were in a cab in front of me. Masked and heavily armed men were stopping the taxis. They dragged the journalists from their taxi, and when I saw what was happening, and knowing that I could also be kidnapped, I jumped out of my taxi, and ran like hell through bushes. I managed to get away, and knew my way to the hotel, where my bags were waiting for me.

"The ship, the *HAUSTRUM* - a products tanker - did not arrive from Fiji for a further couple of days. I was glad to get out of there, and sail for Port Mospby, at Papua, New Guinea. I learned later the ex-President of Haiti helped to secure the release of the three news reporters. The problems in the Solomon Islands then was, I was told, an inter-tribal, inter-island, thing."

His brother Brian was also in the wars, literally, and has a medal to prove it. A petty officer on P&O Ferries, from Dover to Calais, he spent his younger years working deep-sea, and was inadvertently caught up in the Falklands War. He was on the BP oil tanker, *BRITISH WYE* when it was commandeered by the British Government to take supplies down to the aircraft carriers operating in the Falklands War.

The ship was bombed by an Argentine warplane. Fortunately the enemy's aim wasn't quite right. So Brian and 41 other members of the crew survived the incident, and unscathed. He said: "The products tanker, *BRITISH WYE,* left Portsmouth for the Falkland Islands. We arrived there on the day of the start of the Falklands War, and left on the day the conflict ended. Our tanker was down there with supplies, to refuel aircraft carriers.

"We were berthed 300 miles north of South Georgia, but suddenly we were bombed by an Argentinean Hercules transport aeroplane. This 'plane attacked us with bombs that rolled off the back of their aircraft. Fortunately for us, the bombs came in too low, bounced off our deck, and rolled over the side and into the sea to explode. There was some damage to the tank.

"The Falkland's experience was a scary one, more so when I think back at what might have been . . . had the Hercules gunner been more accurate with the bombing. In that case our ship, with all that fuel, would have gone up. We were very lucky. We awaited orders to go in and join the main fleet, and went in to refuel them. We had to wait there until the war was over, before we could return to Portsmouth, Nobody was injured, and we did not lose cargo. For that incident I was later awarded the South Atlantic Medal. The presentation ceremony was by Maggie Thatcher, in London's Guild Hall."

Born in Belfast in 1963, he took what was the routine family route, to a career in seafaring. Hc was a student at Belfast's De La Salle College, before moving to the Antrim Coast, to spend three years at Garron Tower. He added: "Working at sea was what I wanted to do, and after Garron Tower I went to the Sea School at Gravesend, London. I started in the School towards the end of March, 1980, and completed the 12 weeks course that included passing the (EDH) Efficient Deck Hand Certificate and Lifeboat Ticket examinations.

"I was sponsored by British Petroleum, and joined my first ship in mid-June of that year. I travelled to sign on the *BRITISH RENOWN* at Europort, Rotterdam. We moved to Bremerhaven, and then to trade in the Mediterranean, picking up crude oil cargo in Egypt, near Port Alexandria. We traded between Genoa, Italy, and Egypt. The oil was piped from Port Suez to Port Said, and we loaded up there. That was me under way working at sea, my first assignment.

"I was four months on that job. Then I joined the *SAVAN*, a BP boat jointly run by an Iranian shipping company. We took oil from the Persian Gulf round to Europe. I worked on that boat for five months. After that, I joined the *BRITISH RANGER*, another BP oil tanker that traded around South Africa and the Far East.

"After the Falklands adventure, I rejoined the *BRITISH RANGER*, trading to the Far East, and then went to work on the *BRITISH TAMAR*, around Europe and South America. I went coasting for about two years, sailing with the Frank Everard Coastal Shipping Company. It was bulk cargo, trading between England, Ireland, parts of Europe, and the Western Isles. The cargo included coal, and once we took wheat up from France to Donegal.

"During this period on coasters I experienced another very difficult time, when the boat's automatic steering broke in a very bad storm, a Force Ten near Land's End. We were also taking on water. We had a cargo of asbestos tiles from Capella, outside Brussels, and we were bound for Carrickfergus.

"It was tough going up the Irish Sea, as we had to steer her by the big manual wheel, and keep her head into the wind. It wasn't easy. The sea is so powerful, something people out in fun yachts don't truly realise. We managed to get to Carrickfergus."

Brian switched back to deep-sea, in a return to the *BRITISH TAMAR*. He married in 1986, to Ann McCormick of Dunurgan, Cushendun, a daughter of the late Hugh 'Tom' McCormick, and was away on the waves when daughter Erin Rose Blaney was born. The family resides at Knocknacarry. "Erin Rose was three months old by the time I got home to see her for a first time," he said.

"I moved to work on the *BRITISH RESOURCE,* and joined her in Brunei, Borneo. This meant a very lengthy flight, hedge-hopping all the way from Belfast to London, to Sri Lanka, to Singapore, and from there down to Brunei. The oil at Brunei had been held by the Saudi Royal Family, and ships were there for four years. They were VLCC - very large crude carriers.

"The Saudi Royals were afraid of the Iraqis, and this oil was their money in the bank should things go wrong back home. It was their money guarantee, a nest egg, so we were brought in to shift their money/oil. We anchored 50 miles off shore, loaded and took their oil cargo to Penang for discharge, and then our boat went into dry-dock at Singapore."

That intriguing assignment in the Far East was Brian's final deep-sea passage. After working on shore for a time, he joined P&O Ferries in April 1988, on the Dover to Calais run, and has been there since. He is ranked Quartermaster with P&O, working one week on and one week off.

46 BLACK MARKERS

RED BAY-born skipper Dan Black is one of many iconic seamen from the Antrim Coast. The big man, who died on October 25, 1996, aged 77, was a faithful employer of young men from the area. He devoted a lifetime of service on the seas, held a Foreign Masters' ticket, and was master of coasters that traded up the Baltic.

Born on a farm overlooking McQuillan's crumbling castle remains, and with a panorama out towards Garron Point and the more distant Paddy's Milestone (Ailsa Craig) near the Scottish western coastline, the lure of the seas proved too strong to ignore. Captain Black was with Robertson's of Glasgow for decades, and local sailors such as Sean Mort worked under him on the *OLIVINE*, *AGATE*, and the *EMERALD*. Rated a fine seaman, his run, for a time, included taking stones from Llandulus in north Wales up to Norway and Sweden

Before moving to live at Foran, near Garron Point, Captain Dan and wife Eithne settled at Lurig View - at the bottom of Glen Road, Glenariffe. A neighbour in those days was a young Mick Graham, who recalled: "Captain Dan lived next door to the Darragh family. Often he would sail his boat across Red Bay. When we were kids . . . myself, my brother Brendan, and our neighbour Lawrence Darragh - all living at Lurig View - would get word that Captain Dan was about to come up the Bay in his boat.

"We would go down to the beach, and wave a white sheet, and then Captain Dan, a big jolly man, would blow a horn on his boat. He would be on his way to Glasgow with his puffer. At that time two sea captains, Dan Black and Paddy Darragh, and one AB seaman - my father James - lived at Lurig View. The other residents there were John McLaughlin, and Frank and Dan Laverty."

Captain Dan's wife was Eithne McKillop from Glenburn, Cushendall, a sister of Neil McKillop, the accountant. Sadly, Charlie Black Jnr, the only son, died aged 63 of cancer in May 2010. Dan and his brother Charlie were born on the Red Bay farm. Charlie Snr and wife, the former domestic teacher Miss Dillon, had no family. Captain Dan, decided to move from Garron Point to build a new home on the farm, but died in 1996. Eithne was 92 when she died, on the 9th of April 2013.

Charlie Jnr's widow Margaret said: "Captain Dan first intended, after he retired from very many years working at sea, to move from his house, at Garron Point, and come back to his old home and renovate it. His wife, Eithne and a young son Charlie often went on the ships with him. My late husband Charlie was born in 1947, ten years after his cousin

Neil McKillop, whose sister Eithne was a nurse, and worked in London during the Second World War. A sister Annie was the mother of the 'wee' Mariner's wife Margaret. Another sister Kathleen, is wife of house painter, John James McCarry."

Margaret, born in Glasgow, lost an uncle at sea during the Second World War: "His name was Bernard McEnaney. His body was washed up at Rathlin Island, after his ship was sunk in the Second World War. Bernard was from Glasgow, and was 21 years of age when killed on the 21st of January 1942. His parents came over from Scotland to claim the body, and then had him buried at the Bay Cemetery, Glenariffe.

"After the War, my family came over every summer to a holiday home in Glenariffe, and that is how I met my husband, Charlie Black. Bernard had the same name as his grandfather, who left County Monaghan to go to work in Texas, USA, and then came back to live in Scotland. Bernard's brother James, my father, did not work at sea."

Captain Dan managed to secure employment for many Glensmen, including namesake Don Black, one of five Glenariffe brothers to go to the seas. Born in 1936, Don, whose proper Christian name is Daniel, took to the seafaring in 1953. "When I was a youngster, people called me Don for some odd reason - and the name stuck. Seamus, the eldest of the five, was first to go to sea. He was AB, and spent most of his days on coasters, but also worked deep-sea.

"Later, when he left the sea, he lived in Belfast. Seamus also liked to play a bit of hurling. Next in line to go to sea was myself, given a job by Captain Dan Black. Then it was Charlie, who was on coasters. He was on the *TOURMALINE* in the Mersey when there was a collision with another boat. He got out all right, unhurt. I believe all the crew members were rescued at the time, but one died later from exposure - having been too long in the water. Charlie was not all that long working at sea.

"P. J. (Patrick John) was next, and an AB on coasters. He started off an a Robertson oil tanker. He didn't stay too long at sea. P.J. had to make himself a year younger to get to sea in the first place. I think he claimed he was 17, when he was really only 16. The youngest was Malachy, who was also very interested in playing hurling. He was an AB on coasters belonging to Robertson of Glasgow."

The five boys held the distinction of sailing the oceans at the same time, but mostly going their separate ways - apart from the lone accidental pairing of P. J. and Don. Quite often, masters of ships did not like to employ two members from the same family. In this instance the skipper of a small oil tanker, about to sail out of London, decided to let the two Black boys work together.

Don explained: "After starting out one after the other, the five of us were at sea all around the same time. There was just the one occasion when I sailed with one of my brothers. I was reporting back to the KG5 pool in London, and they sent me to work again on an oil tanker. The skipper met me, and asked had I by any chance a relation on board named Black. I said no.

“Afterwards, I looked along the deck and there was P J walking towards me. I had no idea he signed on for work on the same boat. I had to tell the skipper he was my brother, in case there was a problem, but the skipper said he had no concerns about having two brothers working on the same boat.”

Seafaring has been so often the core earner in the Glens. Don could trace family footprints back to his granduncle, Jamie Black. “More than likely, Jamie was on sailing ships,” added Don, who was 17 when he joined another Black, no relation, in Captain Dan, “ I started on coasters with the Robertson company of Glasgow. My first ship was the *FLUOR*, and another I was on was the *TOURMALINE*. The trips were mainly taking cargo of coal, and sometimes cement, from London to Belfast.

“During my spell on coasters, I worked alongside Jamie Murray of Waterfoot. After a while, I wanted to go deep-sea, and so I left Captain Dan. I passed my Lifeboat Ticket, and I had to go for that first and also serve a year of sea time to become an EDH (Efficient Deck Hand). I went deep-sea with Head Line out of Belfast to Canada. I worked on two of their boats, *RATHLIN HEAD* and *RAMORE HEAD*.

“On both of those boats I worked alongside Charlie McKay of Cushendun. That was in the 1950’s, taking cargo of Scotch whisky from Glasgow to Montreal and St John, New Brunswick. Occasionally, we went light ship across the Atlantic, which, at times, was not too nice an experience, and brought back a cargo of grain and timber. I changed my work back and forth, and did not stay too long with Head Line out of Belfast - not a great place to sail from, I felt.

“I went to the KG5 pool in London, where you always got a cosmopolitan crowd making up the crews. I joined Blue Star Line, and sailed to South America. I was also AB on trips to Wellington and Auckland, New Zealand. We took different regular cargo out to New Zealand, and frozen lamb cargo back to England. I was a number of years doing that. Once, when down in New Zealand, I ran into John Preston from Waterfoot. He was at sea here, I believe, before settling in New Zealand to work on the boats down there.

“I started on the boats in 1953, and quit when I married in 1969. During that time I experienced one close shave, while working on a coaster named the *GOREY*. We were carrying a cargo of stone from Rouen, France, to England. I was working for a small London company, trading from there to Paris, and up the River Seine, when we ran into bad weather.

“The cargo was one big heap of loose stone that started to shift during the storm. It was a bad night. I was on the wheel. The old mate came dashing up the steps to the skipper, wanting to know what we were at. It was the weather, and the shifting stones that made the boat roll so much. At times you could put out your hand and touch the water. We turned and went down a canal to LeHavre.”

DOUBLE DESPAIR

MARY ANNE McCormick of Dunurgan, Cushendun, had to bear a cruel cross of twin heartbreak, following the tragic dockside deaths of her husband, Hugh, and around a quarter of a century later the drowning of her young son Patrick.

During the 1930's, Hugh McCormick was killed while working down the side of his ship, when it was berthed on the Clyde. Patrick, better known as Paddy 'Tom' - the family nickname - apparently missed his footing while boarding his boat in Drogheda dock.

Hugh 'Tom' McCormick, Jnr, born on the 28th of January 1923, revealed his mother never recovered from the death of his younger brother, her son Paddy: During a chat on Saturday December 1, 2012, Hugh disclosed his family was left devastated: "The bad news of Paddy's death had a severe effect on my mother, Mary Anne, a McAllister from the Big Bridge, Glendun. She never got over that, became very quiet, and died of a broken heart six years later.

"This, of course, was a second family tragedy at sea that she had to endure, following the death of her husband, a brother of Mrs Charlie (Caroline) Graham of Calishnaugh, Cushendun. Both Paddy and my father were very young men when they were drowned. My father was just in his 30's when he was killed on the Clyde, in 1937, following an accident on a ship. He was down the side, doing some painting work when his ship was struck by another boat coming in, and he fell into the water.

"My brother Paddy was killed at Drogheda, on November 30, 1960. He was 33 years of age. He started at sea in his early 20's. He went away on coasters. Before that, he worked for a time in the then Elliott's Bay Hotel, in Cushendun.

"He sailed on Kelly coal boats for a period, and then changed to deep-sea with the Head Line boats out of Belfast. This meant sailing to Canada, and also to ports along the American coastline. On those trips to America and Canada he worked alongside another Cushendun seaman, John McQuaige. A very quiet man was John, who spent many years working on boats that sailed all over the world. He was often on the Head Line sailings, and also did coasting work with Captain John Mort on the PASS of GLENOGLE.

"I also recall our Paddy sailing with his young cousin, John Graham of Calishnaugh. I think that was on an oil tanker, and some time before John (Graham) became a Captain. Another family connection with the sea was the McKenty family, one that included Nellie, Tessie, and Dan. Their father Neil came from Carnlough, and was a seaman. His wife was another McAllister of the Big Bridge, Teresa, who ran a restaurant in Glasgow with her sister Mary Anne, my mother.

"That is where Merchant seaman Neil McKenty met Teresa. I believe Neil worked on coasters as a fireman, but was also tragically killed. In 1944, during blackout I'm told, he was injured on a boat in the Clyde, and died later in hospital.

"The Glasgow link is also on display in an old faded studio photograph that includes my father before he was about to board his ship. The image was taken in Glasgow during the middle 1920's. Included are Alex O'Hara of Knocknacarry, and a man named John Lewis, who was an orphan. I think Lewis first lived at Tromra, and was then taken down to Knocknacarry to be looked after by Maggie Cameron, the mother of the infamous strong man Jim O'Neill.

"Lewis had a younger brother, Robert, who was cared for by old Charlie McAuley, the blacksmith in Knocknacarry.. I think the Lewis boys came to Cushendun from Belfast during the First World War. They went away, and were never seen again. It was said Robert went to America. It appears, John Lewis went to sea, and worked as a deck hand alongside either Alex O'Hara or my father."

Hugh's cousin, Dan McKillop of the Big Bridge, Glendun, whose mother was Jane McAllister, a sister of Hugh's mother, helped to indentify the body of Paddy McCormick in December 1960. He said: "Paddy 'Tom' was drowned on the 30th of November 1960, but his body was not found until 28 days later. When the news came through to Cushendun that the body turned up on the right-hand side of the mouth of the River Boyne, opposite Baltray and on the Bettystown side, four of us left for Drogheda's Lady of Lourdes hospital, where the body was taken to.

"With me were my brother Jim, Alex O'Hara of Tromra, and Arthur McKay of The Turn, Dunurgan. That was on the 29th of December, 1960. Paddy was buried two days later at Craigagh, Cushendun. We learned that a taxi took Paddy back to his boat around 7.30 on the evening he was drowned. The skipper of the boat told me it was Paddy's habit not to use the gangplank when coming back on board. He jumped from quayside onto the ship.

"This time, in Drogheda Harbour, there was a full flood on the River Boyne. He must have misjudged his jump, hit his head on the edge of the boat, and fell into the river. There was a large bruise on his forehead. It was a dreadful tragedy. At first, I believe, the search for his body was up river, because of the way of the tide at that period. Instead, Paddy's body washed down the river.

"When I was young, I was told of other sea fatalities in the McCormick family circle. I believe two McCormick brothers were drowned in America. One was on a harbour lighter at New Jersey. I heard of an uncle of Hugh 'Tom's' fell overboard while working on one of the lighter/barges. Jack Hernon was with him, and tried to save him. It was said Jack managed to catch hold of his hair, but it was cut so short Hernon couldn't hold the grip sufficiently to get the McCormick man out of the water."

The Cushendun Parish census of 1901, with notes compiled by historians Malachy McSparran and Denis McKillop (Big Bridge), suggest Pat 'Tom' McCormick of Clady was twice involved in torpedo incidents during the First World War. A brother John is listed as 'drowned in New York'..

On a lighter note, Hugh McCormick recalled a forgotten fun time in the valley, long before the intrusion of television on family life and community fervour, when many young man became proficient in playing the violin: "I enjoyed playing the 'fiddle', and other enthusiastic violin players from around the Dunurgan area included Tommy Sharkey and Hugh McGavock." He featured in the Cushedun Ceili Band that also often included John Charles O'Hara, Colm McQuillan, and Johnny McKillop..

One of the proudest possessions in the McCormick house is a portrait by Michael McDaid of Hugh displaying his violin. He is depicted with his fiddle and Belfast docker Gerry Greham Snr, father of one of Hugh's sons-in-law Gerry Greham Jnr. Of even more poignant significance, and in the care of one of Hugh's sons, Paddy McCormick Jnr, is a unique portrait of a teenage Paddy 'Tom' McCormick. The special canvas is by one of Ireland's most accomplished landscape and portrait painters, Maurice Wilks of Belfast.

Following the popular trend of the middle 20th century, when a number of noted artists such as James Humbert Craig flocked to reside in the Cushendun area to satisfy their love of landscape painting in the Glens, a burgeoning Wilks first began to hone his skills when he rented accommodation in Dunurgan. Later, he moved closer to Cushendun Bay, to reside in a green painted corrugated house at the bottom of a field owned by Harry Scally.

The painting of Paddy McCormick may well be one of the first, if not the first, portrait completed in the Glens by Wilks. Hugh McCormick said: "The Wilks family stayed here, in the house I now live in at Dunurgan. They came down from Belfast on holiday, and rented what was then the Youth Hostel owned by old Alex 'Beat Hell' McGavock.

"When Maurice Wilks was here, he did the portrait of my brother Paddy, and presented it to him as a gift. Wilks came here for a number of years, to the Hostel, which then had a thatched roof, before he moved down to reside at Milltown, Cushendun. Wilks spent many summers in the Cushendun area to do his paintings." *The ever helpful, always humble, Hugh McCormick died, following illness, on Friday, August 30, 2013.

48

WALL of WATER

ROGUE WAVES during a sea storm carry life-threatening menace, and it requires nerves of steel from crew members and a sturdy ship to survive. Captain Jim McKay of Mill Street, Cushendall, could have been forgiven for wondering how his tanker, the *PASS of DRUMOCHTER* (2), would stay afloat off the northern Scottish coast.

"This one wave caught us by surprise. It was like a giant black wall coming at you," he said, "It was the roughest sea journey ever I was involved in, certainly the worst I can remember. I was skipper on the *PASS of DRUMOCHTER* when we were taking a cargo of chemicals from Middlesboro to Derry. It was November time, and the weather was really bad. We were off Cape Wrath one night, off the north of Scotland, at the Southeastern Hebrides - on the other side of the Pentland Firth.

"We were right across the top of Scotland, as you are about to turn to go down towards Ireland. We were not too far from the Skerry Vore Lighthouse, up near Barra, when we were more or less heaving to. It was so bad I was in the bridge as well. Conditions were dreadful, and all of a sudden things became worse. We went up on this massive wave. I thought the boat would not come back down again. She turned, and came straight down, vertical, and broke the mast.

"Then she was out in deep water, and time to lift her head. She was a good boat. To this day I still remember that wave. Up to that point the waves were high, but manageable, and then out of the ordinary came this rogue wave. We did not see it coming. It was a shock, but we survived.

"My older brother, Alistair once sailed with me when I was skipper of the *PASS of DRUMOCHTER*. Other locals from the Glens, who sailed with me were Neil O'Boyle from Waterfoot, his brother 'Red' Denis, Jerry McDonald from Tully, John Eddie McAlister from Galbolly, and Arthur Hamilton of Cushendun. I was AB when I worked alongside Arthur (Hamilton) for maybe three months. He was mate of the *AMBER*.

"One of the trips we were on was tough going, coming from Norway and heading for Ancona in the south of France. We ran into a storm. It was a rough journey, as we hit severe conditions when crossing the Bay of Lyons, part of the Bay of Biscay. We had a deck cargo of paper pulp for Ancona, but we lost half of it during the storm. Thankfully, no crew members were hurt."

Captain McKay, who lives in Scotland, first went to work as a deck boy on the cross-channel ferry running from Belfast to Heysham. "I managed to get the job through Archie 'Free State' Murray of Waterfoot. He was a seaman on board the *DUKE of ARGYLE*. I was under the impression he worked in America for a long time before that. Archie was a deck hand on the ferry, and it was through my father, Alex, I took up a career at sea. He knew that nothing would do me but that I would get to sea.

"He mentioned this to the man Murray. A whole lot of different types of jobs were put to me, but - no - I wanted to go to sea. I moved from Cushendall Primary School to St Aloysius School for about one month - and on to Ballymena Technical, for three years. From there, I went to sea, at 16-and-a-half-years-of-age, and on a ferry that sailed overnight.

"You left Belfast at 8 o'clock in the evening, and arrived in Heysham at around 7 o'clock the next morning. From the Heysham side, on the return journey, you left at midnight. You had to wait until late in the evening, to link with train times, and be ready for passengers, before departing for Belfast. I spent 18 months on the ferry, before switching to join Blue Funnel. The skipper of her, the ferry, had a brother who was a recruitment man for Blue Funnel. He spoke to his brother, to get me a job.

"It was deep-sea for me, right away, to the Far East, and I stayed with Blue Funnel for three and a half years. This was in the 1960's. I worked on trips down around Jawa, Indonesia, and was there during the time of trouble. It was a dangerous period. You could only stay in port during the day, because it was a time of crisis. As a precaution, we had to move the ship out of port at night, and anchor well away from the docks because of the danger of getting caught up in the fighting.

"The rebels and government troops were fighting, but we didn't see or hear very much of that. We sometimes brought in a cargo of armoured cars, for the government side. I also sailed to Hong Kong. Usually you went from Liverpool and Glasgow, and loaded Singer Sewing machines, bottles of Guinness, and bottles of Scotch whisky in the hold.

"From there, I left to join Robertson's of Glasgow, working on cargo boats that were constantly running all around Europe. We used to trade down to Spain and Casablanca. I sailed with Robertson's on timber runs up the Baltic, to the White Sea. I used to do three journeys up there during summer time, when weather conditions were good.

"But, on one trip we had to stay at anchor, in a queue, for a month, waiting for a berth, because it was so busy, so many other boats there ahead of us. Because we were there so long, and we hadn't stored up for a month, our food supplies rapidly ran out. We were berthed in a place where there were no roads, just dirt trails.

"We were in the wilds, no food could we buy. With a crew of 12, we arrived back in Cardiff and there was not a thing left to eat. There was not a bit of grub we didn't eat, including the lifeboat stores. The fuel was all right, but no groceries. Still a deck hand then, I went to work on oil tankers - on the Pass ships. I joined my uncle, Captain John Mort on the *PASS of GLENOGLE.* I stayed with him until I got married in 1969."

Born in 1941, he wed Glasgow girl Anne Cannon. "She used to come to Waterfoot on holiday. That is where I met her. She has relations around Glenravel, the Kerr family there, and also McAuley first cousins in Ballymena, including Carl McAuley."

He has a family of three boys - James, Stephen, and Alexander - and one girl, Kathleen. He left the Glens to live in Scotland. "I was on the Pass tankers at that time, living at Carnmunnock, between Glasgow and East Kilbride, and ten minutes from Hampden Park. I decided to go for a Ticket, so I took three months away from work to sit the Mate's Ticket.

"I went to the College in Glasgow, travelling in and out from my home on the bus. When I passed the examination, I rejoined the Pass boats as Second Mate. Uncle John Mort was retired by this time. I worked with a Captain Tommy Templeton of Islandmagee. I was Second Mate on a number of different ships, including the *PASS of GLENCLUNIE.*

"The Pass ships were taken over by P & O, and called Panocean. A number of changes were made to the name of the ships, such as the *PASS of KERNWELL* and the *PASS of DRUMOCHTER.* I was round a good many of them for 18 months, and then decided to take three months out, and sit my Master's Ticket examination, in Glasgow.

"The Pass company paid my college fees, so I returned to their boats, and went as Second Mate again. They only had four to five ships. I didn't want to be a lifetime as Second Mate. I felt I was not going to improve my situation, so I said so to the skipper, George Holstrom, from Newcastle-upon-Tyne. I was leaving, and was going to BP. He said: 'Hang on' - and next word I got was a First Mate's job. I stayed Mate for a further 18 months..

"I got my first shift as skipper in 1975 - on the *PASS of GLENCLUNIE,* and as I sailed out of Granegemouth as captain I remember it being a very proud day for me, but also a very nervous occasion. I was skipper on many Pass boats - *DALBURN, CAIRNWELL. DRUMOCHTER, DERRYMOR,* and back to the *PASS of CAIRNWELL* - a chemical cargo tanker.

"It used to run into Derry and also to Coleraine, where there was the Monsanto Chemical plant. It shut down as well. Suddenly, Panocean finished, just quit, not making enough profit. The bubble burst even with their deep-sea ships, and they sold the lot to Greeks and Italians. Crews were out of jobs. After a couple of weeks, I managed to get a job with Everards of London, and stayed with that company until I retired. I was probably 15 years with them, and they presented me with an engraved glass decanter when I decided to retire.

"I worked on their oil tankers, more coasting than anything else. Sometimes the furthest you would be away was when we'd do runs down to Santander, in northern Spain, to LeHavre in France, and to Germany. When the boat had to go into dry-dock it was always to Gdansk and Gdena in Poland, because it was cheaper to get the job done there. I stayed with the boat until it was ready, to make sure everything was done right - then sail again, around three weeks later.

"My last ship was the *AUTHENTICITY,* and I was 12 years on her, trading around these coasts, and also to the Continent. That was the longest I ever worked on any one ship. My last shift as Master of the *AUTHENTICITY* was in 2002."

49

PLAIN SAILING

GARDINER'S world was the preferred choice of passage for Carnlough-born Patrick Darragh, who successfully steered through the stormy coastal waters where widespread danger lurked during the two major conflicts of 1914-1916 and 1939-1945.

An acting skipper for many years with the Gardiner Shipping Company, Glasgow, he was born on September 29, 1892, and went to work at sea at 16-years-of-age. "He was an active Merchant Seaman during the First and Second World Wars, but I don't recall him discussing what happened in the First World War," said his son Lawrence, who lives near the top end of Glenariffe Glen.

His father was first registered as an Able Seaman, born in Carnlough. His listing is recorded RS2 No 351421. Born in 1946, Lawrence added: "I recall my mother telling me my father had curly flaxen-coloured hair when he was a young man, but after an illness, a gall bladder operation, his hair turned completely white. That is how I remember him. He was with Gardiner's all of his sea career, working his way up from deck hand, through the Mate Tickets, but was never ticketed for ship's captaincy.

"Despite not having sat the examination for a Master's Ticket, he was appointed skipper by Gardiner's when he was 26-years-of-age. For years and years, including through the Second World War, when he was based at Scapa Flow in the north of Scotland, he was a ship's master. The first boat he skippered was the *ARDCHATTAN*, and then he moved to the *SAINT ODHRAN*, which he was on for a long number of years. The cargo was generally coal or scrap metal - all that sort of stuff, and trading along the coasts.

"During a long period at Scapa Flow, the whole time of the Second World War, his job as a skipper was to ship munitions and other supplies from there out to the navy vessels. Once at Scapa Flow, he recounted a very dangerous incident that happened on a dreadfully stormy night. During gale-force winds, a huge violent storm was in full force, the wooden bridge of his boat was blown clean off. He had to tie himself to the wheel.

"My father married Mary Magee of the Big Bridge, Glendun - an aunt of Paddy and Joe Magee of Cushendun. My mother met my father when she worked for the McSparron family at their Carnlough Post Office. I lived in Carnlough until I was four-years-of-age. We moved to the Bay, Glenariffe. Also living with us was a Joe Gibson, who joined the Merchant Navy, but was lost at sea during the Second World War, when his ship in convoy was torpedoed by a German submarine in the Atlantic.

"My father was 65 when he died, after suffering a heart attack in September 1958. We were living at Lurig View, Glenariffe. When we were there, our neighbours included the Graham family, and Captain Dan Black. I moved out of Lurig View at 18. My mother died in 1978, and my sister stayed on there for a while."

The Darragh family also holds blood connection to the late Father Alex Darragh of Carnlough, a former Antrim footballer famous for launching the Ballymena All Saints Boxing Club in the early 1960's. "The recently retired seaman, George Darragh of Carnlough is also a relation," added Lawrence, "I remember seeing Fr Darragh quite often, as I had to bring two old aunts, both spinsters and sisters of my father - Annie and Isabella Darragh, of 38, High Street, Carnlough - out to see Fr Alex."

The aforementioned George Darragh retained a strong interest in the ways of the sea, long after he retired from working on big boats. His love of the oceans never wained, and the veteran Carnlough mariner maintained he would one day sail off into the western sunset, just to look at the Panama Canal one more time.

In November 2012, the 69-year-old said: "Since I retired from sea going I took up a bit of local fishing. I had a 37-feet fishing boat in Carnlough, but recently sold it at Howth, and bought a 28-foot boat. I enjoy the fishing. Now I'm on the look for a decent boat to see if I could sail back to the Panama Canal before I die.

"During my days at sea, I was through the Panama Canal over half-a-dozen times. It is an amazing place. For passages to New Zealand we went through the Panama Canal, and for Australia, where the nearest port from London is Fremantle, the quickest route is through the Suez Canal and the Indian Ocean. Big tankers that couldn't pass through the Panama Canal went around Cape Horn, a trip I never made."

Darragh, also a cousin of the late 'Big' George Darragh, a brother of Fr Darragh who was a deep-sea sailor on tankers and cargo ships, took to a working life on the waves at 14 years of age. It seemed the natural thing to do. He was not interested in remaining at school.

"I made an early move to the sea. I was a student at St Aloysius School in Cushendall, and I was in the same class as Hugh McIlwaine of Waterfoot. We went there the year the school first opened, and are the same age. I went to sea as a deck hand. At that time it was the done thing to work at sea, as almost every other house in Carnlough had some connection with the sea.

"When I started out, the vessel was a puffer carrying limestone out of Carnlough Harbour to Glasgow. It had a total crew of four, including the Master. He was a man named McMullan from Campbeltown, and he owned the boat, which was named *HAYSCHAM.* After one year on the wee schooner I moved to work deep-sea, as AB, because, when you are a young fella you want to see the world, visit all those far-off places I heard so much about. I managed to join the Blue Star line."

Darragh's deep-sea passages took in New Zealand, Australia, South America, California, and other ports along North America's west coast. All with the Blue Line Shipping Company. "I worked with Paddy McNeill of Cushendun on some of those boats," added George, "Paddy and his brother Seamus both were with Blue Star. During my years at sea, as an AB, I experienced the odd bit of bad weather conditions, but nothing serious. I retired from sea work at 60, so I was a seaman for 46 years.

"During that time, I also worked alongside Sean Mort on the *WILLIAM WAINWRIGHT.* I remember a very worrying period during the time of US President John F. Kennedy's problem with the Cuban missile crisis, which began on October 22, 1962. We were sailing back from Australia, and coming out of the Suez Canal, when the news broke there might be a nuclear war.

"We felt war was sure to happen. We seemed to be on the brink of a nuclear disaster. Here we were on a pretty slow-moving tanker. Our main concern was to get home before the world went mad. We got to the Glens just as the tension eased in the Cuban crisis. Also on that trip was Sean McBride of Carnlough, who later jumped ship in Sydney, Australia. He married out there, worked in an oil refinery at Sydney, and died there.

"When I was in London, to board a ship, I often met John O'Neill of Cushendall, who was going to work for the Shaw-Savill line. In later years, I worked with John on the Larne-Cairnryan Ferry. I spent the last ten years of my sea life as AB on the ferry. It was handy to get home."

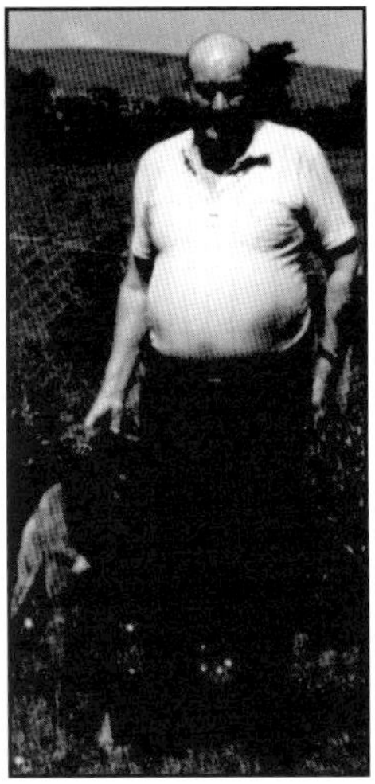

John Stewart of Knockans, Cushendall

Sea cook John Leavey of Southampton and Cushendun

John Scollay, Cushendall

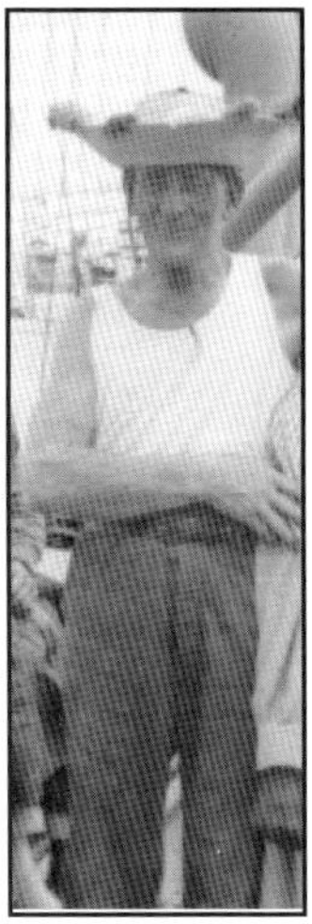

Old salt Tommy 'Shetland' Scollay

Glenariffe AB Patsy Black

Ship's cook Jim McElroy, Cushendall

Hal Harvey, Glenariffe

The PRINCESS VICTORIA

1960- Cairns, Cushendall, Healy brothers, Frank and Hugh, dobieing (washing) jeans before returning to sea work

Teenager Danny Reddington of Glenariffe

Carnlough seamen include Dan McNeill, Don McCart, and Johnny Magill

Taking it easy. Good buddies, John Murphy, left, and Alastair McKay of Cushendall

Charles McKernan, Carnlough

AB seaman James Graham of Lurig View, Glenariffe

Carnlough deck hand Archie McNeill

The McHugh brothers of Cushendun, Eugene (left) and Paul, right, on overseas deck duty

Deck Hands Archie Gore, Mill Hollow, Cushendall, and Glenariffe's Tommy McCollam

Cushleake, Cushendun, deep-sea sailor John Murphy helping on the home farm in October, 1937.

Cushendall's Johnnie O'Hara earned wartime fame while on board the PARKNASILLA

The TORFEY

SS. BRINKBURN

The PACIFIC PRESIDENT

S.S. HERSCHEL

The PASS OF GLENOGLE

Liverpool Ferry Stewardess (right) Mary Monaghan of Glenariffe

Cushendall AB Ian Mort, son of Captain John Mort

Captain Gerry Blaney, Cushendall

Passage on the Panama Canal

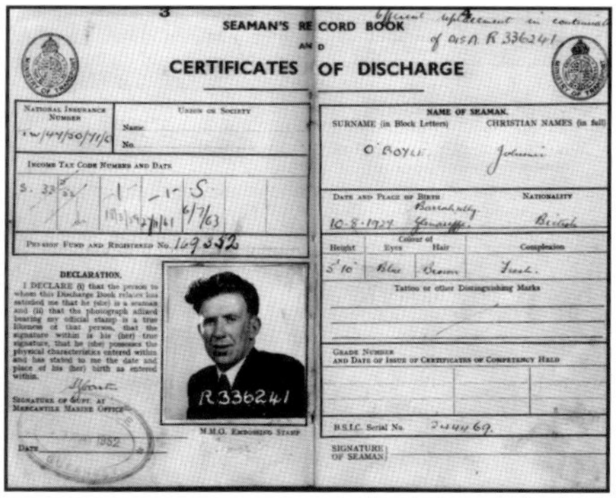
SEAMAN'S RECORD BOOK AND CERTIFICATES OF DISCHARGE

R 336241

Sea chart of Johnnie O'Boyle

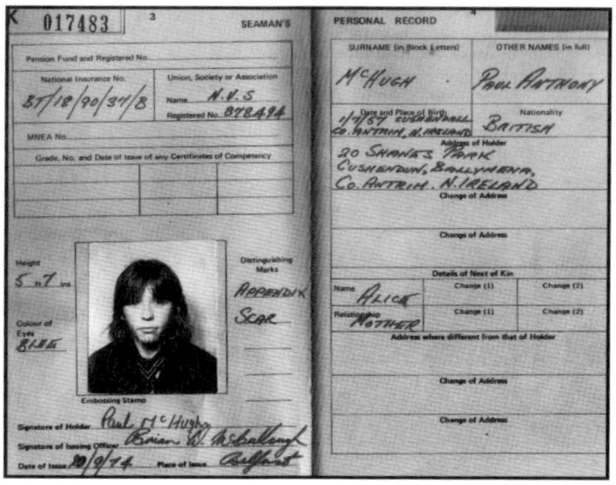
017483

SEAMAN'S PERSONAL RECORD

McHUGH PAUL ANTHONY

BRITISH

20 SHANE'S PARK CUSHENDUN, BALLYMENA, CO. ANTRIM. N.IRELAND

Paul McHugh's Discharge book

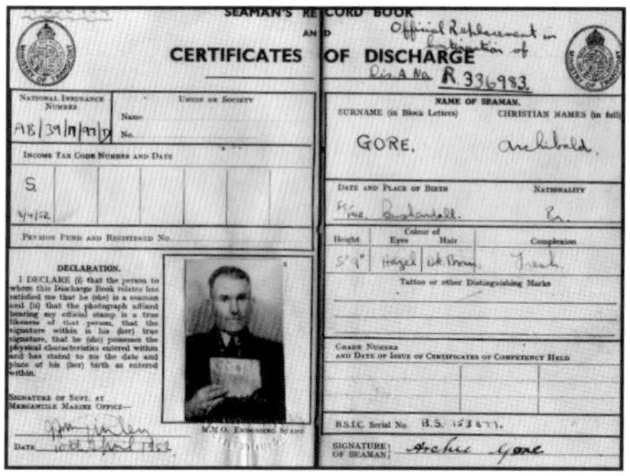
SEAMAN'S RECORD BOOK CERTIFICATES OF DISCHARGE

R 336983.

GORE, Archibald

Discharge Book of Archie Gore,
Mill Hollow, Cushendall.

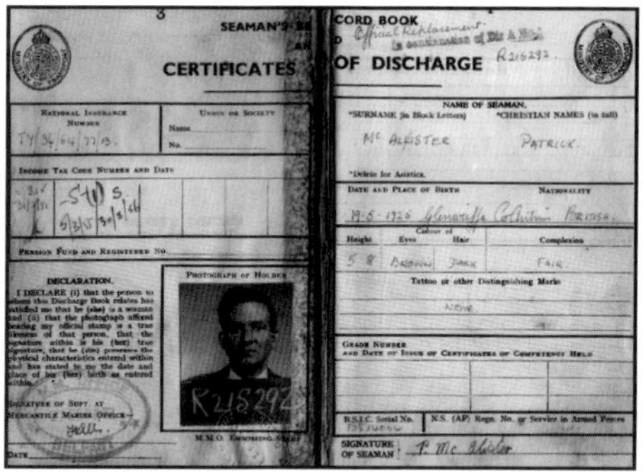
SEAMAN'S RECORD BOOK CERTIFICATES OF DISCHARGE

McALISTER PATRICK

R218294

Glenariffe bo'sun Paddy McAlister's
Discharge Book

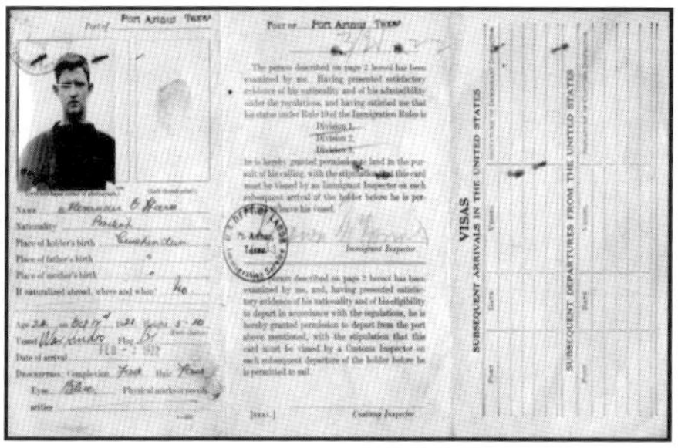
Port Arthur Texas

VISAS

February 1922 - Knocknacarry's
Alex O'Hara visits Texas.

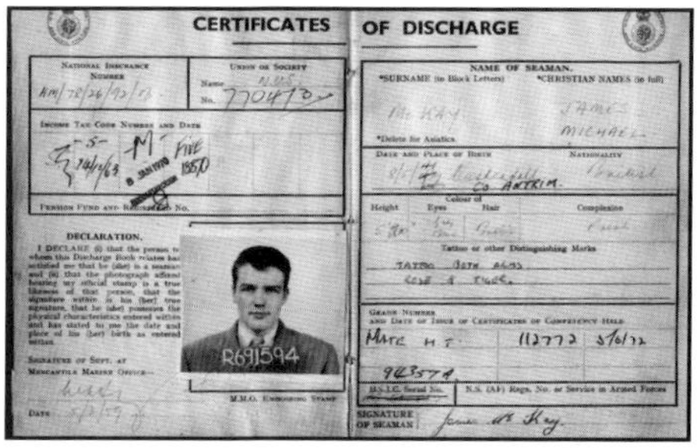
CERTIFICATES OF DISCHARGE

R691594

Discharge Book of Cushendall
teenager Jim McKay.

50

CHARLIE'S CHOICE

FIVE YEARS on a factory floor in Larne would appear an unlikely setting towards securing a switch to a significantly successful career at sea. Charlie McAuley of Cushendall made the move in 1963, while working as an engineer on turbines in the A.E.I. complex overlooking Larne Harbour.

From Glenballyeamon, he pondered the prospect of packing in the factory job and taking to the oceans. After all, he had blood connections with seagoing. "My uncle, Danny McAuley up in Clough, was a seaman on coasters. His father, Daniel, was also at sea for a long time, and I believe he worked deep-sea. Danny was at sea along with Pat Gore," he said. However, it took an unexpected elbow to help make up his mind, when he was overlooked for a job in travelling abroad with exported turbines, to help with the fitting of those turbines at locations in Canada and Brazil.

Born in 1941, and married in 1972 to near neighbour Elizabeth O'Rawe from Tully, he added: "I broke with tradition in the Glens. In olden times, the sailors mostly started as deck hands on small coastal ships, until the period when many, like Paddy 'The Rock' McNeill, went deep-sea, but firstly attending the Sea Training School. It may seem uncommon for shore-based engineers to take up work at sea. This is not the case. Many engineers working on the building of big ships in Belfast Shipyard went on to become top engineers at sea.

"Working on ship engines on land, and then going to sea happened quite often with workers in the 'Yard'. They had the advantage of knowing all about the engines of big ships, and were able to quickly make the transition, and move to become engineers at sea. I worked on land, in a turbine-making factory, and not beside the ships and sea, like the men from the Shipyards. I served an apprenticeship on steam turbines, and went to the Belfast Department of Trade before going to sea as a junior engineer.

"Quite a lot of workers from shore-based industries went to sea, from employment that had nothing to do with the sea. I met up with quite a few when doing Ticket examinations in Belfast, many working deep-sea. There were 25 apprentices in the Larne A.E.I. turbine factory, and a lot of them went to sea. I thought about the idea of also going on the boats, as an engineer, for a good while.

"When B.T.H. and then A.E.I. Turbines from the factory in Larne were being exported overseas, to Canada and Brazil, I applied for one of the posts to go with the engines for assembly, but I didn't get a job. It was then I decided to go another route, to sea. So, I quit Larne. In those days ship companies were on the look-out for engineers, and especially if you had time-engineering behind you.

"Five young engineers left the A.E.I., including me, and went on to become ship's engineers. We were used to working and making ship's turbines in Larne, and that helped. Joe McMaster from Ballymena was an engineer in the A.E.I., and went to work as an engineer on the ferries. Jim King, a big fellow from Belfast, went to the same Blue Funnel Line in Liverpool as I did. We studied in Belfast, and gained a Certificate of Competence.

"While I had those five years on land, I needed 21 months of sea-going time before passing that first level. They eased me in, working up and down the local coasts, out of Glasgow and so on. My near neighbour, Danny McNaughton of Tully, who went to sea with Captain Jim McGonnell, and me were at sea around the same time. I was with him in Belfast when he collected his Ticket

"Dorey's had a couple of new boats then, the *PORTELET* and the *HAVELET*. Garron Point's Joe O'Boyle sailed as Second Mate when Danny was First Mate, and the skipper was McCullough of Larne. I was on the *PORTELET*. While locals such as Danny (McNaughton) went as sailors, and many progressed to achieve mate and captain's tickets, I went for a sea career in engineering.

"Captain Gerry Blaney once told me I was the first man from these parts to get a ship's Chief Engineer Certificate. Later on, his son, Gerry Blaney Jnr became a Chief Engineer. Way back, I remember Scotland-born Bob Mitchell working as a ship's engineer. Then I did part A of the Second Engineer's Ticket, and later part B. I was with the Blue Funnel line, Alfred Holden of Liverpool.

"After they broke me in, by sending me on coasters, I went deep-sea for a first time, on the Blue Funnel's *TAMTALUS,* in 1963. The ship was supposed to go for scrapping, but somebody changed the order, and the ship came home again. It began as a Victory ship, built in the USA during the Second World War to bring troops across the Atlantic. In the States then they were turning out one ship a week. Blue Funnel bought five of them, and ran them as cargo vessels.

"We sailed through the Suez Canal, to Malaysia, Singapore, Hong Kong, Japan, and sometimes up to China. We also traded to Ceylon, now Sri Lanka, to load with big chests of tea out of Trinco Melee, and back to London or Liverpool. During 1963 to 1965, I was on a run down to Australia, and also in 1965 I did my Second Engineer's ticket in Belfast.

"After sea time, I got the Second Engineer Ticket in 1966, and sailed with Blue Funnel as a Third Engineer. I remember once in a chat with Captain Gerry Blaney, Captain John Small, and Captain Alex Blaney of the Crossroads - they kept telling me the best place to go to work was on the China Seas.

"They were working for Chinese companies then. They insisted I would be better off there, that I would get a better job, and better pay. Jim McElroy was also there, during a gathering in the Thornlea Hotel, and he had the opposite view. He advised me to stay where I was. I stayed. I

CERTIFICATE OF COMPETENCY

AS

FIRST CLASS ENGINEER

No. 126831

STEAMSHIP AND MOTORSHIP

To —— Charles McAuley ——

WHEREAS you have been found duly qualified to fulfil the duties of First Class Engineer Steamship and Motorship in the Merchant Navy, the Board of Trade in exercise of their powers under the Merchant Shipping Acts and of all other powers enabling them in that behalf hereby grant you this Certificate of Competency.

Dated this 22nd day of June 1978

Countersigned

Registrar General.

An Under Secretary of the Board of Trade

REGISTERED AT THE OFFICE OF THE REGISTRAR GENERAL OF SHIPPING AND SEAMEN

remained with Blue Funnel, and sat the Chief Engineer's Ticket, part of the test held in Belfast, part in England.

"In 1969, I became Second Engineer on one of the world's biggest high-powered twin-screw container ships. The shipping scene was rapidly changing then, with one big tanker equal to ten old cargo ships. I was on the *PALTHYVIOUS*. All those Blue Funnel ships, from 1945, had Greek names. It did 16 knots, and it held a great amount of cargo. Blue Funnel had the Victory ships altered, and ran them as cargo ships. Those boats, with turbine engines, lasted well into the 1970's."

In the early 1970's, Charlie changed tack, and went on tankers for a short period, still with Blue Funnel. but now with a name change to Ocean Fleet. "I was sailing as Second engineer," he explained, "I did my Motor Endorsement Ticket in Belfast, adding to the Chief Engineer certificate. Now I could sail motor or steam run ships, so I went to motor tankers for a while, and then back to container ships.

"I worked on big refrigerated ships going to New Zealand and Australia. By now, Ocean Fleet was amalgamated with P&O, and became OCL (Overseas Containers Limited). Until 1992, I sailed on those refrigerated ships, taking out mainly general cargo from England. Sometimes there was a little refrigerated cargo going out. I remember once we took out special boxes of fish to Australia. The hatches held the containers, with blowing-air systems. In the fruit season 'Down Under' we would bring back containers of apples, dairy produce, beef and lamb. Sometimes we had a few containers on deck."

One of his most striking memories of this period was the astonishing efficiency of the killing fields of New Zealand. He recalled: "I'd never seen anything like this before. We would go around the New Zealand coast, during what is known as 'the killing season', and collect lamb carcases. We would call in at Auckland, Wellington, and also at Littleton, the nearest we could get to Christchurch. It was an amazing scene in New Zealand during the killing season.

"One moment the hills would be jam-packed with thousands of young sheep, the next the fields would be bare. Our refrigerated cargo held one million lamb carcases, taken back to northern Europe, and unloaded, part cargo, at Hamburg, Bremerhaven, Rotterdam, and then at Tilbury Docks in London.

"I went from the New Zealand run to join new container ship buildings in Japan, where the company had the then biggest container ship in the world, built by MHI (Mitschibushi Heavy Industry). That was in 1998/1999. As Chief Engineer, I was sent to the dockyard in Japan. I had a team of First Mates with me, and we did trials. It was for P&O, which was part of OCL, and I sailed on a single-screw, one-engine ship that could carry 8,000 containers, and had 96,000-shaft horse-power. P&O broke away from OCL, become P&O Containers, and amalgamated with Nedlloyd of Rotterdam. The Dutch company became P&O Nedlloyd."

He retired in 2001, after almost 39 years at sea. The last voyage was memorable. Taking wife Elizabeth with him on a trip that lasted two months, the McAuleys sailed into the rising sun on board a jumbo-sized container ship, one with the long named *P&O NEDLLOYD SOUTHAMPTON*.

While husband had to concentrate on the serious side of sailing Elizabeth enjoyed the smooth cruise-liner style journey on this massive ship. She said: "It was a very pleasant voyage. I enjoyed it - just like being on a huge passenger liner. I was spoiled. Charlie told me of the great cook they had on board, and it was true."

Sea transport progressed in dramatic leaps during recent decades. Behemoth container boats traverse the oceans. McAuley stated: "A huge vessel named *TOKYO BAY* was the first of the new monster container ships, and was made in 1970. It carried 2,800 containers. Cargo sometimes included racehorses housed in special horse-boxes in the holds. The progression continued, the size of ships increasing all the time.

"Later came the *SHENZEN BAY*, which carried 8,000. I was at the building of this ship in Japan. You rode a bike through the shipyard. I stayed in a hotel, was then taken by van each morning to the yard, which was three miles long, and then you picked up one of the bikes to go to the workshop. I was on that ship for her first sea trials.

"For my farewell trip, the ship, *SOUTHAMPTON*, built in 1998 and with a top speed of 24.5 knots, is 299.9 metres long - twice the length of the Cushendall hurling field. She is 42.80 metres wide, and this helped to carry enormous train carriages on the deck for the Hong Kong Metro system.

"The loading started at Southampton, then Hamburg and Rotterdam, and the voyage through the Suez Canal to a first stop at Singapore, where we dropped off some containers. It was on to Japan, with stops at Kobe, Yokohama, and Tokyo. Eventually, it was back to Singapore, Suez, and Southampton.

"It wasn't to be the last moments for me at sea, as I anticipated. I had to leave Elizabeth to go home on her own. The relief engineers didn't turn up, so I had to stay on, along with the second engineer, Frank McAleese. We made a repeat sailing out of Southampton through Hamburg, Rotterdam, and down to Suez. This was where my last job ended, in Egypt, and into retirement. I was able to leave the ship at Port Said, and the Company flew me home out of Cairo. Leave owed took me up to the beginning of February 2001, three weeks before my 60th birthday."

After his retirement, the size of container ships has become staggering. The shipping lanes are regularly dominated by giants of the deep blue seas. McAuley reflected on the trend: "After I left the sea, the Maersk Lines, who took over P&O Nedlloyd, built three container ships that carry 15,000 containers. The engine is now 115,000 SHP. There are now bigger still container ships by the Maersk Line. The changes in shipping have been dramatic.

"When I was on the old cargo ships, such as the *HELENUS*, with a 95,000 ton cargo, we had 20 of an engine-room staff, including seven engineers, two electricians, two Chinese fitters, and nine Chinese engine-room hands. On deck we had the master, four mates, one navigating officer, two midshipmen, a bo'sun, nine deck hands, a chief steward, a second steward, two cooks, two radio officers, and four stewards. The total workforce we had on that ship was 47. We were also carrying 12 passengers.

"Times changed dramatically from that period. Trimming back all the time. For the same trading, I was about to rejoin the last vessel I worked on in Southampton, on a New Year's Eve, when I received a telephone call at home in Cushendall, from headquarters in Rotterdam.

"I was told I would be sailing without an electrician. And this was on a ship that had 400 refrigerated containers on deck, and all were plug-in. The cutbacks were continuing. I was the chief engineer. We had three engineers, the ship's master, three mates, one greaser, a bo'sun, and eight deck hands. In total, the crew was 19. That represented a huge drop in crew, from a workforce of 47."

51 FERRY TALES

PASSENGER trips across the Irish Sea generally prove a relaxing experience, with stabilisers to keep the boats on an even keel. The comforts of the lounge and restaurants somehow create a distilled form of escapism during such pleasant journeys, yet it demands alertness at all times for the crew members.

John O'Neill has been on such trips for close on half a century, keeping a constant vigil as ship's bo'sun. This rock-steady seaman, who joined P&O Ferries in 1971, said: "I have been with them ever since, 42 years as bo'sun. My first job with P&O was on the *BARDIC FERRY*, sailing from Larne to Preston. On a couple of occasions, I was sent to work on the ferry from Felixtowe to Europort, Rotterdam."

Born in 1947 - the year of the really 'Big Snow' - in Dalriada Hospital, Ballycastle, he has, since 1977, been living in Cushendall, where wife Mary (nee McAlister) runs the 'Glendale' B&B on the Coast Road side of the town. He attended St Patrick's Primary School, Ballycastle, and from there to the old Star of the Sea Secondary on Mary Street, and on to the Sea Training facility near Dover.

"In 1964, I went to sea at 17-years-of-age, and along with the late Gerard Black and the McCurdy brothers, Gerard and Dominic from Rathlin Island," said O'Neill, "We went to the Prince of Wales Sea Training School at Dover, and trained there for four months. We were allocated jobs. At that time, the School was attached to about five different shipping companies, including P&O, New Zealand Steamship, Port Line, and the one I started with, Shaw-Savill.

"Gerard Black and I went with Shaw-Savill, and the first ship I worked on, as a deck boy, was the *CORINTHIC*. She went to New Zealand, with 85 first-class passengers and also general cargo. Coming back on this refrigerated ship we took cargo of lamb, cheese, beef, and butter. I was on the *CORINTHIC* for five voyages.

"On one occasion, three years after I joined Shaw Savill, the four sea school boys from Ballycastle were all sailing together on a journey to New Zealand and back - Gerard Black, the McCurdy brothers, and me. Four mad Irishmen! I stayed with Shaw-Savill for four years, moving up the grades to Ordinary Seaman and EDH.

"One of the ships I also worked on was the *GOTHIC*, a first-class vessel that once took Queen Elizabeth on a Commonwealth tour, in 1953. I moved to do a couple of trans-Atlantic runs with Head Line, out of Belfast to Canada, an the *RATHLIN HEAD* and *RAMORE HEAD*. Cushendun seamen, John McKay and Patrick McKendry were on those trips, too. I was on that run for six months, and moved to do some work on a coaster, the *FALLOWFIELD*, taking containers mostly between Larne, Preston, and Ardrossan.

"I decided on another change of direction, and moved to the ferries. Nowadays, there are not the same number of Glens seaman employed, because of big changes in the business. For example, the crew on the ferryboat I work on is made up of many Latvians and Poles. The AB's are probably earning half the pay of the good old days, which are well and truly over"

O'Neill added: "After sailing on the ferries to Preston and Rotterdam, I moved to work, for 20 years, on the Larne-Cairnryan ferry, sailing on the *PRIDE of RATHLIN*. I switched to the Larne-Troon run in 2002, and stayed there until 2011, when they closed down that service. I was moved, in December 2011, to the Dublin-Liverpool run, working on the *EUROPEAN ENDEAVOUR*.

"Of the teenagers who set out to sea from Ballycastle all those years ago, Gerard Black left deep-sea sailing to become Captain of the Belfast-Liverpool ferry, and then the Dublin to Liverpool ferry. Sadly, he died of a heart attack on the boat. Dominic McCurdy left deep-sea to become Captain of the Ballycastle-Rathlin ferry, and retired recently."

Seamen from the Glens mostly stopped trading on far distant routes, and decided on deck work closer to home, by securing posts on passenger ferries. Taking on extensive periods of employment on the roll-on/roll-off services are sailors such as Francis McGinty, the Graham brothers, Hugh McIlwaine, James Kelly, Pat Close, James McKendry, Francis Black, Willie Granville, and Eugene McMullan.

Not many, like John O'Neill, devoted the bulk of their working days on the ferryboats. Closer to home I unearthed another long-serving ferryman, Kevin McHugh. Three sons of Sean and Alice McHugh of Shane's Park, Cushendun, took to the ships. Kevin spent 15 years on the oceans.

"I started at 17-and-a-half-years-of-age, when I attended the Merchant Navy's Sea Training College at Gravesend, Kent," said Kevin, "I spent the first three months at the College, near Tilbury docks, London, where I sat the examinations. I was then five years working deep-sea. About that time my brothers, Eugene and Paul, decided to quit the sea, after spending two years as deck hands on deep-sea voyages down to Australia and back.

"I worked as a steward, bar steward, and relief purser on a variety of ships. My first job was as a steward on a BP oil tanker going deep-sea, sailing across the Atlantic to Curacao in the West Indies . . . and back with oil cargo to ports such as Rotterdam.

"My first ship was the *APPLEBY*, and on that BP tanker was Glenariffe deck hand, big Neil O'Boyle. I was not always on oil tankers, but switched to work long-distance on boats carrying iron ore from Canada to Swansea. That was in 1980, and once when coming back with iron ore from Quebec we couldn't unload the cargo in Swansea, because of the strike in the UK. The ship, owned by Caser Irvine, had to change course and unload the iron ore in Dunkirk."

It was then McHugh changed to work closer to home, and at stabilised sailing. He gained employment as a steward on the Belfast to Liverpool passenger ferry. "I was on the *St COLUM* ferry, and it meant night passage. I spent nine years on that run. The job lasted until 1990, when the crew members were all paid off by the owners, Irish Containers. There was a financial problem, I believe. That service shut down.

"I had to spend 18 months out of work, until a new company bought over the run. I was back on the same cross-channel shift, the passenger ferryboat from Belfast to Liverpool. For the next two years I was Bar Steward and Relief Purser on the *RIVER MERSEY*, before deciding to quit the sea."

His brothers, Eugene and Paul clocked over two years of deck duty before quitting. "I went to work on a Kelly coal boat at 16 years of age," declared Paul, "Eugene was at sea before me, working for a year on passenger ships down to Tenerife. I started as a deck boy on the *BALLYROBERT*. Also working on this Kelly coal boat was John Leech of Waterfoot. We brought coal out of ports such as Garston.

"After one year, I decided to move, and try deep-sea sailing. I managed to get a job on a Texaco oil tanker. I was flown out of Belfast to the Persian Gulf, to join the *TEXACO ROTTERDAM*. I started work on deck from there. We sailed to Karachi, Pakistan, to Panang, Malaysia - and from there to Saigon. It was just coming to the end of the Vietnam War, but I was very glad to get in and out of there quickly.

"We travelled 30 miles up the river, and docked at a jetty beside an American ammunitions ship. Before we arrived another petrol tanker had been blown up at the same jetty. Just beside us you could see the remains of that ship sticking out of the water. We were there overnight, and out. It was my one and only trip to Saigon.

"We returned to the Persian Gulf, and from there to New York, Boston, Portland (Maine), and back to dry-dock at Pembroke, Wales. It was there my brother Eugene joined the ship. My second trip on the *TEXACO ROTTERDAM* was back to the Persian Gulf to load with oil. However, this time we couldn't go through the Suez Canal, because of fighting down there.

"That was in 1975, and we had to sail around South Africa, the Cape of Good Hope, and up to the Persian Gulf. We went from there to Papua, New Guinea. Port Mosley, Sydney, and Darwin. When this trip ended, both Eugene and me quit the sea. I joined the Calor Gas company in Belfast, in 1978, and I've been there ever since."

52

HARBOUR LIGHTS

PATRICK McKeegan began the exacting job of Harbour Master at Coleraine in 2001, and still remembers the first day at work, when he sweated bricks. He left years of conventional seafaring, working abroad and also on coasters and cross-channel ferryboats, to take on what might appear an 'armchair' occupation linked to the waves.

"I found the job more demanding than I expected, and prayed I wouldn't mess it up. The responsibility is severe," claimed McKeegan, whose wife Ann runs the 'Riverside' B & B in Cushendall's Mill Street, "I'm in charge of boats going in and out, and responsible for the safety of all involved - the staff, the pilots, the boats - over a five-mile stretch of the River Bann, down to the Bar Mouth."

McKeegan followed a family trait, taking to seafaring in the footsteps of his father, Patrick and his uncle John. "My McKeegan family originated from a farm up Glenaan, known as the 'McVicker' McKeegan's from near Ossian's Grave. Kate McVicker was an aunt of my father, Patrick McKeegan, who later lived down Shore Street, Cushendall. John McCambridge, connected to Lizzie and John Darragh, bought the small hill farm of around 17 acres from my father, and lived there at the Mill Town, near Ossian's Grave. John went to sea for a lengthy spell, working on coasters.

"My father was a deep-sea sailor. He was a carpenter, and once worked on the Paddy Henderson of Glasgow's passenger/cargo *KEMMENDINE* that ran from Glasgow to Rangoon. He stayed in Glasgow during the Second World War years. My mother once received a letter from the ship's company to state the ship had been torpedoed and sunk, but all aboard, crew and passengers, were safe.

"*The KEMMENDINE* was attacked off Ceylon, on her way to Burma, by a German raider ship. The crew and passengers were first taken off, and then the German's sunk the ship." On Saturday July 13, 1940, the German vessel *ATLANTIS* (known as Raider C to the Royal Navy) opened fire and sunk the 7,769 ton passenger/cargo ship *KEMMENDINE* of the Henderson Line, which was heading for Burma.

It seems a German boarding crew first took people off the ship that carried a crew of 112 and 35 passengers, including 5 women and 2 children. The cargo included whisky and beer. The *KEMMENDINE* was bound for Rangoon, out of Glasgow, and via Gibraltar and Cape Town. The sneaky *ATLANTIS,* often disguised as a harmless looking Soviet or Japanese cargo vessel during 1940, and displaying false identification, sank or captured 22 ships in the south Atlantic and Indian Ocean.

Patrick McKeegan added: "Most of my father's time on ships was on deep-sea passages. In later years, he ended up working as bo'son on coasters, and mainly on an oil tanker skippered by Jim Blaney of Cushendall. I went to sea in 1964, and my father was still working. He took ill in the late 1960's, came ashore, and died at home.

"His brother John also went to sea, and became a captain, He was skipper of the last British-owned ship, a wee coaster, to leave Holland moments before the Second World War started. He ended up owning a nursing home at Southport. He also worked as a pilot on the River Mersey."

A teenage McKeegan took the Sea School route, one that many other young Glensmen followed and became hugely successful in their chosen profession. "I joined the Sea School at Sharpness, and spent three months on the old training sailing vessel, *VINDICATOR*, which was tied up there," he said.

"I went straight from there to deep-sea work, on the Cunard passenger liner, *MAURITANIA*. Normally, she sailed from Southampton to LeHavre, then Cobh, and on to New York, but when I started she was cruising in the Mediterranean. My first job, through the Ships' Federation, was the lowest form of seaman, as a 'Peggy', looking after the needs of the crew members. Indeed, the ship had such a huge crew number I was a 'Peggy's Peggy' to start with. I was Mess Boy, washing dishes, cleaning up, and so forth.

"My first voyage was from Southampton, starting on April 15, 1964, and cruising down to places such as Gibraltar, Tangier, Malta, and Palma. My first pay was £17 a month, and 2/6 an hour for overtime. You were given twelve days a year leave, and for being at sea on a Sunday an extra day of leave. You could be a year at sea, making 52 extra days of leave.

"I spent eight months on the *MAURITANIA*, and then moved to work deep-sea on various other ships, mostly on trampers. On one, I sailed for a year and a day on the oil tanker *RAUDHAAINT*. It traded round South America. I first joined her in Italy, at Genoa. She was normally trading to the Persian Gulf, and that is where we set off for.

"We were heading into the Suez Canal when war broke out there. Fortunately, we were able to turn and get out. Some ships were locked in there for up to three years. Obviously, plans for the passage had to change, and we made for South America, mostly trading along the Pacific - taking cargo from Chile up to San Francisco. We also worked oil cargo out of Lake Maracaibo.

"I did some coasting, on Kelly boats, and a spell of coasting on a Shell-Mex oil tanker. During all the while I sat my Mate's Home Trade Ticket. Later, I passed the Master's Home Trade Ticket, which I then had it upgraded for foreign-going work. My first appointment as a ship's captain was on the *AILEEN MO GRAIDH*, coasting around the Scottish Western Isles. This was a general cargo vessel, and I stayed there for a couple of years.

"On one occasion, I took John Higgins with me. John, who lived down Shore Street, is a cousin of my family, and when he was a young man went to sea for around eight years. He worked as a ship's cook. He worked on the fully air-conditioned passenger liner, the 27,284-ton *EMPRESS of CANADA* that mostly sailed from Liverpool to Montreal.

"Much later, after he finished with sea work, I took him with me for that one trip . . . one month on the *AILEEN MO GRAIDH.* Normally, we did not have a cook, but John did the job during that run out of Red Bay and up the Western Isles, stopping at places such as Stornoway."

The effervescent Higgins, living in Ballycastle, County Antrim, for many years, enjoyed that final working voyage: "It was tremendous fun, a great wee journey up the Isles with my cousin Patrick on the puffer. That was many years after I quit the sea. I worked as a chef on passenger liners, from 1962 until around 1970. My father, Danny Higgins, was at sea for a short time, on coasters - rock dodging, he called it. My uncles, brothers of my mother, were John or Jack McKeegan and Paddy McKeegan.

"It was Jack who helped me get a job at sea. At that time he was skipper of the biggest dredger in Great Britain, the *LEVITHION,* working on the Mersey. Once he worked on the passenger boat, the *KEMMENDINE,* out to Rangoon. Uncle Pat as well. Jack was a lifetime at sea, and was once the skipper of a boat that managed to get out of Antwerp just in the nick of time, as the Second World War was breaking out. German soldiers, through loud hailers, ordered the boat to stop, but the crew worked on, ignored the Germans, and managed to escape. It was a boat belonging to the Limerick Steamship Company.

"My uncles lived at Ballymacdoe, Cushendall village, before the houses were built there on that corner of the Coast Road, and in what was once our garden. Aunt Kate McKeegan lived up Glenaan. Our next-door neighbour at Ballymacdoe had been a First Mate on sailing ships, and was connected to the family of Gerry Blaney. His name was Mawhinney."

Born in January 1943, Higgins went to sea at 19-years-of-age with the Canadian Pacific shipping company, as a chef on the liners, *EMPRESS of CANADA*, the *EMPRESS of BRITAIN*, and the *EMPRESS of ENGLAND.* "They were passenger ships going to Quebec and Montreal, and along with passengers took out cargo of new motor cars from England," added John.

"When the St Lawrence seaway froze over, during the deep winter months, we sailed to New York. The last ship I worked on was the *EMPRESS of ENGLAND*, cruising from Cape Town to South America. To get the work I first went to my uncle Jack in England, and he put me in touch with the Canadian Pacific Company.

"I was 17 when interviewed by them. I was asked what I was doing at that time, and I told them I was a student at the Catering College. They were interested, promised me a job offer when I finished school, and they kept their word. I was in and out of sea work. At one time there was a strike. Once, I spent eight months cruising down to South America. I celebrated my 21st birthday on the famous Copacabana Beach, at Rio de Janeiro. I also made two world cruises."

Patrick McKeegan added: "I went to work for Sealink Ferries after that time in Scotland, and was there for quite a while before moving to take up a job with the South of Ireland's In-shore Fishing Patrol ships. I was skipper of the *COSANTOR BRADAN*, (Salmon Protector), on the look-out for illegal fishing. My run was from Galway to Waterford, along such a beautiful coastline that took in the Cliffs of Moher, west Cork, and Dunmore East. I was on that job for four years.

"I went back to deep-sea for the Dutch firm, Car-carrier. The ship I was on took 1,000 Nissan cars from Barcelona, the main port. The cargo went to places such as Greece - and then back to the UK. The company had three ships chartered to Nissan, one based in Barcelona, and two in the Mediterranean. Sometimes a cargo of cars was taken out of South Shields with car drop offs in Sweden, Denmark, and Poland.

"The vessel I was on was a feeder ship, and shaped like a car ferry. It had seven decks with the cars tied down. The mother ships came in from Japan, each carrying between 5,000 and 7,000 Nissan cars. It was amazing. In 2001, I left the Car-carrier firm to go to Coleraine as Harbour Master."

53

DIVING DILEMMA

LONG before Johnny O'Hara of Tromra, Cushendun, became a chief pipe-laying engineer at sea, working mainly in the Gulf of Mexico, he was involved in a delicate and exacting undersea recovery operation in the North Sea.

Born in 1961, one of three sons of Alex and Mary O'Hara, he started a career in sub-sea construction. During an early assignment, while a 20-year-old with the *UNCLE JOHN*, he was on hand at the rewarding rescue of two deep-sea divers.

On February 1, 2013, O'Hara recalled this excitement as his most satisfying saga on the high seas: "My best and most memorable work happened in 1981, while aboard the *UNCLE JOHN*. It was a pitch-black night in the North Sea, in a January gale. We were running everything 'on the blood' to effect the rescue of two divers who were trapped 140 metres below the surface, in their crippled diving bell.

"Somehow, the life support umbilical to their mother ship, *STENA SEASPREAD,* had been severed. It wasn't the big news story it should have been, because it all happened as Tehran released 52 US hostages, who had been held for 444 days. The rescue of the divers was successfully completed by bringing them, one at a time, through the water to the *UNCLE JOHN's* diving bell - and recovering them to the surface for decompression."

Later in his career, in November 2006, he moved to work on the largest rigid reel-laying ship in the world. "It is a massive ship named *DEEP BLUE*. It has a crew of 160, and our base is Mobile Bay, Alabama. I'm laying pipes for oil, gas, and water, and I've been.the chief pipelay engineer on the Rigid Reel and Derrick Lay vessel. We lay about 65 kilometres of pipe in five days.

"I've been operating in the Gulf of Mexico. I work an average of six weeks on and six weeks off, and return to rejoin *DEEP BLUE*, again down to Brazil. I have completed campaigns in Angola, Gulf of Mexico, Brazil, Ghana, Egypt, Equatorial Guinea. *DEEP BLUE* has set many firsts in the O&G laying pipe and installing structures in up to 3000 metres of water. This is too deep for divers so Remote Operated Vehicles (mini-subs) are used instead."

When on dry land, he lives at Glengormley with wife Briedge, and three sons - Conan, Michael, and Donal. A former student of St MacNissi's College, Garron Tower, his interest in seafaring was due to the influence of his first cousins, captains Seamus and Paddy 'The Rock' McNeill.

O'Hara confessed the early urges to try sea work were the result of visits by his cousins, Seamus and Paddy (McNeill). When they would be going back to sea, they'd often call into the O'Hara house at Tromra. I'd hear of all the places they visited, all the things they saw while at sea. When they sailed to New Zealand they would visit my granny, Belle Davidson (Mrs Masterson). She was a cook in the Agriculture College," added Johnny.

"There was not much that interested me then, and I was fed up staying at school. I left Garron Tower in 1968, after doing 'A' Level Maths, and joined the Merchant Navy. I became an Engineer Cadet with Furness Withy, spending two years at the College of Technology in Belfast. In the third year, I was going to sea. I was sailing to Newfoundland, the eastern seaboard of the USA, Caribbean, Panama, the West Coast of South America, and to New Zealand.

"I spent my final Cadet year at Springburn College of Engineering, in Glasgow. The shipping firm of Furness Withy split up near the end of my connection with them. When I left the college in Glasgow I started working on a diving vessel in the North Sea, on sub-sea construction work.

"In 1975, I was promoted to Second Engineer, and three years later to Chief Engineer. From 1979 to 1995, I sailed on *UNCLE JOHN* in the North Sea - probably the most successful diving vessel ever - built in Oslo, in 1977, and still working in 2013. Those were the days of 'dry transfer' to welding habitats on the seabed, when dives could last anything up to 36 hours.

"Dry transfer allowed hyperbaric welders, breathing a helium/oxygen mix, to weld pipelines up to 36" in diameter on the seabed without getting wet. After a review on diver safety, this practice was no longer allowed. From 1995 to 2006, I was on various sub-sea construction and umbilical lay vessels, and in September 2006 I was asked to transfer from the smallest vessel in the Technip fleet to the largest, the *DEEP BLUE*."

O'Hara recalled some 'hairy' moments for the *DEEP BLUE*: "Before I joined the ship there were two really close shaves, once when the pipe broke on the reel, when unwinding. Apparently, some people were out on lifeboats. They pulled the pipe on like a fishing line on a big reel. First of all, they were abandoning it while lowering it down onto the seabed.

"They paid out the wire off the wench, so the whole pipeline fell of its own accord onto the seabed. They still had pipe on board at that stage. It was passed back to the reel. But, by now, they lost the head clamp. It went to the sea as well. We dived to gather up all the pieces, and rebuild it. Two months later we had the pipe back in the firing line again.

"However, we had a temporary well, and the pipe broke at 65 metres up in the air, and unwound off the reel like a big clock spring. We've not had anything like it since. In my first job, the pipe broke off the other reel, but it didn't break all the way through.

"Such things can happen, and we also have to always be aware if hurricanes are due to happen in the area where we are working. There are loads of hurricanes in the Gulf of Mexico. We just move out of their way. The weather forecasts are so good nowadays."

His brother Jim remembered a phase of early childhood, spent in Australia's outback. "I am the oldest of the three boys. Johnny is next, and Alistair, who is in Canada, is the youngest. When we were small children, the family decided to emigrate to Australia, where Alistair was born, but stayed there just a little over one year. It seems I kept picking up illnesses, taking too many fevers, so my parents decided to return home, in 1954.

"The one thing I remember was while we were in Australia, and I was around four-years-of-age. We had this big dog, and it came to Johnny's rescue out the back garden. The very clever dog saw the danger, and raced in front of Johnny to pounce on a snake. When we returned to the Antrim coast, I went to live with my aunt in Carey, at Coolnagopagh, not far from Ballypatrick. I was reared there.

"My father, Alex O'Hara, met my mother, then Mary Davidson of Ayr when she was a nurse in Glasgow. That was during a time when my father worked at sea. Also with him on coasters was Frank McAlister of Glendun, but Frank didn't stay at sea all that long, as far as I recall.

"I think my father, who went to Glendun Primary School from his home at Knocknacraw, was at sea mostly during and after the Second World War. He gave up the sea when he married, and after we came back from Australia he worked for a time with the Forestry

"As a very young man, he and Francis McKillop of Gortacreggan went to America to work, but came home after the start of the Depression, in the early 1930's. He later went to sea here, and on coasters." Also to dabble in sea work with Alex O'Hara was McKillop. Both were stokers, and apparently worked on the same boat alongside Neil McKenty of Carnlough.

Sean 'The Rock' McNeill, a nephew of Alex O'Hara, added: "I remember my uncle Jim O'Hara telling me of his brother Alex and Francis McKillop working for a time in New York. Unfortunately, the Depression happened. Alex and Francis returned to Cushendun. Jim stuck it out in America, working an eight-hour shift for the Standard Rubber Company, and also an eight-hour shift as a barman.

"That happened seven days a week, just to survive. In the summer weather he slept out in Central Park, New York, to avoid paying room and board. He went inside during the cold winter weather. After Alex worked at sea here, he had a spell with his young family in Australia. He once told me he cut sugar cane with a machete in north Queensland. The target cut was 15 tons a day. That was some going, in dreadfully hot conditions. It was very tough work, not to mention having to kill snakes as you went along through the cane field."

55

CABLE GUY

KIERAN McNeill of Cushendun likes living on the edge. The son of Captain Paddy McNeill qualified as a Master Mariner in 2007, and relishes working on specialised assignments. From 2000, he has been involved with Global Marine in the exacting task of seabed cable laying and cable repairing, and since 2002 has been based at Panama City.

In 2012, before taking a holiday break in Cushendun, Kieran was close, but well out of danger, when the devastating 'Hurricane Sandy' hit North America's east coast. It was the largest Atlantic hurricane ever, taking the lives of over 250 people, and causing an estimated $74 million in damage.

He said: "When we hear warnings of really bad weather conditions are on the way, especially news of hurricanes, we shelter out of the way. Our ship was on call in Baltimore, Maryland, just before the arrival of 'Hurricane Sandy'. On the way down to Panama City, we completed one major repair job in Nicaragua, and two in Honduras. It is crucial to keep the cable lines working. It means enormous amounts of money to big companies, such as NTL and SKY, and other communications companies."

However, the hair-raising adventure that fascinates me the most is a time when Kieran worked on globally important enterprises under the auspices of NATO (North Atlantic Treaty Organisation). It wasn't quite cloak and dagger, James Bond-esque, yet of a fairly clandestine nature, especially when one of the tasks was linked to testing missiles. There had to be a high level of risk.

From the moment he decided to make a career of seafaring, in 1990, he was attached to the Denholms Ship Management Company, and it was through this firm he landed the exciting NATO experience. He said: "Denholms had just taken management of a NATO Reserve vessel, the *ALLIANCE*, based in Italy, at Genoa. It was certainly one of the most challenging jobs I was involved in . . . testing hardware that only came to light in 2012, yet stuff we tested all those years ago. This was probably the most interesting job I ever had. My rank then was Third Officer. I enjoyed the job so much I stayed until I became Second Officer.

"The ship carried 50 to 60 of the world's top scientists at any one time, doing all kinds of tests, including military hardware tests - and a lot of research for the British, as well. They also worked with Harvard University, and closely with the world's navy. The ship was very well protected. She worked all around Italian ports, including Sicily, and up as far as northern Norway, Iceland, and Greenland.

"The vessel also doubled as a diplomatic ship. Very important meetings were held on board. The Allied Supreme Commander, for example, would be there - also the head of NATO - and some of the generals from the Russian fleet, and others from across the world. The ship was not affiliated with any out and out navy, but with the German Auxiliary Forces, and one of the few entities owned by NATO. We would also travel up the Black Sea to Bulgaria."

There is a sniff of major mystery and suspense about this overall trip. The passage alone, from the captivating city of Istanbul, and into the salt-water Black Sea, has magnetic appeal. It is an area of rich historic value, the Black Sea surrounded by the countries of Bulgaria, Ukraine, Russia, Georgia, and Turkey - and with fascinating ports along the 3,000-year-old shoreline such as Odessa, Yalta, and Sevastopol.

McNeill added: "It was a wonderful experience for me, but there came a time to move on. I progressed as far as possible. The Master and the First Mate had to be German - to keep everybody happy. The crew members were Italian, and the rest of the officers were British. Because I could advance no further than Second Officer I asked Denholms for a change."

He switched from one specialised job to another. He secured work on a ship involved in Seismic Survey. This probe of rock formation beneath the seabed, is part of the exploration phase of trying to find oil or gas. "Ironically," he added: "I joined the ship when it was aground at Killybegs, County Donegal - the 2,800 gross tons *SIMON LABRADO*R. It was the biggest ship to get into Killybegs Harbour.

"We worked for an American-based company, and made the gas discovery off the coast of County Mayo. We made recordings to determine if there were any worthwhile gas or oil deposits under the seabed. It is all about noise travelling through the water. We were based at Rockall, and gathered seismic data to sell to the biggest oil bidders.

"All this brought Greenpeace down on us. Our work was blamed for damaging whales, through the noise. I did a few trips, and in-between I decided to go back to college, sit the First Mate's examination, and hopefully make it forward up the ranks. I went to Glasgow for nine months, and passed the First Mate's test."

He was 19 when he went to sea, on February 13, 1990, and in 2007, he qualified as Captain, after going to the South Shields College to complete his final examination for the Master's Ticket. Born on July 2, 1970, his early schooling was at St Ciaran's Primary, Knocknacarry, and then St MacNissi's College, Garron Tower, where he sat a special written test, arranged by the Denholms Company.

He recalled the career move: "Denholms were recruiting sea cadets. I decided that was the way I wanted to go. My dad was advised by sea bo'sun Mervyn Kirkland, from the Greencastle-Moville area of County Donegal, to approach Denholms. So. I took and passed the examination.

"Denholms, an Isle of Man-based company, wanted to make sure I was good enough at Physics. They gave me a four-year sponsorship to train me up as a cadet. I was sent to the Glasgow Nautical College. The course was split up. I had to do so much time at College, and so much time at sea. It was quite a novel way to do it, as Denholms could get you work on different types of ships - on containers, bulkers. I ended up with a Second Officer's Ticket.

"My first job was on a ship of 1,599 gross tons, named the *CITY of PLYMOUTH.* I joined her in Dublin. It had a British crew and British officers. It was strictly run, and you had to wear uniform. She was Cunard element. The ship ran from Dublin to Ellsmere Port, Liverpool, and down to Lisbon, then through the Mediterranean Sea, to Cyprus, and then she would go over to Israel on occasions - to Haifa. We once took a container filled with explosives from Beirut, during the end of that war, to Dublin for the Irish Army. Out of Dublin we mainly took potatoes back there.

"I moved to a bigger container ship of around 14,000 tons net, the *ADVISOR.* I was working for the Harrison company of Liverpool, on a ship that did the Caribbean Sea, Central, and South America. It was an absolute hoot of a job. I loved it. We called into different ports every couple of days, and visiting nearly every island in the Caribbean. We took on board cargo such as ferns, fruit. We took a lot of lobster tails, rum, and chemicals back to Europe. I was on that run for seven months.

"For a time, I was on the container ship, the *CITY OF DURBAN*, which was over 52,000 tons gross and was one of the biggest ships of the period. It was a wonderful run that carried passengers as well, down along the South African coast. On a trip back we had a very important and interesting passenger - a White Rhino for Lisbon Zoo. The rhino was obviously penned in, and had two men to look after it, feed it."

He switched from the warm climes of the west African coast to chilly Canada, working for the Alcan Company - for a time a substantial sponsor of top professional golf tournaments such as the Alcan International and Junior Alcan events once staged at Portmarnock, Dublin.

"I was on the Alcan-owned *NORTHERN VENTURE* and *NORTHERN PROGRESS*, bulk containers going up to Port-Alfred, at Quebec. We also went up the Saginaw River. I was third officer on the *NORTHERN VENTURE*, a 21,500 tons bulk carrier. I did quite a few of those long trips, running with bauxite from up the Amazon River, where we would be four or five days. We loaded at Trombetas, a place deep in the Amazon jungle.

"We picked up alumina at Jamaica. This is a very hard dust used in the Alcan productions. We would not be permitted to discharge that cargo when there was a strong wind blowing of over 20 mph. A lot of the farmers and growers in Canada objected, because the dust is so fine it would carry for long distances in a strong breeze. It cannot be seen, but because it is of such an abrasive quality it would wear down the teeth of cattle.

"During one such trip, I met Captain Arthur Hamilton of Cushendun. There was no internet in those days. It was all letter mail, and we picked up mail in Port-Alfred. Quebec. Arthur was then involved on Canadian coastal ships, and was a man who knew the territory like the back of his hand. He heard I was there, came down to see me, and took me out to dinner in Port-Alfred.

"It was minus-25 every day up there. Arthur later moved down to Toronto, where it is 'only' minus-20 a day. The winter temperature in Vancouver is merely two or three below, but up in northern Quebec it is really cold. I remember once we tried to take a large container ship through the Great Lakes Valley with a cargo of special fuel for the Eskimos up in Churchill. That is right up the Hudson Bay. We stove in the ship in the ice, and that was in the middle of summer. We thought we could make it, but didn't.

"I worked the trip to Canada for a couple of years. I enjoyed the part of it when we were in the Caribbean and Brazil, but what drove me away from that container-ship journey was the extremes of weather conditions, the cold in Canada. One week I would be working in temperatures of 35-plus in Brazil, and shortly afterwards in temperatures of 20 or 30-below in Canada. That sheer change of temperature wreaked havoc with your system.

"When I came out of there, Denholms had no ship for me, so to keep active I went as AB on the *PRIDE of RATHLIN* ferry, from Larne to Stranraer. The ship's captain was Paddy McAlinden of Ballycastle. He was the senior skipper. I was a few weeks there before going back to the *SIMON LABRADOR* for one more trip. I was promoted to Chief Officer

"It was off to the Gulf of Mexico, to do surveys for oil and gas in the Galveston, Texas, area. But, in December 1999 people were being laid off. It was my very last seismic survey, because the price of oil dropped below 50 dollars a barrel. The ship's name was changed to *LABRADOR HORIZON*. Two days before Christmas 1999 I was paid off her in Liverpool, and handed the keys over to the Administrators.

"Shortly after that I ended up with Global Marine. Denholms were in a transitional period, around the end of 1999. An Asian company took over. All British people were made redundant. I enjoyed working with British crews, but crews were changed around. It was very disappointing. The crews were made up of Filipinos, Portuguese, Spanish. So, I was home for Christmas."

At the start of the 21st century, Kieran connected with his present long-lasting occupation, as Master and sometimes First Mate of cable-laying vessels that help to maintain crucial world-wide communication systems through underwater cables. The seabed assignments, including exacting repair work, have taken him all over the globe, including the laying of cables in Alaska, where ice breakers cleared passage for his ship.

Sonar checking tells about the sea bed, where the big cable, the size of your thigh, can be ploughed in at up to 300 metres. The ploughing-in process of cable laying is done at 2.5 knots. It is a specialised job. In recent years he has been berthed mainly in the Panama City area.

"On February 16, 2000, I joined Global Marine, who had an array of ships. I started on the 2,700 gross tons cable ship *LA BONNA*. It was very busy, working around the English Channel doing a lot of repair work. I went to the *CABLE INSTALLER*, repairing cables along Japan and California. I changed to the *PACIFIC GUARDIAN*, based in Fiji.

"The *GUARDIAN*, a beautiful white vessel, old style, included our own bars on board, which is a feature disappearing from all ships. Alcohol on board is now mainly 'persona non grata', although Global Marine ships retain the facility. We would berth right in the heart of cities like Darling

Harbour, Sydney, and Long Beach, California. No expense spared. The *GUARDIAN* guarded cables along the Pacific islands.

"I went to the *WAVE ALERT* in Brazil, where we also guarded cables. It was a great ship to be on. It made up for the time on the *MONARCH INSTALLER,* when we were always busy, always at sea repairing cables. On September 9, 2002, I joined the *MAERSK RESPONDER,* also a state-of-the-art cable ship that was based in Panama City. It is a wonderful place. I was mesmerised by Panama City."

It was there he met his wife, Kathia, and also met one of his favourite sportsmen. A fanatical fight fan, he was invited to a special party in Panama City, where he was introduced to two icons of professional boxing. "One of the biggest thrills of my life was to meet two of Panama's legendary world champions, Roberto 'Hands of Stone' Duran, and Ismael Laguna.

"Not often will you have two such boxing greats together. It was a special occasion for me. Duran had a bar-cum-snooker club for a time. I have always taken a keen interest in the sport. While in Panama City I've been to a lot of big title fights, mostly in the featherweight division. Fifteen years ago you could have a ringside seat at a world title boxing show in Panama City for 40 dollars, and a bottle of champagne thrown in."

It has not been all fight fun and games. Stormy weather in the Atlantic, cruel conditions of the worst possible kind, caused havoc to his boat. It was a very worrying experience: "I was back with the ship, the *PACIFIC GUARDIAN,* and based in Bermuda. We did a very difficult repair job in the north mid-Atlantic ridge.

"We ran into a nasty storm, one that wrecked our sail boats, rescue rafts, and so on. We got a right battering. It was the worst storm I was ever caught in - those first few days of January 2007. That experience will live in the memory forever. We managed to get back to port for repairs to the damage, costing up to $50,000.

"My first experience of cable laying was for a Canadian-based cable company, Sekundia, based up in Halifax. I was transferred to the *BOLD ENDURANCE,* for the new adventure. Cable laying means every cable road on the seabed has to be grappled and cleared of debris. We once did a job at Seward, Alaska, a town that features a pub where the bar is made entirely from the jawbone of a whale. Up there, polar bears at times roam wild through the streets, and they can be quite vicious.

"We also did a small job at Valdez. It is a very bleak and cold place, where there is an American oil refinery. Our task was to retrieve a Remote Observation Vessel. We use them to plough in the cables. Up there, you could enjoy seeing the fantastic Northern Lights.

"I joined the *BOLD ENDEAVOUR,* a brand new and very powerful cable ship. It was down at Mobile, Alabama, where she was converted to a multi-purpose vessel. A similar ship was the *ATLANTIC GUARDIAN,* a powerful new cable ship. I also went back to the *MERSCK RESPONDER* for a couple of trips, and as superintendent.

"In 2006, I was with the *CABLE RETRIEVER* in the Philippines, the ship involved in a lot of deep-water, earthquake-type fault repair work, after the tsunami that followed the Surinam earthquake. She was one of the most active cable ships in the world. Also, while in Asia, I joined the *WAVE MERCURY*, based in Shanghai. It was a big converted Danish ferry ship turned into a busy cable vessel.

"We were commissioned to do a job at Papua, New Guinea, for underwater diamond mining in the Bismarck Sea. We did an underwater survey, in an area between New Britain and New Ireland - close to the Solomon Islands, where there had been underwater volcanoes in very deep water reaching nearly 3,000 metres deep.

"There were volcanic eruptions all the time. Where there are eruptions there are always precious minerals and metals thrown up. We drilled into rocks. We punctured the rocks, and coming up out of those eruptions were pure minerals. I was one year there, before returning to work on cables at northern Japan.

"I was Chief Officer on the *WAVE MERCURY*, based at Nagasaki. We also did a few cable-laying and ploughing jobs in between Indonesian islands. It was there, in November 2008, the company gave me my first job as a ship's Master, on the *MERCURY*. Sometimes I would go as Chief Officer if they needed me for cable lays.

"In June 2009, I did a job at Jeddah and Oman, while on the *CABLE INNOVATOR*. Down there we saw pirates, and had to dodge them. We had no arms on the ship at that time, unlike the Chinese who were also working there. For security, the Chinese had 14 soldiers on board their boats. They don't mess about.

"I went back to Shanghai on the *WAVE MERCURY*, and joined the sister ship, the *WAVE VENTURE* in laying cables in the Philippines. I was also on the 14,500 gross tons *CABLE INNOVATOR* for some years as Mate, moving to Chief Officer, and took her back to England through the Suez Canal. That was on March 31, 2011, and it was my first time to go through the Suez.

"Later that year, I was sent to the *JOHN LETHBRAGE*, working for a rescue company searching for shipwrecks, and using scan sonar. It was a very interesting period. However, mostly it was cable laying through 2011 and into 2012, with the *INNOVATOR*, and I was involved in the laying of the first cable for an Irish company - from Dublin to near Holyhead. There was a lot of fanfare when that job was completed.

"Another fascinating time for me was when laying cable in the Mediterranean, from northern Libya to Crete. It was during the unrest, the war in Libya, and security was tight. We had to do our work right in the middle of the Arab Spring. We laid very expensive fibre optic cables.

"I was appointed a ship's superintendent officer, based in Singapore, and I hired a ship and a crew to work on an Indonesian ship. Off I went with a laptop and a mobile telephone to prepare routes, to be cleared before cable laying through the Indonesian islands - Java, Jakarta. It was a very busy run. I joined the *PACIFIC GUARDIAN*, a powerful new ship, to do cable repair work along the US east coast."

55 CREWS CONTROL

SPORTING outlets in boat racing are diverse, ranging from rowing to powerboats, to the natural throwback of the past, sailing vessels. Moving to the more sophisticated age of recent decades we discover ever-improving methods to help speed times on the waters in specialised boats made for rowing or yacht racing.

Ever since a bygone time, when summer Regatta days were plentiful along the Antrim seaboard, there remains the lure of testing ability on the water. Gone are those old-fashioned fun rowing races. Instead, there are high-octane events such as the Olympic Games, the Oxford and Cambridge annual spectacular, and other such outings on the River Lagan and River Bann.

A direct descendent of the glorious tall-masted sailing ships of the 19th century is yacht racing. Locally, there are ways to learn how to safely sail small, medium, and large craft. Fulfilling that need is the Cushendall Sailing and Boating Club, and from there young folk are tutored in the subtle skills required in the intricately precise ways of sailing.

Making waves of their own are the Rowan brothers, Terry and Gareth of The Bay, Glenariffe, and Cushendun's Barry McCartin. Son of Gerry and Catriona (nee O'Hara) of Knocknacraw, he is often a lone sailor, pitting his wits against sailors from more fashionable and long-established clubs in demanding competition at the highest level.

Born on July 13, 1989, talented McCartin, when coached at Cushendall Sailing and Boating Club by Josie Farrell, made an early impact. At 14, he launched what was to be a meteoric march, he clinched the Irish Schools' Sailing title at Skull in West Cork.

In 2005, he was the leading Irish Junior - finishing second in the European Topper UP-16 Championships, and fifth overall. Over two consecutive years (2005-2006) the exciting prospect won every event in Ireland in both the Topper and Laser 4.7 classes. For his opening Topper title, he was the first person from any country to beat the whole of the Great Britain national side, when a Dave Cockerel-coached team guested at the Irish event.

He became the Topper National Coach, and explained: "I have been coach at every Topper World event from 2009-2012, and in 2009 and 2010 I coached two sailors to win the British Topper Championships, out of a 360 entry. For three months, June to August of 2012, I was in the United States, as coach to the Laser Racing team from Newport, Rhode Island."

In between, in 2006/2007, he competed internationally at Laser 4.7/

Radial World Championships, and was recognised by Moyle District Council as their 2006 Young Sportsperson of the Year. Two years later, when 18, McCartin was Moyle's Adult Sportsperson. In 2007, the 18-year-old lorded the Irish National Championship at Howth, and was also awarded the Mary Peters Sports Scholar prize.

In 2011, he competed individually in testing Olympic 470 Class at Grade 1 regattas in the UK, Germany, and the Netherlands - including the 470 World Championships.. For three years, from 2010, he was at the helm on the UCD 1st team that won the UCD/TRINITY Colours. During that period the team was ranked first in the Ireland Universities SA circuit, following wins of the Eastern, Western, and Southern Championships.

During 2012, UCD's leading sailor McCartin helped the team to top ranking, when UCD won the IUSA Intervarsity Championship. He proudly claimed nine Irish National Champion victories, and multiple Provincial titles across six different classes - Toppers, Laser 4.7, Laser Radial 2000, 470, and Fireballs.

McCartin stated: "In November 2012, after qualifying as the Irish entry in the Student Yachting World Championships, I was the Team Tactician on the UCD-Ireland 10-man boat that won the title at La Rochelle, France." Also that year, he was one of three helms representing UCD and Ireland when the team plundered bronze medals in the prestigious British Universities National Championships at West Kirby, Liverpool. This was the highest ever placing by an Irish boat.

A year later, he was awarded the Sailing Sports Scholarship to study at Dublin Institute of Technology. This funded Barry to undertake a Masters Degree in Management Energy, adding to the Mechanical Engineering Degree he completed in 2012.

The Rowan brothers set their collective compass on a different sea route out of the Cushendall Club. Terry and Gareth are professional yachtsmen. That is their trade. They skipper big sailing boats that compete in ocean yacht racing. They often deliver yachts from a harbour in one continent to one in another, and all at the whim of a multi-millionaire boat owner.

They are handsomely rewarded by well-heeled owners. It is a bewitching business, and one that offers a lifestyle of mixing a high element of risk, the requirement of exacting skills, and meeting the rich and famous of a somewhat exclusive global club in the world of seafaring.

Regarded the ultimate in boat racing is the Americas Cup, which is, arguably still the most prestigious event of its kind. The first race was in 1851, between the New York Yacht Club and the Royal Yacht Squadron. The calendar of special events also includes the Sydney to Hobart Race, and closer to home is the Fastnet Race.

The sons of Tommy and Margaret Rowan keep the family's sea-flag flying. It can be a glamorous yet exacting and disciplined career for the bachelor brothers, who first took an interest in specialised sailing while youngsters attending coaching sessions on sailing at the Cushendall Club.

Tommy Rowan, who sails his own *OISIN* at the Cushendall Club, said: "I like the sailing, and that is how the boys began in the sport. Terry is the eldest of the family, then Gareth, and daughter Lorraine, who also sails. Terry was interested in getting in boats with me, in boats made of carbon fibre. It is very light, but harder than steel. It looks and feels like plastic. You could hit it with a sledgehammer, and not break it. Such boats have to be tough to cross the Atlantic.

"In the beginning of their sea careers the boys sailed for the Northern Ireland Youth squad. They sailed Lasers. The Northern Ireland squads race against the Republic and England. From junior racing the young people can progress to compete in the Olympic Games.

"Cushendall Sailing and Boating Club has a School of Excellence, where youngsters are instructed in the ways of sailing. Lessons are given by trained coaches. This is where the two boys started. The courses cane be graded - one, two, three, and powerboats. This is where young Barry McCartin also started, and went sailing as a single man on the likes of Laser boats.

"Terry and Gareth did Youth yacht racing competition. It took off from there, into the Northern Ireland Youth squad, for competition against Scotland and England. They didn't take the Olympic Games route, like Barry McCartin. Instead, they are hired to do big boat races such as the Sydney to Hobart.

"Gareth has a gold medal as a member of an eight-man crew that won the King's Cup Regatta at Phuket, on the 29th of November 2008. The boat owner, from Sydney, flew the crew up to Thailand from there, put them up in a hotel, and flew then back after the win. The crew members were paid professional seaman.

"For the boat owner it was a prestige victory, but very little money for winning. That is what it is like when racing yachts in the premier events, such as the Americas Cup. It is all about pride for the owners, not money. When you see the New York Yacht Club, at Newport, Rhode Island, you know you need to be one of the super rich to become a member and race yachts.

"I once sailed down by it, and right at the end of the lawn, at the water's edge, were these burly bodyguards stationed to make sure nobody uninvited attempted to get into the Club. Terry once managed to receive an invitation into the Club, along with other crew members of a yacht owner, who was one of the members of that elite and exclusive club."

The nephews of retired Merchant sailor Danny Rowan, and cousins of Captain Hugh O'Mullan, the Rowan boys were students at St MacNissi's College, Garron Tower. In July 2013, their mother Margaret said: "Terry is based in Dublin. He was 21 when he went to sea ten years ago. He did the Sydney to Hobart yacht race, and also from Newport, Rhode Island, to Hamburg - the Norbank Race.

"He was also on a boat that won the Fife Regatta in Scotland, a race named after a yacht designer and not the area, on the east of Scotland. This race is held once every five years, and he was on the winning yacht in 2008. He was not involved in the 2013 race. Instead, he was doing a delivery of a yacht from Amsterdam to Stockholm. He delivers yachts for clients, and from time to time is involved in races.

"After Garron Tower, he went to Glasgow University, but didn't finish the degree in Commerce. He decided on a career at sea, and took to delivering yachts and also racing them. His younger brother Gareth, now 28, left Garron Tower and went to UCD, where he completed a degree in Commerce before also deciding on a sea career, in yachts.

"Last year (2012), he was First Mate on the yacht, *GENEVIEVE* that left the Mediterranean to sail through the Panama Canal; and onwards to the Pacific Ocean, to stop off for an escorted tour of the Galapagos Islands. It costs 700,000 Euros to hire the privately-owned *GENEVIEVE* for a week.. The yacht had a captain and a crew of six. Gareth also did the Sydney to Hobart race when the yacht *GEORGIA* appeared to hit something, likely a big sunfish, and sunk. All crew members were rescued."

The cause of the wreck of the expensive American-owned *GEORGIA* was officially put down to colliding with a large shark. The Sydney to Hobart Race, over 600 miles, always starts on Boxing Day, and was launched in 1945. Margaret Rowan said: "Terry did the race a few years before the sinking of the *GEORGIA*. So, Gareth decided he had to have a go when the chance came up. The Sydney to Hobart race sinking of the yacht Gareth was on was extensively reported in the *Daily Telegraph* of Australia. Gareth is now a member of a special club in Sydney, to honour seamen who survived a sinking during the race."

Gareth, who stands 6'2", is listed 'Yachtmaster Offshore'. Born on December 10, 1984, he has also been a First Mate on numerous yachts.

Crew rescued by race competitor after late-night drama sinks ship

NOEL TOWELL
28/12/2008 9:55:00 AM
GARETH ROWAN will have some stories to tell his mates when he gets home to Ireland in a couple of weeks.

As a crew member on the Georgia, the first casualty of this year's Sydney to Hobart yacht race, the 23-year-old student from county Antrim will be the only one in his class with a shipwreck to his name.

Rowan and his 13 crewmates were relaxing on land at Batemans Bay yesterday after Georgia lost her rudder and sank about 45 nautical miles off the coast of Ulladulla late on Friday night.

The crew believe that the 53-footer struck a large fish a whale is thought unlikely at this time of year about 8.45pm. The impact ripped the rudder from the vessel, leaving her stranded with a fractured hull and taking on water fast.

Until the impact, the crew of the New Zealand-built Georgia had been enjoying a smooth run down the South Coast.

"We were up on deck about three-quarters of the way into our watch and we were just cruising, really comfortable," Rowan said yesterday.

"The boat was going well and we were really happy. And the next thing, there was this really loud bang and a crash and we knew that there was something seriously wrong.

"We didn't know at first what had happened, and then the guy who was steering lost steerage, so we kind of figured out we'd lost the rudder."

But according to the Georgia's skipper, Graeme Ainley, there was no panic among the mostly Melbourne-based crew.

"The crew, when it happened, knew exactly what to do, they stepped into the emergency procedures and everything went like clockwork," the skipper said.

"These guys have probably done about 300 Sydney to Hobart races between them and they really kicked into place."

The Georgia's distress signal was answered by another race competitor, Merit, which came to the rescue.

"By a quarter past nine we had tidied up, by 10 o'clock, Merit was alongside," Ainley said.

"We took everybody across in a life raft over to Merit and by 10.30 we were all on Merit, down below, warm and tidy.

"About half-an-hour later, the boat sank."

The crew was transferred from the Merit to NSW Police launch Nemesis which landed them at Batemans Bay at 6.30am.

By 8.30am, the crewmates were relaxing in a Batemans Bay cafe{aac}, calling friends and family and figuring out a way to get back to Melbourne.

Ainley, a veteran of 25 Sydney to Hobart races, was full of praise for the race organisers' safety procedures.

"We all have training in sea safety and survival which is structured by the Cruising Yacht Club of Australia," the skipper said.

"The procedures and systems are very well formatted and everything just kicked into place and everyone who needed to be called was called."

He spent a year based at Melbourne, and joined the crew of the New Zealand-built *GEORGIA*, and was responsible for the big race preparations. Unfortunately, the yacht hit a whale or shark, causing major structural damage to the rudder area, and sank. He remarked: "The impact of the crash against what was suspected a whale or a large shark ripped the rudder from the vessel, leaving her with a fractured hull."

The caption of the newspaper photograph of the crew printed on December 28, 2008, stated: 'Graeme Ainley and his 14-man crew of the sunken yacht *GEORGIA*, after a narrow escape on the previous Friday night - taken ashore by a NSW Maritime Police Rescue boat, *NEMESIS*. They were rescued by the crew of another competitor, the yacht*TELCOINBOX MERIT*, and transferred to the above. It was Ainley's 25th time to race in the bluewater classic. The *GEORGIA*, a 53-foot Victorian boat, was one of 100 starters in the race. It suffered rudder damage, and began taking on water through a large hole in the boat.'

Tommy Rowan added: "The American owner of the *GEORGIA* bought new and very expensive sails for that Sydney to Hobart race. When the yacht was sinking, the owner was trying to take the sails off the boat, to save them. He had to be urgently taken away in the rescue without the sails. The boat went down that deep there was no way of getting her up again. She was never salvaged.

"Other big races include the Americas Cup. Terry once captained one of the Americas Cup yachts. The boys competed in the Fastnet Race of 2007, on the American-owned yacht, *SNOW LION* - the same boat Terry raced that year in the Newport-Hamburg event."

Before that prestigious event, Terry, who is based in Dublin, and intends to remain in the yacht enterprises, sailed on *SNOW LION* from Newport, Rhode Island, to Hamburg. Six weeks later, Gareth joined him to compete in the famous Fastnet Race, which is part of the magnetic attraction of Cowes week. Six-footer Terry was the skipper.

The bi-annual August race from Cowes for 600 yachts to sail 600 miles around the Fastnet Rock on the south coast of Ireland and back to Plymouth is regarded one of the most exhilarating and heart-stopping experiences of world-class yacht racing. The yachts for this testing race, established in 1924 when it featured merely seven boats, is a swift light vessel, crewed by professional sailors. Tommy Rowan revealed: "After a race such as the Fastnet the sail is taken down, packaged carefully, and sent back to America."

OBVIOUSLY, it would be nigh impossible to winkle out the name and story of every Glensman who went to work at sea during the past three millenniums. Many of the old timers have been accorded rightful acclaim in other publications, and by qualified and valued historians.

My random ramblings provide, I feel, a microscopic insight ranging from the exploits of the highest ranked officer to the ever-willing deck hand, all given equal status. The enthusiasm of all interviewees was refreshing, all memories and cherished faded photographs generously given to a project I hope will go some way to a belated honouring of past and present seafarers of the Glens.

It was a touching exercise, as some of the ancient mariners still afloat seemed to have their old grey cells awakened. A glint returned to their eyes, and a sea swagger resurfaced as they brought to life spell-binding descriptions of epic sea passages.

FIN

'Day after day, day after day

We stuck, nor breath nor motion

As idle as a painted ship

Upon a painted ocean

Water, water, everywhere

And all the boards did shrink

Water, water, everywhere

Nor any drop to drink.'

(Extract from - 'The Rime of the Ancient Mariner'
- by Samuel Taylor Coleridge)